School Foodservice Management

for the 21st Century

School Foodservice Management
for the 21st Century

Fifth Edition

Dorothy Pannell-Martin, MA
President, inTEAM Associates, Inc.

inTEAM Associates, Inc.
Alexandria, Virginia
1999

Library of Congress Cataloging-in-Publication Data
Pannell-Martin, Dorothy
    School foodservice management/Dorothy Pannell-Martin.—5th ed.
    Rev. ed. of: School foodservice management, 4th ed., Van Nostrand Reinhold. 1990.
    Includes bibliographical references and index.
    ISBN 0-9666121-1-6
    1. Food service management.   2. School cafeterias, etc.   3. Child Nutrition programs

Cover Designer: Suzanne Gore Reynolds
Cover Photo: Randy Wyant
Editorial Assistance: Gloria Johnson
Text Designer: Florene Love

Library of Congress Catalog Card Number: 99-095222

Copyright © 1999
Published by inTEAM Associates, Incorporated
PO Box 15237
Alexandria, Virginia 22309
e-mail: inteamdot@AOL.com

Orders: 800-494-0023
Information: 703-799-7306

Printed in the United States of America

10 9 8 7 6 5 4 3 2 1

ISBN 0-9666121-1-6

Contents

Contents

Contents

Contents

Contents

Preface

The first edition of *School Foodservice Management* (then titled simply *School Foodservice)* was published in 1975 and was revised every five years after that through 1990. This new fifth edition has expanded upon the fourth edition of *School Foodservice Management* and is a major revision. Throughout this edition the chapters have been updated to reflect current trends and practices in school foodservice. The financial and operational areas have been enlarged upon because of philosophical change and local budget restraints, which have influenced changes in the attitudes of people toward operating school foodservice programs.

The first five years after the Child Nutrition Act of 1966 brought about tremendous changes and expansions in school foodservice programs. More changes, however, have taken place during the 1990s in the way school foodservice programs are administered than in the prior 30 years. The changes of the 1990s included heightened nutrition awareness, a technological explosion, increased competition from management companies, use of branding, financial crises, tightening district/school budgets, escalating costs of both food and labor, and population growth.

School foodservice directors and managers will see equal or greater changes in the next decade. The financial crunch, inroads of management companies, technology expansion, and the shortage of sophisticated and experienced foodservice directors/business managers and short-hour employees to operate the programs will influence the program in several ways.

Since there are many good sources of information on nutrition, personnel management, principles of food preparation, and writing food specifications, these subjects are not discussed in any detail. Instead a general overview of school foodservice management is the emphasis, and all the areas that influence that management are touched upon.

I approached the writing of this book as a teacher and as a former foodservice director. Thus, I have attempted to bring together information on financial management, on staffing, and on operating a school foodservice as a business. Explanations of federal regulations are woven throughout this volume so readers will understand how the regulations influence school foodservice programs.

It is my hope that this edition will continue to meet the needs of foodservice directors and managers as a reference and of students who are preparing to fill the many exciting career opportunities in school foodservices during the 2000s.

Acknowledgments

I gratefully acknowledge permission granted for the use of illustrations and quotes throughout the text. Many people have contributed directly and indirectly to this book. I wish especially to thank the many fine school foodservice directors who have allowed me to learn from them in my role of trainer and sometimes consultant. The experiences of the last seven years (working with school

Preface

foodservice programs across the country) have broadened my approach to school foodservice management. I've learned there are many ways to accomplish the same results—providing food to children at school. Since June of 1992, when I left my position as director of foodservice for the Fairfax County (Virginia) Public Schools, my business partner, Gertrude Applebaum, and I have presented cost control seminars and inTEAM Food System training and provided school districts with program evaluations and assistance in more than 40 states.

I wish to especially thank the many people at the U.S. Department of Agriculture who furnished pictures, information, and materials. Particularly helpful in my understanding of the federal regulations was my opportunity to be a part of the Nutrition and Technical Services staff at the U.S. Department of Agriculture on an Introgovernmental Personnel Agreement contract some years ago.

Many thanks go to the peer reviewers, who questioned, challenged, and made suggestions to the manuscript prior to publishing. Their input strengthened this as a text and as an introduction to managing school foodservice. I gratefully acknowledge their contributions.

Gertrude Applebaum, inTEAM Associates, Inc., Corpus Christi, TX
Mary Kate Harrison, Hillsborough School District, Tampa, FL
Dr. Patricia Luoto, Framingham State College, Framingham, MA
Paul McElwain, Kentucky State Department of Education, Frankfort, KY
Carol Miller, R.D., Adams Twelve Schools, Northglenn, CO
Elizabeth Soares, Creative Choices, Richmond, VA

My special thanks and appreciation to my husband, Clyde, who helped make time for me to write and supplied patience and encouragement, and to my son , Stephen, and daughter, Katherine, who were involved in different ways. Special thanks go to my dear friend and business partner, Gertrude Applebaum, who has reviewed and edited each chapter of this book, and to my friend Elizabeth Soares, who spent endless hours helping update the historical data and helping me understand all the new menu planning options.

Dot Pannell-Martin

About the Author

Dorothy "Dot" Pannell-Martin, MA, is President of inTEAM Associates, Incorporated, and former director of foodservices for the Fairfax County (VA) Public Schools. Her Bachelor's degree is from Mississippi College in Clinton and her Master's degree is from the University of Mississippi in Oxford. Mrs. Pannell-Martin began her professional career in college foodservices as assistant director at Morrison's Food Management Company. She is a former instructor of Food, Nutrition, and Institutional Administration at the University of Maryland in College Park and former director of school foodservices for Chapel Hill City Schools, North Carolina, and assistant school foodservice director for Prince George's County Schools, Upper Marlboro, Maryland. She headed the Management System and Training Section of Food and Nutrition Services, United States Department of Agriculture (USDA) for one year under an "Intragovernmental Personnel Act" appointment, where she was in charge of the development of guidance materials for the Child Nutrition programs. She is winner of many industry awards, including Food Service Executive of the Year from the Restaurant Association of Metropolitan Washington, Most Distinguished Pacesetter Award from the National Roundtable for Women in Foodservices, Silver Plate from the International Food Manufacturers Association, Fame Award from the American School Food Service Association, Eagle's Award for Outstanding Service to Schools from the Association of School Business Officials International and the ServiceMaster Company and Distinguished Alumni at Mississippi College. She is an active member of the American School Food Service Association, the Association of School Business Official International, and the National Restaurant Association. Mrs. Pannell-Martin is the author and coauthor of several books and articles in the field, including four prior editions of *School Foodservice Management (1975, 1981, 1985, and 1990),Controlling Costs in the Foodservice Industry* (1998), *Assisted NuMenu Manual* (1995), *Cost Control for School Foodservices* (1992 with updates and revisions periodically), *Menu Planning Guide (USDA, 1980).* She is recognized as an inspiring speaker and innovator. She and her business partner, Gertrude Applebaum, have developed the inTEAM Food System a standardized approach to foodservice management that extends across the industry.

InTEAM Associates, Incorporated, is a foodservice consulting company that specializes in inTEAM Food System franchise training, as well as training in cost control and problem solving for foodservice operations in trouble financially.

1
INTRODUCTION TO
SCHOOL FOODSERVICE

Overview and History of School Foodservice
School Foodservice From 1853 to 1940
    Volunteer Groups
    Depression and Unemployment
Growth From 1940 to 1966
    National School Lunch Act of 1946
    Limited Funding
    National School Lunch Week
The Child Nutrition Program From 1966 to 1981
    Poverty Revisited
    Universal Free
    Free and Reduced-Price Eligibility
The Uncertainties From 1981 Through 1990
    Federal Budget Cuts of 1981
    Threats of Block Grants
Emphasis of the 1990s
    Healthy School Meals
The Administration of Child Nutrition
National School Breakfast Program
Donated Commodity Program
    Requirements of the Commodity Program
    Processing of Commodities
    Re-Engineering of the Commodity Program
Special Milk Program
After-School Snack Program
Special Needs of Children
    Children With Disabilities
    Children With Allergies
Meeting Regulations
Special Assistance—Provisions 1, 2, and 3
Operating Without Federal Programs
Nutrition Education-Related Training
Present and Future Trends
Selected References

OVERVIEW AND HISTORY OF SCHOOL FOODSERVICE

Over 90 percent of all public schools offer the National School Lunch Program (NSLP), and 24 percent of all private schools do—totaling more than 94,000 schools. Fifty-seven percent of the students eat at school and over half of those students are served meals free or at reduced prices. For that reason many pages of this book are devoted to foodservice management in schools with the NSLP, or the Child Nutrition programs, as well as to the total management of foodservices in elementary and secondary schools.

The NSLP, established by legislation in 1946, is over 50 years old and yet it is thriving today. Serving food at school didn't start in 1946 but can be traced back nearly 150 years. Some of the highlights of that history are covered in this chapter. For a more detailed historical account, see Martin and Conklin (1999).

School Foodservice From 1853 to 1940

Serving food at school began in New York with the volunteer efforts of the Children's Aid Society in 1853 and similar groups in Philadelphia, Milwaukee, Boston, and other cities. In the early years of the twentieth century two books, *Poverty* (Hunter 1904) and *The Bitter Cry of the Children* (Spargo 1906), brought to public attention the hunger and malnutrition that existed in this country. Hunter estimated that at least 10 million persons were living in poverty in 1904. He observed that poverty's misery fell most heavily upon children. He also estimated that in New York City alone, 60,000 to 70,000 children "often arrive at school hungry and unfitted to do well the work required." Spargo described case after case of deplorable poverty in New York City. He pointed out that the land where these people fondly dreamed that their Utopia might be realized had been instead, "poverty through plethora."

Volunteer Groups

The people feeding lunch to children in the early 1900s were primarily volunteer groups. Soon, many schools over the country assumed responsibility for serving lunches. The lunchroom in 1913 in Lower Merion (PA) was described by Cronan (1962) as "under the main stairway." The menu usually consisted of soup, sandwiches, beans, and ice cream.

By 1918, lunch of some type was being provided in schools in approximately one quarter of the larger cities. It could hardly be compared to the "Type A" lunch or the "Nutrient Standard" lunch. For example, a health officer in Pinellas County (FL), who knew that milk was valuable to children, placed a large white cow on the school playground as an advertisement for his milk program. He was so pleased with the results that a bowl of hot soup was added to go with the milk.

In 1921 Chicago claimed it had "the most intensive school lunch system in America." All high schools and 60 elementary schools were serving lunches paid for or authorized by the Chicago Board of Education.

Depression and Unemployment

School lunches expanded during the Depression. For the first time federal funds were appropriated for such programs. The first federal funds came from the Reconstruction Finance Corporation in 1932 and 1933. These funds paid labor costs for preparing school lunches in several towns in southwestern Missouri. In the 1930s there was high unemployment and little money for buying food, so Congress found it necessary to give federal assistance to support agriculture, provide employment, furnish lunches for children at school, and to aid the general economy. By 1934 the funding had been extended to 39 states under the Civil Work Administration and the Federal Emergency Relief Administration.

The Works Progress Administration (WPA), a relief measure established in 1935, assigned women in needy areas to jobs, some in the schools preparing lunches. This resulted in school lunches becoming organized and being supervised by each state. Standardization of menus, recipes, and procedures resulted. By 1941 the WPA program (sometimes referred to as the Works Project Administration) was operating in all states, the District of Columbia, and Puerto Rico. At least 23,000 schools were serving an average of nearly 2 million lunches daily and employing more than 64,000 people (see Figure 1.1).

The school lunch program began growing in the early 1940s. Often food came directly from the farms to the schools. One school superintendent in North Carolina remembered receiving a carload of cabbage on the Tuesday before the Thanksgiving holidays. The weather was warm, and by the following week the classroom used to store the vegetable was reeking with the odor of rotten cabbage. Later, canneries were established in schools to prevent the spoilage of fresh foods.

Figure 1.1. Lunch at School Became a Major Employer of Women in the 1940s and 1950s

Courtesy of the U. S. Department of Agriculture.

GROWTH FROM 1940 TO 1966

In 1942 surplus foods and federal funds were being used by 78,841 schools in order to serve some type of food to over five million children. Federal funds that year were used to purchase $21 million worth of food for the schools. According to Gunderson (1971), the food was available to a school if the school administration signed an agreement with the state distribution agency including the following provisions:

- Commodities would be used for preparation of school lunches on the school premises.
- They would not be sold or exchanged.
- The food purchases would not be discontinued or curtailed because of the receipt of surplus foods.
- The program would not be operated for profit.
- The children who could not pay for their meals would not be segregated or discriminated against and would not be identified to their peers.
- Proper warehousing would be provided and proper accounting would be rendered for all foods received.

The effects of World War II were felt by every part of the economy, especially on the school lunch program. The programs receiving federal funds and surplus foods decreased to only 34,064 schools, hardly a third of those that were participating prior to the war. Federal assistance was cut and commodities were no longer available. WPA workers were not available for preparing school lunches, but were now employed to produce supplies needed for the war. The lunch program had become so much a part of the child's school day that it was not destroyed but temporarily halted.

The school lunch program quickly recovered following World War II with the passage of the National School Lunch Act in 1946, which made it possible to provide 4.5 million children lunch at school. This legislation provided funding that year of $231 million for the National School Lunch Program, compared to $6,490.4 in 1996 (50 years later).

National School Lunch Act of 1946

The National School Lunch Program (NSLP) Act was signed into law in 1946 by President Harry S. Truman (see Figure 1.2). It became a law primarily because (1) during physical examinations for military service, many young men had been found to be malnourished, (2) there was a need for an outlet for agricultural commodities produced by flourishing farms after World War II, and (3) lunch at school was needed for learning to take place. The purpose was stated in the introduction to the law: "...as a measure of national security, to safeguard the health and well-being of the Nation's children and to encourage the domestic consumption of nutritious agricultural commodities and other food. . . ." (See Appendix A for excerpts from the National School Lunch Act.)

By the end of 1946, the Lunch Program had surpassed the size it had been prior to World War II and schools were serving nutritious lunches meeting the established meal requirements (see Figure 1.3). However, the uncertainty of the program and the limited funds caused school administrators to be cautious in starting the program.

Figure 1.2. The National School Lunch Act Was Signed Into Law on June 4, 1946, by President Harry S. Truman (Seated)

Witnesses were (left to right): Rep. Clarence Cannon (Missouri); Clinton Anderson, Secretary of Agriculture; Rep. Malcolm Tarver (Georgia); Sen. Richard Russell (Georgia); Sen. Allen Ellender (Louisiana); Rep. Clifford Hope (Kansas); Sen. George Aiken (Vermont); Rep. Ron Flanagan (West Virginia); Nathan Koenig, Assistant to the Secretary of Agriculture; Paul Stark, Director of the Food Distribution Division, USDA; Robert Shields, Administrator, Product and Marketing Administration, USDA; and N. E. Dodd, Under Secretary of Agriculture.

Courtesy of the American School Food Service Association.

Figure 1.3. Schools Were Serving Nutritious Lunches From the Beginning of the National School Lunch Program

Courtesy of the U. S. Department of Agriculture.

The National School Lunch Program was from the beginning administered by the state education agency and the individual schools in the state participating had to agree to do the following:

1. Serve lunches which met minimum nutritional requirements prescribed by the U. S. Secretary of Agriculture
2. Serve meals without cost or at a reduced cost to children who were determined by local school authorities to be unable to pay the full cost of the lunch
3. Make no discrimination against any child because of his inability to pay the full price of the lunch
4. Operate on a nonprofit basis
5. Utilize foods declared by the U.S. Secretary of Agriculture as being in abundance
6. Utilize free commodities as donated by the Secretary
7. Maintain records of receipts and expenditures and submit this report to the state agency as required

Lunches meeting minimum nutritional requirements were defined by the Secretary as three types of lunches: Type A, Type B, and Type C. Originally the Type A lunch was defined as containing:

½ pint of fluid whole milk
Protein-rich food consisting of one of the following or a combination:
    2 ounces (edible portion as served) of lean meat, poultry, or fish
    2 ounces of cheese
    1 egg
    ½ cup of cooked dry beans or peas
    4 tablespoons peanut butter
¾ cup serving of two or more vegetables or fruits, or both
1 portion or serving of bread, cornbread, biscuits, rolls, muffins, etc., made of whole-grain or enriched meal or flour
2 teaspoons of butter or fortified margarine

The Type A meal pattern lasted 35 years (1946-1977) with only three changes.

The Type B lunches contained smaller quantities of the components in the Type A lunch and were served primarily in those schools with inadequate cooking facilities. Type C lunches consisted only of ½ pint of fluid whole milk served as a beverage.

Limited Funding

In the 1950s and 1960s many school foodservice programs were feeding free lunches out of funds from the paying student. If the paying student paid 25 cents in 1963, one can imagine how difficult it was to pay the cost of preparing two lunches (one being free) out of that 25 cents with a federal cash reimbursement of only 4 cents and commodities valued at another 6 cents. Making students work for their lunches, scrutinizing free-lunch applications, and serving a different lunch to the free lunch student all sound inhumane, but the lack of funds forced adoption of such practices in some parts of the country. It was a matter of pure survival for the school lunch programs.

National School Lunch Week

National School Lunch Week was first celebrated in 1963 by a proclamation signed by President John F. Kennedy. It showed the general acceptance of the program when Congress passed PL 87-780 and established National School Lunch Week, which stated that "the seven-day period beginning on the second Sunday of October in each year is hereby designated as National School Lunch Week, and the President is requested to issue annually a proclamation calling on the people of the United States to observe such a week with appropriate ceremonies and activities."

At first a universal menu was planned for Wednesday of that week. This was replaced when the American School Food Service Association and some of the states encouraged a nationwide menu for the week to be the focal point for National School Lunch Week.

THE CHILD NUTRITION PROGRAM FROM 1966 to 1981

During the mid-1960s there was great interest in Congress regarding nutrition and poverty in various parts of the country. As a result, the Child Nutrition Act of 1966 became law. It provided the first substantial funding for needy children's meals, guidelines for identifying the needy, and a pilot breakfast program.

Poverty Revisited

Included under the Child Nutrition Act was the continuation of the Type C lunch which was known as "Special Milk Program." The Act provided for a pilot breakfast program, funds to purchase school foodservice equipment in low-income areas, and state administrative funds.

In 1968 several groups brought national attention to poverty with the stories they told. The publication of *Their Daily Bread* (Fairfax 1968), said poverty was identified as one of the main reasons for unrest in America. That same year the Citizens Board of Inquiry into Hunger and Malnutrition in the United States focused on poverty in their book, *Hunger, USA* (1968).

Beginning with the Child Nutrition Act of 1966 and adequate funding which really began in 1969 needy children were provided meals free and at reduced prices

Universal Free

During the 1970s Hubert Humphrey (Democrat from Minnesota) in the Senate and Carl Perkins (Democrat from Kentucky) in the House of Representatives introduced legislation for the first time to make the school foodservice program a "Universal Food Service and Nutrition Education Program." The bills never made much progress because of the high price tag and the difficulty of determining what a "universal" program would actually cost.

The Child Nutrition programs were popular with Congress, which rejected the annual budget cuts proposed during most of the 1980s and block grants in the mid 1990s. The Child Nutrition programs provided nutritious meals to countless undernourished children over the years either free or at reduced prices, as can be seen in Table 1.1. The "paid" meals provided under the National School Lunch Program are usually priced from 50¢ to $1 less than at schools not participating in the NSLP as a result of the federal subsidy and USDA commodities received.

Table 1.1. National School Lunch Program Average Participation and Total Meals Served

Fiscal Year	Number of Schools (thousands)	Average Daily Participation (9-Mo. Avg.) (millions)				Total Annual Meals Served (millions)				Percent F/RP[1] of Total
		Free	Reduced	Paid	Total	Free	Reduced	Paid	Total	
1969	74.9	2.9	b[2]	16.5	19.4	507.7	b	2,860.5	3,368.2	15.1
1970	75.6	4.6	b	17.8	22.4	738.5	b	2,826.6	3,565.1	20.7
1971	79.9	5.8	0.5	17.8	24.1	1005.7	b	2,842.6	3,848.3	26.1
1972	83.3	7.3	0.5	16.6	24.4	1,285.3	b	2,686.8	3,972.1	32.4
1973	86.4	8.1	0.5	16.1	24.7	1,363.9	38.5	2,606.4	4,008.8	35.0
1974	87.7	8.6	0.5	15.5	24.6	1,432.8	45.3	2,503.5	3,981.6	37.1
1975	88.9	9.4	0.6	14.9	24.9	1,545.4	92.5	2,425.1	4,063.0	40.3
1976	88.6	10.2	0.8	14.6	25.6	1,650.2	138.0	2,359.7	4,147.9	43.1
1977	91.3	10.5	1.3	14.5	26.2	1,696.4	209.0	2,344.6	4,250.0	44.8
1978	93.8	10.3	1.5	14.9	26.7	1,659.3	248.7	2,386.1	4,294.1	44.4
1979	94.3	10.0	1.7	15.3	27.0	1,623.4	277.9	2,456.1	4,357.4	43.6
1980	94.1	10.0	1.9	14.7	26.6	1,671.4	308.0	2,407.6	4,387.0	45.1
1981	94.0	10.6	1.9	13.3	25.8	1,736.7	311.7	2,162.2	4,210.6	48.6
1982	91.2	9.8	1.6	11.5	22.9	1,621.6	261.7	1,871.7	3,755.0	50.2
1983	90.6	10.3	1.5	11.2	23.0	1,713.5	252.9	1,836.9	3,803.3	51.7
1984	89.2	10.3	1.5	11.5	23.3	1,701.7	248.0	1,876.5	3,826.2	51.0
1985	89.4	9.9	1.6	12.1	23.6	1,656.6	254.5	1979.0	3,890.1	49.1
1986	89.9	10.0	1.6	12.2	23.8	1,678.0	257.0	2,007.5	3,942.5	49.1
1987	90.2	10.0	1.6	12.4	24.0	1,656.1	259.0	2024.8	3,939.9	48.6
1988	90.6	9.8	1.6	12.8	24.2	1,651.1	261.8	2121.0	4,032.9	47.4
1989	91.4	9.7	1.6	12.7	24.2	1656.8	263.3	2114.8	4004.9	47.2
1990	91.3	9.9	1.6	12.8	24.1	1661.6	273.0	2074.5	4009.1	48.3
1991	91.6	10.3	1.8	12.1	24.2	1748.4	292.5	2010.0	4050.9	50.4
1992	92.7	11.2	1.7	11.7	24.5	1891.2	284.8	1926.0	4101.9	53.0
1993	92.7	11.8	1.7	11.3	24.8	1981.1	287.4	1869.2	4137.7	54.8
1994	93.6	12.2	1.8	11.3	25.3	2049.5	298.1	1854.2	4201.8	55.9
1995	94.2	12.5	1.9	11.3	25.6	2090.3	308.5	1854.6	4253.4	56.4
1996	93.7	12.7	2.0	11.3	25.9	2128.4	326.5	1858.5	4313.3	56.9

F/RP = free and reduced-price meals compared to total.
[2]Included with free meals.

Source: U.S. Department of Agriculture, *Annual Historical Review of FNS Programs, Fiscal Year 1998,* and *1996 Green Book* (Committee on Ways and Means, 1996).
   Residential child care institutions (eligible to participate since FY 1977) are included. Schools alone are FY 1977-88, 800; FY 1978-90, 700; FY 1979-90, 800; FY 1980-90, 400; FY 1981-89, 000; FY 1982-87, 200; FY 1983-86, 800; FY 1984-85, 400; FY 1985-85,500; FY 1986-85, 900; FY 1987-86, 200; and FY 1988-86, 200.

Free and Reduced-Price Meal Eligibility

Prior to the Child Nutrition Act of 1966 there were few guidelines for determining who should qualify to receive a free (or reduced-price) meal. This Act established the reduced-price meal (officially) and the free and reduced-price meal eligibility was to be determined on the basis of federal poverty guidelines. These same basic guidelines are used today—they are revised annually and published in the *Federal Register* in February or March for the following school year. The peak in number of children served at school under the National School Lunch Program was in fiscal year 1979, when 27 million children were served in 94,399 schools and residential institutions.

THE UNCERTAINTIES FROM 1981 THROUGH 1990

The 1980s were full of changes and threats for the Child Nutrition programs. It was characterized by declines in funding, stricter federal regulations (including the requirement that applications for free and reduced-price meals include social security number and that some applications be verified), and more audits of school foodservice operations by state and federal agencies. Many school foodservice programs experienced their first deficits during the 1980s.

Federal Budget Cuts of 1981

The reimbursement rates have increased annually based on the Consumer Price Index for food away from home (see Table 1.2), except in 1981, when the Omnibus Budget Reconciliation Act (Public law 97-35) was implemented (and in 1998-99 when the rates were not increased for the paying child). The reduced-price meal reimbursement rates started at 10¢ less than the rates for free-meals in the 1970s, increased to 20¢ in 1981, and jumped to 40¢ in 1982 and has continued at that level ever since. The paying child's subsidy has been at risk several times during the budget-cutting years.

Participation in the National School Lunch Program dropped from a high of 27 million in 94,300 schools in fiscal year 1979 to 22.9 million in 91,200 schools in fiscal year 1982. With declining enrollment in the 1980s and the 1981 budget cuts, participation has increased only slightly since (Table 1.1).

In 1982 nearly 3,000 schools dropped out of the National School Lunch Program and another 2,000 over the next two years, as a result of the budget cuts and the participation dropped accordingly. Federal funding decreased drastically in most categories as can be seen in Tables 1.2 and 1.3. At the same time the percentage of the students served free and reduced-price meals increased (Table 1.1). This decline continued until 1989, when a slight increase was realized, but the program has never regained the numbers of 1979, the peak year. (See Figure 1.4.)

Table 1.2. National School Lunch Program National Average Payment and Commodity Rates by Type of Meal (cents per lunch)

Period	Paid Section 4	Free Sections 4 and 11	Reduced-Price Sections 4 and 11	Commodities All Lunches
01/76-06/76	12.50	69.25	59.25	11.00
07/76-12/76	13.00	71.50	61.50	11.75
01/77-06/77	13.25	73.25	63.25	11.75
07/77-12/77	14.00	77.00	67.00	12.75
01/78-06/78	14.50	79.50	69.50	12.75
07/78-12/78	15.25	83.50	73.50	13.75
01/79-06/79[a]	15.75	87.25	77.25	13.75
07/79-12/79[b]	17.00	93.25	83.25	15.75
01/80-06/80	17.75	97.25	87.256	15.75
07/80-12/80	18.50	102.00	92.00	15.50
01/81-06/81[c,d]	16.00	99.50	79.50	13.50
07/81-08/81	17.75	109.25	89.25	11.00
09/81-06/82[e]	10.50	109.25	69.25	11.00
07/82-06/83	11.00	115.00	75.00	11.50
07/83-06/84	11.50	120.25	80.25	11.50
07/84-06/85	12.00	125.50	85.50	12.00
07/85-06/86	12.50	130.25	90.25	11.75
07/86-06/87	13.00	135.50	95.50	11.25
07/87-06/88	13.50	140.50	100.50	12.00
07/88-06/89	14.00	146.25	106.25	12.25
08/89-06/90	14.75	153.25	113.25	13.25
07/90-06/91	15.50	160.75	120.75	14.00
07/91-06/92	16.00	166.25	126.25	14.00
07/92-06/93	16.25	169.50	129.50	14.00
07/93-06/94	16.50	172.50	132..50	14.00
07/94-06/95	17.00	175.75	135.75	14.50
07/95-06/96	17.25	179.50	139.50	14.25
07/96-06/97	17.75	183.75	143.75	14.50
07/97-06/98	18.00	189.00	149.00	15.00
07/98-06/99	18.00	190.00	150.00	14.75

[a]During January 1, 1979-December 31, 1980, the reduced price could be up to 10 cents less than indicated depending on the state pricing polices.
[b]Alaska has been reimbursed at lunch rates equal to 162 percent of the national average payment rates since July 1979.
[c]Hawaii has been reimbursed at lunch rates equal to 117 percent of the national average payment rates since January 1, 1981.
[d]Between January and August 1981, payment rates were 2.5 cents higher for those school food authorities that served 60 percent or more of lunches free or at a reduced price in the second prior school year.
[e]After September 1981, payment rates were 2 cents higher for school food authorities that served 60 percent or more of their lunches free or at a reduced price in the second prior school year.

Source: U. S. Department of Agriculture, *Annual Historical Review of FNS Program,* Fiscal Year 1998, and *Federal Register* 1998.

Table 1.3. Federal Cost of All School Food Programs (millions of dollars)

Fiscal Year	NSLP Section 4	NSLP Section 11	NSLP Total Cash	School Break-fast	Special Milk	Total Cash	Entitle-ment[b]	Commodities Bonus	Commodities Total	Total Federal Cost
1969	162.0	41.8	203.8	5.4	101.3	310.5	272.0	—		582.5
1970	168.0	132.2	300.2	10.8	101.2	412.2	265.2	—	265.2	677.1
1971	224.7	307.5	532.2	19.4	91.2	642.8	277.3	—	277.3	920.1
1972	225.7	513.0	738.7	24.9	90.3	853.9	312.1	—	312.1	1,166.0
1973	225.7	656.4	882.1	34.6	90.8	1,007.5	331.0	—	331.0	1,338.5
1974	409.0	676.4	1,085.4	59.1	49.2	1,193.7	316.1	—	316.1	1,509.8
1975	463.4	825.6	1,289.0	86.1	122.9	1,498.0	423.5	—	272.0	1,921.5
1976	513.0	978.5	1,491.5	113.7	138.5	1,743.7	418.6	—	418.6	2,162.3
1977	560.1	1,010.2	1,570.3	148.6	150.0	1,868.9	540.8	—	540.8	2,409.7
1978	618.0	1,190.3	1,808.3	181.2	135.3	2,124.8	485.3	57.6	542.9	2,667.7
1979	684.6	1,299.1	1,983.7	231.0	133.6	2,348.3	675.3	69.6	744.9	3,093.2
1980	772.4	1,507.0	2,279.4	287.8	145.2	2,712.4	765.5	139.0	904.5	3,616.9
1981	708.6	1,672.0	2,380.6	331.7	100.8	2,813.1	578.9	316.3	895.2	3,708.3
1982	421.3	1,764.1	2,185.4	317.3	18.3	2,521.0	426.2	330.8	757.0	3,278.0
1983	446.2	1,955.6	2,401.8	343.8	17.4	2,763.0	426.8	374.1	800.9	3,563.9
1984	470.9	2,036.8	2,507.7	364.0	16.0	2,887.7	440.5	386.9	827.4	3,715.1
1985	497.9	2,080.5	2,578.4	379.3	15.8	2,973.5	456.0	345.2	801.2	3,774.7
1986	524.1	2,190.4	2,714.5	406.3	15.5	3,136.4	445.8	376.2	821.9	3,958.3
1987	541.5	2,255.7	2,797.2	446.8	15.5	3,259.5	448.5	439.6	888.1	4,147.6
1988	574.9	2,344.9	2,919.8	483.7	19.0	3,422.5	462.7	340.6	803.3	4,225.8
1989	592.3	2,413.3	3,005.6	513.2	18.5	3,537.3	471.4	292.5	763.9	4,301.2
1990	622.6	2,591.4	3,214.0	596.2	19.2	3,829.4	465.9	153.8	619.7	4,449.1
1991	658.6	2,866.2	3,524.7	685.0	19.8	4,229.5	590.1	109.1	699.3	4,928.8
1992	686.8	3,169.7	3856.5	786.7	19.5	4,662.7	583.4	123.9	707.2	5,369.9
1993	705.4	3,33759	4,081.3	868.8	18.7	4,968.9	577.8	90.5	668.4	5,637.2
1994	731.5	3,559.3	4,290.8	959.0	17.8	5,267.6	629.2	96.2	725.3	5,992.9
1995	762.6	3,704.2	4,466.8	1,048.3	17.0	5,532.1	611.8	81.8	693.6	6,225.7
1996	787.8	3,874.0	4,661.8	1,118.8	16.8	5,794.4	647.2	445.8	693.0	6,490.4

[a]Includes commodity schools (cash).
[b]Includes cash-in-lieu-of commodities and commodity schools.

Source: U.S. Department of Agriculture, *Annual Historical Review of FNS Programs, Fiscal Year 1998.*

Threats of Block Grants

Off and on during the 1980s, the threat of block grants were feared. The potential developed more during the United States House of Representatives debates in 1994. With block grants the federal money would be given to the state for the states to decide how the money would be distributed. School foodservice directors feared children would lose in such an arrangement.

Figure 1.4. Lunch at School Was Popular With Students of All Ages in the 1980s

Courtesy of U. S. Department of Agriculture.

EMPHASIS OF THE 1990s

The emphasis of the early 1990s has been on meeting the nutritional requirements of students, referred to as the "School Meals Initiative."

Healthy School Meals

In October 1994 the "Healthy Meals for Americans Act" (PL 103-448) established nutrition standards for the National School Lunch and School Breakfast Programs. No legislation in recent years has caused such a stir as this has for the Child Nutrition programs. The regulations for the "School Meals Initiative" were finalized in June 1995 with the flexibility to choose from the four different menu planning systems. Then a fifth option was added — "any reasonable approach" to meeting the nutritional standards. The nutritional standards are the same for all five menu planning options. Many directors have selected the option that is easiest to carry out and that means the least change, which is the "traditional food-based." These menu planning options are discussed in detail in Chapters 3, "Dietary Guidelines and Nutritional Requirements," and 4, "Planning Menus and Food Offerings."

Since July 1996, schools under the Child Nutrition Program have been required to comply with the *Dietary Guidelines for Americans*. Under the regulations of the School Meals Initiative there are five types of meal-planning systems:

Traditional Food-Based Menu Planning
Enhanced Food-Based Menu Planning
Nutrient Standard Menu Planning
Assisted Nutrient Standard Menu Planning
Any Reasonable Approach to Menu Planning

The differences in the five systems are described in Chapter 3, "Dietary Guidelines and Nutritional Requirements." Public Law 104-149 established the "School Meal Initiative," which is the means of accomplishing the nutritional goals and standards for analyzing the meals served. The state depart-ment administering the Child Nutrition Programs checks the school districts for compliance with a review of the School Meal Initiative (SMI). The menus and production records are evaluated for a period of time, and nutrient analyses are performed regardless of the method used for menu planning.

In 1998 the NSLP served 26.6 million children daily in 94,000 schools. Millions of other children were being served under unsubsidized programs. Due to declining school enrollment (see Table 1.1) and the implementation of the budget-cutting law, Omnibus Budget Reconciliation Act (see Table 1.2), there was a decline in the number of school lunches served during the 1980s. This trend slowed in the years to follow. According to the Government Accounting Office (GAO) report, "Schools that left the NSLP," only 300 schools left the NSLP between July 1989 and February 1993. Many fear the enforcement of the Dietary Guidelines, and sale of foods of minimal nutritional value, and high costs of operating the program will cause more high schools to drop from the program. Enrollment among the younger age groups increased in the 1990s (as can be seen in Table 1.4) and is expected to rise slightly between 2000 and 2010.

The total foodservice industry (as a whole) has grown rapidly in the 1990s to over $350 billion by the end of the 1990s; school foodservices were in excess of $14 billion of that in 1999 (representing four percent of the industry). Although school foodservice is no longer considered the third largest foodservice industry (as it was in the 1960s and 1970s), it has the opportunity to expand if school foodservice management desires to meet some of the growing needs for foodservice in communities. School district foodservice programs can become the community nutrition centers meeting the food needs of the elderly and preschool children. Also, the enrollment rates of the school-age children are expected to grow by 8 percent through 2006.

Table 1.4. Population Change for Five Age Groups 1980-2000 (population in millions)

Age Groups	1980 (millions)	1990 (millions)	2000 (millions)
Children Under 5	16.4	18.9	19.0
5-9	16.6	18.3	20.0
Youths 10-14	18.2	17.2	19.3
15-19	21.1	17.8	19.6
20-24	21.6	19.1	17.8

Source: U.S. Bureau of Census based on 1985, 1990, and 1998 data.

THE ADMINISTRATION OF CHILD NUTRITION

The Child Nutrition programs are administered at the federal level by the United States Department of Agriculture (USDA), see Chapter 7 for the USDA structure, and at state level by state departments of education. One exception is in New Jersey where the Child Nutrition programs are administered by the New Jersey Department of Agriculture. Locally the school food authority (SFA) is responsible for the Child Nutrition programs and an SFA may be as large as the New York City School District, with 1,417 schools serving 138 million meals a year, or as small as one school serving 100.

The school year is commonly considered nine months (180 days), however, year-around education has become rather common in over four percent of the schools districts nationwide, with at least 40 percent of those in California.

Any public or nonprofit private school (high school level or under) is eligible to participate in the Child Nutrition programs, except for private schools with tuition of more than $2,000. Cash reimbursement and commodity assistance are provided to public and nonprofit private schools that agree to comply with federal regulations of the Child Nutrition programs. Federal funding over the years is shown in the Table 1. 2.

The reimbursement rates have been extended to a fraction of a cent in the past as can be seen in Table 1.2. The cash reimbursement and commodity rates for lunch (by category) in the 1998-99 school year were as follows:

Beginning July 1999, the rates will be rounded down, which could result in a considerable loss to the foodservice program. For example, if the free reimbursement for 1999-2000 was to be $1.9875 for each student lunch, the rounding would result in it being $1.98, a loss of $.0075 per free lunch (for a school district serving 25,000 free lunches a day, that is a loss of $33,750 that year).

Federal Reimbursement Rates for Lunch in 1998-99	
Paid	$0.1800
Free	$1.9425
Reduced-Price	$1.5425
Entitlement Commodities (all student lunches)	$0.1475

Schools qualifying and serving more than 60 percent of their students lunches at free or reduced prices quality for the "severe need" reimbursement rates, which is an additional 2 cents per student lunch in 1999-2000.

In 1998-99, the Chicago Public Schools began serving a third meal three days a week to 35,000 students in 248 schools in what the school district calls the "Light House Program." The federal funding is provided through the USDA Child and Adult Care Food Program.

The earned federal reimbursement for the NSLP, the School Breakfast Program (SBP), and Special Milk program is based on performance participation, that is, an assigned rate per meal or half pint of milk served. The federal reimbursements are funneled through the states, except for private schools in a few states, and are received as a reimbursement after the meals are served.

To qualify for cash reimbursement for the SBP and cash reimbursement and commodity assistance for the NSLP, numerous federal regulations must be followed by a school district or the school food authority. (See the Appendix for the texts of the regulations.) The main regulation centers around meal requirements, handling of free and reduced-price meal applications, and meal accountability. The regulations that are relevant to subsequent chapters of this book will be discussed in those chapters, particularly Chapters 3 and 4, which addresses the nutritional requirements.

NATIONAL SCHOOL BREAKFAST PROGRAM

Breakfast was provided at school for the very needy long before a program became law. Sometimes breakfasts are at the expense of the lunch program. Food costs for the breakfast program may exceed the food costs for the lunch program because of meal requirements and the trend toward using convenience foods. The Child Nutrition Act of 1966 established funding for a pilot breakfast program, which was made permanent in 1975.

Today 27% of the children who participate in the National School Lunch Program (NSLP) also participate in the School Breakfast Program (SBP). More than two-thirds of the schools (65,000 in 1998) that participate in the NSLP participate in the breakfast program as well, serving an average of 7 .8 million a day in early 1999. Children qualifying for free and reduced-price meals account for more than 87 percent of the breakfasts served in 1998. Between 1976 and 1997, participation in the SBP more than tripled, and almost four times as many schools are in the program today as in 1976 (Table 1.5).

The benefits of breakfast to students have been proven in several studies. One of the most quoted is a study conducted in 1998, by a team of researchers from Tufts University School of Nutrition Science. This study showed that children who participated in the SBP performed better on standardized tests and were on time and in school more often than children who did not. Also, studies done by the Harvard Medical School, Massachusetts General Hospital, and the state of Minnesota found that children who ate breakfast performed better both academically and socially.

In 1998 a group of superintendents told USDA why the breakfast programs were not one of their major emphases, giving such reasons as: (1) breakfast is not seen as a part of the overall educational process, (2) no staff is available to supervise students that early in the day , and (3) bus schedules do not allow sufficient time for children to eat breakfast. Other reasons the breakfast program has not grown any larger in some parts of the country are: (1) there is a lack of interest on the part of the students, (2) foodservice personnel are not available to serve breakfast, (3) the reimbursement rates are not adequate to cover the costs, and (4) principals' opposition—many consider breakfast a family responsibility, not the school's responsibility .

The federal reimbursement rates for free, reduced-price, and paid meals escalate annually and are indexed to change as the Consumer Price Index for food away from home changes. The income eligibility guidelines for free and reduced-price meals for the lunch and breakfast programs are identical.

Additional funding for breakfast is available for schools designated as "severe need" for federal funding purposes, which are those schools serving in excess of 40 percent of their lunches free or at a reduced price two preceding years and with costs that exceed the regular breakfast program rates. Most schools that qualify for "severe need" based on participation also qualify for full allowable funding. How the cost of a breakfast is determined in some states prevents the schools in those states from qualifying for full funding. Fourteen states provide financial incentives for the breakfast program, and 22 mandate the breakfast program. Generally the mandate is that breakfast be provided in any school where the number of free and reduced-price lunches served exceeds a specified percent of those served.

Table 1.5. School Breakfast Program Participation From 1977 Through 1997 by Category

Fiscal Year	Free (Millions)	Reduced-Price (Millions)	Full-Price (Millions)	Total (Millions)
1977	2.0	.1	0.4	2.5
1978	2.2	.2	.4	2.8
1979	2.6	.2	.5	3.3
1980	2.8	.2	.6	3.6
1981	3.0	.2	.5	3.8
1982	2.8	.2	.4	3.3
1983	2.9	.1	.3	3.4
1984	2.9	.1	.4	3.4
1985	2.9	.2	.4	3.4
1986	2.9	.2	.4	3.5
1987	3.0	.2	.4	3.7
1988	3.0	.2	.5	3.7
1989	3.1	.2	.5	3.8
1990	3.3	.2	.5	4.0
1991	3.6	.2	.6	4.4
1992	4.0	.3	.6	4.9
1993	4.4	.3	.7	5.4
1994	4.8	.3	.7	5.8
1995	5.1	.4	.8	6.3
1996	5.3	.4	.9	6.6

Source: U. S. Department of Agriculture, *Annual Historical Review of FNS Programs, Fiscal Year 1998.*

The costs of preparing and serving breakfast must equal or exceed reimbursement rates in order to receive the "severe need" rates, or rates are adjusted accordingly. The state departments of education provide school districts with current federal rates of reimbursement for the breakfast program. For example, in the 1998-99 school year, federal reimbursements were as follows:

Federal Reimbursement Rates for Breakfast in 1998-99	
Paid breakfast	$0.2000
Non-severe need, reduced-price	$0.7725
Severe need, reduced-price	$0.9775
Non-severe need, free	$1.0725
Severe need, free	$1.2775

Commodities for the breakfast program were eliminated in 1981 as a part of the Omnibus Budget Reconciliation Act. In 1989-90 the reimbursement rates were increased by 3 cents (in addition to escalation increases) to assist in improving the nutritional quality of meals served.

A universal breakfast program was promoted by the American School Food Service Association in 1998, but many are afraid of the potential price tag. A universal school breakfast pilot program was proposed in the 1999 federal budget but was not funded by Congress.

DONATED COMMODITY PROGRAM

The USDA, Food and Nutrition Service, is in charge of the Food Distribution Program, which purchases food with funds provided through:

- direct appropriations from Congress
- surplus removal
- price support

The USDA donated commodities are distributed to state agencies for schools eligible under the National School Lunch Program and commodity-only schools. Schools that operate a non-profit foodservice program are also eligible to receive donated food assistance if they do not participate in the National School Lunch Program. The overall donated food values are based on the annual percentage change in a three-month average value of the Price Index for Food Used in Schools and Institutions, which sets prices for cereal/bakery products, meat/poultry/fish, dairy products, processed fruits/vegetables, and fats/oils. The state agencies may be charging for handling donated commodities, as high as $5 per case. This becomes an undesirable expense, particularly if the commodity received isn't needed or wanted by the school district.

Two types of commodities have been provided to schools under the National School Lunch Program: (1) "entitlement" commodities, which are based on the number of lunches served multiplied by the annual per meal commodity rate (see Table I.2), and (2) "bonus"commodities, which has been additional foods acquired through the price-support and surplus-removal programs. Bonus commodities will be a part of entitlement commodities beginning with the 1999-2000 school year, which means a reduction in commodities.

Entitlement commodity value, unlike the federal cash reimbursements that generally increases annually, increases occasionally based on changes in the Consumer Price Index for food away from home (see Table 1.2 for the value of entitlement commodities from 1976 through 1999). The USDA acquires foods for donation under three authorizations:

1. Section 6, National School Lunch Act of 1946
2. Section 32, Public Law 320 as amended in 1936
3. Section 416, Agricultural Act of 1949

The bonus commodities vary according to the market and in the 1980s were based on how much the school district can use. In the 1970s and through most of the 1980s, there were surplus dairy products that government officials thought would never be completely used. These products were distributed to schools as bonus commodities in unlimited quantities. With the increased popularity of pizza using cheese and the distribution of dairy products to the needy and drought victims, the "unlimited"supply was used up by 1988. Suddenly the world market price was above the surplus removal price paid by the USDA. In July 1988 the USDA cut back on cheese and dry milk allocations to the schools and limited the quantities schools could receive.

The role of donated commodities has changed substantially since the mid-1980s when donated commodities accounted for about 30 percent of the total value of foods used by the schools. In 1996-97, they accounted for less than 13 percent. The total quantity of donated commodities was about 50 percent of what it was in 1984-85. The dollars spent was at its peak in 1987 with $439.6 million and dropped in 1989-90 to $153.8 million, and in 1997 it was a mere $28.8 million.

Requirements of the Commodity Program

Schools receiving commodities are required in many states to submit inventory reports during the school year to the state department responsible for commodity distribution. In all states schools are required to maintain records of the amounts received and used for a period of three years, plus the current year. The USDA foods cannot be sold or traded. It is the duty of the school receiving the commodity to inspect the delivery, noting the amount received, and the condition of the food before signing the receipt. The school is then held responsible for properly storing and using the commodity.

Federal regulations allow a school district to refuse up to 20 percent of the total value of a donated commodity and receive substitute commodities when available. Most school districts do not utilize this federal regulation to their full advantages and many of the states can not handle the refusals and substitutions because of storage and delivery systems used within the states. In addition, often the lead time between notification and receipt of a donated commodity does not allow for refusals. Some commodities are unpopular in parts of the country and difficult for school districts to use. Figure 1.5 provides a breakdown of the percentage of commodity dollars spent by category in 1998-99. Over 50 percent of the commodity dollars is spent on protein-rich foods, 21 percent on fruits and vegetables, and 16 percent for dairy products.

Processing of Commodities

Processing of commodities is a way to obtain variety and flexibility and utilizing more donated foods and processing is discussed further in Chapter 9, "Procurement and Inventory Management."

States usually have processing contracts whereby the commodity can be converted into another product before delivery to the school district. It is ideal when the conversion can be arranged before the state receives the products. Approximately four percent of the foods used by schools is processed using a commodity as an ingredient. The USDA discontinued the National Commodity Processing, which allowed school districts to convert raw products into different food items, during the early 1990s. This is unfortunate because some state departments do not have processing contracts in place and do not encourage school districts to use them. Foodservice directors in California have organized and cooperatively process their commodities.

Figure 1.5. Variety of USDA Commodity Foods Received

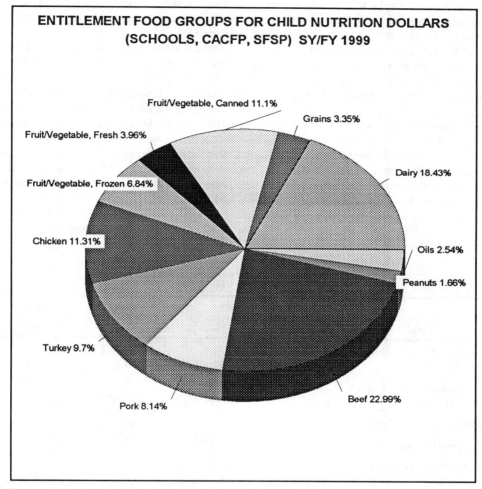

ENTITLEMENT FOOD GROUPS FOR CHILD NUTRITION DOLLARS
(SCHOOLS, CACFP, SFSP) SY/FY 1999

Fruit/Vegetable, Canned 11.1%

Grains 3.35%

Fruit/Vegetable, Fresh 3.96%

Dairy 18.43%

Fruit/Vegetable, Frozen 6.84%

Chicken 11.31%

Oils 2.54%

Peanuts 1.66%

Turkey 9.7%

Pork 8.14%

Beef 22.99%

Source: U. S. Department of Agriculture, Food Distribution 1999.

Re-Engineering of the Commodity Program

Schools and food distributors had various complaints which were strongly voiced in the early 1970s about commodities related to quality, delivery, quantities, timing, size and type of packaging, waste, and other problems.

Some people argued that since the early 1930s, when the commodity program was started, foodservice at schools had changed, but the commodity program had not kept pace with the changes.

For example, commodities were usually delivered in the raw state, and some school districts did not have the equipment and/or labor to prepare meals from raw ingredients. For some it was no longer cost-effective to accept a commodity that would require excessive labor hours to prepare or an unpopular food item that would negatively affect participation.

As a result of the complaints in the late 1970s, Congress authorized a study of alternatives to the commodity program. During the 1978-79 school year, eight school districts took part in a one-year pilot program and received all cash from USDA's budget for their lunch programs in place of donated commodities. A study done by Kansas State University and financed by the National Frozen Food Association found that schools realized more from the money available and could serve lunches that cost less if they received cash instead of commodities. The study projected a potential annual savings $162 million in 1979 if this program was extended nationwide. The cost of using commodities has become more of an issue than ever before for some directors—the food is not free. For example, in 1998-99 the cost of obtaining the commodity may equal $2 to $3 per case more than the identical commercially-purchased product. As a result of distributor storage and delivery costs (up to $5 per case), many school districts have established warehouses. The cost of warehousing and delivery may be greater than paying a distributor. Many school districts could purchase foods received from USDA for less. Based on Colorado prices in 1997-98, three commodity items as delivered to the district are compared to the commercial market in Table 1.6.

Table 1.6. Colorado 1997-98 Commodity Versus Purchased Food Prices

Food	Cost/Value	State Fee	Distributor Fee	Total Cost/Value
Commodity Peanut Butter 6/No. 10 cans	$ 32.95	$ .37	$1.97	$35.29
Purchased Peanut Butter, 6/No. 10 cans	$ 32.76	N/A	N/A	$32.76
Commodity Flour, 40 lb	$ 5.31	$ .37	$1.97	$ 7.65
Purchased Flour, 40 lb	$ 5.60	N/A	N/A	$ 5.60
Commodity Green Beans, 6/No. 10 cans	$ 13.07	$ .37	$1.97	$15.41
Purchased Green Beans, 6/No. 10 cans	$ 10.79	N/A	N/A	$10.79

Source: Miller, C. 1999. "The Case for Commodity Letter of Credit," California School Food Service Association Annual Meeting (Palm Springs, CA).

Pro-commodity groups still argue even today that cashing out commodities would defeat the whole purpose of the agricultural support programs. As a result of unrest and concerns about commodities, during the spring of 1980 the "voucher" system, or "commodity letter of credit" (CLOC) system, was promoted by the National Frozen Food Association and some school districts. Congress listened and passed legislation to fund a small national study to test two alternatives—CLOC and CASH. Ninety-six school districts participated in the three-year study; with 32 receiving CLOC, 34 receiving CASH, and 30 continuing commodities as control sites.

The impact of the different alternatives on school districts and on the stock of surplus food was analyzed. The sites receiving CLOCs proved that a voucher system could work effectively with the smallest and the largest school districts. Those testing CLOCs saw that the main advantage to such school districts is that the system is flexible and permits the purchase of food products (generic food that USDA designates as price support or surplus) in the form the local school district can use best. For example, a CLOC for "apples" can be used to purchase fresh apples, canned apples, canned apple pie filling, canned applesauce, apple turnovers, and so on.

Sixty of the 66 school districts opted through legislation to continue following the study to receive the alternative (CLOC or CASH) they tested, and it was made permanent for those few school districts in 1994. Also, all the schools in the state of Kansas have received cash for entitlement commodities since the late 1970s.

Though USDA Food Distribution has responded to request for more processed foods, which has tripled over the last ten years—34.4 of the value of donated foods are being further processed before reaching the school districts (USDA 1998). But yet, the complaints have not gone away, and the groups have organized again. USDA does realize they need to make change and they are planning change under the heading of "re-engineering" of the commodity program.

As a part of the "re-engineering" efforts, the USDA has appointed a group to work on the "reforms." The group is referred to as CORE (Commodity Order Re-Engineering) Team with the goals to find more efficient ways to deliver services and commodities to schools in a more predictable and timely manner. Unfortunately, the results will be a complicated process that will be a logistical challenge (or nightmare).

Though the purpose of the commodity program has changed over the years, and efforts have been made to improve the program, it is doubtful that the USDA can continue to successfully (cost effectively) purchase food for 92,000 school districts in 50 states. The Adams 12 (Northglenn, CO) School District director (1999) said, "The commodity program is like a dinosaur—it is large, cumbersome, tough to turn around, insensitive, terribly out of date and soon to be extinct if it doesn't change." The future of the commodity program and its alternatives is hard to predict since it continues to be a sensitive political issue.

SPECIAL MILK PROGRAM

The Special Milk Program was first authorized in 1954, and in 1966 was made a part of the Child Nutrition Act. The program provided subsidy for milk purchased by children in addition to the milk served as part of lunch and breakfast. For example, if a school purchased milk for 9.1 cents per half-pint in 1972, the child would pay 4 cents and the federal subsidy would be 5 to 6 cents. In 1980 funding was drastically cut, and from 1981 to 1986 the Special Milk Program was restricted to schools and institutions that did not participate in any other Child Nutrition programs.

In 1986 Congress authorized subsidizing milk for split-session kindergarten children who did not have the option of breakfast or lunch at school. The milk served "paying" students (those not qualifying for free milk according to the federal guidelines) is subsidized by the established rate, which is determined annually (the 1998-99 rate was 13 cents). The subsidy for free milk covers only the average cost of the milk from the dairy. The school district must cover the cost of labor to handle the milk storage, equipment depreciation, paper supplies, and other overhead costs.

This program has dwindled in the 1990s. Many directors want it eliminated and the money used in other ways to benefit more universally.

AFTER-SCHOOL SNACK PROGRAM

The After-School Snack Program (Public Law 105-336) was a part of the Child Nutrition Reauthorization Act of 1998. It puts a special emphasis on snacks served to children through age 18 who participate in organized educational/enrichment programs after school. The intent is to help reduce or prevent children's involvement in juvenile crime or other high-risk behavior.

For a school to be eligible for the After-School Snack Program and receive federal reimbursement, a school must operate the National School Lunch Program. The agreement is between the school food authority and the state agency. Snacks served during or before the school day, on weekends, during school vacations, or on holidays are not eligible to receive reimbursement under this provision. Under no circumstances can organized athletic programs receive this After-School Snack Program . The scheduled school day for some children may end at noon, as in the case of a kindergarten program or older children in split sessions. If the children remain in school under a care program, snacks served to these children are reimbursable. The food content of the snack is provided in Chapter 4, "Planning Menus and Food Offerings." The rather low reimbursement rates will limit what can be offered unless it is subsidized by another group. See Table 1.7 for the 1998-99 funding levels. Directors will need to carefully plan the snack and maintain low labor costs if this program is to break even.

After-school programs that operate in schools/areas where 50% or more students are eligible for free and reduced-price meals may receive the free rate of reimbursement for all snacks served to children in those programs are eligible for the After-School Snack Program. When the program receives the free rate of reimbursement for all children, the children cannot be charged for the snacks. If the program is not receiving the free reimbursement for all children, the children can be charged. The charges for the reduced-price snacks may not exceed 15 cents. Schools may claim reimbursement for one snack per child per day. The forms for applying for the After-School Program may be obtained from the state agency with more details about the requirements of the program.

Table 1.7. Funding in 1998-99 for Snacks Served in After-School Snack Program

	Paid	Reduced-Price	Free
Contiguous States	$.0400	$.2675	$.5325
Alaska	$.0700	$.4325	$.8625
Hawaii	$.0500	$.3125	$.6225

SPECIAL NEEDS OF CHILDREN

The Rehabilitation Act of 1973, the Individuals with Disabilities Education Act of 1990, and the Americans with Disabilities Act of 1990 call for providing nutrition services to children with special needs at no additional cost to the student. According to a survey done by the National Food Service Management Institute, there is at least one child in each school with special food and nutrition needs at no additional cost to the student. The parents and the child (children) often handle the needs without the school getting involved. The most common special food and nutrition needs are alternative beverages for children with milk allergies. Under the NSLP and SBP, a formal "prescription" from the doctor is required for a food or beverage substitution to be made.

Children With Disabilities

Disabled children's nutritional needs at school are to be met through the National School Lunch Program in accordance with Public Law 94-142, with only slight menu modifications. (See the National School Lunch Program regulations in the appendix for meal pattern adjustments that can be made in menus.)

In accordance with Public Law 94-142, both public and private education programs are prohibited from discriminating in the operation of foodservice programs. The slight modifications to the meals are to be made at no extra charge to the students whose handicaps restrict the diet. If a child has a medical request for a food substitution that the school does not have available, the parent may have to furnish the food. States may have additional regulations, and it is always wise to check with the state supervisor for such requirements.

Children With Allergies

Allergies are becoming more common among students. Regulations governing the National School Lunch and Breakfast Programs allow for food substitutions for individual students with medical or other special dietary needs when supported by a statement from a recognized medical authority. Such a statement should include recommended alternate foods. When a state supervisor or other auditor representing the USDA reviews the school foodservice in a district, the reviewer will ask to see the statements. As far as federal regulations are concerned, a medical statement regarding the allergy can be used so long as the student is in school and the statement does not have to be updated annually. State regulations should be checked for interpretation of these regulations.

MEETING REGULATIONS

At the local level, each school food authority (SFA), which is the entity signing the National School Lunch and Child Nutrition programs agreement with the state, is responsible for meeting the federal and state regulations of the programs that the school district is participating in. The relevant federal regulations are provided in the appendix and addressed in the checklist in Figure 1.7 which appears later in this chapter. Under the Coordinated Review Effort (CRE) reviews, the "auditors" of the program are checking schools for compliance with federal and state regulations.

The state department administering the Child Nutrition program monitors programs through several means; Administrative Review Service (ARS), Coordinated Effort Review (CRE), and School Meals Initiative (SMI). The latter two are used primarily today and are independent of each other, although they can be done at the same time, and in most states these reviews are performed every five years. CRE focuses on accountability and is involved with areas that affect the claim for reimbursement. The SMI review determines if a school district is meeting the goals of the Dietary Guidelines and Nutrient Standards regarding the foods offered.

SPECIAL ASSISTANCE—PROVISIONS 1, 2, AND 3

The Child Nutrition program regulations have a clause known as "Special Assistance"—Provisions 1, 2, and 3. Under these provisions a school district may opt to implement one of the provisions in all schools or in specific schools for breakfast or lunch or both. It is generally for schools with a high number of students qualifying for free and reduced-price meals—the closer to 100% of the enrollment the better. The federal funding is no greater for the school districts adopting Provision 2, for example, than for any other school districts.

The purpose of the provisions is to reduce the requirement for free and reduced-price meal applications, notifying the public, and counting meals by category for schools that agree to serve all enrolled students free meals. A school district that opts to meet the requirements and agrees to pay for other meals that federal funds do not cover should contact their state agency for information regarding the provisions. The administrative cost of handling the paperwork, and accountability is reduced and participation generally increases, which may offset some of the cost of serving all students free.

Under "Special Assistance—Provision 2," for example, schools provide lunch (or breakfast) free to all children in their schools. The advantages to the district are that the regulation reduces the requirement for taking applications to every five years and eliminates counting meals by category for school districts that agree to serve all students free meals. (See the National Lunch Act, Appendix A, for further details.) When a school district or a school goes this route, the school district agrees to pay the difference for those children who do not qualify for free meals. Some school districts with as few as 88 percent of their students qualifying for free have meals—lunch and/or breakfast—found "universal free" works well for them, e.g., the Brownsville (TX) Independent School District. On the other hand, some schools/school districts find they cannot make up the difference for cost even when 90 to 95 percent of their students qualify for free meals.

Philadelphia (PA), Jersey City (NJ), and National (CA) school districts have been testing different approaches to reducing paperwork and serve students at no cost to the customers. These paperwork reduction approaches are similar to Provision 2 in that the school districts testing them serve students at no cost and do not have to collect free and reduced-price meal applications every year.

OPERATING WITHOUT FEDERAL PROGRAMS

In the last ten years a number of school districts have elected to remove their high schools from the National School Lunch Program. Generally the reason has been because of the federal restrictions regarding those foods a school may offer for sale. Under the federal regulation regarding sale of foods containing minimal nutritional value, carbonated beverages cannot be sold in the cafeteria at breakfast or lunch. Those school districts that leave federally subsidized program usually restrict this to their high schools, and allow the schools to sell carbonated drinks at lunch. Some other school districts have found they can compromise at the high school level and stay on the program by offering fountain juice-based drinks over ice and putting in food courts, thereby keeping the high school students happy.

When a school district goes off the NSLP it no longer receives federal funds and donated commodities, not even for the free students. Nor does the school foodservice program have to carry out the federal regulations. It depends on state and local regulations or policies as to what is done about the students who are needy.

The Glendale (AZ) High School District took its high schools off the program in 1990 and is happy with its decision. Mountain Brook (AR), who has never operated under the National School Lunch program, re-examined the advantages recently of being under the program, but decided against it. Some districts have come back on the program when the number of students qualifying for free and reduced-price meals have increased, for example, the Pulaski County (AR) Special School District went off the National School Lunch Program but came back on the program in 1995.

NUTRITION EDUCATION-RELATED TRAINING

The Nutrition Education and Training (NET) Program is state-run but federally funded. Its purpose is to provide nutrition education to students and foodservice employees. Another program is the "Team Nutrition," a federal program administered by USDA that develops nutrition materials for promoting nutrition education.

"Team Nutrition" was introduced with vigor in 1995 with a group of "Team Nutrition" schools. It promotes food choices for a healthful diet. The USDA allows states to apply for grants under the "Team Nutrition" program. For example, the Arizona Department of Education received a 1997 Team Nutrition training grant to use in the development of three-day train-the-trainer modules and the California Department of Education received a Team Nutrition grant for two projects:

Local training grants for Team Nutrition
Laptop computer laboratory for NSMP training

The future of NET is uncertain. Many have suggested combining the state's NET program efforts with USDA's Team Nutrition to have a better organized and efficient approach to nutrition education.

PRESENT AND FUTURE TRENDS

Foodservice in the public and private schools takes many forms; however, over 90 percent of the schools that qualify have elected to participate in the National School Lunch Program because of the funding provided. Figure 1.6 shows students of different ages with some of the all-time favorite school menu items.

Many private schools cannot qualify for the NSLP because of the tuition they charge. Some administrators of private schools that do qualify prefer to be in total control of their schools and their lunch program and do not elect to participate. The same is true of a few public schools, usually high schools that want to have total control of their foodservice offerings.

Though this book will focus on carrying out the regulations of the NSLP, and operating a successful program, Chapters 2 and 15 will address operating the school foodservice program off the National School Lunch and School Breakfast Programs. Basically, the following chapters in this book covers subjects related to running a cost-effective, successful foodservice, meeting the challenges of the 2000s.

Enrollment in the schools is not expected to grow substantially between 2000 and 2005 (Table 1.4), nor is federal funding for the Child Nutrition program expected to increase substantially. In spite of enrollment, the foodservices operated in the schools throughout the country have an opportunity to grow by expanding into other areas of service (see Chapter 15, "Other Sources of Revenue and Serving the Community").

The challenges facing the school foodservice industry in the 2000s include tighter budgets, labor shortages, customers who are more demanding and knowledgeable, tough federal reviews (referred

Figure 1.6. The Customers of the 2000s Know What They Want and Continue to Enjoy Lunches at School

to as Coordinated Review Effort [CRE] and School Meals Initiative [SMI]), and stiff competition. They also are faced with changes in education philosophies within school districts which have caused challenges to school foodservices, such as, site-based management, open campus, sale of competitive foods to pay for school activities, and block scheduling.

There is also the change in philosophy by administrators on who should operate the support services—and more and more there are those that believe privatizing is the way to go. Commercial management companies and school district management will be in competition as financing of school foodservice becomes more of an issue. School district foodservice management in many school districts are handicapped by high payscales, high costs of fringe benefits, and poor financial management.

Large urban school districts are going outside to management companies to solve their financial problems or for other reasons, e.g., those in Chicago (IL), Houston (TX), and Duval County (FL). This trend is expected to continue through 2005, according to McKinsey and Company's report (1996), *Foodservice 2005: Satisfying America's Changing Appetite.*

Regardless of who manages school foodservice programs, the successful programs will have to be customer-oriented, cost-effective, and able to utilize technology. Figure 1.7 provides a checklist for school foodservice managers on meeting regulations.

Figure 1.7. Checklist for Meeting Regulations

YES	NO		
❏	❏	1.	Has the annual agreement with the state department of education (or department of agriculture) been executed?
❏	❏	2.	Is a copy of the school district's policy statement for provision of free and reduced-priced meals on file in each school?
❏	❏	3.	Has the application for free and reduced -price meals been distributed to all students?
❏	❏	4.	Are the free, reduced-price, and paid students treated the same?
❏	❏	5.	Are nondiscrimination posters displayed where students can see them?
❏	❏	6.	Are only students who qualify for free or reduced-price meals receiving them?
❏	❏	7.	Are edit checks being done daily?
❏	❏	8.	Are the applications for free and reduced-price meals that are approved complete and in accordance with regulations?
❏	❏	9.	Is verification of an approved sampling of free and reduced-price meal applications being completed annually?
❏	❏	10.	Has an appropriate hearing procedure been developed and implemented for use if the family does not agree with the free and reduced-price meal determination?
❏	❏	11.	Are ticket posters displayed in the school if tickets are used?
❏	❏	12.	Is a procedure used for obtaining an accurate meal count by category— free, reduced-price, and paid?
❏	❏	13.	Are the school's financial data and meal counts consolidated monthly and submitted by the twentieth of the following month (or in accordance with the state's requirements)?

Figure 1.7. Checklist for Meeting Regulations (continued)

❏ ❏ 14. Are the purchasing procedures used in compliance with state and federal regulations?

❏ ❏ 15. Are the state's requirements for inventory being followed?

❏ ❏ 16. Are commodities and purchased foods being stored properly? Off the floor? At the correct temperature? Properly rotated? Used within a reasonable time period?

❏ ❏ 17. Do the menus meet the requirements of the planning system selected?

❏ ❏ 18. Are whole milk and lowfat milk available to all students as choices? (Or, is there documentation that shows amount served in prior school year was one percent or less?)

❏ ❏ 19. Is "offer-versus-serve" carried out in senior high schools?

❏ ❏ 20. Is a medical statement on file for every student receiving a substitute for milk as a part of the federal school lunch or breakfast program?

❏ ❏ 21. Is food waste low?

❏ ❏ 22. Are leftover foods being handled properly?

❏ ❏ 23. Is the temperature of all cold food kept at 40° F or below?

❏ ❏ 24. Is the temperature of all hot food kept at 140° F or hotter?

❏ ❏ 25. Is the temperature of all refrigeration being recorded at a minimum of three times a week?

❏ ❏ 26. Are production records completed daily?

❏ ❏ 27. Is there parent involvement, and is it documented?

❏ ❏ 28. Is there student involvement, and is it documented?

❏ ❏ 29. Are all foods in the storage area labeled, dated, and covered properly?

❏ ❏ 30. Are cleaning supplies stored separately from food?

❏ ❏ 31. Is the lunch priced as a unit?

❏ ❏ 32. Are records kept and available for audit for the three previous years?

❏ ❏ 33. Are all components of the breakfast program offered?

❏ ❏ 34. Is the fund balance no greater than three months' operating costs?

❏ ❏ 35. Is the school foodservice fund kept separate from other school funds?

❏ ❏ 36. Is interest earned by the foodservice fund credited to the fund?

❏ ❏ 37. Are school foodservice funds used only for the benefit of the school foodservice program?

❏ ❏ 38. Is the adult meal price sufficient to cover costs and at least equal to the federal and state subsidies and commodity entitlement for the free lunch?

❏ ❏ 39. Do all adults except foodservice employees and those who qualify for free meals pay for meals?

❏ ❏ 40. Is the competitive food regulation being carried out?

SELECTED REFERENCES

American School Food Service Association. 1997. *School Foodservice—The Little Big Fact Book.* Alexandria, VA: American School Food Service Association.

Briggs, H, and C. Hart. 1931. "From Basket Lunches to Cafeterias—A Story of Progress." *Nation's Schools* 8:51-55.

Cronan, M. 1962. *The School Lunch.* Peoria, IL: Charles A. Bennett Company.

Dwyer, J., M. Elias, and J. Warren. 1973. "Effects of an Experimental Breakfast Program on Behavior in the Late Morning." Master's Thesis, Harvard School of Public Health, Cambridge, MA.

Fairfax, J., 1968. *Their Daily Bread.* Atlanta, GA: McNelley-Rudd Printing Service.

Gunderson, G., ed. 1971. *The National School Lunch Program: Background and Development.* FNS 63. Washington, DC: U.S. Department of Agriculture.

Hunter, R. 1904. *Poverty.* (Reprinted, 1965, as *Poverty: Social Conscience in the Progressive Era.*) New York: Harper & Row.

Kotz, N. 1969. *Let Them Eat Promises: The Politics of Hunger in America.* Englewood Cliffs, NJ: Prentice-Hall.

Martin, J., and M. Conklin, editors, 1999. *Managing Child Nutrition Programs: Leadership for Excellence.* Gaithersburg, MD: Aspen Publishers.

McKinsey & Company. 1996. *Foodservice 2005: Satisfying America's Changing Appetite.* Falls Church, VA: Food Distributors International-NAWGA/IFDA, Inc.

Miller, C. 1999. "The Case for Commodity Letter of Credit." Presentation at the California School Food Service Association Annual Meeting (Palm Springs, CA).

National Education Association. 1989. *The Relations between Nutrition and Learning : A School Employee's Guide to Information and Action.* Washington, DC: National Education Association.

Spargo, J. 1906. *The Bitter Cry of Children.* New York: Macmillan Publishing Company.

U.S. Bureau of the Census. 1985, 1990, and 1998. "United States Population Estimates by Age, Sex, Race, and Hispanic Origin, 1990-1997." Washington, DC: U.S. Bureau of the Census, Population Division.

U.S. Department of Agriculture 1970. *Chronological Legislative History of Child Nutrition Program.* Washington, DC: U.S. U.S. Government Printing Office.

_____ . 1983. *The National Evaluation of School Nutrition Programs: Final Report.* Vols. 1 and 2. Washington, DC: U.S. Government Printing Office.

_____ . 1988. "National School Lunch Program: Accountability; Proposed Rule." *Federal Register*: 7CFR, part 210 (September 9, 1988). Washington, DC: U.S. Government Printing Office.

_____ . 1994. *School Lunch and Breakfast Cost Study.* Washington, DC: Author.

_____ . 1998. *Annual Historical Review of FNS Programs, Fiscal Year 1998.* Washington, DC: Author.

_____ . 1998. "National School Lunch Program Revision; Final Rule." *Federal Register*: 7CFR, part 210. Washington, DC: U.S. Government Printing Office.

_____ . 1998. *School Food Purchase Study: Final Report.* Washington, DC: Author.

_____ . 1999. *USDA, Food and Consumer Service Food Distribution Program: Facts about USDA Commodities.* Washington, DC: U.S. Government Printing Office.

2
FINANCIAL MANAGEMENT

Importance of Managing Finances

Budget

Financial Reports
    Balance Sheet
    Profit and Loss Statement
    Statement of Changes
    Allowable Fund Balance

Revenue Management
    Sources of Revenue
    Pricing School Breakfast and Lunch
    Pricing Adult Meals
    Pricing A la Carte and Other Extra Food Sales

Expenditure Management
    Costs of Food and Service
    Fund Balance

Establishing The Break-Even Point
    Determining the Break-Even Point for Individual Schools

Audits/Compliance Requirements
    Compliance Requirements

Selected References

IMPORTANCE OF MANAGING FINANCES

Directors and managers have needed to manage school foodservice finances in the 1980s and 1990s because the funds have been more limited than in the 1970s. The importance of managing finances has been a major emphasis of school districts nationwide, and this will continue to be true. The goals of successful school foodservice management are to provide customer satisfaction and cost containment. The first step in managing a financially successful operation is to know the financial objectives and goals of the school board. Is the foodservice program to be self-supporting? Is the program to be a source of revenue for the general fund budget? Or is it more important that the prices charged to students be kept very low?

The next step toward managing a financially successful operation is to have a good accounting system. An accounting system that provides accurate data on a timely basis is essential for management to be able to "manage finances." Without accurate, timely financial information, no one should be held responsible for financial management. With the slim margin that most school foodservices have to run on, it is essential for the information to be accurate and also in a form that can assist management in making decisions. Timing is critical. It is of little value to a person who is trying to "manage tight finances" to receive data five months after the expenditures are incurred. A financial report should be available no more than 30 days after the month is over. Computerization of the different financial functions (discussed in Chapter 14) will be necessary in the year 2000 and beyond for school foodservices to survive.

There are uniform systems of accounting for restaurants, hotels, and clubs, but no one universal guide for school foodservice. Seminars on cost control held by inTEAM Associates and *Cost Control Manual for School Foodservice,* 2nd edition (Pannell-Martin 1995), have been sources of financial management information for many school districts. The state departments of education in Kentucky, Massachusetts, New York, Texas, Mississippi, and Virginia have supplied guidance materials and established standards for financial management for the school foodservice programs in their states. Currently the National Food Service Management Institute is developing a prototype for financial management that can be used by school districts in managing foodservice finances.

As a result of the lack of uniform national guidance, the financial information provided to foodservice directors/managers/supervisors varies greatly from school district to school district and from state to state. If the finance officer for the school district is handling the school foodservice account, the account may not get the attention needed. The school foodservice account is a small fund in comparison with the school district's general fund and may not be considered very important (so long as there is no financial problem), when in fact, it is one of the most challenging funds to manage.

The kind of information needed for an "enterprise fund," which generates its own income, is very different from what is needed for a "budgetary fund." The school foodservice fund parallels an enterprise account in that foodservice produces goods, provides services, and charges for those goods and services and should be handled as an enterprise fund account. These two terms—"budgetary funds" and "enterprise funds"—need to be defined.

Definitions:

BUDGETARY FUNDS—Revenue generally received from taxes, e.g., a school district's educational budget is referred to as the "general fund;" the funds do not generate revenue as with a business and are generally in a preset amount.

ENTERPRISE FUNDS—Revenue generated by producing goods and services that are sold, e.g., school foodservice and book store; sometimes referred to as proprietary or revolving funds.

If a school district is receiving federal funds and donated commodities for the school foodservice program, the accounting system has specific federal requirements to meet. In order to meet the federal requirements, the accounting system should:

- Provide accurate meal counts by category (free, reduced-price, and paid) at the *point of sale*.
- Ensure that those served a free or reduced-price meal have approved application on file..
- Ensure that the school foodservice is in compliance with state and federal program requirements.
- Ensure that the school foodservice funds (which include federal funds) are safeguarded against unauthorized, improper, or wasteful use.
- Comply with federal and state regulations in purchasing.
- Provide an accounting system whereby the revenues, expenditures, and all other fund transactions are properly managed, recorded, and accounted for.
- Accrue all interest earned by the school foodservice funds to the school foodservice account.
- Maintain records for three years plus the current year.

BUDGET

A budget is a financial management plan. It helps a manager/director to forecast revenue and expenses based on prior year's data and estimates and planned changes. By comparing the projected revenue and expenses during the budget year with actuals on a monthly basis, a manager can determine if the budget is going to be met. The budget is an important management tool for the following reasons:

- Provides a constant reminder of projections, throwing up red flags to identify potential problems (if estimated income is not being generated monthly, then expenditures may need to be reduced, or a deficit may result)
- Sets performance standards for management
- Provides basis for comparison (monthly profit and loss can be compared to budget)

- Controls erratic expenditures
- Helps a manager determine if a program can afford to make an expenditure (e.g., purchase a piece of equipment or attend a national convention)

Many centralized school districts do a district-wide budget (the "top-down" approach) without individual schools being involved in the budget process. When a budget is developed at the top and "passed down" for implementation, top management is totally responsible for meeting the budget. Therefore, it is desirable for a school district made up of more than one school to start with the individual school's budget—the "bottom up" approach. The latter approach provides a separate budget for each school foodservice, and the total of each school's budget becomes the district's budget. For example, the Jackson (MS) Public Schools' foodservice director provides budgets to each of the managers and trains them in comparing how they are doing financially compared to their budget. Most commercial foodservice operations use a bottom-up approach. The lower the level, the greater the feeling of ownership, which yields more involvement and helps in meeting the budget on the part of the site-based manager and employees.

There are a few definitions that are needed, as provided below:

Definitions:

BASELINE BUDGET—A budget based on the assumption that all the previous year's expenditures were necessary and will be duplicated.

ZERO-BASED BUDGET—A budget planned as if for the first time by determining revenue for number served and sources of revenue and determining expenditures by costing out all line items.

BOTTOM-UP APPROACH—A decentralized approach to budget planning, whereby each cost center (school) plans a budget and the school district's budget is made up by combining all the budgets together.

TOP-DOWN APPROACH—An approach whereby a centralized budget is planned for a combination of cost centers.

Budgets are usually prepared a year in advance and involve several processes before final approval. Figure 2.1 gives an example of a school district's budget with details as to the projected revenues and expenditures. In this example, the value of donated commodities are considered both a revenue and an expenditure, but that is optional. The advantage to including the value of commodities is that decreases or increases are reflected and help explain changes in food costs.

Since the estimated figures are based on an "educated guess" that far in advance, the figures may be incorrect because of unexpected changes in costs and/or revenues. In either case, corrective action may be needed to avoid a deficit from occurring.

Figure 2.1. Example of a Detailed School District Budget Showing the Sources of Revenue

REVENUE (1)	TOTAL (2)	PERCENT (3)
BREAKFAST:		
18,000 Number Paying Elementary x $ .60 Price Charged	$ 10,800	
15,300 Number Paying Secondary X $ .60 Price Charged	9,180	
13,500 Number Reduced Price x $ .30 Price Charged	4,050	
7,000 Number Paying Adult x $ .95 Price Charged	6,650	
33,300 Number Student Paid x $ .1875 Federal Reimbursement	6,188	
13,500 Number Reduced Price x $ .6450 Federal Reimbursement	8,708	
108,000 Number Free x $ .9450 Federal Reimbursement	101,849	
TOTAL REVENUE FROM BREAKFAST	$ 147,425	7.4%
LUNCH:		
432,000 Number Paying Elementary x $1.00 Price Charged	$ 432,000	
243,000 Number Paying Secondary X $1.25 Price Charged	303,750	
27,100 Number Reduced Price x $ .40 Price Charged	10,840	
19,800 Number Paying Adult x $1.75 Price Charged	34,650	
675,000 Number Student Paying x $ .1625 Federal Reimbursement	109,688	
27,100 Number Reduced Price x $1.2950 Federal Reimbursement	35,095	
288,000 Number Free x $1.6950 Federal Reimbursement	488,160	
990,100 Number Reimbursable x $ .05984 State Reimbursement	59,248	
TOTAL REVENUE FROM LUNCH	$1,473,431	74.3
OTHER REVENUE:		
A La Carte Sales	$ 142,200	
Special Functions or Catering	28,000	
Interest	4,200	
USDA Donated Commodities	103,000	
USDA Commodity Rebates	2,020	
Other	42,150	
State Matching	41,152	
TOTAL REVENUE FROM OTHER SOURCES	$ 362,722	18.3
TOTAL REVENUE	$1,983,578	100.0%

EXPENDITURES	TOTAL	PERCENT
FOOD COSTS (Including value of commodities used)	$ 725,973	36.6%
SCHOOL STAFF:		
Wages and Salaries $652,800		
Fringe Benefits, Employer's Share 143,800		
LABOR AND FRINGE BENEFITS	796,600	40.2
LABOR AND FRINGE BENEFITS CENTRAL OFFICE STAFF SALARIES	147,112	7.4
SUPPLIES, DETERGENTS, AND DISPOSABLES	95,264	4.8
SMALL EQUIPMENT AND OFFICE SUPPLIES	1,920	0.1
LARGE EQUIPMENT	52,060	2.6
OTHER OPERATING EXPENSES	44,209	2.2
TOTAL EXPENDITURES	$1,863,138	93.9%

Some of the factors to be considered in making revenue projections and expenditure estimates are:

Historical data
Goals and plans
Economic indicators
Demographic changes (school openings or closings and new housing in the area)
Projected enrollment
Effects of menu changes
Changes in operating procedures
Changes in food and labor costs
Meal price changes
Operational changes

Since the projections (or estimates) have so many variables, it is important that the budget be updated in the late summer before the school year begins and again after the trends in participation and cost have been established (around December). It is not possible to predict the variables a year ahead with 100 percent accuracy—how many students will be served a day, what the federal reimbursement rate will be, and what the costs of food will be. When a price increase is involved, the number that will be served usually drops, which is important to revenue as well as expenditures. The decreases in participation and expenditures are not usually parallel.

There are two basic methods of preparing a budget: zero-based and baseline. Zero-based budgeting assumes no function or expense is absolutely required, and all expenses must be justified. This means determining income by extending out the numbers and dollars (e.g., the number of lunches served for year multiplied by (×) the amount of the federal reimbursement).

With the baseline budget, it is assumed that all the activities of the previous year are necessary and a "baseline" is provided. Generally this kind of budget is a projection of the costs based on the percentage of increase or decrease over the previous year. Normally this is the method used by most school districts. It is wise, however, to check the figures occasionally by using the zero-based method.

The steps to planning a budget are as follows:

1. Forecast participation and sales.
2. Forecast federal reimbursements and other subsidies.
3. Forecast all other income.
4. Forecast the percentage increase (or decrease) in food costs.
5. Forecast the increase (or decrease) in labor costs based on raises and staffing.
6. Forecast equipment needs and other costs.

Some basic questions a manager and supervisor should ask regarding budget are the following:

*   What is the daily revenue (including reimbursements)?
*   Will the daily income multiplied by the serving days equate to what is in the budget?
*   How much can be spent on food each day?
*   How much does labor (including fringe benefits) cost per day? What is the average cost of one hour of labor?

- What percentage of the income is spent for labor?
- How much do the salaries of managers cost? How much does central office staff in a centralized foodservice cost? What percentage of the labor costs go for management?
- How much are overhead and other costs in dollars? What percent of the income?

Along with the yearly budget, forecasting revenue and expenditures over the following five years is important to long-range planning. This can give management enough warning of upcoming problems that action can be taken to correct them. With increases in labor costs, which occur annually in most school districts, and the rising costs of fringe benefits, lunch price increases need to be evaluated annually. A 5¢ or 10¢ increase annually may be needed to cover increases in expenses. It is not a good business practice to operate at a deficit unless the operation balance provides more than enough to function for one to two months.

School districts are charging foodservice programs today for things they never charged them for before. For example, starting in 1998-99 the Boston (MA) Public Schools' foodservice budget contributes $1.5 million, or 9 percent, of the budget for trash removal and utilities.

By comparing the projected and actual revenue and expense on a monthly basis, a manager can determine if the budget is going to be met. A convenient form for budget analysis is shown in Figure 2.2. Month-to-month financial statements should be checked against the budget. The budget needs to be prorated over the days of service (e.g., 175 days, 180 days) when there is revenue. In Figure 2.2, October is 11.1 percent of the budget year. The revenue in the example for August/September and October were below the projections, and this has resulted in a deficit. Corrective action has been taken in November, but more reductions in expenditures or increases in revenue are needed for the foodservice program to end the year with a profit.

FINANCIAL REPORTS

According to Tidwell (1986), the three financial statements needed by an enterprise account, such as a school foodservice account, are (1) a balance sheet, (2) a statement of revenue and expenditures (on an accrual bases) or profit and loss, and (3) statement of change in the fund balance. An accrual-based income statement using accrual-based accounting will provide the true financial position for any given period of time. It shows the amount of cash earned and the amount of food, labor, supplies, and so forth, that was expended. "Cash-based accounting" reflects the cash in the account at the time of the month the account is closed out. The accrual income statement shows how a school foodservice is doing financially when credit is extended and revenue hasn't been received—the school foodservice program usually has an outstanding federal reimbursement. **It is important for foodservice management to know which type of accounting system—accrual-based or cash-based—is being used for the school foodservice account.**

ACCRUAL-BASED ACCOUNTING—A system of accounting whereby revenues are recorded in the period earned and expenses are recorded in the period they occur.

CASH-BASED ACCOUNTING—A system of accounting whereby revenues are recorded when received and expenses are recorded in the period they are paid.

Figure 2.2. Example of the High School Budget Projected by Month by Main Categories and Compared with Actual

Revenue %Budgeted	Aug/ Sept 17.0%	Oct 11.1%	Nov 10.0%	Dec 8.3%	Jan 11.7%	Feb 10.0%	March 11.7%	April 8.9%	May 10.5%	Total
Breakfast Budget	$ 5,336	$ 3,328	$ 2,998	$ 2,488	$ 3,507	$ 2,998	$ 3,508	$ 2,668	$ 3,148	$ 29,979
Breakfast Actual	$ 5,002	$ 3,123								
Lunch Budget	39,573	24,678	22,232	18,452	26,011	22,232	26,011	19,766	23,345	222,318
Lunch Actual	37,436	21,567								
Other Budget	6,123	3,819	3,440	2,855	4,025	3,440	4,025	3,062	3,611	34,400
Other Actual	5,980	3,142								
Projected Revenue	$51,032	$31,825	$28,670	$23,795	$33,543	$28,670	$33,544	$25,516	$30,102	$286,607
Actual Revenue	$48,418	$27,832								
Expenditures										
Food Costs Budget	$20,412	$12,729	$11,468	$ 9,518	$13,417	$11,468	$13,417	$10,206	$12,040	$114,675
Food Costs Actual	$21,890	$12,567								
Labor Costs Budget[1]	20,778	12,957	11,673	9,608	13,657	11,673	13,657	10,389	12,257	116,729
Labor Costs Actual	19,547	11,509								
Other Costs Budget	9,491	5,919	5,332	4,426	6,239	5,332	6,239	4,746	5,599	53,322
Other Costs Actual	8,453	5,478								
Total Expenditures Budget	$50,681	$31,605	$28,473	$23,632	$33,313	$28,473	$33,313	$25,341	$29,896	$284,726
Actual	$49,890	$29,718								
Budget Gain or (Loss)	$ 351	$ 220	$ 197	$ 163	$ 230	$ 197	$ 230	$ 175	$ 206	$ 1,961
Actual Gain or (Loss)	$(1,472)	$(1,886)								

Balance Sheet

A balance sheet is a basic financial statement that shows the financial condition of a fund at any given point and compares current balances with balances at the end of the prior year (Figure 2.3). Described as a "snapshot," it reports assets, liabilities, and net worth of the program (fund balance) at the end of the accounting period (generally a month or a fiscal year). It shows cash on hand (including the value of inventory). A school district may or may not include the value of equipment as an asset.

The revenues (assets) include cash, accounts receivable, and inventories. Expenditures (liabilities) include accounts paid during the accounting period, accounts payable, accrued payroll, and taxes payable. Many of these items need to be defined.

---

[1] If employees' salaries are annualized or in equal installments, this would be reflected. The costs will need to be charged over the school year (August-May/June).

Figure 2.3. Example of a Balance Sheet

	FY 1998	FY 1999
ASSETS		
Current Assets		
Cash	$ 171,516	$ 166,957
Investments	114,989	67,437
Accrued interest receivables[1]	—	7,111
Other miscellaneous receivables	—	29
Federal reimbursements receivable[2]	—	31,272
Inventory	79,755	83,403
TOTAL OF CURRENT ASSETS	$ 366,260	$ 356,209
Equipment		
Total	179,178	175,357
Less accumulated depreciation	112,317	101,545
NET EQUIPMENT	$ 66,861	$ 73,812
TOTAL ASSETS	$ 433,121	$ 430,021
LIABILITIES AND FUND BALANCE		
Liabilities		
Accounts payable	$ 274	$ 1,164
Fund Balance		
Retail earning	432,847	428,857
TOTAL LIABILITIES AND FUND BALANCE	$ 433,121	$ 430,021

Source: Principal of School Business Management by S. Tidwell, ed., 1986, Reston, VA: Association of School Business officials International. This report received the Certificate of Excellence in Financial Reporting by School Systems awarded by the Association of School Business Officials (1986). Used by permission.

---

[1]Interest earned but not received.

[2]Federal reimbursement is generally received within 20 days after a claim form is completed and sent to the state agency administering the school foodservice programs.

ACCOUNTS PAYABLE—The amount owed creditors for goods and services, e.g., food and supplies and unpaid payroll. "Prepaid" student tickets may be considered accounts payable.

ACCOUNTS RECEIVABLE—The amount that is owed the foodservice program for food and services rendered, e.g., federal reimbursement and contract meals.

EXPENDITURES (LIABILITIES)—The costs that are incurred for food, supplies, services, etc.

REVENUE (ASSETS)—Moneys that are received for food and services and accounts receivable.

Profit and Loss Statement

A profit and loss statement (referred to as a revenue and expense statement, or operating statement) shows the financial results at the end of an accounting period—usually the end of the month. Some directors, school boards, and administrators do not like to use the term "profit" referring to the financial statement because school foodservice is not suppose to be profit making. Since school foodservice needs to operate as a business, the commercial terminology is used in this book. The goal should be to have a profit, which goes back into the school foodservice program to purchase equipment, etc.

The profit and loss statement provides (1) the cost of goods and services, (2) a summary of the income or revenue, and (3) net income (see Figure 2.4). Since the philosophy is that school foodservice programs are not profit making, many school districts refer to it as a revenue and expense statement.

The "bottom line" reflects either a profit (gain) or a deficit (loss)—it is the balance once the expenditures are subtracted from the revenues. Large school districts with central office staffs may want to show the labor costs for the office under administrative expenses rather than all the labor costs lumped together.

Comparisons of data—with the current month, with previous months and the previous year, and with industry standards—are very useful. Comparison analyses with previous year's participation in the foodservice program and with revenue will show when unusual increases or decreases in revenue or participation should be a concern. For example, the highest participation may be during January, and February, therefore, the revenue will usually be higher. However, the cost of labor may be highest in September and June because of the days when employees are paid with no revenue coming in (holidays, inservice training days, days paid for "setup" time prior to opening and

Figure 2.4. Profit and Loss Statement for a School District

	SEPT. 1997	%	OCT. 1997	%	NOV. 1997	%	DEC. 1997	%	YTD	%
REVENUE										
Breakfast:										
Students Paid	$ 4,681	.8%	$ 4,975	.7%	$ 6,364	1.0%	$ 6,660	1.4%	$ 22,680	.9
Students Reduced-Price	430	.1	495	.1	506	.1	512	.1	1,943	.1
Federal Reimbursement	8,990	1.5	9,270	1.3	10,435	1.7	10,979	2.2	39,674	1.6
Lunch:										
Students Paid	117,318	19.9	186,975	26.2	148,653	24.3	119,644	24.6	572,590	23.8
Students Reduced-Price		.8	5,270	.7	4,020	.7	3,927	.8	18,137	.8
Federal Reimbursement	284,474	48.2	310,983	43.5	244,884	40.0	193,509	39.7	1,033,850	43.0
State Reimbursement	14,300	2.4	14,300	2.0	14,300	2.3	14,300	2.9	57,200	2.4
Adults	19,233	3.3	25,720	3.6	32,206	5.3	19,400	3.9	96,559	4.0
A la Carte Sales	92,801	15.7	112,185	15.8	96,201	15.7	86,204	17.6	387,391	16.1
Special Functions	2,648	.4	4,110	.6	6,329	1.0	4,263	.9	17,350	.7
USDA Commodities	16,515	2.8	11,625	1.6	22,979	3.7	10,572	2.2	61,691	2.6
Contracts—Day Care	24,220	4.1	28,260	3.9	25,690	4.2	18,021	3.7	96,191	4.0
TOTAL REVENUE	$590,530	100.0%	$714,168	100.0%	$612,567	100.0%	$487,991	100.0%	$2,405,256	100.0%
EXPENDITURES										
Labor Cost:										
Wages—School Based	$165,159	27.9	$186,398	26.1	$172,131	28.1%	$161,037	33.0%	$684,725	28.5
Fringe Benefits	37,986	6.4	41,007	5.7	37,869	6.2	34,428	7.1	151,290	6.3
Salaries—Central Office	52,020	8.8	61,002	8.5	53,293	8.7	52,460	10.7	218,775	9.1
Fringe Benefits	12,625	2.2	15,250	2.1	13,323	2.2	12,005	2.5	53,203	2.2
TOTAL LABOR COST	$267,790	45.3%	$303,657	42.4%	$276,616	45.2%	$259,930	53.3%	$1,107,993	46.1%
Food Used:										
Purchased	$170,072	28.8%	$207,108	29.0%	$180,094	29.4%	$139,077	28.5	$696,351	29.0
USDA	42,518	7.2	57,133	8.0	49,618	8.1	37,555	8.2	186,824	7.8
Paper & Supplies	29,526	5.0	39,279	5.5	34,308	5.6	24,887	5.1	128,000	5.2
TOTAL FOOD & SUPPLIES	$242,116	41.0%	$303,520	42.5%	$264,020	43.1%	$201,519	41.8%	$1,011,175	42.0%
Equipment	$ 16,000	2.7%	$ 19,264	2.7%	$ 17,800	2.9%	- 0 -		53,064	2.2
Overhead	17,715	3.0	4,920	3.9	26,400	4.3	25,400	5.2	97,367	4.0
Indirect Cost	23,621	4.0	29,995	4.2	25,040	4.1	22,040	4.5	100,696	4.2
TOTAL EXPENDITURES	$567,242	96.0%	$684,288	95.7%	$609,876	99.6%	$508,889	104.8%	$2,370,295	98.5%
NET INCOME (OR LOSS)	$ 23,288	4.0%	$ 29,880	4.3%	$ 2,691	.4%	($20,898)	(4.8%)	$ 34,961	1.5%

"cleanup" time prior to closing). Comparative percentage analysis is more meaningful than figures for many managers and supervisors. This is illustrated in Figure 2.4. It is important to know what percentage of the revenue/income is being used for food and for labor. It can be helpful to compare these analyses with those of other school districts.

Definition:

LOSS (DEFICIT)—The expenditures exceed the revenue and result in a loss or decrease in the fund balance.

PROFIT (GAIN)—The revenue is in excess of the expenditures, resulting in an increase in the fund balance.

Profit and loss statements by school district and by individual school are needed on a monthly basis. The food cost in Figure 2.5 totals 39.1 percent of the revenue and the labor cost is 41.3 percent (year-to-date). Though this school in Figure 2.5 is showing a profit now, the labor cost is about to be a problem and the manager needs to increase productivity in the future (discussed in Chapters 6 and 12). The profit and loss statement for each location will provide the manager incentives for improving and the central office with the data to determine where problems are or are about to occur. Also, management can do comparisons of similar-sized schools and determine exactly where the problems are if any of the schools are operating at a deficit (Figure 2.6). If a school is operating at a deficit, preparing a daily or weekly profit and loss statement will help pinpoint problems.

In Figure 2.6 Jefferson Elementary School is operating at a deficit and it is caused by a combination of high food and labor costs. All three schools in Figure 2.6 have high food and labor costs, which could be reduced for increased profits. Reducing cost is discussed in Chapter 12, "Reducing Cost and Increasing Productivity." Food cost or labor cost that is one or two percentages over 80 percent can make the difference in a profit or a loss.

Each school's profit and loss statement needs to be evaluated monthly and compared with other schools in the district or nearby schools. This is becoming a common practice in school districts across the country. For example, Adams Twelve Schools in Northglenn (CO) does a detailed monthly and year-to-date profit and loss statement by school recognizing each school as an independent revenue and cost center, as does the Clarkstown Central School District in New York.

When school districts are running a deficit, corrective action needs to be taken, as discussed in Chapter 12, "Reducing Costs and Increasing Efficiency." There are many success stories of school districts that have turned around their financial situations. For example, the Hillsborough County (FL) School Board director reported in 1990 an annual loss of $2.5 million. By 1994 that had been turned into a $3.5 million surplus by increasing productivity from 12.3 meals per labor hour to 16.8 meals per labor hour (discussed in Chapter 6, "Organizational Structure and Personnel") and implementing competitive bidding practices. The district now runs a food cost of 36 percent and labor cost of 52 percent. Standardization has been critical to this turnaround and increased revenue.

Figure 2.5. Profit and Loss Statement for a School

School: ___Oakview High___   Month: ___December 1998___

	For Month	Percent of Income	Year to Date	Percent of Income
REVENUE ACCOUNT				
BREAKFASTS				
Full Price Paid	$ 112.50	0.4	$ 487.50	0.4
Reduced-price	90.00	0.3	387.00	0.3
LUNCHES				
Full Price Paid	15,000.00	48.8	65,000.00	45.2
Reduced-Price	180.00	0.5	11,700.40	8.0
Adults	525.00	1.7	2,275.00	1.6
Federal Reimbursement	6,048.00	19.7	26,208.10	18.3
State Subsidy	837.00	2.7	3,627.46	2.5
Special Functions	418.50	1.4	1,813.50	1.3
A la Carte Sales	6,375.00	20.7	27,625.00	19.2
Other sales	425.00	1.4	1,435.60	1.0
Value of Commodity Received	697.50	2.3	3,022.50	2.0
Other Income	50.25	0.1	290.00	0.2
TOTAL REVENUE	$ 30,758.75	100%	$ 143,872.06	100%
EXPENDITURES				
Purchased Food: Beginning Inventory	$ 2,821.40		$ 4,430.20	
+ Purchased Food	11,478.00		52,204.46	
- Ending Inventory	3,240.50		5,240.50	
TOTAL FOOD COSTS	$11,,058.90	36.0	$ 51,394.16	35.7
Commodity Food: Beginning Inventory	$1,100.00		$1,140.00	
+ Value Received	697.50		6,201.20	
- Ending Inventory	989.50		2,405.00	
TOTAL COMMODITY FOOD COSTS	$808.00	2.6	$4,936.20	3.4
Paper Supplies	1,230.35	4.0	5,431.52	3.8
Labor Costs				
Payroll	$ 9,995.91	32.5	$ 47,048.94	32.7
Fringe Benefits	2,798.77	9.1	12,320.67	8.6
TOTAL LABOR COSTS	$ 12,794.68	41.6	$ 59,369.61	41.3

Figure 2.5. Profit and Loss Statement for a School (continued)

School: Oakview High   Month: December 1998

	For Month	Percent of Income	Year to Date	Percent of Income
Operating Expenses				
Cleaning Supplies	$ 768.96	2.5	$ 3,383.42	2.4
Maintenance	320.00	1.0	1,500.00	0.9
Administrative Costs				
Administrative Salaries	350.90		1,754.50	
Office Supplies	28.00		201.00	
Delivery Charges	27.00		320.60	
Travel	12.00		49.00	
Data Processing	25.00		125.40	
TOTAL ADMINISTRATIVE COSTS	$ 442.90	0.3	$ 696.10	0.4
Utilities and Trash Removal	695.00		$ 3,475.00	
Large Equipment	2,230.00		5,350.00	
TOTAL EXPENDITURES	$ 30,248.79	98.3	$ 137,290.41	95.4
PROFIT (LOSS)	$ 509.96	1.7	$ 6,581..65	4.6

The goal is to maintain a food cost (including the value of donated commodities) and labor cost (including fringe benefits) of no more than 80 percent of the revenue/income—40 percent for food and 40 percent for labor or any combination. Many school districts are operating below 80 percent, which allows funds for other items.

Figure 2.7 is an example of a school district that is keeping their secondary schools' cost within the guidelines. The food costs are averaging 41 percent of the revenue and labor costs are at 40 percent of the revenue, which results in a profit for all of the secondary schools. By comparing these schools' food costs and labor costs the supervisory staff know which schools need attention. For example, North Secondary School is running a 53 percent labor costs. The question becomes: "Why?" and "Are they over staffed?" South, Southwest, and Washburn schools are running high food costs. Some questions to be asked are: "Why?," "Is portion control being practiced?," and "How are leftover being handled?" See Chapter 12, "Reducing Costs and Increasing Productivity," for additional ideas for solving these problems.

Statement of Changes

A statement of changes or fund balances (Figure 2.8), also known as a **statement of financial position**, provides a summary of the fund to date, showing changes in working capital from one year to the next.

Figure 2.6. Comparison Analysis of School Profit and Loss

	Oakview Elementary School		Jefferson Elementary School		Central Elementary School	
	$	%	$	%	$	%
REVENUE						
Student Breakfasts	$ 202.50	0.7	—		—	
Student Lunches	15,800.00	49.3	$ 11,250.00	41.7	$ 18,375.00	47.0
Federal Reimbursement						
and Commodity Rebates	6,745.50	22.0	10,963.00	40.7	2,246.05	5.7
State/Local Subsidies	1,255.50	4.1	1,716.12	6.4	541.40	1.4
A la Carte Sales	6,375.00	20.7	2,502.00	9.3	14,480.00	37.0
Other Income	1,000.25	3.2	507.50	1.9	3,500.00	8.9
TOTAL REVENUE	$ 30,758.75	100.00	$ 26,938.62	100.00	$ 39,142.45	100.0
EXPENDITURES						
Purchased Food Used[1]	$ 13,158.80	42.8	$ 11,852.00	44.0	$ 15,500.41	39.5[2]
Commodity Value Used	$ 4,215.89		$ 3,010.55		$ 4,485.90	
Labor Costs	14,294.68	46.4	12,903.62	47.9	16,635.54	42.5
Paper Supplies	1,230.35	4.0	1,212.24	4.5	1,996.26	5.1
Administrative Costs	92.00	0.3	107.75	0.4	156.57	0.4
Operating Costs	1,088.96	3.5	1,050.61	3.9	1,409.13	3.7
TOTAL EXPENDITURES	$ 29,864.89	97.0	$ 27,127.21	100.7	$ 35,697.91	91.2
PROFIT (LOSS)	$ 893.86	3.0	($ 188.59)	(0.7)	$ 3,444.54	8.8
COMMODITY VALUE						
Beginning Inventory	$ 9,500.00		$ 8,700.90		$ 9,880.00	
+Commodities Received	2,460.00		2,200.80		2,510.00	
-Ending Inventory	7,744.11		7,891.15		7,904.10	
TOTAL COMMODITY VALVE USED[3]	$ 4,215.89		$ 3,010.55		$ 4,485.90	

[1]Percent of purchased food cost.

[2]In this example, the value of donated commodities used is not included in the food cost. The value or may not be included as an expense. If it is considered an expense the value of donated commodities received must be included as revenue.

Figure 2.7. Example of Profit and Loss Summary for Secondary Schools (For School Year 1998-99, as of April 1999)

	Total Bkfst Serv	Total Lunch Serv	Bkfst Rev	Lunch Rev	A la Carte Revenues	Total Revenues	Total Expense	MTD PROFIT/ (LOSS)	YTD PROFIT/ (LOSS)	FOOD %	LABOR %	SUPPLY %
ANTHONY	1,914	6,655	$ 2,523	$ 12,639	$ 7,353	$ 22,514	$ 17,312	$ 5,202	$ 17,232	37%	37%	3%
ANWATIN		NUMBERS DO NOT REFLECT TRUE PROFIT AND LOSS DUE TO REMODEL AT SITE							19,821	43%	40%	4%
FOLWELL	3,117	10,209	4,143	20,261	4,648	28,953	25,706	3,247	2,453	44%	40%	4%
FRANKLIN	2,618	8,108	3,471	15,708	4,238	23,417	20,609	2,808	18,826	42%	43%	3%
OLSON	3,054	9,040	3,996	17,971	4,918	26,888	21,838	5,048	26,347	42%	37%	2%
SANFORD	3,132	7,717	4,089	14,552	3,955	22,596	17,683	5,013	17,805	37%	37%	4%
EDISON	3,199	9,519	4,228	19,114	12,423	35,765	26,680	9,185	32,574	34%	37%	3%
HENRY	3,454	9,918	4,566	19,223	8,072	31,862	23,093	7,969	26,874	32%	39%	3%
NORTH	4,267	5,939	5,672	11,623	5,365	22,660	21,721	940	1,181	39%	53%	3%
NORTHEAST	4,653	9,977	5,548	19,239	6,312	31,099	26,137	4,962	16,582	39%	42%	3%
ROOSEVELT	5,462	11,110	7,263	22,120	11,730	41,113	33,350	7,763	26,997	38%	40%	3%
SOUTH	3,034	7,790	4,038	15,126	21,637	40,802	35,680	5,114	26,598	49%	37%	2%
SOUTHWEST	3,544	7,014	4,690	13,423	14,110	32,223	29,748	2,476	18,145	53%	37%	3%
WASHBURN	2,620	6,715	3,488	12,539	18,268	34,293	33,801	491	9,395	51%	43%	4%
TOTALS FOR ALL SITES	47,780	116,789	$ 62,613	$ 227,459	$ 129,555	$ 419,628	$ 356,026	$ 63,601	$ 256,830	41%	40%	3%
										AVERAGE OF ALL SITES		

Source: Minneapolis (MN) Public Schools. Used with permission.

Figure 2.8. Example of a Statement of Change

	FY 1998	FY 1999
SOURCES OF WORKING CAPITAL		
Operations		
Net income	$ 3,315	$ 33,585
Depreciation not requiring an outlay of funds	14,205	14,352
TOTAL SOURCES OF WORKING CAPITAL	$ 17,610	$ 47,937
USES OF WORKING CAPITAL		
Purchase of fixed assets	$ 7,146	$ 21,299
NET INCREASE IN WORKING CAPITAL	$ 10,464	$ 26,638
ELEMENTS OF NET INCREASE (DECREASE) IN NET WORKING CAPITAL		
Cash and investments	$ 51,634	$ 2,247
Receivables	(31,300)	2,623
Accrued interest receivable	(7,112)	(4,571)
Inventories	(3,648)	25,374
Accounts payable	890	965
NET INCREASE IN WORKING CAPITAL	$ 10,464	$ 26,638

Allowable Fund Balance

The difference between revenue and expenses is either a profit (gain) or a deficit (loss). The profits accumulate and become the fund balance. If a deficit occurs, it decreases the fund balance. Though school foodservice is considered a nonprofit foodservice operation, it is not a good management practice to take this concept literally. Since federal funding is on a reimbursement basis and may be received six to eight weeks after a meal is served, it is advisable to maintain a two-to-three month operating balance. This enables a school foodservice to meet payrolls and pay vendors on a timely basis without needing financial assistance from the school district's general fund. Federal regulations limit the funds in the account at the end of a school year to three months of operating cost, except when major equipment replacement is planned. Then special permission should be obtained from the state department administering the Child Nutrition programs when the fund balance is in excess of three months.

REVENUE MANAGEMENT

Sources of Revenue

The revenue, or income, for school foodservices usually comes from five sources: cash payments from customers, federal (cash reimbursement and commodity value), state subsidy, possibly local subsidies, and interest earned.

Figure 2.9 shows the sources of revenue as reported in 1994 in the U. S. Department of Agriculture "School Lunch and Breakfast Cost Study." Table 2.1 provides an example of the income received for a lunch, which includes prices charged customers, and federal, state and local subsidies. In the 1999 school year, slightly over 40 percent of the students participating in the National School Lunch Program paid for their meals (that is, they did not qualify for free or reduced-price meals).

An additional source of revenue for some districts, particularly middle and high schools, comes from a la carte sales. Other services, such as, day-care meals, senior citizen meals, vending, and special functions/catering, may provide revenue (see Chapters 15 and 16). However, none of the services mentioned should operate at the expense of the federally subsidized school foodservice program. Any profits from these sources can be used to subsidize the school breakfast and/or lunch programs or assist with the purchase of equipment.

Figure 2.9. Source of Revenue for a School District Serving Reimbursable Lunches and Breakfasts

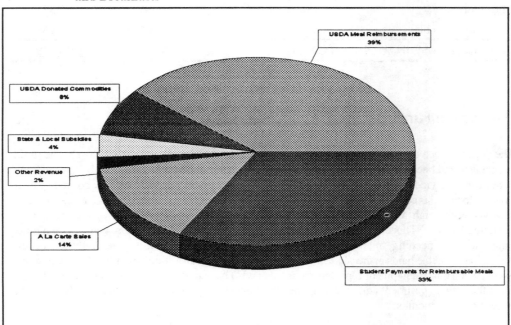

Table 2.1. Example of Income Received for a Lunch

Source	Paying Students		Reduced-Price Students	Free Students	Adults
	Elementary	Secondary			
Cash Payment	$ 1.5000	$ 1.7500	$ 0.4000	$ 0.0000	$2.25
Federal Reimbursement[1]	0.1800	0.1800	1.5425	1.9425	0.00
Commodity Value[2]	0.1475	0.1475	0.1475	0.1475	0.00
State Subsidy[3]	0.0570	0.0570	0.0570	0.0570	0.00
Local Funds	0.0000	0.0000	0.0000	0.0000	0.00
TOTAL INCOME	$ 1.8845	$ 2.1345	$ 2.1470	$ 2.1470	$ 2.25

Pricing School Breakfast and Lunch

In accordance with federal regulations, breakfast and lunch under the National School Lunch and Child Nutrition programs must be priced as a unit. Individual food items may be sold a la carte or separately.

Prices charged for breakfast and lunch, unfortunately, are often a local political issue. Some states have restrictions on what can be sold separately. The costs of the breakfast and lunch should certainly be a prime consideration. In 1996-97 the median price charged for lunch was $1.25 for elementary school lunch and $1.35 for middle/secondary lunch. Most school districts charge the maximum for reduced-price lunch, 40 cents, but some charge as low as 25 cents. The median price charged for breakfast in 1996-97 was $.65 for elementary schools and $.70 for middle/secondary schools. Again most school districts charge the maximum for reduced-price breakfast, 30 cents.

Items sold a la carte and services provided in addition to the federally subsidized lunch and breakfast should be priced so that they do not compete with the lunch or breakfast program. Most school districts price a la carte and other services to make a profit, which is used to subsidize the school lunch and breakfast programs.

There is an "art" to pricing, which the restaurant industry knows well, and it should be used in school foodservices. This requires a combination of intuition, knowledge of customers and competitors, and knowing the real costs of the products being priced. Some call it using "the psychology of pricing," which means arriving at a price the customer will pay without great

---

[1]Federal reimbursement is different for Hawaii and Alaska, and it changes annually.

[2]Value of entitlement commodities usually changes annually.

[3]State subsidy differs from state to state with some states providing none.

resistance. It is important that the customer not perceive the price as too high. On the other hand, if it is too low, the customer may perceive food as being of low quality or having something wrong with it.

Pricing for school foodservice should be competitive with the surrounding school districts and less than prices at local restaurants, convenience stores, and grocery stores. School foodservices are expected to charge less for an a la carte item than is charged by a commercial foodservice operation. A price rise that is too rapid or too large can result in huge drops in participation. Timing is crucial. It is better to raise prices over the school break (summer) than in the middle of the school year. The menus should not be negatively changed at the time an increase goes into effect.   Some school districts have expanded menu choices and made positive changes in the program to correspond with a price increase. Across the country lunches prices range from a low of 60 cents to $2.75 (and higher).

According to a USDA study (1982), participation decreases one percent for every cent the price of lunch increases. This may not always be true, and if a drop in participation occurs, it is often only temporary. Timing and other happenings influence reactions to a price increase.

Pricing Adult Meals

What should an adult be charged for breakfast or lunch? The guidelines have been loose over the years. However, in 1988 the USDA did provide written guidelines to the states, as follows:

> Breakfast and lunches served to teachers, administrators, custodians and other adults must be priced so that the adult payment in combination with any per-lunch-revenues, from other sources designated specifically for the support of adult meals (such as states or local fringe benefits or payroll funds, or funding from voluntary agencies) is sufficient to cover the overall cost of the lunch, including the value of any USDA entitlement and bonus donated foods used to prepare the meal. If cost data are not available, the minimum adult payment should reflect the price charged to students paying the school's designated full price, plus the current value of federal cash and donated food assistance (entitlement and bonus) for a full-price meal. (See FNS-782-5, 210.6 and 220.6)

Some states have even stiffer or more specific guidelines for pricing an adult meal. For example, Mississippi has a minimum price of $2. Some school districts use a la carte prices for adults.

Pricing A la Carte and Other Extra Food Sales

A la carte sales include any items sold in addition to the unit-priced breakfast and lunch. In some states, a la carte sales are discouraged, and the sale of individual items may be referred to as "extra food sales." In some states it is limited to the sale of milk and items on the menu. Over 70 percent of all school districts offer food separate from the meal . More and more school districts are finding that a la carte sales provide revenue needed to stay in business and provide funds for subsidizing the school lunch program. A la carte sales may be a service that is needed by the students who cannot afford or do not want an entire meal, particularly in high schools. It also provides an option for school districts to provide a "super-sized" meal, meaning a second portion at a la carte prices. Federal competitive food regulations and state regulations specify what can be sold.

There are a number of methods (Pannell-Martin, *Controlling Food Cost in the Foodservice Industry* 1998) used in the foodservice industry for arriving at the prices charged for a la carte items. A "combination of factors" is probably the safest, since it considers actual cost, perceived value, and desired profit. All costs of producing and serving food are discussed later in this chapter. Many commercial foodservices use a "food-cost-percentage markup." Since labor costs may be consuming more than 40 percent of the school foodservice income, it is important that labor-intensive items include sufficient costs for that labor. Otherwise an item may really be costing more than priced using the food-cost-percentage markup method. If the price that management needs to charge in order to cover costs and obtain the profits desired is too high for the students to pay, management needs to decide: (1) Can we afford to sell the item for less than it cost (bearing in mind that no other program should be run at a cost to the National School Lunch Program)? (2) Can costs be reduced?

According to the School Lunch and Breakfast Cost Study (1994) by U. S. Department of Agriculture, federal funding is sometimes used to subsidize a la carte and catering services. It shows that most school districts represented in the study priced their services too low, which resulted in the school lunch programs revenue subsidizing the services. Catered events are difficult to price and are frequently under priced. Some school districts have preprinted catered menus, prices, and established policy regarding projected numbers for use when scheduling, which helps.

Pricing of food at the right price is an art, but it does requires some basic information, such as, precosting of food products, determining how much labor is involved, and knowing what the competition is charging for the same items. There are alot of creative ways to use pricing, for example, loss-leader pricing is pricing an item at cost, or even below, for a reason. It may be an item on hand that needs to be moved (because it has sold too slowly or has a brief shelf life), it may be a "come on" that will encourage purchasing something else ("go-togethers"), a new food product, or it may be an item that management wants to promote, such as fresh fruit and yogurt.

Any items sold a la carte should be carefully priced, so they are not in competition with the lunch and breakfast programs unit prices. A la carte prices should be determined on the basis of (1) product cost, (2) prices charges by commercial competitors, and (3) how much the customer will pay (the value of the product to the customer). Figure 2.10 provides an example of a few items that are priced out. Consider the cost of French fries and the a la carte price for French fries—French fries may cost only 10 cents for food, 10 cents for labor and 5 cents for overhead, but pricing French fries at 25 cents would yield no profit and would take away from the lunch program. Consider what the "perceived value" of French fries is by the customer by checking prices at the popular commercial restaurants, and then price the school's French fries just under the commercial restaurant's price. Foods like French fries should have a high profit margin; whereas fresh apples wouldn't. To encourage their sale, the price may hardly be above actual cost (including labor).

When setting a la carte prices, it can be helpful to group items at a particular price—for example, all entrees at $1.25 or $1.50, all vegetables at 60 cents a portion (except French fries, which may be priced higher), all similar-sized cookies at 50 cents each. Group pricing of items is easier for the customer and the cashier to remember (25¢ increments, e.g., 50¢, 75¢). This is particularly true when the cashiering is done without an automated cash register. Even when using a programmable cash register, it is more efficient to limit the number of different priced items and easier for the customer to remember.

Figure 2. 10. Example of Factors to Consider When Pricing A la Carte Items

FOOD ITEM	FOOD COST	LABOR COST[1]	CURRENT PRICES CHARGED	PRICES CHARGED OUTSIDE	PRICES SET	FOOD COST %
Milk, ½ pt	$ .146	X	$ .30	FF $ .55	$ .30[2]	48.7%
Ice Cream Sandwich	$ .17	X	$ .50	CS $ .60	$ .50	34.0%
Cookies, Large	$ .14	X	$ .30	FF $ .79	$ .50	28.0%
Pretzel, Soft	$ .18	XX	$ .50	SM $ .89	$ .60	30.0%
Popcorn	$ .15	X	$ .50	VM $ .50	$ .50	30.0%
Yogurt, 8 oz	$ .39	X	$ .65	GS $ .39	$ .65[2]	60.0%
Apple	$ .16	XX	$ .25	GS $ .29	$ .35[2]	45.7%
Milk Shake, 12 oz	$ .13	XXX	$ .75	FF $1.08	$ .85[3]	15.0%
Salad, Small	$ .12	XXX	$ .50	FF $ .79	$ .50	24.0%

Abbreviations used to designate outside sources:

CS =   convenience stores
FF =   fast-food restaurants
GS =   grocery stores
SM =   shopping malls
VM =   vending machines

---

[1]If labor is required only for ordering, counting, and selling, it is indicated with "X"; if minimal labor is also required to prepare product, it is indicated with "XX"; and "XXX" indicates a lot of preparation and/or cleanup time is required, e.g., school-baked cinnamon rolls and salads (lot of preparation) or milk shakes (machine cleanup).

[2]Nutritional items that are priced low to encourage increased consumption.

[3]One factor not shown as a column in chart above, but that is considered in the price set, is "what the traffic will bear" or what the customer will pay. It is the value perceived by the customer. Popular commercial-brand items can usually be priced higher than others.

EXPENDITURE MANAGEMENT

In expenditure management, expenses are categorized usually as fixed and variable and direct and indirect. Direct expenses are related to the services provided, such as food, paper supplies, and the labor involved in preparation and service. Indirect expenses are often charged by the school administration for services they provide, such as maintenance of equipment, costs of running the central foodservice office, printing, utilities, and so on.

Definitions:

FIXED COSTS—Costs that remain relatively constant or the same during a given period of time regardless of the number served.

VARIABLE COSTS—Costs that vary in direct proportion with volume of sales or numbers of customers served, e.g., food and disposable products.

DIRECT COSTS—Items of cost that can be specifically identified, e.g., food and paper supplies and equipment maintenance.

INDIRECT COSTS—Costs that cannot be directly identified because the amount is prorated across several programs, e.g., utilities.

The charges that a school district expects the foodservice program to pay vary greatly across the country. For the most part, they are limited to the most identifiable costs incurred in providing the services. In many cases, custodial services, maintenance of equipment , and all utilities are paid for by the school district's budget. In some cases, charges are prorated for utilities and custodial, maintenance, personnel, and financial services. In some school districts, the foodservice programs are expected to cover a greater share of the costs than if a management company operated the foodservice program. (Contract management is discussed in Chapter 5.) In some cases, the indirect costs may be returned to the school district at the end of the school year if the management company has a "profit" for the year.

Any profits that are earned by the school foodservice fund can be used only for the school foodservice program and cannot be transferred to other school operation funds.

Costs of Food and Service

For a foodservice director and manager to know the costs of each food item and each service may be impractical. However, management does need to know the overall costs in order to make such decisions as whether to add a new food product to the menu or how much to charge for a service provided. In actual costing of meals and individual items, the following should be calculated:

- Direct labor costs associated with the production of the food or providing the service
- Ingredient (food and supplies) costs required to produce the finished product or service
- Proportionate share of all other costs to operate the foodservice program (fixed costs, administrative costs, management salaries, miscellaneous costs of operating)
- Proportionate share of the indirect costs and depreciation cost of equipment

To determine a "cost of operating" or a "fixed cost" may mean adding together all expenditures besides direct labor, food, and supplies (including expenditures in the summer months). These costs are frequently called overhead costs. In order to charge the operating costs or overhead costs against each product and service, it may be useful to determine the costs of operating per dollar of revenue and to use this rate to arrive at the pro rata share for each service. In this way the operating costs are changed proportionately.

This may be far more than a school foodservice manager or supervisor wants to know; however, these costs do need to be considered. Subjective pricing of products and services can be dangerous. One can be fooled into believing a food item or service is costing less than it does and even be selling the product below cost.

Actual product cost is needed in order for management to make decisions and other aspects should be considered, such as:

- If a food item should be purchased already prepared or should be prepared by foodservice employees
  (Note: When using this data for deciding to purchase prepared items, some labor costs must be eliminated to realize savings by reducing labor hours and increasing productivity.)
- Price to be charged for a product or service, such as the a la carte price to be charged for a food product or the price per person for a special banquet
- Whether management can support the prices charged (in the public sector, a manager often has to have good documentation for making a decision)
- If the product or service should be continued
- If the price of lunch and breakfast should be increased or decreased
- If the customer will consider the price reasonable and be willing to pay the price

The cost of producing a lunch varies greatly from one school district to another. A study done by the National Food Service Management Institute (1998) showed the cost of a lunch at a low of $1.74 and a high of $2.40. The comparison of costs are shown in Figure 2.11. The costs of those school districts varies almost as much as does the revenue for school districts. Prices charged by the school district and the state subsidy can make a real difference in the revenue of a school district. In states like Utah and Louisiana, where state subsidy is high, the revenue per meal is some of the highest in the country. Whereas, three states have no state cash subsidy. Efficient use of com-modities will also help the revenue, for example, school districts in Georgia average over 15 cents commodity value per lunch.

Figure 2.11. Comparison of Lunch Production Costs for Four School Districts

Category	District A	District B	District C	District D
Food Costs	$ 0.56	$ 0.60	$ 0.70	$ 0.71
Labor Costs	1.40	0.61	0.89	0.81
Supplies	0.06	0.21	0.07	0.06
Commodities	0.14	0.22	0.17	0.12
Equipment, Capital	0.08	0.15	0.02	0.00
Overhead	0.07	0.12	0.08	0.04
Indirect Costs	0.09	0.00	0.12	0.00
Total Costs	$ 2.40	$ 1.91	$ 2.05	$ 1.74
MPLH[1]	12.5	15	19	15

Source: National Food Management Institute 1998. Used with permission.

The School Lunch and Breakfast Study (1994) by the U. S. Department of Agriculture captured the costs charged to school foodservice (reported cost), as well as those costs incurred by the school district in support of the school foodservice operation (unreported costs). The study showed the median (based on 1992-93 data) "reported" cost of producing a reimbursable lunch was $1.63, compared with a federal subsidy of $1.84 for a free lunch in 75 percent of the school districts. When the unreported costs are included, the median cost of producing lunch goes up to $1.88. Figure 2.12 shows a break-out of cost. This study also shows that in two-thirds of the schools, the costs of producing and serving a reimbursable breakfast exceeded the federal subsidy for a free breakfast. The median cost was $1.05, compared to federal subsidy of $ .95 for a free breakfast ($1.12 for a "severe need" breakfast). When the unreported costs are included, the cost of producing breakfast went up to $1.38. The study reported costs of producing a reimbursable lunch ranged from $0.93 to $2.50. InTEAM Associates, who has done financial analyses for many school districts, reports this type cost variance exists even within a few school districts.

---

[1]MPLH is the acronym for "meals per labor hour;" MPLH are discussed in Chapter 6, "Organizational Structure and Personnel." The higher the MPLH the better it is and the higher the labor costs the more important it is to have high productivity. District A's high labor costs were due to very low productivity, but the district took corrective action and reduced labor costs the following year.

Figure 2.12. Composition of Reported Cost of a Reimbursable Lunch

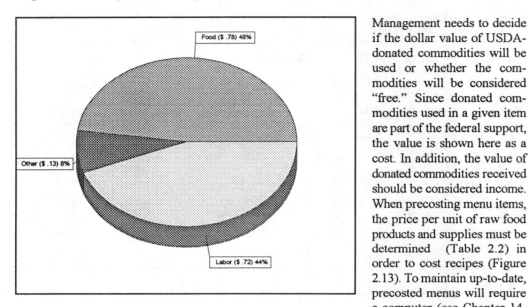

Management needs to decide if the dollar value of USDA-donated commodities will be used or whether the commodities will be considered "free." Since donated commodities used in a given item are part of the federal support, the value is shown here as a cost. In addition, the value of donated commodities received should be considered income. When precosting menu items, the price per unit of raw food products and supplies must be determined (Table 2.2) in order to cost recipes (Figure 2.13). To maintain up-to-date, precosted menus will require a computer (see Chapter 14, "Computerization and Automation"). Precost information is useful in menu planning; however, what something really costs, the "postcost," is the cost that is important in pricing or determining whether the product can be served. Records of all foods removed from inventory or a good requisition system is needed to provide this information.

It is not easy to arrive at the "real cost," or the postcost, because there are so many variables. It is important to know the precost of preparing and serving a lunch and the real cost of preparing and serving a lunch. One without the other misses the full value of the exercise. If the precost and postcost are very different—more than two percent—management needs to find out why and reduce the difference.

To determine the percentage of labor costs (payroll plus fringe benefits), divide the cost of labor by the total revenue:

$$\frac{\text{Labor Cost}}{\text{Revenue}} = \text{Labor cost \%}$$

If employees are provided annual leave and their salaries and benefits are paid over 12 months, the salaries, taxes, and benefits need to be accrued within the number of days the school foodservice served within the year (e.g., 175 days, 180 days). Using percentages help to make the financial reports more meaningful, and it is easier to compare one school with another or one month's data with another.

To determine the percentage of revenue used for food cost, divide the cost of food by the total revenue, as follows:

$$\frac{\text{Cost of food}}{\text{Revenue}} = \text{Food cost \%}$$

Table 2.2. Determining Unit Prices of Food Products to Be Used in Costing Recipes/Menus

Item	Purchase Unit	Purchase Price	Unit	Unit Cost
Sugar, 6/5 lb	case	$10.80	lb.	0.36
Applesauce (6/10)	case	14.54	can	2.43
Fruit Cocktail (6/10)	case	25.75	can	4.30
Peaches, Slices (6/10)	case	23.13	can	3.86
Pears, Halves (6/10)	case	29.10	can	4.85
Beans, Green (6/10)	case	12.17	can	2.03
Corn, Yellow (6/10)	case	16.02	can	2.67
Peas, Green , Frozen (12/2.5 lb.)	case	15.25	lb.	0.51
Catsup (1000/9 gm)	case	9.73	packet	.01
Mayonnaise (4/1 gal)	case	15.90	gal.	3.98
Salad Dressing, Light Ranch (4/gal)	case	23.58	gal.	5.90
Pickle Relish (4/1)	case	18.64	gal.	4.66
Potatoes, Oven Fries (6/6 lb)	case	13.62	lb.	0.38
Beef Pattie, 2.4 oz, Cooked 67/2.4 oz	case	18.89	each	0.28
Turkey Roast, Preroasted 225/2 oz	case	77.14	portion	0.34
Cheese, American, Grated 4/5 lb	case	38.79	lb.	1.94
Strawberries, Frozen (6½ lb.)	package	6.05	lb.	0.93

Fund Balance

The profits of the school foodservice program become the fund balance. The difference between the revenue and expenses is either a profit (gain) or a deficit (loss). The profits accumulate and increase the fund balance. If a deficit occurs it decreases the fund balance. Though school foodservice is considered a nonprofit foodservice operation, it is not a good management practice to take this concept literally. Since federal funding is on a reimbursement basis and may be received six to eight weeks after a meal is served, it is advisable to maintain a two or three month operating balance. This enables a school foodservice to meet payrolls and pay vendors on a timely basis. Federal regulations limit the funds in the account at the end of a school year to three months of operating cost, except when major equipment replacement is planned. Then special permission should be obtained from the state department administering the Child Nutrition programs when the fund balance is in excess of three months.

Figure 2.13. Example of a Precosted Recipe

TACO SALAD BAR (Chili with UDSA-Donated Beef)	
Number portions: 336 ⅓ cup	Portion cost : $ 0.203
Recipe yield: 7 gal.	Total cost: $ 22.69
Portion: ⅓ cup, 3 oz	Preparation time: 45 minutes for 7 gal
Plan group: Meat/meat alternate	
Cooking utensil: Kettle	
Cooking time: 30 minutes	
Cooking temperature: 170° F	

Food File Number	Ingredient Name	Quantity	Item Cost
156	Vegetable protein	14 oz	$ 0.521
0	Water	2½ cup	
520	Beef, ground USDA	5 lb	6.900
17	Onions, dehydrated	1 cup	0.182
157	Flour, all purpose	1 cup	0.042
0	Water	1 cup	
76	Beans, kidney	4½ gal	9.950
122	Chili powder, ground	10 Tbsp	0.499
85	Tomato paste	1 gal	4.593
0	Water	2 qt	

Instructions

1.   Add water to textured vegetable protein.

2   Brown beef, onions, and reconstituted textured vegetable protein; drain.

3.   Make a paste of flour and water, add to meat, stir constantly.

4.   Add beans, chili powder, tomato paste, and water to meat mixture; simmer until internal temperature reaches 170° F.

5.   Transfer into soup crock for service; reduce heat to prevent thickening (add water to thin).

ESTABLISHING THE BREAK-EVEN POINT

The break-even point (BEP) is the ultimate determiner in knowing the daily financial situation, particularly when the director/manager establishes the BEP and sets goals to meet that point. This can be done for a school district and by school. In some cases, one may decide that it is impossible to break even at some school locations, because the revenue will not cover the basic operating costs. This section takes the BEP formulas taught by Professor Mickey Warner of Florida International University and applies it to school foodservice.

The daily BEP can be established for the school district and for each of the schools. Since the controlling of costs and increasing of sales are most affected at the school level, ending the school year with a small profit or gain in fund balance can best be accomplished by involving the managers of the individual schools in the process. The following example is of a high school in a centralized school district.

To determine a BEP for the school (and school district) the following basic formula (Warner 1989) is used:

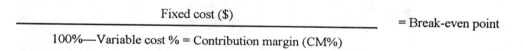

$$\frac{\text{Fixed cost (\$)}}{100\% - \text{Variable cost \%} = \text{Contribution margin (CM\%)}} = \text{Break-even point}$$

Fixed costs (FC) are the costs that do not vary with the day-to-day or week-to-week volumes of sales or numbers of customers served, e.g., manager's salary, maintenance cost. The most common FC items are:

- Central office cost
- Manager's salary
- Basic telephone charge
- Core staff
- Trash removal (unless by weight)

The FC are always expressed in dollars and include: management salaries and fringe benefits, telephone service, depreciation (if currently being used by the school district in profit and loss), utilities (if applicable), and office supplies. To be included are the costs that stay relatively constant regardless of whether a school serves, for example, 600 or 700 lunches.

Variable costs (VC) are the costs that vary in direct proportion with volumes of sales or numbers of customers served, e.g., food, some supplies, and some labor. VC are those costs that increase and decrease in direct ratio to the sales. The most common VC items are:

- Food
- Supplies, paper goods
- Some labor (that is, if numbers of hours are adjusted according to numbers served or amount of revenue)

The **contribution margin (CM)** is the percent of the revenue that can be used to pay the FC. In other words, if the CM is 49 percent, then 49¢ of every dollar in revenue goes to paying the FC (manager's salary, indirect costs, etc.) as shown in the formula that follows.

$$\frac{FC\ \$}{CM} = BEP\ \$_____$$

If daily FC are $400 and VC are 51%, the CM is 49%, or .49 (the percentage is converted to a decimal point .49), and the FC figure of $400 is divided by .49 to arrive at the BEP of $817.

$$\frac{\$400\ \ FC}{100 - 51\% = 49\%\ CM} \quad OR \quad \frac{\$400\ \ FC}{.49\ CM} = \$817$$

Determining the Break-Even Point for Individual Schools

The BEP is the amount of sales (revenue/income) needed to cover the FC and VC. It is that point where total revenues and total expenses are equal. Any sales beyond that point will provide some profits. When the revenue does not reach the BEP or surpass it, the operation will have a loss (deficit).

When establishing a BEP for the individual schools, the labor costs for the foodservice central office and those expenses that are charged to the central office must be charged against the schools—as overhead costs. A decision to be made is whether this cost will be "fixed" or "variable." It is easier to compile when considering overhead as a fixed cost. Annually the central office can allocate the cost to be charged to each school based on meal equivalents served or dollars. If the a la carte sales contribute considerably to the revenue, then the percentage should be based on dollars. (All revenue should be included—such as, value of donated commodities, federal and state subsidies, and cash sales.) For example, if the school district's revenue for the year was $ 1,450,000, the percentage of overhead costs a high school in that school district (with a revenue for the year of $ 250,000) would be charged is $ 250,000 ÷ $ 1, 450,000 = .17 or 17 percent. If the number served is going to be used to determine the percentage share of overhead that is to be charged to each school, then the total meals served in the school district and the total number of meals served by each school are to be used.

If the school district or school determines what profit it wants to make, the profit would be added to the fixed cost.

The BEP seems to be more meaningful when broken down by the day, versus by month or year. The BEP can help management determine where financial problems are and how much change is necessary to resolve a financial problem. Figure 2.14 provides an example of using the BEP for a high school.

If the BEP is higher than is possible to reach, the options are to subsidize the school foodservice program or do one or more of the following:

Reduce FC—Reduce fixed costs, e.g., reduce the manager's salary, trash removal, or telephone

> **Reduce VC**—Lower the percentage of revenue used for food, substitute labor, supplies, and paper
>
> **Increase revenue**—Increase the number of lunches served and services offered (e.g., add breakfast program) without increasing FC

Figure 2.14. Example of Determining the Break-Even Point

The BEP can be determined for this high school with the following information:

1. Average revenue per day, e.g., average of $1,301.74 (serving 520 lunches and selling $400 in extra food sales a day)
2. Fixed costs—e.g., manager's salary $96, plus $28.80 fringe benefits; staffed with 43 labor hours @ $7 per hour ($1.76 fringe benefits); overhead cost (central office, salaries, utilities, etc.)—$200 per day; trash removal—$1.50 per day, and telephone—60¢ per day
3. Variable Costs—e.g., use last month's or year's data; determine percentage of revenue spent for food, substitute labor, and paper supplies

ITEM (1)	FC ($) (4)	VC (%) (5)
Revenue for Day—$1,301.74		
Food Costs		39%
Labor Costs		
Management	$ 96.00	
Core Staff	301.00	
Benefits	104.48	
Total Fixed Labor	$ 501.48	
Overhead	200.00	
Substitute Labor Costs		5%
Telephone	.60	
Trash Removal	1.50	
Paper/Supplies		6%
TOTAL COSTS	$ 703.58	50%

$$\frac{\$703.58 \text{ FC } (+ \text{Profit } \$25)}{100\% - \underline{50\%}\ \text{VC} = \underline{50\%}\ \text{CM}} = \frac{\$1,407.16 \text{ BEP without profit}}{\text{or } \$1,457.16 \text{ BEP with profit}}$$

Lowering the variable cost is usually the easiest and can possibly be done by reducing waste. Lowering the fixed cost will probably mean reducing labor, which may be less desirable than increasing revenue.

In the example in Figure 2.14, the difference in the revenue and the BEP is $105.42. It will take a combination of all three means to obtain a BEP for this school. The food cost is within 40 percent of the revenue and may be difficult to reduce more than one percent. The fixed cost has in it $501.58 of labor cost, which is slightly under 40 percent of the revenue. The salaries are relatively low but the school is over-staffed (which will be discussed in Chapter 6). The staff is producing at 13 meals per labor hour, when the school should be producing at 16 to 17 meals per labor hour. With this in mind, management may choose to put a freeze on the use of substitutes (reducing that cost by one to two percent) and increase participation by adding a breakfast program (without adding labor) and increasing participation and extra food sales at lunch by five percent. The school did break even when the BEP is refigured in Figure 2.15.

Figure 2.15. Determining the Break-Even Point After Making Changes

ITEM (1)	FC ($) (4)	VC (%) (5)
Revenue for Day—$1,366.82		
Food Costs		38%
Labor Costs		
Management	$ 96.00	
Core Staff	301.00	
Benefits	104.48	
Total Fixed Labor	$ 501.48	
Overhead	200.00	
Substitute Labor Costs		3%
Telephone	.60	
Trash Removal	1.50	
Paper/Supplies		6%
TOTAL COST	$ 703.58	47%

$$\frac{\$\ 703.58\ FC\ (+Profit\ \$\ 25.00)}{100\%-\underline{\ 47\%\ }\ VC=\underline{\ 53\%\ }\ CM}=\begin{array}{l}\$\ 1,327.51\ BEP\ without\ profit\\ or\ \$\ 1,374.68\ BEP\ with\ profit\end{array}$$

AUDITS/COMPLIANCE REQUIREMENTS

The Child Nutrition Act and National Lunch Program regulations require compliance in order to receive federal funds. Audits (though the federal and state agencies call them reviews) are done by the state agencies administering the Child Nutrition programs. Occasionally the USDA regional offices are involved in audits.

In an effort to ensure that the accountability system used in the school districts is meeting the objectives of Congress and in an effort to reduce the cost of the Child Nutrition programs, Congress ruled in 1988 that federal regulations were to be adhered to more strictly. The assessment, improvement, and monitoring system (**AIMS**) review, a state review system that was being required by the USDA, was determined inadequate and failed to detect meal-count deficiencies and over-claims. The system of audit that resulted later was called **AccuClaim procedures**, which was a modification of AIMS. AIMS was replaced with Coordinated Review Effort (CRE), which is now used—along with a check on the nutritive value of meals served, called a School Meals Initiative (SMI) review. CRE and SMI are two completely different and separate reviews. See Appendix B for an example of SMI form used by most state agencies.

Basically the purpose of the state audits is to improve accuracy and accountability in the counting of school meals served and the claiming of those meals for federal reimbursement. The state agencies will be comparing numbers claimed monthly against numbers approved and present at school (using an attendance factor). In addition, the audit reviews will be performed by the state on schools claiming large numbers of meals served free and at reduced prices. Action will be taken against a school or school district when violations exceed $600, even the first time the violations occur, whereas in the past the school or school district was given an opportunity to correct violations or errors the first time. (The checklist in Figure 1.7 will be helpful to the manager concerned with meeting the federal regulations.)

Compliance Requirements

It is important to emphasize that CRE audits are intended to determine if a school foodservice program is in compliance with federal and state requirements. The meal counts and cash collection systems should provide an accurate claim for reimbursement. McCullen (1989) offers criteria for a model meal count system.

- *Guidance, including written detailed instructions, on the operation of the meal count system is developed and provided to all responsible personnel.*
- *All personnel involved in the meal count system are knowledgeable and can adequately perform their duties and responsibilities.*
- *All applicants (for free and reduced-price meals) have been approved in accordance with the regulations and in a timely manner.*
- *Category determinations are accurately recorded on the master roster and maintained*

throughout the year with frequent updates as changes occur.

- *Tickets, tokens, IDs, etc., and master roster accurately reflect the student's eligibility for free, reduced-price or paid meal.*
- *Reimbursable meals are clearly identifiable.*
- *All meals are correctly counted at the point of service and recorded by category.[1]*
- *The cash collection system for reimbursable meals and other sales ensures that appropriate amounts of cash are collected and recorded for each sale category.*
- *A cash reconciliation system is used that : (1) determines on a daily basis whether cash collected reconciles with meal counts as recorded; (2) ensures that all differences are documented; (3) ensures that corrective action is taken where needed.*
- *A system is in place to safeguard cash and tickets, tokens, IDs, etc., from loss, theft, or misuse.*
- *Reports of daily meals and cash collected are complete and are compiled for the Claim for Reimbursement.*
- *Edit checks for individual schools are implemented to identify potential problems in the meal count systems.[2]*
- *Periodic monitoring and technical assistance are provided for each school to ensure compliance with the approved meal count system.*

If a child is receiving free meals and the auditor determines that the application is not complete or is incorrectly acted upon, or if there are verification problems a school district could be required/requested to return the overclaimed federal reimbursement. Not all states handle these problems the same. The Appendix A provides the text of the regulations relating to these reviews.

---

[1]Only one meal per student is claimed.

[2]Edit checks compare number of students qualified for free and reduced-price meals who are present (at school) with the numbers of meals served (and claimed).

SELECTED REFERENCES

Boeher, J. 1993. "Managing to Meet the Bottom Line." *School Business Affairs* 59 (10): 3-8.

Cater, J., and N. Mann. 1997. *Revenue Generation and Cost Control Measures Currently Used in Financially Successful Child Nutrition Programs.* University, MS: National Food Service Management Institute.

Cater, J., N. Mann, and M. Conklin. 1999. "Financial Management: A Growing Concern for Child Nutrition Program Administrators." *School Business Affairs* 65(5): 45-49.

The Educational Foundation. 1992. *Basic Accounting for Food Services.* Chicago, IL: National Restaurant Association.

_____. 1992. *Management Accounting for Food Services.* Chicago, IL: National Restaurant Association.

Kehoe, E. 1986. "Educational Budget Preparation: Fiscal and Political Considerations." In *Principles of School Business Management,* edited by R. Craig Wood. Reston, VA: Association of School Business Officials International.

McCool, A, F. Smith, and D. Tucker. 1994. *Dimensions of Noncommercial Foodservice Management.* New York , NY: Van Nostrand Reinhold, Inc.

McCullen, G. 1989. "AccuClaim Means Better Accountability." *School Food Service Journal* 43(2): 44-45

Miller, J., and D. Hayes. 1994. *Basic Food and Beverage Cost Control.* New York, NY: John Wiley & Sons, Inc.

Miller, J. and D. Pavesic. 1996. *Menu Pricing and Strategy.* 4th ed. New York, NY: Van Nostrand Reinhold Company.

National Food Service Management Institute. 1998. *Revenue Generation and Cost Control Measures Currently Used in Financially Successful CNPs.* University, MS: Author.

National Restaurant Association. 1996. *Uniform System of Accounts for Restaurants.* 7th ed. Washington, DC: National Restaurant Association.

"National School Lunch Program: Accountability." 1989. *Federal Register* 54(58): 12575-12583.

Pannell-Martin, D. 1998. *Controlling Costs in the Foodservice Industry.* Alexandria, VA: inTEAM Associates, Inc.

_____. 1995. *Cost Control Manual for School Foodservice.* 2nd ed. Alexandria, VA.: inTEAM Associates, Inc.

Pavesic, D. 1998. Fundamental Principles of Restaurant Cost Control. Upper Saddle River, NJ: Prentice Hall, Inc.

Tidwell, S. 1986. "Educational Accounting Procedures." *Principal of School Business Management,* edited by R. Wood. Reston, VA: Association of School Business

U. S. Department of Agriculture. 1994. *School Lunch and Breakfast Cost Study.* Washington, DC: Author.

Warner, M. 1989. "Break-Even Analysis and Profit Volume Charting: Function and Use by Restaurant Managers." Presentation at the National Restaurant Association Convention in Chicago, IL.

3
DIETARY GUIDELINES
AND
NUTRITIONAL REQUIREMENTS

Nutritional Requirements and Goals

Nutrients and Menu Planning Regulations
    Traditional Food-Based Menu Planning for Lunch
    Enhanced Food-Based Menu Planning
    Nutrient Standard/Assisted Nutrient Standard Menu Planning
    Any Reasonable Approach to Menu Planning
    Comparison of the Lunch Menu Planning Methods
    School Breakfast Meal Requirements
    Milk Requirements
    Offer Versus Serve

Trends and Health Concerns
    Assessment of Nutrient Standard Menu Planning

Special Nutritional Concerns
    Fats
    Sodium
    Dealing with Current "Nutritional Concerns"
    Allergies

Nutrient Analysis Programs

Food Production Records

USDA Child Nutrition (CN) Labeling Program

Selected References

NUTRITIONAL REQUIREMENTS AND GOALS

The goals of the USDA's *School Meals Initiative for Healthy Children* are addressed in this chapter, which covers the nutritional requirements of the National School Lunch and Breakfast Programs, and in Chapter 4, "Planning Menus and Food Offerings," which puts dietary guidelines into foods/menus. In recent years the goals of the National School Lunch Act and Child Nutrition Act have become more exact and spelled out, with emphasis on meeting the Recommended Dietary Allowances (RDA)[1] and the recommendations of the Dietary Guidelines for Americans (see Table 3.1). The RDAs are discussed later in this chapter. Much emphasis has been placed on controlling the number of calories from fat and saturated fat. Schools are encouraged to plan menus based on nutrients but have been given alternatives.

On the basis of nutrient intake data, students who participate in the school lunch program have nutritionally superior meals as compared to those not participating. Congressional studies also show that the school lunch program provides nutritionally superior meals more efficiently than providing additional cash benefits through social programs to the families directly.

With the increased interest in nutrition, the nutritional aspects of menu planning are expected to receive continued emphasis by the customer in the coming years. The basic guidelines used by school foodservice menu planners between 1979 and 1994 were the "School Lunch Meal Patterns," which replaced the "Type A Lunch Pattern." The meal requirements went from two different reimbursable "Meal Pattern" formats—one for lunch and another for breakfast, which were already complicated, to five menu planning methods for lunch and two for breakfast.

Now there are five approaches to meeting the lunch nutritional requirements of the students, which make an already complicated program much more complicated. Using nutrients to plan menus is not totally new to school foodservice. Nutrients were used by a few school districts as far back as the late 1970s as a part of USDA pilots. The current rules for the menu planning requirements were issued in June 1995 in the *Federal Register* (Volume 60, Number 113).

The basis for all the planning methods is that the lunch meal should meet one-third of the RDAs, and breakfast one-fourth of the RDAs. It was the hope of the USDA administration in the early 1990s that school foodservices would be limited to Nutrient Standard Menu Planning (or Assisted Nutrient Standard). There are many schools out of 94,000 participating in the National School Lunch Program that could not have managed Nutrient Standard and the necessary computer analysis. This point was finally made with Congress and food-based alternatives were added as a means of meeting the nutritional meal requirements.

The Healthy Meals for Healthy Americans Act of 1994 mandated the Dietary Guidelines be followed by 1996-97, though waivers were granted by states.

---

[1]The Dietary Guidelines for Americans are recommended dietary allowances established by the Food and Nutrition Board of the National Research Council of the National Academy of Sciences.

Table 3.1. Dietary Guidelines for Americans

> 1. Eat a variety of foods.
> 2. Balance the food you eat with physical activity—maintain or improve your weight.
> 3. Choose a diet with plenty of grain products, vegetables, and fruits.
> 4. Choose a diet low in fat, saturated fat, and cholesterol.
> 5. Choose a diet moderate in sugars.
> 6. Choose a diet moderate in salt and sodium.
> 7. If you drink alcoholic beverages, do so in moderation.

Source: Nutrition and Your Health: Dietary Guidelines for Americans, 4th ed.. U. S. Department of Health and Human Services and U. S. Department of Agriculture 1995.

NUTRIENTS AND MENU PLANNING REGULATIONS

There are five approved methods of meeting the nutritional guidelines under the "School Meal Initiative:"

Traditional Food-Based
Enhanced Food-Based
Nutrient Standard
Assisted Nutrient Standard
Any Reasonable Approach

In order for a school district to claim meals for reimbursement, the school foodservice must carry out one of the five methods of meeting the meal requirements. A comparison of the first four methods which are the most used begins in Figure 3.1 with a comparison of the nutritional requirements of the methods. Figure 3.2 compares the food requirements of the four methods of planning menus. Chapter 9, "Procurement and Controlling Inventory," compares the cost of meeting the meal requirements for four of the menu planning methods.

Traditional Food-Based Menu Planning for Lunch

Traditional Food-Based Menu Planning is based on food and is not new. If this method of menu planning is selected, the menus may meet the Dietary Guidelines for Americans and the RDAs. The National School Lunch Meal Patterns, which are the basis of the traditional food-based menu planning, were developed and implemented in 1980 as a part of the guidelines of the National School Lunch Act, replacing the "Type A" lunch pattern. The School Lunch Patterns, which have been revised four times since then and are the foundation for the Traditional Food-Based Menu

Figure 3.1. Comparison of Lunch Menu Planning Methods Nutritional Requirements

NUTRIENT STANDARDS	COMPARISON OF LUNCH MENU PLANNING SYSTEMS											
	FOOD BASED								NUTRIENT STANDARD/ ASSISTED NUTRIENT STANDARD			
	TRADITIONAL[1]				ENHANCED							
Age/Grade Group:	Preschool	Grades K-3	Grades 4-12	Grades 7-12 Optional	Pre-school	Grades K-6	Grades 7-12	Grades K-3 Optional	Pre-school	Grades K-6	Grades 7-12	Grades K-3 Optional
Energy Allowances (Calories=cal)	517 cal	633 cal	785 cal	825 cal	517 cal	664 cal	825 cal	633 cal	517 cal	664 cal	825 cal	633 cal
Protein (grams=g)	7 g	9 g	15 g	16 g	7 g	10 g	16 g	9 g	7 g	10 g	16 g	9 g
Calcium (milligrams=mg)	267 mg	267 mg	370 mg	400 mg	267 mg	286 mg	400 mg	267 mg	267 mg	286 mg	400 mg	267 mg
Iron (milligrams=mg)	3.3 mg	3.3 mg	4.2 mg	4.5 mg	3.3 mg	3.5 mg	4.5 mg	3.3 mg	3.3 mg	3.5 mg	4.5 mg	3.3 mg
Vitamin A (retinol Equivalents=RE)	150 RE	200 RE	285 RE	300 RE	150 RE	224 RE	300 RE	200 RE	150 RE	224 RE	300 RE	200 RE
Vitamin C (milligrams=mg)	14 mg	15 mg	17 mg	18 mg	14 mg	15 mg	18 mg	15mg	14 mg	15 mg	18 mg	15 mg
Total fat	No more than 30 percent of total calories should come from fat.											
Saturated fat	Less than 10 percent of total calories should come from saturated fat.											

Source: U.S. Department of Agriculture, Team Nutrition, *A Menu Planner for Healthy School Meals* 1998.

[1] Note the grade grouping differences for Traditional, Enhanced, and Nutrient Standard/Assisted Nutrient Standard.

Figure 3.2. Comparison of Menu Foods for Different Lunch Menu Planning Methods

COMPARISON OF LUNCH MENU PLANNING SYSTEMS*

MEAL PATTERN	FOOD BASED — TRADITIONAL					FOOD BASED — ENHANCED					NUTRIENT STANDARD (NSMP)/ ASSISTED NUTRIENT STANDARD (ASSISTED NSMP)
	Ages 1-2	Ages 3-4	Grades K-3	Grades 4-12	Grades 7-12	Ages 1-2	Pre-school	Grades K-6	Grades 7-12	Grades K-3	A LUNCH PLANNED WITH NSMP OR ASSISTED NSMP MUST INCLUDE AT LEAST THESE *THREE* MENU ITEMS: REQUIRED COMPONENT
COMPONENT Lean Meat, poultry or fish	1 oz	1-1/2 oz	1-1/2 oz	2 oz	3 oz	1 oz	1-1/2 oz	1-1/2 oz	2 oz	3 oz	**1) AN ENTREE. An entree is a combination of foods or a single food item offered as the main course. The entree is the central focus of the meal and forms the framework around which the rest of the meal is planned.** For NSMP and Assisted NSMP, a school week is defined as a minimum of 3 consecutive days and a maximum of 7 consecutive days. If there are fewer than 3 consecutive days in a week, the days in that week are combined with the coming or prior week for nutrient analysis. Using customized age groups? If you choose to use age groups in planning meals with NSMP or Assisted NSMP, you may want to stay with the established age groups. These will already be programmed into any USDA-approved software. As we've seen, there are four established age groups. In years, they are: • Ages 3-6 • Ages 7-10 • Ages 11-13 • Ages 14 and older However, since not all school districts are divided into these four age groups, the NSMP software will also allow you to create your own customized age groups. In fact, to most accurately target the nutrient needs of the children you serve, this is the recommended method.
Cheese	1 oz	1-1/2 oz	1-1/2 oz	2 oz	3 oz	1 oz	1-1/2 oz	1-1/2 oz	2 oz	3 oz	
Large egg	1/2	3/4	3/4	1	1-1/2	1/2	3/4	1	1	3/4	
Cooked dry beans or peas	1/4 cup	3/8 cup	3/8 cup	1/2 cup	3/4 cup	1/4 cup	3/8 cup	1/2 cup	1/2 cup	3/8 cup	
Peanut butter or other nut or seed butters	2 Tbsp	3 Tbsp	3 Tbsp	4 Tbsp	6 Tbsp	2 Tbsp	3 Tbsp	4 Tbsp	4 Tbsp	3 Tbsp	
Yogurt	4 oz or 1/2 cup	6 oz or 3/4 cup	6 oz or 3/4 cup	8 oz or 1 cup	12 oz or 1-1/2 cup	4 oz or 1/2 cup	6 oz or 3/4 cup	8 oz or 1 cup	8 oz or 1 cup	6 oz or 3/4 cup	
Peanuts, soy nuts, tree nuts, or seeds	1/2 oz =50%	3/4 oz =50%	3/4 oz=50%	1 oz =50%	1-1/2 oz =50%	1/2 oz =50%	3/4 oz =50%	1 oz =50%	1 oz =50%	3/4 oz =50%	
COMPONENT VEGETABLES/ FRUITS	1/2 c	1/2 c	1/2 c	3/4 c	3/4 c	1/2 c	1/2 c	3/4 c plus extra 1/2 c over a week	1 c	3/4 c	**2) A SIDE DISH. This can be any other food except a condiment or a food of minimal nutritional value.**
COMPONENT GRAINS AND BREADS: Minimum per DAY	1/2 serv	1 serv	1 serv	1 serv	1 serv	1/2 serv	1 serv	1 serv	1 serv	1 serv	
Minimum per WEEK	5 serv	8 serv	8 serv	8 serv	10 serv	5 serv	8 serv	12 serv	15 serv	10 serv	
COMPONENT MILK**	6 fl oz	6 fl oz	8 fl oz	8 fl oz	8 fl oz	6 fl oz	6 fl oz	8 fl oz	8 fl oz	8 fl oz	**3) FLUID MILK SERVED AS A BEVERAGE MUST BE OFFERED.**

*Meets the nutrient standards for the appropriate grade or age groups when averaged over one school week's menu.

**Under Offer versus Serve it does not have to be one of the side dishes.

Planning (see Figure 3.2). The School Lunch Patterns provide the simplest way of planning nutritionally adequate meals that most people are familiar with.

The School Lunch Meal Patterns state minimum portion sizes for the five age/grade groups, these groups being:

Group I	—	ages 1-2
Group II	—	ages 3-4
Group III	—	ages 5-8, grades K-3
Group IV	—	ages 9 and over, grades 4-12
Group V	—	all ages

For group V, recommended (not required) quantities are given for grades 7-12 students (age 12 and over), but the menu will meet (or exceed) the nutritional requirements for all ages. Group IV quantities will meet the requirement for all age groups. Group IV will provide approximately one-third of the daily RDAs for all nutrients for a student between the ages of 10 and 12 years. The School Lunch Meal Patterns encourage varying the portion size according to the age of the child.

Schools/school districts **are not** required to run the nutrient analysis on the menus planned using the traditional food-based meal planning method; however, the state agency administering the Child Nutrition programs will evaluate the menus when reviewing the school district's foodservice program using nutrient analysis.

Enhanced Food-Based Menu Planning

The Enhanced Food-Based Menu Planning is very similar to the Traditional Food-Based Menu Planning with increased servings of vegetables/fruits and grain/breads. The menu must contain food from the four components. It is the number of servings and the sizes of servings that have changed. It will probably be easier to meet the nutritional goals because of those additional calories, vitamins and iron. These may be the nutrients short when running the nutritional analysis on the Traditional-Food-Based Menu Planning.

A grain-based dessert may be credited to meet one of the grain/bread servings **each day**. The creditable foods under the grain/bread section or component of the Enhanced Food-Based Menu Planning have been expanded to include a number of foods not previously credited. See USDA's *A Menu Planner for Healthy School Meals (1998)* for the list of grain/bread credits.

Nutrient Standard/Assisted Nutrient Standard Menu Planning

Nutrient Standard Menu Planning (NSMP) and Assisted Nutrient Standard Menu Planning (Assisted NSMP) have the same nutritional requirements. The difference is in who plans and analyzes the menus. Nutrient Standard menus are those the school or school district plans and analyzes itself. With Assisted NSMP, an outside consultant or agency performs the function. Several state agencies have planned and analyzed statewide menus for the school districts to use, e.g., Mississippi. A number of consultants provide the nutrient analysis services. InTEAM Associates, Incorporated, has published *Assisted NuMenu Manual with Database on Disk*, which provides popular menu cycles, enhanced food files, and recipes (Pannell-Martin 1996).

NSMP sets specific goals for calories, fat, calcium, iron, protein, and Vitamins A and C that menus must provide when averaged over a week. The menus planned by this method must be analyzed for nutrients using simple weighting to determine if the requirements have been met.

Under NSMP one of two grade groupings may be selected when planning menus and they are:

Group One	Group Two
Grades K-6; Grades 7-12	Grades K-3; Grades 4-6; Grades 7-12

OR

Age Groups of 3-6 years, 7-10 years, 11-13 years, and 14 and older

Any Reasonable Approach to Menu Planning

"Any Reasonable Approach to Menu Planning" is the fifth method approved by Congress. It was approved later than the four methods previously discussed. It is a method that enables foodservice to comply with all statutory and regulatory requirements without exactly following either of the four other methods of menu planning listed. Guidelines for using this method can be obtained from the state agency administering the Child Nutrition programs or USDA Food and Nutrition Services, since *A Menu Planner for Healthy School Meals* (1998) does not address how to use this option.

Comparison of the Lunch Menu Planning Methods

Figures 3.1, 3.2, and 3.3 show comparisons of the four different lunch menu planning methods in the following areas:

- Nutritional requirements
- Food requirements
- Basic menu that has been adjusted to meet each of the different menu planning requirements
- Cost of each menu as planned (Chapter 4 will compare the menus and the menu costs.)

With all of the menu planning methods, the nutrients are to meet the nutritional goals as required by the federal regulations. When analyzing the menus, the nutrients are to be averaged over a week, which means one day's menu can be high in fat as long as over the week the average is within the requirements. The same is true of costs—one or more menus within the week may cost more than the others. The costs should be averaged over a week and be within the amount of money available. As shown in Figures 3.1 and 3.2, the major differences are:

Age groups
Nutrients
Exactness of food quantities
Components

There are many aspects of each of these menu planning methods that are discussed in this text. Chapter 4, "Planning Menu and Food Offerings," uses the nutritional guidelines in a practical way to plan menus. To fully understand these methods of planning and particularly to plan menus, three essential USDA publications are: *Food Buying Guide for Child Nutrition Programs*, (1984, revised 1990, new edition to be released in 2000), *A Menu Planner for Healthy School Meals* (1998), and *A Tool Kit for Healthy School Meals: Recipes and Training Materials (1998)*.

Figure 3.3. Comparison of Menu Planning Systems Food Requirements

FOOD REQUIREMENTS /CRITERIA FOR A REIMBURSABLE MEAL		
Traditional Food Based	**Enhanced Food-Based**	**Nutrient Standard/ Assisted Nutrient Standard**
Four food components for lunch **must be offered** Five food items for lunch	Four food components for lunch Five food items for lunch	A minimum of three menu items (However, the three menu items are not be the same for both meals.)
Three food (or four) components for breakfast **must be offered** Four food items for breakfast	Three (or four) food components for breakfast Four food items for breakfast	In addition, a reimbursable meal must meet the nutrient standard for the appropriate age or grade group when the nutrients in those foods are nutritionally analyzed and averaged over a
In addition, a reimbursable meal must meet the nutrient standard for the appropriate age or grade group when the nutrients in those foods are nutritionally analyzed and averaged over a school week. This can be accomplished by following the instructions in the USDA-approved software.	In addition, a reimbursable meal must meet the nutrient standard for the appropriate age or grade group when the nutrients in those foods are nutritionally analyzed and averaged over a school week. This can be accomplished by following the instructions in the USDA-approved software.	school week. This can be accomplished by following the instructions in the USDA-approved software. A reimbursable meal under Offer versus Serve: –Contains at least two menu items –Breakfast-- no more than one may be declined –Lunch must contain an entree and no more than two menu items
A reimbursable meal: –Contains at least three food items under Offer versus Serve	A reimbursable meal: –Contains at least three food items under Offer versus Serve	may be declined if more than three are offered as a meal A menu item may be any single food or combination of foods except: (1) Condiment (2) Food of minimal nutritional value not included in a menu item There are three categories of menu items: ✦ Entrees ✦ Side Dishes ✦ Milk

School Breakfast Meal Requirements

There are two methods of meeting the school breakfast meal requirements, using (1) the Nutrient Standard/Assisted Nutrient Standard Menu Planning Method or (2) the Traditional Food-Based School Breakfast Meal Pattern. There is one established age or grade group, 3 years of age up or Grades K-12. An additional optional age/grade group is Grades 7-12, and the recommended portions are slightly larger.

The federal School Breakfast Program requires that a breakfast for Grades K-12 contain the following as a minimum:

Component One (one serving)	½ pint of fluid milk (as a beverage or on cereal or both)
Component Two (one serving)	½ cup of fruit or vegetable or fruit juice or vegetable juice
Component Three (two servings)	2 servings of grain/bread *or* 2 servings of meat/meat alternate *or* 1 serving of grain/ bread and 1 serving of meat/ meat alternate

Studies in the early 1980s of the breakfast program showed that the breakfast pattern needed more protein and iron-rich foods than had been specified. Congress increased the reimbursement for the breakfast program by 3 cents in 1989 for the purpose of increasing the protein and iron-rich foods. The breakfast pattern was revised in 1989, though the funding was not adequate to cover the costs.

Milk Requirements

Section 9(a)(2)(B) of the National School Lunch Act requires that schools offer, as part of a reimbursable lunch, "...a variety of fluid milk consistent with prior year preferences unless the prior year preference for any such variety of fluid milk is less than 1 percent of the total milk consumed at the school." Schools must offer fluid whole milk and fluid unflavored lowfat milk, previously stipulated in the law, as well as other types of fluid milk, such as flavored milk or skim milk, that have been proven popular with children. This statutory mandate was incorporated into the National School Lunch Program regulations in 1995.

The Food and Drug Administration's labeling requirement for "lowfat" and "reduced-fat" milk (effective January 1, 1998), defines the terms as follows: "Lowfat applies only to milk with a designated fat content of about 1 percent or less; 'reduced fat' applies only to milk with a designated fat content of about 2 percent." The USDA states that schools may offer children milk meeting the new definition of lowfat in place of milk meeting the prior definition. Chocolate and strawberry milks, which are popular with students, often contain as little as one-half to one percent fat.

Offer Versus Serve

"Offer versus serve" is the regulation that allows students in any grade to choose fewer than all of the food items within the breakfast and lunch menus planned. This has always been a difficult regulation to communicate to employees and students. It has been made harder with the additional menu planning methods. Offer versus serve is the same for Traditional Food-Based Menu Planning and Enhanced Food-Based Menu Planning. The regulation states that at lunch offer versus serve is required of high schools and is a local school foodservice authority option for the other grades. At breakfast, offer versus serve is a local option for all grade levels. Over 85 percent of all school districts report they carry out offer versus serve. It is not an easy regulation to teach, but the advantages are strong enough reasons to encourage the option and to do the training necessary.

Offer Versus Serve at Lunch

The regulation means different things under the different menu planning options as explained below:

Traditional Food-Based and Enhanced Food-Based Menus—The student must be offered all five food items, but may refuse any two. Offer versus serve is required for high school students, optional and local food authority's decision for other grade levels.

Nutrient Standard/Assisted Nutrient Standard Menus—The student must be offered three menu items, and those three must include an entree, fluid milk, and another menu offering. The student must select at least two of the required menu items, and one must be an entree. Offer versus serve is required for high school students, but is optional at other grade levels. It is the local school foodservice authority's decision for other grade levels. A hamburger served under Nutrient Standard is consider an entree only, whereas, under Traditional Food-Based it counts as two food items.

Offer Versus Serve at Breakfast

Traditional Food-Based Menus—Offer versus serve is optional and the local school food authority's decision at all grade levels. Four food items are to be offered, and one item may be refused.

Nutrient Standard Menus—Students may decline a maximum of one menu item regardless of how many are offered. Offer versus serve is optional and the local school food authority's decision at all grade levels.

All the above meals must be priced as a unit regardless of whether the student takes all the offerings or declines some of the foods offered under offer versus serve.

Reasons for Carrying Out Offer Versus Serve

There are many reasons for a school district to carry out offer versus serve at all levels, such as the following:

- Increases customer satisfaction by giving students some say in what is put on the tray or plate.

- Reduces food waste.
- Reduces food costs.

The biggest drawback to offer versus serve is the difficulty in training employees to carry it out. It takes constant reinforcement and going over each menu with the key employees (server and cashier) to make certain they understand what makes a breakfast or a lunch. It is also difficult to communicate to teachers, principals, and parents the intent of the federal regulations and options. There are many creative ways of communicating "offer versus serve" to the customers, and some will be discussed in Chapter 4. The person who decides if a meal qualifies as a reimbursable meal will find it helpful to have a few items with easy reach and help the student customer to meet the requirements, rather than sending the student back and hold up a serving line.

TRENDS AND HEALTH CONCERNS

In less than 30 years, school foodservice has moved from one extreme to another in regards to fat in the school lunch program. The pendulum swung from the 1960s and early 1970s, when two teaspoons of butter and whole milk were requirements of the School Lunch Meal Pattern, to the late 1970s and most of the 1980s, when lowfat milk was a required offering (see Table 3.2). In 1985 Congress listened to the milk lobbyists and passed legislation that schools had to offer whole milk as a beverage. Those concerned about good nutrition were shocked by the passage of this legislation. Much progress had been made by school foodservice toward influencing students to drink lowfat milk as a result of a 1979 regulation requiring that lowfat, unflavored milk be offered as a beverage with lunch. Excess butterfat was becoming a problem for the dairy industry; therefore the whole-milk offering became law.

A lot of emphasis has been put on nutrition and content of food during the 1990s. With all the emphasis on nutrition in the media as well, student customers (and their parents) in many school districts have an opportunity to be better informed today than in previous years—about the nutritional value of the meals served.

During the late 1970s, and more so during the 1980s, school foodservice meals had a reputation (not necessarily deserved) for being loaded with fat, particularly saturated fat, and sodium. During those periods USDA-donated commodities continued to consist mainly of unlimited quantities of butter, ground pork, and cheese, which encouraged the negative image. In the 1990s the emphasis was on correcting this; however, some people learned it would not be as easy as they thought to change the eating patterns of all children and to accomplish the sophisticated levels of menu planning using nutrient analysis by all schools.

Over 81 percent of all school districts are using either Traditional Food-Based Menu Planning or Enhanced Food-Based Menu Planning methods to plan menus (USDA 1998). Many of the management companies carry out the Assisted Nutrient Standard and they realize the food cost reduction that can be realized (see Chapter 9, "Procurement and Controlling Inventory," for the cost comparison). Some of the school districts that use Nutrient Standard for lunch use the Traditional Food-Based Planning method for breakfast. Regardless of the method used to plan menus, the dietary guidelines are to be met with the menu as planned (approved through September 2003). After September 2003, the guidelines may apply to weighted average (based on portions served).

Table 3.2. History of National School Lunch Program Federal Laws and U.S. Department of Agriculture Meal Regulations

1946-1968	2 tsp (9 g) butter or fortified margarine required[1]
1946-1968	½ pint (240 ml) whole, fluid milk required
1946-1975	All meal components required to be served (no OVS)[2]
1946-1994	2 oz of meat, poultry, fish, or meat alternate had to be offered
1968-1975	1 tsp (4.5 g) butter or fortified margarine required
1973-present	½ pint (240 ml) skim milk and lowfat milk allowed
1975-present	Butter or fortified margarine requirement dropped
1976-present	Offer versus serve for high school students[3]; an option for elementary and middle school levels
1980-1994	"Type A Pattern" replaced with School Lunch Meal Patterns No butter or margarine Expansion of bread portions At least one of the following forms of milk made available: unflavored lowfat milk, unflavored skim milk, and unflavored buttermilk
1986-present	Whole milk required to be offered as an option on the School Lunch Meal Pattern Lowfat milk required to be offered[4]
1998-present	Offer a variety of milk based on preferences[5]
1994-1995	Nutrient Standard Menu Planning option required by 1996-97
1995-1996	Nutrient Standard or Enhanced Food-Based Menu Planning options must be used
1997 - present	Nutrient Standard/Assisted Nutrient Standard, Traditional Food-Based, Enhanced Food-Based, or Any Reasonable Means Menu Planning options required to meet Dietary Guidelines (each having nutritional and food requirements, but all limited to no more than 30 percent of the calories from fat and to less than 10 percent from saturated fats)
1998-2003	Postponed implementation of weighted average

[1]Under the USDA commodity program, unlimited quantities of butter were available.

[2]Offer versus serve (OVS) gave students the right to decline foods they did not want.

[3]All four components/five food items of the lunch pattern must be offered, and a minimum of three food items must be served for the meal to be reimbursable.

[4]Skim milk was not listed as meeting the School Lunch Meal Patterns' milk requirement at one time because it did not have enough fat to be considered "lowfat" milk.

[5]National School Lunch Act was amended to read that the reimbursable lunch should include a variety of fluid milk consistent with prior year preferences unless the prior year preference of any such variety of fluid milk is less than one percent of the total milk consumed at the school.

Assessment of Nutrient Standard Menu Planning

A recently released study, "Evaluation of the Nutrient Standard Menu Planning (NSMP) Summary of Findings" (USDA, 1998), reported on 15 school districts that had fully implemented Nutrient Standard and showed the following results:

- No change in participation in the NSLP
- Approximately the same number of daily options provided
- More skim milk, flavored lowfat milk, fresh fruits and vegetables, extra bread and choices, pasta-based entrees, and rich desserts than prior menus included
- Less whole milk, french fries, breaded meat, poultry and fish, burgers, nachos, hotdogs, and snack chips than for prior menus
- Cost comparable or lower than for prior menus (see Chapter 6)

According to most reports, the efforts of Congress and the U. S. Department of Agriculture administration and thousands of school foodservice professionals during the 1990s, meals served have been nutritiously improved.

School foodservice has had more than its share of criticism because of serving meals with more than 30 percent of the calories from fat. The School Nutrition Dietary Assessment Study by the U. S. Department of Agriculture (1994) showed that school meals were "high" in fat (38% of the energy was from fat and 14% from saturated fat). The Bogalusa Heart Study found that typical children consumed 35.6 percent of their calories from fat.

The National Food Service Management Institute (1995) used a modified Delphi process or technique[1] to determine the barriers to achieving the Dietary Guidelines for Americans (DGA), and 95 percent of the participants agreed that the main barriers were:

" • No benchmarks exist for nutritional quality of school meals in relation to the DGAs
- Eating habits of many children are inconsistent with the DGAs
- Limited time is available for foodservice personnel to evaluate products, develop new recipes, and compare products"

There are still school foodservice critics out there in 1999. For example, the Associated Press article by Karen Gullo, entitled "Schools Still Serving 'Fat' Lunches," charged that many school districts had not changed the menus or production methods at all as a result of the emphasis on meeting the DGAs. On the other hand, *Consumer Report* (September 1998) reported in an article entitled "Is Your Kid Failing Lunch?" that schools were making progress.

Regardless of the option chosen, the foods served over a week are required to meet the Dietary Guidelines. Until September 2003, meeting the Dietary Guidelines will be based on the menus as planned, not on what the students selected. School districts using the Traditional Food-Based Menu Planning and Enhanced Food-Based Menu are not required to analyze the menus for the nutritional content, however, the state staff who performs a "School Meal Initiative" review on the school

---

[1]The Delphi technique is a non face-to-face procedure for aggregating group members' opinions.

district will preform analysis on the menus. This review is to be performed at a minimum of every five years.

SPECIAL NUTRITIONAL CONCERNS

Present awareness about food safety and the potential link between diet and disease have made it more important than ever that the menu planner consider the special nutritional concerns of the customer. Although the controversy over restricting fats and sodium during the growing years has not been settled, it is good business for the menu planner to develop menus that provide moderate or controlled amounts of these nutrients—fats and sodium.

Another health concern is obesity. In addition to fighting heart problems, scientists at the National Institutes of Health have declared obesity as a killing disease in America (IFMA 1985).

Because of the health concerns, there have been significant changes in Americans' food habits since 1975; there has been increase in consumption of leaner, lowfat types of foods, such as fish and poultry. People have responded to the information on diet and disease. As early as 1987, the affects could be seen by changes per capita in consumption of certain foods (USDA, 1987). Food consumption changes listed for the period per person between 1975-85 were:

- Lowfat milk increased from 6.4 pounds per year to 77.8 pounds.
- Whole milk decreased from 251.7 pounds per year to 132.9 pounds.
- Yogurt increased from 0.3 pounds per year to 3.2 pounds.
- Butter decreased from 6.9 pounds per year to 3.2 pounds.
- Fresh broccoli increased from 0.4 pounds per year to 1.9 pounds.
- Eggs decreased from 40.3 pounds per year to 33.1 pounds.
- Chicken increased from 30.7 pounds per year to 53.9 pounds.
- Sugar decreased from 97.3 pounds per year to 71 pounds.

The *School Food Purchase Study* (USDA 1998) reported there has been a striking change in the composition of the school food market basket between 1984-85 and 1996-97 as shown below:

Increase	Decrease
Breakfast cereals	Vegetable oils and shortening
Prepared foods	Lard and other animal fats
Yogurt	Mayonnaise and salad dressing
Fruit drinks	Fluid milk
Margarine	Butter

This study showed a dramatic drop in fluid milk and nearly as dramatic an increase in fruit juices, fruit drinks, carbonated beverages, and bottled water.

Fats

The American Academy of Pediatrics is advising doctors for the first time to test for cholesterol among children with family histories of premature heart attacks or high cholesterol levels. Public health officials are considering 140 to 150 milligrams the desirable cholesterol level for children. The American Academy of Pediatrics recommends that children get no more than 40 percent of their total calories from fat. However, if total fat intake drops below 30 percent of needed calories, children may not be consuming enough calories to sustain normal growth.

Calculating fat calories, using 1,800 calories as the total daily intake, is done as follows:

Step 1. Determine calories from fat by calculating 30% of 1,800 (1,800 x .30), which equals 600 calories from fat.

Step 2. Divide 600 calories by 9 to determine how many grams of fat. (Every gram of fat provides 9 calories.)

$$\frac{600}{9} = 66.6 \text{ grams of fat}$$

Step 3. Divide the grams of fat over the day—an average of 10-20 grams for breakfast, 20-35 grams for lunch, and 20-35 grams for dinner.

Step 4. Calculate the caloric content of the food and the fat content, and pay special attention to those fats with high cholesterol content.

Much of the controversy concerning fat centers around the four different types of fat, which are described below. Sources of each of the fats, shown in Tables 3.3 and 3.4, may be useful to the menu planner.

1. *Saturated* fat tends to increase blood cholesterol levels. It comes from animal fats and palm and coconut oils. It is recommended that the menu calories be limited to 10 percent from saturated fats. Most American food processors have removed tropical oils from their products.

2. *Polyunsaturated* fat lowers blood cholesterol. It comes from vegetables such as corn, safflower, sesame seeds, and fish.

3. *Hydrogenated* fat is processed to convert oil to saturated fat.

4. *Monounsaturated* fat lowers blood cholesterol. It comes from olive, peanut, and avocado oils.

The reason for the concern over fat is primarily because of the danger of high cholesterol and low density lipoproteins (which is found only in animal foods) elevates blood cholesterol when consumed in excessive amounts and the body can convert dietary fats into undesirable fats.

Sodium

Sodium is a fundamental nutrient, but because of the attention it has gotten, some think it is bad. Much is being learned about the medical effects of a high-sodium diet, and the school meals should give the student the option of a diet with a moderate amount of sodium or whatever amount is considered safe for the student. As with fat, the RDAs do not specify exact quantities for sodium. It is known that some groups of people suffer from sodium deficiencies, while others are oversensitive to excess quantities. Salt is sodium, and foods that are high in sodium include cured and smoked foods; cold cuts; hot dogs; sausages; canned vegetables and vegetable juices; canned and dehydrated soups and broths; canned meat and fish; pickled foods; and salted crackers, snacks, and nuts.

Table 3.3. Percentages of Polyunsaturated and Saturated Fats in Foods

Type of Oil or Fat	% Polyunsaturated Fat	% Saturated Fat
Safflower oil	74	9
Sunflower oil	64	10
Corn oil	58	13
Mayonnaise-type salad dressing	53	14
Italian dressing	58	14
Thousand Island dressing	55	16
Blue cheese dressing	54	19
Soybean oil	40	13
Margarine		
Soft (tub)	42	16
Hard (stick)	32	18
Peanut oil	30	19
Vegetable shortening	20	32
Lard	12	40
Olive oil	9	14
Beef fat	4	48
Butter	4	61
Palm oil	2	81
Coconut oil	2	86

Source: Facts About Blood Cholesterol, U.S. Department of Health and Human Services, Public Health Service, National Institutes of Health Publication No. 85-2696 and *Eating Moderate Fat and Cholesterol*, The American Heart Association 1988.

Table 3.4. Quantities of Cholesterol Found in Foods

FOOD	CHOLESTEROL (mg)
Fruits, grains, vegetables	0
Oysters (cooked, about 3 ½ ounces)	45
Scallops (cooked, about 3 ½ ounces)	53
Clams (cooked, about 3 ½ ounces)	65
Fish, lean (cooked, about 3 ½ ounces)	65
Chicken and turkey, light meat (skinned and cooked, about 3 ½ ounces)	80
Lobster (cooked, about 3 ½ ounces)	85
Beef, lean (cooked, about 3 ½ ounces)	90
Chicken and turkey, dark meat (skinned and cooked, about 3 ½ ounces)	95
Crab (cooked, about 3 ½ ounces)	100
Shrimp (cooked, about 3 ½ ounces)	150
Egg yolk, one	270
Beef liver (cooked, about 3 ½ ounces)	440
Beef kidney (cooked, about 3 ½ ounces)	700

Source: Facts About Blood Cholesterol, U.S. Department of Health and Human Services, Public Health Services, National Institutes of Health Publication No. 85-2696.

Dealing with Current "Nutritional Concerns"

Foodservice managers and directors should address current nutritional concerns and be as responsive as possible within the regulations of the Child Nutrition programs. During the 1990s it was important that school foodservices create in the minds of customers and parents a reputation for serving good, high-quality, safe, nutritious food. Some of the ways that this positive image can be maintained are through expert menu planning, efficient and proper preparation practices, and effective advertising of what has been done. Some very basic practices should be changed:

- Discontinue the use of fatback pork meat and lard in the preparation of breads and pie crusts and in seasoning vegetables. Avoid purchasing prepared foods such as pie crusts and bakery products that have lard and tropical oils as ingredients.
- Cut down on hidden calories supplied by large quantities of butter and sugar and other sweeteners.
- Discontinue the use of high-sodium soups and mixes (such as salad dressings and

gravies); pressure the food industry to provide products with acceptable levels of sodium by organizing school foodservice as an industry.

- Avoid salt-cured foods.
- Use more fresh fruits and vegetables; when using canned fruits, specify those packed in natural juices or light syrup.
- Request nutritional analyses from a reputable laboratory on processed foods such as food mixes (e.g., taco seasoning), pizza, burritos, and cookies. Know what is in the food served.
- Offer lower-fat milk as a choice.

Allergies

Either food allergies are being diagnosed earlier, or there is actually an increase in the number of school-age children with food allergies today in comparison to the 1970s. The most common allergy that school-age children have is to milk. Other common allergies to natural foods are those to soy, wheat, and peanuts.

In order for a breakfast or a lunch, under the National School Lunch Program, to qualify for federal reimbursement, the meal must meet the meal requirements, or the foodservice manager must have a statement on file from a medical authority stating the child's allergy. A stated "acceptable replacement" in the medical statement is also helpful. The reason is, when the school foodservice is audited or reviewed by federal or state personnel, the foodservice manager will need to support substitutions being made with the medical statements for each child.

In addition to allergies to natural food products, many people are allergic to the chemicals in the preservatives, additives, artificial colorings, and artificial flavorings put into food. (Also, a number of pesticides cause reactions.) Monosodium glutamate (MSG) is a chemical that people are commonly allergic to. MSG is used to accentuate flavor, and it may cause dizziness, headache, facial pressure, and a burning sensation on the back and the neck.

A menu planner cannot find any food to which some person is not allergic, except perhaps for refined sugar. Thus, a school foodservice manager may be asked by parents for a list of menu items that contain certain ingredients. Ingredient lists on all food products may be required by the foodservice director from manufacturers and processors in bid specifications. This information may be needed to assist the allergic child in identifying foods he or she cannot eat.

NUTRIENT ANALYSIS PROGRAMS

The National Food Service Management Institute in 1997 evaluated four of the first nutrient analysis programs (softwares) approved by USDA for use by the Child Nutrition programs, and they were:

Computer Assisted Food Service (CAFS)
Horizon Software (LUNCHBOX)
Lunch Byte Systems (NUTRIKIDS)
School Nutrition Accountability Program (SNAP)

The objectives of the U. S. Department of Agriculture regulations are for the school foodservice programs to start with the same database when analyzing menus. The USDA has developed and made available free to the software developing companies a database referred to as the "National Nutrient Database." Five areas were reviewed by the National Food Service Management Institute when evaluating the software programs. The review found that NUTRIKIDS appeared to require the least amount of time in five of the five areas presented. The National Food Service Management Institute study stated, "It is important to note that every nutrition analysis software program reviewed is issuing new updates. NUTRIKIDS may or may not have the same findings in the future." The same menus were analyzed on all four software programs, and it was concluded that even though the same database was used, the programs were not all the same.

There are now at least 16 nutrients analyzed by the software programs approved by the USDA, and each should be considered carefully before committing to a program. It makes sense to purchase one program that will do more than analyze recipes and menus. Entering the recipes, menus, and new food data is too time-consuming to do twice in different programs. Some of the approved nutrient analysis programs interface with other packages and have many features, such as: precosting, inventory, postcosting, and providing a finished production record. See Chapter 14, "Computerization and Automation," for a detailed comparison of six of the nutrient analysis software.

The "National Nutrient Database" includes the nutrients for all commodities, a wide range of processed foods, many standard reference food items, and all USDA-developed recipes.

FOOD PRODUCTION RECORDS

A food production record must be kept daily on food prepared and served by a school. This is a federal requirement and is a good business practice because it makes an excellent audit trail for determining how foods purchased have been used. It serves as a document stating enough food was prepared to serve "x" of servings of each food item and it serves as a record of where the food received was used. The information to be kept for Traditional Food-Based and Enhanced Food-Based Menu Planning and Nutrient Standard and Assisted-Nutrient Standard Menu Planning are basically the same. The information required are as follows:

    School name
    Meal date
    Type menu—breakfast, lunch, snack
    Food components
    Condiments
    Recipe number or identifier or food product used
    Planned/projected number of portions and serving sizes
    Total amount of food prepared
    Actual number of reimbursable meals served
    Actual number of nonreimbursable meals or portions served
    Leftovers and substitutions

Two different production records are provided in *A Menu Planner for Healthy School Meals (1998).*

USDA CHILD NUTRITION (CN) LABELING PROGRAM

The Child Nutrition (CN) Labeling Program is a voluntary federal labeling program, which is discussed in Chapter 9, "Procurement and Controlling Inventory." It requires an evaluation of a product's formulation by USDA Food and Nutrition Service to determine what the product contributes toward the Food-Based Menu Planning requirements. It allows the manufacturer to use the CN logo and to state the contribution. The only products that are eligible for CN labels are main dish products, juice and juice drink products. The CN label can still be used by Traditional Food-Based Menu Planning and Enhanced Food-Based Menu Planning, but it does not apply to Nutrient Standard Menu Planning or Assisted Nutrient Standard.

SELECTED REFERENCES

Carr, D. 1997. *An Evaluation of USDA-Approved Nutrient Analysis Programs.* University, MS: National Food Service Management Institute.

Federal Register. June 1995, 60 (113).

Gullo, Karen. 1999. "Schools Still Serving 'Fat' Lunches." *Associated Press.*

"Is Your Kid Failing Lunch?" 1998. *Consumer Report.* September 1998.

National Research Council. 1989. *Recommended Dietary Allowances.* 10th ed. Washington, DC: National Academy Press.

Pannell, D. 1995. "Why School Meals Are High in Fat and Some Suggested Solutions." *American Journal of Clinical Nutrition.* American Society for Clinical Nutrition.

Pannell-Martin, D. 1996. *Assisted NuMenu Manual with Database on Disk.* Alexandria, VA: inTEAM Associates, Inc.

U. S. Department of Agriculture.1983. *Nutrient Standard Menu Planning Computer Coding Programs.* PA 1331. Washington, DC: U. S. Government Printing Office.

____. 1984 (with 1990 revisions). *Food Buying Guide for Child Nutrition Programs.* PA 1331. Washington, DC: U. S. Government Printing Office.

____. 1987. *School Lunch Patterns.* Washington, DC: Food and Nutrition Services, U. S. Department of Agriculture.

____.1994. *The School Nutrition Dietary Assessment Study.* Washington, DC: U. S. Government Printing Office.

____. 1998. *Assisted NuMenus—A Resource Guide.* Washington, DC: U. S. Government Printing Office.

____. 1998. *Evaluation of the Nutrient Standard Menu Planning Summary of Findings.* ABT Associates for U. S. Department of Agriculture. Washington, DC: U. S. Government Printing Office.

____. 1998. *A Menu Planner for Healthy School Meals,* FNS-303. Washington, DC: U. S. Government Printing Office.

____. 1998. *School Food Purchase Study.* Washington, DC: U. S. Government Printing Office.

____. 1998. *A Tool Kit for Healthy School Meals: Recipes and Training Materials.* Washington, DC: U. S. Government Printing Office.

U. S. Department of Health and Human Service and U. S. Department of Agriculture.*1995. Nutrition and Your Health: Dietary Guidelines for Americans.* 4th ed. Washington, DC: U. S. Government Printing Office.

4
PLANNING MENUS
AND FOOD OFFERINGS

Menu Planning

Factors to Be Considered
Nutritional Requirements and Federal Regulations
Customer Preferences
Amount of Money Available
Facilities and Equipment
Staff: Labor Hours and Skill Levels
Purchased Food Supplies and USDA-Donated Foods
Aesthetics
Style of Service

Types of Menus
Standard No-Choice Menu
Choice Menu for Elementary/Middle Schools
Choice Menu
Multiple Menus
Salad Bars
Cycle Menus
Student and Parent Involvement
Tips for Menu Planning
Frequency Charts

Breakfast Menus

A la Carte Offerings

Snack Programs and Other Programs

Selected References

MENU PLANNING

The menu is the single most important factor in the success of a foodservice operation. It is the driver of all aspects of the foodservice operation, and is a particularly critical consideration in a school foodservice operation participating in the Child Nutrition programs. Many planners do not realize the importance of the menu, or more emphasis would be placed on the planning of the menu. Consider some of the successful chain restaurants, such as the Olive Garden, the Outback Steakhouse, McDonald's, and Wendy's, and the important role the menu has had in their success.

Successful menu planning takes time, concentration, reference materials, and knowledge. Menus should be planned far enough ahead so that orders can be placed and received before needed. It is poor management to plan the menus by the day depending on what is on hand. A few decentralized school districts, where individual managers make all the decisions and do all the jobs, may still function on a day-to-day basis. This is not the norm, however. Menus need to be planned a month in advance so that ordering can be cost-effective and efficiently done.

In the 1970s school menus in different regions of the country were all different, but by the 1990s the school menus had become fairly universal. Five of the most popular entrees in Maine will also be five of the most popular entrees in Colorado. McDonald's and Pizza Hut have made the food choices of the student-age customer so universal that, except for a few regional foods, one could plan a menu model that would be universally popular. The menus of other school foodservices can be useful as guides and can provide ideas for planners.

A well-planned menu will go a long way toward making a foodservice program successful because of its impact on all aspects of the operation. The well-planned menu will:

- Help control food costs
- Emphasize what the customer wants and will eat
- Determine participation in the programs and sales (revenue)
- Meet the nutritional goals of the foodservice program
- Determine how much labor is needed
- Determine the employee skills needed
- Utilize staff and equipment efficiently
- Determine what needs to be purchased (specifications and orders)
- Lead to more accurate forecasting of menu items
- Make carrying out offer versus serve easy

An electronic feedback survey taken at the American School Food Service Association's Industry Seminar in 1999 showed that over 40 percent of the attendees believed that the menu is the most important factor that influences children eating in the school cafeteria. (The second was food quality.)

An essential to planning menus for the Child Nutrition programs is the USDA publication, *A Menu Planner for Healthy School Meals (1998)*, which interprets the federal regulations for the menus. There are a number of excellent publications by the National Food Service Management

Institute that can assist with planning and producing healthy school meals, such as *A Tool Kit for Healthy School Meals: Recipes and Training Materials (1998)*. This publication contains recipes, as does *Quantity Recipes for Child Nutrition Programs* (USDA, 1988).

FACTORS TO BE CONSIDERED

As stated earlier, the menu is the single most important factor in any foodservice operation. In school foodservice this is especially true for the lunch menu. Breakfast and lunch menus should be planned before food is purchased, the labor needs are determined, and the price of the meal to the customer is decided. Planning menus requires a great deal of knowledge about the operation. It would be ideal if the kitchen layout were planned around the menus and the equipment purchased for the menus to be prepared; however, this is seldom the case.

When planning menus, the following factors should be considered: nutritional requirements and federal regulations; customer preferences; whether choices will be offered; the amount of money available; facilities and equipment; staff-labor hours and skill level; the type of service; the purchased food supplies and USDA donated commodities; aesthetics; and style of service. These topics are discussed in this chapter, primarily as they relate to breakfast and lunch menu planning.

Nutritional Requirements and Federal Regulations

Federal regulations and nutritional requirements have been emphasized during the 1990s resulting in the "School Meal Initiative," which has had an impact on most school districts and the menus they plan. To meet the caloric requirements of students of different ages and reduce fat are challenging if the goal is also to plan popular menus that students will eat. Many menu planners find the need to increase calories by putting desserts back on the menu. During the 1980s, with the emphasis on meeting the Dietary Guidelines for Americans, many directors reduced sodium, fat, and sugar in the menus by using fruits packed in light syrup or natural juices and removing desserts from the menu.

Menu planning is challenging because there is probably no perfect menu. Meeting the Recommended Dietary Allowances (RDAs) is the same regardless of the menu planning method selected, and the least amount of change is realized by using Traditional Food-Based Menu Planning, which is what 85 percent of the schools are using. According to the critics, little has changed in the amount of fat in the students' diets after all the talk and money spent by the USDA to promote lowering fat and "NuMenus" (another name for menus planned using Nutrient Standards).

The first step to carrying out federal regulations is for a school district to determine what method of meeting the Dietary Guidelines/School Meal Initiative will be used. Some state agencies have influenced the decisions within their states, e.g., Mississippi with preplanned statewide menus, called "Ms Cycles."

The main choices are Traditional Food-Based Menu Planning, Enhanced Food-Based Menu Planning, and Nutrient Standard/Assisted Nutrient Standard Menu Planning. Regardless of the method, the nutrients are averaged over a week based on what is planned. The "weighted average"—based on what students take—was originally to be enforced, but has been deferred by Congress until September 2003. Many people are hoping that weighted averaging will never be required because students often do not select the fruits and vegetables needed to meet the vitamin A and C requirements. Iron may also be deficient in some menus selected by students when the analyses is based on weighted averages.

Meeting the nutritional requirements through menus that students will eat is not easy, and teaching the concept to all the people who need to learn it is even harder. The Texas Education Agency which administers the Child Nutrition programs in Texas, has developed a set of color-coded menu cards to help foodservice directors meet the federal nutritional goals for fat, as follows:

Blue ------------------------ Up to 25% of calories from fat   (Excellent)
Green------------------------ 15-30% of calories from fat   (Okay)
Yellow---------------------- 30-32% of calories from fat   (Apply caution)
Red-------------------------- 32-34% of calories from fat   (Time to apply brakes)
Purple---------------------- 34-36% of calories from fat   (Vein cloggers)

Foods from each group may be selected and it is recommended that one blue, three greens, one red over a week and usually the menus are within 30% of calories from fat. These cards show how to combine high fat with lowfat and meet nutritional goals.

Categories of Foods of Minimal Nutritional Value—There are four food categories that may not be sold by the school foodservices participating in the Child Nutrition programs. They are:

1. Soda Water
2. Water Ices
3. Chewing Gum
4. Certain Candies—hard candy, jellies and gums, marshmallow candies, fondant, licorice, spun candy and candy coated popcorn

When planning menus, the USDA publication, *A Menu Planner for Healthy School Meals* (1998), can be referred to for detailed instructions. Also, *Assisted NuMenu Manual* (Pannell 1996) will be helpful.

Customer Preferences

The food habits and beliefs of different religious groups, the cultural differences of the students, and the fads of the time need to be considered by menu planners. Minorities are projected to make up over 50 percent of the students participating in the school lunch programs in most major cities by 2005. For instance, the Hispanic population has grown considerably and the influence of Mexican food on the menus across the country can be seen. By 2005, the Hispanic population is expected to make up 25 percent of the students in the Western region of the United States (McKinsey & Co. 1996). In some parts of the country the Asian and Muslim population has influenced the menu offerings. If there is a large Jewish population in the community, it will be important to consider whether the products purchased were prepared under Kosher standards. Though a public school caters to all, it is a good menu-planning practice (and good business) to consider the population it hopes to serve.

Student preferences play an important part in satisfaction with a school's foodservice. Food preferences can be defined as the foods selected when options are made available. Factors that influence preferences include (1) intrinsic characteristics—color, texture, flavor, quality, and method of preparation; (2) extrinsic characteristics—environment, expectations (for example, a banquet is expected to be very good); (3) biological, physiological, and psychological considerations—age, sex, appreciation, perception, and appetite; (4) personal likes and dislikes—familiarity, expectation, importance of food, influence of peers, mood, and emotions; (5) socioeconomic status of family—acceptance, prestige, and conformity; and (6) cultural and religious beliefs—including religious restrictions (for example, Muslims and Jews restrict consumption of pork and pork products). Khan (1987) provides an excellent discussion of each of these factors.

According to the *FoodService Director* (March 1999), pizza was America's number one favorite food. A survey of 400 school foodservice directors of what students' favorite foods were did not uncover many surprises (see Table 4.1). Pizza was by far the most popular entree (66.2%), corn the most popular vegetable (40.6%)—beating out French fries (27.7%), cookies the most popular dessert (47.8%) , and apples/applesauce (22.6%) the most popular fruits, with peaches a close second (19.3%). Unfortunately this is not a survey of the students that these directors represent. There may be a difference.

Table 4.1. Results of a Survey of the Most Popular Lunch Menu Items

Favorite Lunch Foods Among Students							
Entrees		**Vegetables**		**Desserts**		**Fruits**	
Pizza	66.2%	Corn	40.6%	Cookies	47.8%	Apple/Applesauce	22.6%
Chicken Nuggets	20.2%	French Fries	27.7%	Cake	15.9%	Peaches	19.3%
Mexican Food	6.4%	Potatoes	7.7%	Ice Cream	10.3%	Pineapple	15.2%
Hamburgers	2.6%	Broccoli	5.6%	Crisp/Cobbler	8.0%	Oranges	11.2%
All Others	4.7%	Green Beans	5.2%	Brownies	6.4%	Bananas	8.5%
		Mashed Potatoes	5.2%	Pie	1.6%	Grapes	7.8%
		Green Salad	3.9%	All Others	10.0%	Strawberries	5.4%
		Carrots	2.6%			Watermelon/Melon	2.7%
		All Others	1.1%			Kiwi	2.2%
						Mixed Fruit	2.0%
						All Others	3.1%

Source: American School Food Service Association 1999. Used with permission.

When planning menus—regardless of the menu planning system to be used—the planner needs two guides: *Food Buying Guide for Child Nutrition Programs* (U.S. Department of Agriculture, 1984, revision, 1990), which provides the yields of food by purchased units; and *A Menu Planner for Healthy School Meals* (U.S. Department of Agriculture, 1998). Also a *Menu Planner* provides good instructions for carrying out the Nutrient Standard and for good menu planning tips for healthy school meals.

As discussed above, there are many points to consider when planning menus—and customer preference is an important one. However, the goals are to ensure that the nutritional needs of the children are met within the guidelines set and that students will eat the food offered.

Amount of Money Available

In order to operate a sound foodservice, the amount of money available to be spent on food must be determined accurately, not left to guesswork. Recipes and menus need careful precosting and postcosting, as discussed in Chapter 2.

In calculating food costs, it must be determined what percentage of income is to be spent on labor and other expenses and what percentage can be spent on food in order to break even. For example, if the goal is to keep food costs at 40 percent of revenue available (or less) and if the price charged students for lunch is $1.50, the revenue available in 1999 would be approximately $1.8275 (including federal subsidies only, not including any state subsidies). Thus, the amount of money available for food would be slightly over 73 cents ($1.8275 X 40%). It should be determined how the 73 cents could be divided among the food items. If milk cost 15 cents per half pint, this would leave 58 cents to cover all the other foods in the menu. If the cost of one menu were greater than the amount of money available, the next day's menu would cost less, so that it averaged out. Like nutrients, costs should be averaged over a week.

Protein-rich foods are expensive and may consume one-third or more of the food dollar. For economy reasons, a combination of meat, poultry, or fish and one of the less expensive meat alternates such as eggs, dry beans or peas, or peanut butter may be used in meeting the nutritional needs. The use of soy protein to meet a part of the protein requirement is a practical solution to rising food costs, lowering fat and saturated fat. Soy protein can be used to meet up to 30 percent of the meat and meat alternate component. The economy of using soy is discussed in Chapter 10. The increased popularity of Mexican foods has the advantage of being a lower-cost sources of meat/meat alternates.

Shaping Health as Partners in Education (SHAPE), a network of California school districts and child care agencies, reported an increase in food costs using the Traditional Food-Based Menu Planning and the Enhanced Food-Based Menu Planning over using Nutrient Standard of 1 to 8.5 percent. Many school districts in California had a head start at using the Nutrient Standard Menu Planning option, and many are using that method of menu planning with ease today. The San Diego (CA) Unified Schools' foodservice program has used the Nutrient Standard to plan since 1978 (under a pilot program); however, the new guidelines and the emphasis on fat and saturated fat and what makes a reimbursable lunch has resulted in higher costs. San Diego has continued to use Nutrient Standard Menu Planning option for lunch, but is using the Traditional Food-Based Menu Planning to plan breakfast menus because it costs less.

A recent USDA study, "Evaluation of the Nutrient Standard Menu Planning," by ABT Associates, Inc., verified that the average cost of lunch was less in the demonstration schools using the Nutrient Standard Menu Planning method. (See Figure 4.1.)

Since 1996 milk is taking a larger portion of the food dollar as the Milk Price Support Program, which began in 1981 and extended through the 1996 Farm Bill, has had its effects. Also, the popularity of flavored milks and new packaging has added to the cost of milk. The price of ½ pint of milk has gone from 11-12 cents to as high as 22 and 23 cents in some parts of the country.

Figure 4.1. Comparison of Food-Based Menu Planning with Nutrient Standard Menu Planning—Lunch Costs

Costs	Elementary School	Middle School	High School
Before NSMP[1]	$ 1.36	$ 1.44	$ 1.56
After NSMP[1]	$ 1.23	$ 1.46	$ 1.49

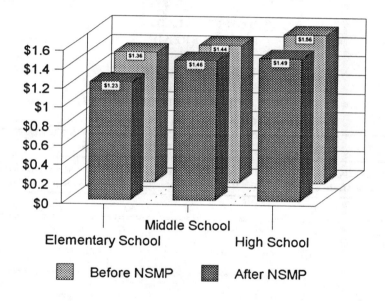

Figure 4.2 shows a comparison of a menu planned to meet the minimum requirements, and implementing offer versus serve; it is conceivable that a student would take what is listed under each option. The only thing that would prohibit the planning of the Nutrient Standard Menu Planning option would be the customers' demands for certain foods and the average nutrients over a week must meet the calorie levels for the different age students. The calorie levels are higher than many of the popular menus provide.

---

[1]Nutrition Standard Menu Planning.

Figure 4.2. Comparison of the Lunch Menu Planning Methods That a Student Could Select and Meet Minimum Meal Requirements

LUNCH MENU WITH CHOICES—OFFER VERSUS SERVE—PLANNED
SPAGHETTI WITH MEAT SAUCE or **TACO WITH BEEF** **LETTUCE—ONION—TOMATO** **TOSSED SALAD** **FRENCH BREAD** **APPLESAUCE** **ORANGE SHERBET** or **CHEF SALAD** **CHOICE OF MILK WITH A LUNCH**

MINIMUM TO MEET REQUIREMENTS

TRADITIONAL—Possible Reimbursable Meals		ENHANCED—Possible Reimbursable Meals		NUMENUS—Possible Reimbursable Meals	
#1	Cost	#2	Cost	#3	Cost
Spaghetti/Meat Sauce (2 oz Meat/Meat Alternate 1 serving of Grain)	$.3173	Spaghetti/Meat Sauce (2 oz Meat/Meat Alternate 1 serving of Grain)	$.3173	Spaghetti/Meat Sauce (1.5 oz Meat/Meat Alternate)	$.2626
Applesauce - ½ cup	.1220	Applesauce- ½ cup	.1220	Sherbet, Orange - 1 cup	.1562
Total Cost	$.4393	Total Cost	$.4393	Total Cost	$.4188
#1	Cost	#2	Cost	#3	Cost
Taco with Beef/Cheese (2 oz Meat/Meat Alternate 1 serving of Grain) Lettuce, Onion, Tomato (1/4 cup Vegetables)	$.2805	Taco with Beef/Cheese (2 oz Meat/Meat Alternate 1 serving of Grain) Lettuce, Onion, Tomato (1/4 cup Vegetables)	$.2805	Taco with Beef (1.5 oz Meat/Cheese)	.1975
				Salsa - 1 portion	.04
Total Cost	$.2805	Total Cost	$.2805	Total Cost	$.2375

Facilities and Equipment

Unfortunately, the facility and the equipment often are menu controlling factors. It would be ideal if the equipment could be selected to fit the menus planned; however, this is seldom the order of events. In many instances, menus will be determined by the equipment. If oven space is limited, a menu that includes baked potatoes, oven-fried chicken, and yeast rolls may be physically impossible. Also to be considered is whether the serving line will accommodate the food.

The question becomes, "How many choices can you offer and be able to keep hot food hot and cold food cold during service?" Maintaining food under safe conditions is essential in quantity food production and service. There are many ways of solving the facility and equipment deficiencies without major outlays of money.

Staff: Labor Hours and Skill Levels

The skills and training of the staff may limit the menus. In areas with heavy staff turnover and employees with low educational levels, menus will need to be simpler. Even with skilled staff, it may not be cost-effective for complex items such as stuffed eclairs to be on the menu, and it may be necessary to plan menus using some convenience foods.

A balance from day to day in the amount of preparation required is desirable, so that the workload is not impossible one day and very light the next. The person planning the menus needs to be very familiar with how to schedule, the labor hours available, and the amount of preparation that can be accomplished.

Purchased Food Supplies and USDA-Donated Foods

The frequency of purchased food deliveries and what the USDA-donated foods are have to be considered when planning menus. The availability of food will limit menus only slightly in this country today, but the delivery schedules, and the type and quantity of storage space available will influence the types of food that can be put on a menu. The season of the year will influence the prices of some foods. Produce prices will vary greatly over the year and in relationship to the season; for instance, fresh strawberries may be affordable at the peak of their season but not at other times.

Schools participating in the National School Lunch Program and receiving USDA-donated food will find that the menus are greatly influenced by USDA-donated foods, and sometimes this is not to the benefit of the School Lunch program. In order to obtain the full value from USDA-donated foods and keep the price of the lunch to the students as low as possible, it is necessary to utilize the donated foods well. This may be the greatest challenge of menu planning. For the most part, USDA-donated foods are of good quality, but may not be desirable to students and may be in a form the menu planner can not use because of labor shortages. In addition, predicting when the donated commodities will arrive is risky, particularly for a large school district.

The processing of USDA-donated foods into other, more usable products can increase the variety and acceptability (see discussion in Chapter 7). In this regard, the USDA has responded to some of the needs of the schools; for example, frozen whole turkeys are seldom if ever distributed to schools, but instead turkey roast is provided—but even the turkey roast has limited use in planning favored lunches. Processing by a commercial manufacturer can convert the turkey into turkey ham, nuggets, hot dogs, turkey pot pies, and varieties of cold cuts.

Aesthetics

Aesthetics—color, flavor, aroma, shape, and texture of food are important to the customer. "People eat with their eyes" is a true saying. A meal can be nutritionally adequate and also contain favorite foods, but if it is not attractively served and visually appealing, it may not be eaten. When planning menu "eye appeal," the planner should use some basic principles employed by artists in obtaining good design.

Color is a particularly powerful marketing tool to a child. Warm colors are usually preferred in foods. The flavor of food is also important—it is enhanced by fat and sodium to the extent that if too much of a change (reduction) is made, the food will be considered not good. McDonald's and Taco Bell learned this when they tried to introduce menu items with drastically reduced fat content. Aroma and smell are strong marketing tools, too. However, what is pleasant to one may not be to another, so this must be considered. If a food smells foul, the brain tells the person to move away from it. However, children don't respond as strongly to smell as adults do.

To put all the factors influencing a menu together and plan a menu that satisfies all is not an easy job. The number of choices to be offered is a decision to make early in menu planning. Recognizing that all students and staffs do not like the same foods, it is important to offer choices, but not more than students and staff can handle are considerations to be dealt with.

Style of Service

The facilities may have a lot to do with the style of service selected; however, some school districts have converted the typical two-serving line cafeterias into "scramble" systems, or food courts, with great imagination. The Brownsville (TX) Unified School District and the Colquitt County (GA) School District have achieved this.

Cafeteria-Style—Cafeteria-style service is by far the most common used in schools, and at one time it may have been the only type used. (Cafeteria-style service has become outdated in the commercial world, in colleges and universities, and even in hospitals.) With this style of service, generally the employees serve the food onto plates or trays as the students move in front of the serving area. For many years in most school districts there was the menu for the day. Before "offer versus serve" became a law in 1978, all menu items for the day were served onto the plate, even if the student was protesting, "I don't want any of that."

Today there are a number of innovative ways of carrying out the cafeteria-style service. "Scramble" cafeteria-style service is a variation of the typical cafeteria-style service where several separate stations are serving different food items. Students go from one station to another making their selections, then exit by the cashier. This style has varying degrees of success. In fact, it can appear to an observer to be a disorganized approach.

Self-Service Bars—With "self-service," sometimes called "buffet-style" service, food can be offered buffet-style from a cafeteria line with the students serving themselves. Self service was new in the first half of the 1980s, but it has gained popularity, particularly in schools (elementary through secondary) in southeastern states such as North Carolina and Tennessee. Elementary school children handle this style beautifully in schools where administration and teachers are involved in the foodservice program.

Self service will continue to be a popular trend, in part because of the present labor shortage. Another advantage is that when students serve themselves, they are a part of the decision-making process and they do not blame the foodservice workers for the selections they make. The style also allows preportioning of foods.

"Self-service bars" became popular in the early 1980s as a result of the customer's desire to make selections, and their use was to the foodservice industry's advantage because of high labor costs and the beginning of a labor shortage. Self-service bars caught on and have flourished in school foodservices with students of all age levels. The types of bars offered and the percentage of school districts providing bars (American School Foodservice Association 1987) are:

Type of Bar	Percent
Salad	75.3
Snack	46.6
Dessert	45.8
Sandwich	40.0
Breakfast	31.4
Baked Potato	30.8
Taco/Ethnic	30.4

Bars may be planned to meet the meal requirements if offer versus serve is carried out. For instance, in order for a salad bar to qualify for meal reimbursement, all the components of a lunch must be offered and the student must take at least three of the food items. A concern may be the sanitation with children serving themselves and theft that may occur.

Several types of specialty salad bars have been successfully used by school foodservices: (1) the taco salad bar (discussed later in this chapter); (2) the potato bar, serving a large baked potato with various toppings; (3) the sandwich bar, or deli bar, with a choice of meats and cheese served by the ounce or number of slices; (4) the pasta bar, with different toppings; and (5) the dessert bar, serving ice cream or cake with toppings.

There are many attractive pieces of equipment for salad bars; however, some schools have simply turned a regular serving line into a salad bar with success. It is important that there be a "sneeze guard" for sanitation purposes. In addition, the cold food should be kept cold and the hot food kept hot.

Self-service bars should be carefully costed out to determine if it is better to offer the bars a la carte or as a meal. This is discussed later in this chapter.

Fast Foods or Food Courts—The term "fast foods" denotes a type of service that one might find in a food court; however, it has also become synonymous with hamburgers and other types of sandwiches, pizza, and French fries. This type of food is very popular with students today, and the food court arrangement has developed out of it as the customers ask for more say in what they will eat. Food courts are discussed in Chapter 16, "Marketing and Promoting School Foodservice," in more detail.

Len Frederick, who was director of foodservices for the Las Vegas, Nevada, School District in the 1970s, was one of the first to deviate from the traditional school menu. He developed the fast-food concept to fit the school lunch program and meal pattern requirements. Frederick (1977) commented, "It continues to puzzle me that a school foodservice director persists in thinking that a school lunch operation can't be 'super efficient, a real money saver,' and still 'feed youngsters something that's good and that's good to them'." He referred to his lunch as "Type A Combo." It was basically a choice of sandwiches, French fries, sandwich fixings (lettuce, tomatoes, and so on), and a choice of milk, including an enriched or vitamin-fortified milkshake. It provided one-third of a students' Recommended Dietary Allowances, according to Frederick.

Since 1977 fast-food menus have become a nationwide trend because of the popularity of the foods. It appears that the philosophy of school foodservice director/manager and principal has the most influence over whether a school will offer a fast-food menu.

TYPES OF MENUS

For many years the school menu offered no choices but in recent years that is an exception as foodservice professionals have realized students are customers and not all students like the same foods. Today there are only a few schools offering no choice menus but choices within the menu and multiple menus are common.

Standard No-Choice Menu

A standard no-choice menu is one menu that meets the school lunch or breakfast menu planning guidelines. This was the most common menu until the 1980s, when menus with choices became popular in many school districts. When using this menu, it is important to serve foods *most* students will like and eat—although it is impossible to plan one menu that all students like. Older students particularly object to having someone else decide what they will eat; therefore, a standard no-choice menu is more acceptable in elementary schools than in secondary.

The menu variety has to be somewhat limited when this type of menu is served —to foods most students like. Offering unpopular items results in fewer students eating a school lunch, and if "offer versus serve" is not an option for elementary- and intermediate-age students, there can be heavy food waste. The most common problem with no-choice menus is that students eat an unbalanced meal. For example, in the South, when the vegetable is turnip greens, most students will not take them if offer versus serve is in practice or they become plate waste. Items that are not popular with most students need to be offered as a choice.

The advantages of using a standard no-choice menu are (1) greater productivity and lower labor costs (though not always the results), (2) faster moving lines, (3) less equipment needed, and (4) ease in determining quantities of food needed.

Menu Choices for Elementary/ Middle Schools

Elementary school menus should be more limited in choices than high school menus, but choices should be provided. Middle school children can usually handle more choices than elementary school children. Three choices can be handled without major problems by most staffs, and the children can learn the concept quickly. The suggested choice menu has one hot lunch, one cold , and a salad lunch (premade or at self-service salad bar), or a choice of two hot lunches, a cold lunch, and a salad lunch.

Figure 4.3 shows a scheme used when planning the menu either no choice or choice—this will not work for everyone, but another like it might make menu planning easier for the planner.

Figure 4.3. Example of a Menu Scheme for Planning Menus

Monday	Tuesday	Wednesday	Thursday	Friday
Choice of Two: Sandwich-type food[a]	Mexican-type food[b]	Chicken or Turkey[c]	Italian-type food[d]	Pizza or fish[e]
Student Selects Two: Selection of four to six items each day that include fresh fruit, chilled canned fruit, vegetable salad or vegetable soup, cooked vegetables or potatoes				
Bread and bread alternates				
Milk, lowfat, whole, and chocolate				

[a]Burgers, hot dogs, steak subs, grilled cheese, peanut butter and jelly, ham and cheese
[b]Tacos, burritos, nachos, etc
[c]Chicken nuggets or fingers, fried chicken, barbecued chicken, sliced turkey, turkey/chicken pot pies
[d]Spaghetti, lasagna, ravioli, macaroni and cheese with fish sticks, etc
[e]French bread pizza; cheese, pepperoni, and sausage pizza; a sandwich option—tuna fish salad sandwich; batter-fried fish, and fishburger

Put the local special or manager special on weekly as a choice—which uses commodities, gives an opportunity for students to plan menus.

Choice Menu

The choice menu takes careful planning and is more difficult to produce than a no-choice menu but it has several advantages:

- The number of lunches served usually increases.
- Plate waste decreases.
- Students complaints are less.
- There is greater opportunity to meet students' nutritional requirements.
- More variety can be offered.

Figure 4.4 gives an example of a choice menu for a day.

Care must be taken in offering choices within the menu planning federal guidelines, since all combinations possible must meet requirements. For example, under the Traditional Food-Based and Enhanced Food-Based Menu Planning methods potato chips cannot be offered as a choice with mashed potatoes, because potato chips are not a creditable vegetable. Communicating with the customer what the offerings are and what they need to take for the menu to be considered a reimbursable breakfast or lunch takes training of employees and understanding of the menu planning federal guidelines. Students are turned off by adults saying "You have to take. . . ." and this should be avoided by making available foods that look good, that are good, and that students want to eat. Many schools' food costs go up when menus are planned with the goals that students will eat the fruits and vegetables as well as the entrees.

Figure 4.4. Choice Elementary or Middle School Menu

Customer Choice:	Nachos/Chili and Cheese Sauce/Dinner Roll
	or
	Hot Dog on Bun
Customer Select Two:	Golden Corn Fiesta
	Chilled Apple Juice
	Fresh Grapes
	Fresh Kiwi
Customer Choice:	Chocolate Milk
	Whole Milk
	Lowfat Milk
or	
Customer Optional Lunch:	Crisp Chef Salad with Ham and Cheese/Hot Dinner Roll
	and Choice of Milk

With choices on the menu the challenges will be:

- Forecasting the number of servings
- Planning production whereby all foods are ready to serve at the same time
- Having a means of displaying food and maintaining proper temperatures
- Communicating with the customer with signage to avoid adults having to help the students through the choices
- Keeping the service fast
- Training employees

In the sample menu shown in Figure 4.4, the apple juice, fresh grapes, fresh kiwi, and dinner rolls can be proportioned for self-service. One server can keep up with the line flow.

Offering choices is particularly desirable when an unpopular item is on the menu. Offering choices also makes it possible to increase the variety. Since cooked vegetables are the least preferred food for most students, choices of fresh and cooked vegetables can lessen plate waste and in turn help meet nutritional goals.

Providing choices usually reduces food complaints. It is common for people to complain about food, but a student who chooses what he or she will eat is less critical. Figure 4.5 provides an example of a two-week elementary lunch menu cycle, which would repeat every two weeks. The choice menus should contain popular menu items whereby the participation will be high all week—not just on the days when pizza or chicken nuggets/fingers are offered. At the same time the goal should be to introduce some new food and offer a variety, but know that putting those items on the menu will not guarantee they will be eaten. Small samples of foods may be offered as "extra" to introduce new foods. Notice that some days in the cycle menu have a "special of the day," which gives some flexibility in centralized school districts for local favorites and seasonal items, e.g., chili in the winter.

Figure 4.5. Two-Week Elementary School Lunch Menu Cycle

MONDAY	TUESDAY	WEDNESDAY	THURSDAY	FRIDAY
Week One: Offer 2—3 Entree Choices —— Customer Selects 1				
Hamburger or Cheeseburger	Spaghetti/Meat Sauce/French Bread/Garlic Butter or Make Your Own Taco with Meat/Beans and Cheese	Chicken Nuggets/ Muffin or Peanut Butter and Jelly Sandwich	Special of Day or Breaded Steakettes with Gravy	Cheese Pizza or Pepperoni Pizza or Peanut Butter and Jelly Sandwich
Choice of two: French Fries Sandwich Fixings Sliced Peaches Fresh Fruit or Melon in Season	**Choice of two:** Tossed Salad/ Dressing Applesauce Fruit Sherbet	**Choice of two:** Mixed Vegetables Pineapple Chunks Fresh Fruit	**Choice of two:** Mashed Potatoes Special Green Vegetable Fruit Gelatin Fresh Fruit	**Choice of two:** Tossed Salad School-Made Soup Fruit Cup Fresh Fruit
Week Two: Offer 2—3 Entree Choices —— Customer Selects 1				
Burrito or Barbecue Rib Sandwich	Chicken Fillet /Spaghetti/ French Bread or Peanut Butter and Jelly Sandwich	Nachos/Chili and Cheese Sauce or Hot Dog on Bun	Special of Day or Fried Chicken	Cheese Pizza or Sausage Pizza or Deli Sandwich
Choice of two: Curly Fries Coleslaw Fresh Fruit or Melon in Season	**Choice of two:** Green Vegetable Fruitsicle	**Choice of two:** Golden Corn Fiesta Apple Juice or Fresh Fruit	**Choice of two:** Special Potato Special Green Vegetable Canned Fruit Fresh Fruit	**Choice of two:** Tossed Salad Tomato Soup Fruit Cup Fresh Fruit
Choice of: Lowfat Milk, Chocolate Milk, or Whole Milk				
Alternate Lunch: Chef Salad, Bread, Milk				
Chef Salad/ Cheese Texas Toast	Chef Salad/ Eggs and Cheese Bread of Day	Chef Salad/ Turkey and Cheese Pretzel	Chef Salad/ Ham and Cheese Dinner Roll	Chef Salad/ Cheese Dinner Roll

Source: Pannell-Martin, et al. 1995.

Multiple Menus

Multiple menus are made up of more than one complete menu that students may select. Multiple menus are usually served at different serving areas/lines. Examples are shown in Figure 4.6 that would be appropriate for an elementary school. High school managers will frequently offer the popular sandwich/pizza (fast-food) type foods at one serving area or line and more traditional foods on another area or line. See Figure 4.7 for a high school one-week menu cycle, which repeats every week.

The goal is that the menus offer many combinations and be balanced nutritionally. Many school foodservices are serving multiple menus with four or ten choices daily and are very successfully. However, it probably isn't necessary to offer ten choices, and may not be cost-effective. It certainly takes a well-organized manager to plan and carry out this many choices cost effectively.

Desserts may or may not be a part of the lunch menu. If cost is a factor, desserts should not be a part of the menu unless they contribute to the menu plan for the day or are served on a special day. Desserts can be sold a la carte (in the states where regulations will allow) to those who want them. Having wrapped, freshly baked cookies at the point of sale (cashier) can increase the revenue for the day and help offset the costs of the lunch menu.

Since inactive teenage girls are often concerned with their weight, and their calorie needs are less than for other more active students, it may be desirable to offer a salad plate that meets meal requirements if a salad is not available.

The menu cycle for high schools shown in Figure 4.7 gives an example of numerous choices for multiple menus or a food court arrangement

Figure 4.6. Example of a Multiple Menu

Choice of One:	*Choice of One:*
Hamburger or Cheeseburger	Spaghetti with Meat Sauce
Battered Breast of Chicken on Bun	Freshly-Made Tuna Salad
	with Garlic French Bread
Choice of Two:	*Choice of Two:*
Crispy French Fries	Tossed Salad with Dressing
Soup Special of the Day	Soup Special of the Day
Sandwich Fixings	Green Beans
Chilled Sliced Peaches	Chilled Sliced Peaches
Choice of One:	*Choice of One:*
Lowfat Milk	Lowfat Milk
Chocolate Milk	Chocolate Milk
Whole Milk	Whole Milk

Figure 4.7. Sample High School Master Lunch Menu Cycle

Day of Week	Global Fare (or Fiesta)	Grille Stop	Pizzeria	Mama's Kitchen	Sub Shoppe
Monday	Beefy Bean Burrito Egg Roll with Fried Rice Taco Basket	Hamburger/ Cheeseburger Hot Dog or Coney Island Hot Dog Chicken Fillet	Pizza by the Slice and/or Pan Pizza Chicken Parmesan with Pasta and French Bread	Crispy Chicken in Basket/ Biscuit or Barbecue Rib on Steak Roll	Ham and Cheese Sub or Chicken Salad Sub
Tuesday	Enchiladas Red Beans and Rice	Hamburger/ Cheeseburger Hot Dog or Coney Island Hot Dog Barbecue Rib on Steak Roll	Pizza by the Slice and/or Pan Pizza Spaghetti with Meat Sauce with Bread Stick	Hot Wings with Roll or Hot Ham and Cheese on Croissant	Italian Sub or Sliced Turkey Sub
Wednesday	Beefy Bean Burrito Frito Pie	Hamburger/ Cheeseburger Hot Dog or Coney Island Hot Dog Chicken Fillet	Pizza by the Slice and/or Pan Pizza Cheese Ravioli with Tomato or Meat Sauce and French Bread	Chicken Nuggets with Roll or Local Special	Roast Beef Sub or Italian Deli Sub
Thursday	Chicken Fajita Nachos with Cheese and Chili	Hamburger/ Cheeseburger Hot Dog or Coney Island Hot Dog or Half Smoke Steak Sub	Pizza by the Slice and/or Pan Pizza Lasagna and Bread Stick	Baked Potato with Broccoli/ Cheese, Chili, and Bacon or Local Special	Ham and Cheese Sub or Local Special
Friday	Crunchy Tacos with Meat and Cheese Jumbo Tostado	Hamburger/ Cheeseburger Hot Dog or Coney Island Hot Dog Fishburger	Pizza by the Slice and/or Pan Pizza Macaroni with Cheese and Ham and Roll	Country Fried Steak with Mashed Potatoes and Gravy Macaroni with Cheese and Ham and Roll	Tuna Salad or Sliced Turkey and Cheese Sub

Combo Lunch: Includes two fruits and/or vegetables and ½ pint of milk

A Deli Lunch to go (bag lunch) and Chef Salad Lunch are available every day.

Source: Pannell-Martin, et al. 1995.

Salad Bars

Salad bars can be presented as a lunch or offered for sale a la carte. If the salad bar (or any other self-service bar) is to meet the menu requirements of the chosen menu planning option, careful planning and supervision may be necessary. The following should be considered when setting up a salad bar:

1. Meat and meat alternates are the most expensive part of the meal, and proportioning may be necessary to control costs.
2. Controlling portions must be considered. This may be done with the size of the bowl or plate to be filled, by number of scoops, or by weight. The bowl or plate capacity is probably the easiest.
3. The required eight to ten servings of bread and bread alternates a week may be slightly difficult to serve on the salad bar. Croutons, pasta products, and crackers add variety and can contribute toward meeting the bread requirement.
4. A cashier should be stationed at the end of the salad bar, where the tray can be checked to ensure that the school lunch meets the minimum requirements. With the Traditional Food-Based Menu Planning, students have to take a minimum of three food items under offer versus serve. With the Nutrient Standard Menu Planning option, only two items have to be taken.

Figure 4.8. Self-Service Taco Salad Bar—Suggested Salad Bar Setup

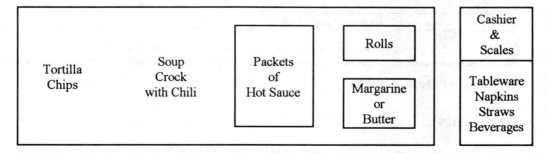

Source: Pannell-Martin, et al. 1995.

The cashier has to be alert and well-versed regarding the school lunch requirements to determine if the foods taken are in sufficient quantities to meet the requirements (see Chapter 3). Some managers prefer portioning the meat and meat alternate to ensure that the component is met and to control costs. However, some school districts have found that when students are allowed to help themselves, the cost is not that much different.

An example of a popular taco salad bar setup is shown in Figure 4.8 (see the USDA guide, *A Menu Planner for Healthy Schools Meals*, for details on meeting the meal requirements in a self-service situation). The meal is priced as a unit and counts as a lunch under the National School Lunch Program. Many schools make it a policy that the student can have all he or she can put into a 12-ounce bowl. Chili is often served on top of the salad items (doesn't sound good, but this is the idea). To keep costs down, a chili recipe can be developed to utilize the maximum amount of vegetable protein (soy) permitted and more kidney beans than normally used. The nacho chips come in bulk sizes and one-ounce packages—maintaining portion control, and waste may make the packages most cost-effective. The cost may be further reduced by using sour cream dressing rather than sour cream (the sour cream dressing tastes almost identical). The popularity of the taco bar (began by Wendy's restaurant chain) may be enough to warrant this bar weekly.

A variety of foods can be offered at a salad bar. A five-day salad bar menu is recommended. This helps prevent sameness and provides a better guide to ordering. Four or more of the following can be offered for a variety of colors, shapes, and textures:

Bean sprouts	Cucumber slices
Chick peas	Broccoli florets
Cauliflower florets	Celery, chunks or chopped
Radishes, sliced	Spinach leaves
Julienne beets	Green peas
Carrots, sliced or grated	Beans, green, waxed, or kidney
Green pepper, sliced	Pickle chips

Offering two or more of the following daily will provide variety in meat/meat alternates. If "offer versus serve" is being carried out, the meat/meat alternate does not have to be preportioned.

Cheese, grated or cubed	Canned salmon or tuna flakes
Eggs, sliced or wedged	Julienne turkey
Cottage cheese	Macaroni salad (protein fortified)
Chicken, tuna, or egg salad	Three-bean salad (made with dry beans)
Julienne ham or salami	Peanuts

At least one serving of the following should be offered daily and eight/ten servings in a week to meet requirements:

Enriched or whole-grain bread	Soft pretzels
Crackers	Croutons
Pasta products	Muffins
Bread sticks	

A choice of salad dressings should also be offered.

Cycle Menus

The process of menu planning can be made easier by using cycle menus. Children, particularly seventh and eighth grade students, tend to like routine, and they like having their favorites often. Variety is not as important to students as to adults. A sample menu cycle is provided in Figure 4.5 for elementary children and in Figure 4.7 for high school children.

In the inTEAM Food System, the menus are planned as follows: a one-week cycle lunch menu with eight to ten choices for high schools; a one-week cycle lunch menu for chef salads and salad bars; and a one-week breakfast menu cycle with three to four choices every day. The system includes a suggested two- week menu cycle for elementary schools with a minimum of three choices each day. Middle school menus may be more like the high school menus or the elementary school menus. Routinely serving favorite foods on particular days has become such an accepted practice, that changing a food to another day of the week can be disturbing to students. For instance, a foodservice director reported that when pizza, usually served on Friday, was changed to another day, she received letters and signed petitions from the PTAs to put pizza back on Fridays. For high school students, who often do not keep up with the printed menus, the plan described in Figure 4.7 very quickly becomes a memorized menu—whereby the student says, " It's Friday it must be Pizza."

Since some foodservice directors think that it is desirable to avoid menus that repeat the same meals on the same days of the week, they go to great lengths to ensure that this doesn't happen—and this philosophy is often taught in colleges. Along with "scrambling" the same basic menu offerings to get a different looking menu, they try to include the unpopular "healthy" foods. Such efforts are not always popular with the students and usually do not accomplish the goals.

Due to differences in food prices and availability, there are some advantages to planning the menu in three seasonal cycles: (1) September-October-November, (2) December-January-February, and (3) March-April-May-June. However, if the menu cycle is planned with some generic terms, e.g., "fresh fruit," "chilled canned fruit," "green vegetables," and "special of the day," the seasons and USDA commodities can be worked into a cycle without changing the cycle. The monthly menu sent home with elementary children, however, should be more specific, and should be a marketing tool. In the schools, daily specials or the vegetable of the day, soup of the day, or fresh fruit of the day can be advertised on a changeable menu board.

Menu planning is a complicated process that controls every aspect of foodservice and is too important to take lightly. Cycle menu planning with student-appealing choices is a recommended way because of the advantages, which include:

- Time saved in planning and on NSMP/nutrient analysis
- Forecasting and purchasing made simpler
- Scheduling employees made easier
- Training employees made easier
- Better use of leftovers
- Increased productivity results
- Increased student participation

The job of the menu planner has only just started when the food items are put on a menu form. The menu then needs to be(1) costed, (2) part of the production record form (can be completed ahead with menu items, portion size, and notes), and (3) layout of the serving line planned. All the steps can be "recycled" with the cycle menu and reduce the work involved in planning menus.

Student and Parent Involvement

Federal regulations suggest student and parent advisory committees. Student committees can be involved in menu planning; however, it is probably not feasible or good business to involve them in planning all menus since so many factors have to be considered. Serving "student-planned" menus once a month usually gives students enough feeling of involvement.

Student groups, and also parent groups, can act as advisers in menu planning, tasting new foods, testing recipes, selecting qualities of foods to be purchased, and suggesting policy changes. Surveys conducted by student leaders can provide valuable information to menu planners. Student assistance in menu planning should not be limited to the upper grade levels since elementary school students also enjoy this type of activity. When classes are studying a country, it can be meaningful to provide a theme menu and tie it in with what has been learned in the classroom.

Tips for Menu Planning

A checklist can make the job of meeting meal requirements easier (see Figure 4.9) The following features of the school meal planning methods and the accompanying regulations should be noted:

- Minimum quantities of the four lunch components (five foods) in the Traditional Food-Based and Enhanced Food-Based Menu Planning methods are stated for four age/grade groups. (see discussion earlier in this chapter) All age groups must be offered all four components (five foods, at the minimum quantity specified) in order to meet the meal requirements under Traditional Food-Based Menu Planning and Enhanced Food-Based Menu Planning.
- Preschoolers can be served in two sittings.
- If the choice is made to serve the larger portions of Group V, smaller portions should be made available for those who prefer less; however, minimum quantities for that age/grade must be offered.
- Offer versus serve[1] required in high schools, may be extended to other age groups as a local option.
- The grain/bread lists of creditable foods has been increased to include a number of new items. See Appendix 4 in *A Menu Planner for Healthy School Meals* (U.S. Department of Agriculture 1998) or FCS 783-1, Rev. 2 (USDA directive).
- Vegetable protein products and enriched macaroni products with fortified protein may be offered.
- For Traditional Food-Based Menu Planning option, the bread requirement is for a minimum of one serving a day and a total of eight servings per week. The weight and portion sizes become important to meeting the bread and bread alternate requirement.

---

[1]Students are offered a complete meal but they may choose to select only three or four of the five items offered.

Figure 4.9. Menu Checklist for Traditional/Enhanced Food-Based Menu Planning Options

	YES	NO	COMMENTS/SUGGESTIONS
1. Are all components of the lunch/breakfast included each day?			
2. Are serving sizes sufficient to provide:			
Meat or meat alternate as specified in the appropriate meal planning option?			
Two or more vegetables or fruits or both?			
Appropriate servings of enriched grain/ bread per week needed?			
Fluid milk as a beverage?			
3. Is a Vitamin A vegetable or fruit included at least twice a week?			
4. Is a Vitamin C vegetable or fruit included 2 or 3 times a week?			
5. Are foods rich in iron included?			
6. Are foods planned and included to satisfy the appetites of the age group?			
7. Are the combinations of foods pleasing and acceptable to this age group?			
8. Do lunches have a good balance of:			
Color—in the foods themselves or as a garnish?			
Texture—soft, crisp, firm?			
Shape—different sizes and shapes?			
Flavor—bland and tart, or mild and strong?			
9. Are most of the foods and food combinations ones children of this age have learned to eat?			
10. Have children's cultural, ethnic, and religious food preferences been considered?			

Figure 4.9. Menu Checklist for Traditional/Enhanced Food-Based Menu Planning Options (continued)

	YES	NO	COMMENTS/SUGGESTIONS
11. Is a popular food or dish planned for lunch that includes a "new" or less popular food?			
12. Are foods varied from day to day?			
13. Are different kinds or forms of foods (fresh, canned, frozen, dried) included?			
14. Are seasonal foods included?			
15. Have "new" foods or new methods of preparation been included occasionally?			
16. Can lunches be prepared and served successfully by employees in the time available?			
17. Are lunches planned so that some preparation can be done ahead?			
18. Is the workload balanced among employees from day to day?			
19. Can lunches be prepared and served with facilities and equipment available?			
20. Is oven, surface-cooking, or steam-cooking space adequate for items planned for each lunch?			
21. Can foods planned for each lunch be easily served?			
22. Will foods "fit" on dishes or compartment trays?			
23. Have USDA-donated foods been used to best advantage?			
24. Do high- and low-cost foods and lunches balance?			

Under Enhanced Food-Based Menu Planning option ten servings of grain/bread per week are required. One grain-based dessert each day can be used to meet the grain/bread requirement.

- Nuts and seeds can be used to meet 50 percent of the meat and meat alternate requirement for Food-Based Menu Planning option.
- Yogurt may be used to meet the meat and meat alternate. Frozen yogurt and yogurt bars are not creditable for Food-Based Menu Planning option.
- The milk as a beverage requirement states that flavored milk may be offered as a choice but a student must be offered the choice of whole milk and an unflavored lowfat milk (skim milk, buttermilk, or lowfat milk), unless prior year preferences of one percent rule warrant discontinuing.
- Choices from a variety of foods should be offered children to meet their needs better, appeal to their likes, and introduce them to new foods.
- Fruit and vegetable requirements must be met with at least two sources.
- The minimum creditable serving of fruits and vegetables is 1/8 cup—under the Traditional Food-Based Planning option.
- Juice can meet only ½ of the total fruit and vegetable component requirement for Food-Based Menu Planning option.
- Nutrient analysis of planned menus is not required for Traditional Food-Based Menu Planning or Enhanced Food-Based Menu Planning. The state agency administering the child Nutrition programs will check compliance with the nutritional goals through nutritional analysis. The school/school district will need production records and recipes used (discussed in more detail in Chapter 10, "Managing Production and Service") and nutrient data on products for each menu item.
- Nutrient analysis of planned menus is required for those schools/school districts using Nutrient Standard Menu Planning to meet the requirements.

Frequency Charts

A frequency chart lists the number of times foods appear on the menu. Such charts, which provide a record for meats, vegetables, breads, fruits, and desserts, show at a glance which foods are repeated most often (see Figure 4.10). If a food is repeated frequently on the menu, the reason should be that the item is popular and students will eat it.

If there are limited choices, more variety is needed to avoid students from becoming bored with the food offerings. For example, menu offerings made with ground beef should not be served consecutively if there are few choices. When there are a number of choices, the repeating of items, such as pizza and hamburger/cheeseburgers, is usually the custom. Many high schools offer pizza every day as a choice with three to eight other choices.

The frequency chart is helpful in determining the quantities of different foods that will be used during the cycle or year. This information is needed in estimating quantities for the bid process and for placing orders.

Figure 4.10. Frequency Chart of Menu Items

	Week 1					Week 2					Week 3					Week 4				
	M	T	W	T	F	M	T	W	T	F	M	T	W	T	F	M	T	W	T	F
Beef:																				
Steak Sandwich														x						
Tacos		x										x								
Hamburger	x										x									
Meat Loaf, Beef/Pork																				
Lasagna									x									x		
Spaghetti with Meat Sauce		x										x								
Meat Ball Sub													x							
Burritos, Beef/Bean						X										x				
Roast Beef Sandwich																			x	
Cheeseburger	x										x									
Nachos, Cheese and Chili								X										x		
Steakette				x										x						
Cheese:																				
Macaroni with Cheese																				
Grilled Cheese Sandwich			x															x		
Pizza, Cheese Topping					X					x					x					x
Pizza, Cheese/Pepperoni					X					x					x					x
Grilled Ham and Cheese Sandwich								x										x		
Burrito with Cheese/Bean																				
Cheddar Cheese for Chef Salad	x	x	x	x	x	x	x	x	x	x	x	x	x	x	x	x	x	x	x	x

Figure 4.10. Frequency Chart of Menu Items (continued)

	Week 1					Week 2					Week 3					Week 4				
	M	T	W	T	F	M	T	W	T	F	M	T	W	T	F	M	T	W	T	F
Pork:																				
BBQ Pork on Roll																x				
Ham Slices		x					x					x					x			
Barbecue Rib Sandwich						x										x				
Smoked Sausage Links																				
Smoked Sausage with Red Beans over Rice						x										x				
Pizza, Cheese/Sausage										x										x
Poultry:																				
BBQ Chicken							x													
Chicken Nuggets		x									x									
Chicken or Turkey Salad																	x			
Oven-Fried Chicken								x									x			
Chicken Fillet						x										x				
Chicken or Turkey Pie																				
Hot Dog (Turkey)							x													
Sliced Turkey	x						x													
Seafood:																				
Breaded Fish Sticks																				
Salmon Patty																				
Tuna Salad					x								x							
Other:																				
Egg Salad						x										x				
Peanut Butter/Jelly Sandwich	x				x	x					x			x		x				
Sub with Deli Meat										x										x

BREAKFAST MENUS

There are two methods of meeting the reimbursable meal requirements for breakfast under the National Breakfast Program: the Traditional Food-Based approach and the Nutrient Standard approach. Those who use the latter approach usually analyze the menus for breakfast and lunch together. However, the foods for meeting breakfast requirements tend to be more expensive when the Nutrient Standard Menu Planning approach is used; therefore, most school districts have stayed with the traditional means of meeting the requirements. When planning the menus, see Chapter 3 for details regarding the meal requirements and the USDA publication, *A Menu Planner for Healthy Schools Meals* when planning the menus. Figure 4.11 provides an example of a breakfast combo menu cycle.

The school breakfast is designed to meet, at a minimum, 1/4 of the Recommended Daily Allowance (RDA) for Grades K-12, which is:

Calories	554 cal
Protein	10 grams
Total fat	18 grams (total fat not to exceed 30% of calories over a school week)
Saturated fat	6 grams (to be less than 10% of calories over a school week)
Iron	3 mg
Calcium	257 mg
Vitamin A	197 RE
Vitamin C	13 mg

The breakfast and lunch menus should be coordinated so that the same foods are not on both menus the same day. The *Commodity Menu Alert ® Newsletter* surveyed foodservice directors across the country and found that the favorite breakfast foods are:

1. Breakfast pizza
2. Cold cereal
3. Cinnamon rolls, pancakes and sausage, french toast, biscuit/gravy

A study by the USDA (1992) found basically the same items popular—except breakfast pizza was not a menu item at that time. The breakfast menu in Figure 4.11 has breakfast pizza, cold cereal, and cinnamon rolls within the cycle.

A LA CARTE OFFERINGS

A la carte offerings are usually limited at the elementary school level, whereas in high schools they range from limited to widely varied choices. State regulations and the philosophy of the school district will have a lot to do with the types of foods sold a la carte. As a cost-savings measure, many school districts have taken desserts off the menus and sell them a la carte. Some states have tight controls on the sale of food, e.g., Mississippi and Louisiana.

Figure 4.11. Breakfast Combo Menu Cycle

MONDAY	TUESDAY	WEDNESDAY	THURSDAY	FRIDAY
GROUP I = 2 Components ⇨ Customer Selects 1				
GROUP I **Customer Choice of:** 1. Hot Cinnamon Rolls (2)[1] 2. Cereal with Toast or Bulk Cereal 3. Belgian Waffle with Sausage 4. Toast with Sausage 5. Hot Bran Muffins (2)[1] Condiments: Syrup, Jelly, Butter	**GROUP I** **Customer Choice of:** 1. Hot Cinnamon Rolls (2)[1] 2. Cereal with Toast or Bulk Cereal 3. French Toast with Link Sausage 4. Toast with Link Sausage 5. Blueberry Muffins (2)[1] Condiments: Syrup, Jelly, Butter	**GROUP I** **Customer Choice of:** 1. Hot Coffee Cake[1] 2. Cereal with English Muffin or Bulk Cereal 3. Egg and Ham on English Muffin 4. Toast with Ham 5. Apple-Cinnamon Muffins (2)[1] Condiments: Jelly, Butter	**GROUP I** **Customer Choice of:** 1. Hot Cinnamon Rolls (2)[1] 2. Cereal with Toast or Bagel or Bulk Cereal 3. Breakfast Sausage Pizza 4. Bagel and Cream Cheese 5. Hot Bran Muffins (2)[1] Condiments: Jelly, Butter	**GROUP I** **Customer Choice of:** 1. Whole Wheat Donuts[1] 2. Cereal with Hot Biscuit or Bulk Cereal 3. Ham and Hot Biscuits (2)[1] 4. Toast and Ham 5. Blueberry Muffins (2)[1] Condiments: Jelly, Butter
GROUP II = 1 Component ⇨ Customer Selects 1				
GROUP II **Choice of:** 1. Orange Juice 2. Apple Juice 3. Banana	**GROUP II** **Choice of:** 1. Orange Juice 2. Grape Juice 3. Applesauce	**GROUP II** **Choice of:** 1. Orange Juice 2. Apple Juice 3. Fruit Cup	**GROUP II** **Choice of:** 1. Orange Juice 2. Grape Juice 3. Banana	**GROUP II** **Choice of:** 1. Orange Juice 2. Apple Cranberry Juice 3. Apple Slices
GROUP III = 1 Component ⇨ Customer Selects 1				
GROUP III **Choice of** Milk	**GROUP III** **Choice of** Milk	**GROUP III** **Choice of** Milk	**GROUP III** **Choice of** Milk	**GROUP III** **Choice of** Milk

Source: Pannell-Martin, et al. 1995.

Note: Offer a minimum of two items from Group I (each item should meet two meal pattern requirements), two to three selections from Group II, and a minimum of lowfat and whole milk from Group III each day. Students need to select one from Group I and one from either Group II or III for the meal to qualify as a reimbursable breakfast—under "offer versus serve," only three meal pattern components must be served to qualify as a reimbursable breakfast, though four must be offered. If bulk cereal is offered, two components can be met with the one item.

It is always wise to check with the state agency (over Child Nutrition programs) to learn that state's regulations.

Many school districts are increasing their a la carte sales to help with the increased revenue needed. According to *FoodService Director* (June 1998), Charlotte Mecklenburg (NC) School District sells 12 to 15 different sandwiches, juices, waters, homemade desserts, and pizzas in the secondary schools. The Lubbock (TX) Independent School District, which is operated by Aramark, a management company, reports that 65 percent of the high school meals are a la carte items. The San Bernardino City (CA) Unified Schools generate 22 percent of its sales from a la carte sales.

A big seller is water—sparkling-flavored water and non-flavored, non-sparkling and flavor water and non-flavored. Ten years ago very few schools had water for sale. Today it is commonplace.

Another form of a la carte sales is vending, which has much potential for growth, especially in parts of the country where labor shortages are experienced. Vending machines can be merchandisers of good nutritious foods, such as fresh fruits, yogurt, salads, sandwiches, and fruit juices. They allow foodservice to be available over extended hours when otherwise it would not be economically feasible. This is discussed further in Chapter 16, "Marketing and Promoting School Foodservice."

SNACK PROGRAMS AND OTHER PROGRAMS

Snack programs for kindergarten children, Head Start children, and after-school "extended" day-care programs can be a source of revenue for school foodservice, and there may be a need for these services.

A snack program that operates under the After-School-Snack program regulations receives federal reimbursement must meet the federal requirements. Table 4.2 provides the minimum amounts of food components to be served. Two different components must be served, and juice may not be served when milk is served. Typical menus are shown in Figure 4.12.

The food costs on the menus should average no more than the revenue for the week will allow. If the guidelines in Chapter 2, "Financial Management," are applied and if the revenue for a snack averages $.5325 (reimbursement rates for 1998-1999 school year), the food costs should not exceed $.213 (if kept at 40 percent of the revenue) or $.2662 (if kept at 50 percent of the revenue), as shown below:

Food Cost 40% ----------- $ .2130	50%------------ $ .2662
Labor Cost 40% ------------- .2130	30% ----------- .1598
Other 20%------------------ .1065	20%------------ .1065
Average Revenue $ .5325	$ .5325

There is probably little labor involved in preparing and serving the snack, and allowing 30% of revenue for labor may be adequate. Many school district directors reason that serving the after-school-care snack program is increasing revenue without increasing fixed costs (labor and other costs). For many this is a way of increasing low productivity of the existing staff.

The after-school-care snack program is being encouraged by the USDA and may be needed in some parts of the country. Care has to be taken when planning the menu offerings because of the very

Table 4.2. After-School-Care Supplement/Snack Components

MEAL SUPPLEMENT CHART FOR CHILDREN			
SNACK (SUPPLEMENT) FOR CHILDREN	CHILDREN GRADES 1 AND 2	CHILDREN GRADES 3 THROUGH 5	CHILDREN GRADES 6 THROUGH 12
(Select two different components from the four listed)			
Milk, fluid	½ cup	½ cup	1 cup
Meat and meat alternate[1]	½ ounce	½ ounce	1 ounce
Juice or fruit or vegetable	½ cup	½ cup	3/4 cup
Bread and/or cereal: enriched or whole grain bread or	½ slice	½ slice	1 slice
Cereal: cold dry or hot-cooked	1/4 cup[2] 1/4 cup	1/3 cup[4] 1/4 cup	3/4 cup[5] ½ cup

limited funding—in many cases the after-school-care snack program reimbursement will not be adequate to cover the costs. There are grants available for start up that many school districts have received. The snack service may have to be provided with the idea that someone other than the school foodservice staff will handle distribution of the snack. If this be the case, the menu will be greatly affected by what can be prepared and served later. There are still some fun approaches that can be taken, such as letting the children make the no-baked cookies, or paint their own hard cooked eggs before eating them, or popping the popcorn, if supervision is available.

Under the food requirements for the snack program, the sizes of portions may be regulated by age, and this could be to the planner's advantage because of the costs. See Figure 4.13 for a menu that has been adjusted to the age group using only two age groups (1-2 year old children have been included with 3-5 year old children). The costs could be reduced by using the three age groups because some serving sizes are smaller.

---

[1]Yogurt may be used as meat/meat alternate in the snack only. Four ounces (weight) or ½ cup (volume) of plain, or sweetened and flavored, yogurt may be served to fulfill the equivalent of 1 ounce of meat/meat alternate component. For younger children, 2 ounces (weight) or 1/4 cup (volume) may fulfill the equivalent of ½ ounce of the meat/meat alternate requirement.

[2]1/4 cup (volume) or 1/3 ounce (weight), whichever is less.

[4]1/3 cup (volume) or ½ ounce (weight), whichever is less.

[5]3/4 cup (volume) or 1 ounce (weight), whichever is less.

Figure 4.12. Snack Menu for Children 6 through 12 Grades

Monday	Tuesday

Honey Wheat Doughnut   1
Milk   ½ pint
   or Juice   6 oz
Napkin, Straw
	Honey Oatmeal Granola Bar 1
	Milk ½ pint
	   or Apple Juice 6 oz
	Napkin, Straw

Wednesday

Fresh Fruit   3/4 cup
   Select One:
     Apple
     Banana
     Grapes
     Melon
     Orange
Milk   ½ pint
Napkin, Straw

Thursday	Friday

Popcorn   1 pkg
Milk   ½ pint
   or Orange Juice   6 oz
Napkin, Straw
	Cheese 1 oz
	Crackers 2 pkts
	Milk ½ pint
	   or Juice 6 oz
	Napkin, Straw

Figure 4.13. Sample Snack Menu with Varied Portion Sizes for Grade Groupings

Component	Monday		Tuesday		Wednesday		Thursday		Friday	
Grades	1-5	6-12	1-5	6-12	1-5	6-12	1-5	6-12	1-5	6-12
Milk	½ cup	1 cup					½ cup	1 cup		
	Chocolate Milk, 1% fat						2% Unflavored Milk			
Meat/Meat Alternate	3 Tbsp	1/4 cup			6 oz	8 oz				
	Peanut Butter				Strawberry Yogurt					
Juice or Fruit or Vegetable			½ cup	3/4 cup					½ cup	3/4 cup
			Apple Juice						Orange Juice	
Bread Cereal	4	8	1 oz	2 oz	2	3	1/3 cup	3/4 cup	½ sl.	1 sl.
	Saltine Crackers		Muffin		Graham Crackers		Granola Trail Mix		Raisin Bread	
Cost	$0.16	$0.31	$0.21	$0.32	$0.22	$0.43	$0.14	$0.27	$0.19	$0.29

SELECTED REFERENCES

Federal Register. June 1995, 60 (113). Washington, DC: U.S. Government Printing Office.

National Food Service Management Institute. 1995. *Purchasing Decisions for Cost Effective Implementation of the Dietary Guidelines for Americans.* University, MS: Author.

_____. 1998. *A Tool Kit for Healthy School Meals: Recipes and Training Materials.* University, MS: Author.

National Research Council. 1989. *Recommended Dietary Allowances.* 10th ed. Washington, DC: National Academy Press.

Pannell, D. 1996. *Assisted NuMenu Manual.* Alexandria, VA: inTeam Associates, Inc.

Pannell-Martin, D., and G. Applebaum. 1995. *inTEAM Food System: School Foodservice Manager's Manual.* Alexandria, VA: inTEAM Associates, Inc.

Pouwels, Marie K. 1988. "The Battle Over A la Carte." *Food Management* 24(9): 75.

"Survey Reveals School Food Facts." 1987. *School Food Service Journal* 41(8): 17+.

U. S. Department of Agriculture. 1983. *Nutrient Standard Menu Planning Computer Coding Programs.* Washington, DC: U. S. Government Printing Office.

_____. 1984 (with 1990 revisions; new edition mid-1999). *Food Buying Guide for Child Nutrition Programs.* PA 1331. Washington, DC: U. S. Government Printing Office.

_____. 1987. *School Lunch Patterns.* Washington, DC: Food and Nutrition Services, U. S. Department of Agriculture.

_____. 1994. *The School Nutrition Dietary Assessment Study.* Washington, DC: U. S. Government Printing Office.

_____. 1995. *Healthy School Meals Training.* Washington, DC: U. S. Government Printing Office.

_____. 1998. *Assisted NuMenus—A Resource Guide.* Washington, DC.: U. S. Government Printing Office.

_____. 1998. *Evaluation of the Nutrient Standard Menu Planning Summary of Findings.* ABT Associates for U. S. Department of Agriculture. Washington, DC: U. S. Government Printing Office.

_____. 1998. *A Menu Planner for Healthy School Meals,* FNS-303. Washington, DC: U. S. Government Printing Office.

U. S. Department of Health and Human Service and US Department of Agriculture. 1995. *Nutrition and Your Health: Dietary Guidelines for Americans.* 4th ed. Washington, DC: U. S. Government Printing Office.

5
SYSTEMS OF OPERATING FOODSERVICES

Foodservice Systems

On-Site Production System
    Conventional Foodservice System
    Convenience Foodservice System

Kitchenless or Ready-Cooked System

Central Kitchen or Satellite System
    When and Why the Satellite System Is Used
    Cook-Chill/Freeze Preparation System
    Methods of Transporting Food
    Preplated Meals

InTEAM Food System

Selected References

FOODSERVICE SYSTEMS

According to the *Webster's II New College Dictionary (1995)*, a system is "a set or arrangement of things so related or connected as to form a unity or organic whole." A foodservice system is a unit comprised of an arrangement of things or elements that are related and connected: planning menus, purchasing, receiving, storing, issuing, preparing, cooking, serving, and cleaning up. There are various types of foodservice systems.

In a conventional or traditional school foodservice, the kitchen that prepares and cooks the food is on site. School foodservice does more raw ingredient cooking than do college and university foodservices, primarily because many of the USDA-donated commodities are in a raw form. In a multi-unit foodservice operation, the preparation may be done at another school, in a "central kitchen," or at a "commissary."

Minor and Cichy (1984) classify foodservice systems "on the basis of the degree to which the use of processed foods takes place." Four categories of foodservice systems are presented in this book. Three are based on where/how the food is processed and one is based on how the operation is managed. The categories of systems discussed herein are as follows:

1. On-site production system: food preparation on the premises.
2. Kitchenless or ready-cooked system: convenience foods or fully prepared foods purchased, assembled, and served.
3. Central kitchen system (sometimes referred to as a "satellite system" or "commissary system"): production in a central location for distribution to schools and other service outlets to serve.
4. InTEAM Food System: a standardized approach or system for managing school foodservices regardless of the system used to produce the food.

ON-SITE PRODUCTION SYSTEM

The on-site production system is the most prevalent system used by 81.5 percent of the schools across the country, although not the prevalent one in intercity and large suburban school districts (USDA 1998). The on-site system is broken down further into (1) conventional foodservice system (cooking from raw ingredients), and (2) convenience foodservice system or a mixture of conventional and convenience food systems.

Conventional Foodservice System

The conventional foodservice system of preparing and serving food may mean cooking and baking foods using raw ingredients and all reusable dishes. It is the most labor-intensive and often the most expensive system; however, if costs are within the desired range and desired quality can be maintained, this system may be the preferred one for a school or school district. Rural school districts usually use the conventional system of preparing and serving food because of geographic location, tradition, and over-staffing.

The advantages of the conventional food system are as follows:

- A manager can determine the ingredients (e.g., sodium, additives, and preservatives) in a product.
- More full-time jobs are provided for the community.
- The manager can utilize USDA-donated commodities in the form received.

The disadvantages of the conventional food system are as follows:

- There is less efficiency and lower productivity than with other systems.
- Labor costs are higher.
- Better-trained employees are required—a good cook and a good baker—for good-quality products to be produced.
- Products may not be of the type or quality today's students prefer.

Many school foodservices that consider themselves users of the conventional system serve a number of convenience items—probably more than they realize.

Convenience Foodservice System

As labor costs increase, labor shortages plague the industry, and labor turnover leaves some school districts without skilled labor, the convenience food system becomes an attractive option. A convenience food is a menu item in a preserved state that with using the finishing instructions, allows the serving of the menu item without the need for a skilled cook or baker to ensure customer acceptance of the item.

The advantages of this system are:

- More consistent quality
- Better quality in many instances
- Lower labor costs
- Reduced need for skilled employees or training
- Increased productivity
- Products that today's students prefer

Convenience food is usually higher in cost than the sum of the ingredient costs because labor is "stored" in the product. Therefore, it is important when increasing the use of convenience foods that a concurrent reduction in labor hours occur for overall cost control.

The convenience food system may involve the following: assembling sandwiches made with bakery bread, presliced sandwich meats and cheese, and portion "pak" of mayonnaise; making hamburgers from bakery buns and pre-charcoal-broiled hamburger patties that have been reheated;

heating premade and preportioned pizza to melt the cheese; heating prefried chicken, baking "proof and bake" cinnamon rolls.

Formal banquets can be served with this system. Like schools, many specialty restaurants have considerable numbers of convenience items on the menu, such as spinach souffle, pepper steak with gravy, chicken Napoleon, and fancy desserts like cheesecake.

Convenience food systems need a lot of storage space (mostly in freezers), an assembly area, an oven for heating, and space for serving (preferably a serving line).

Most convenience foods can be purchased in two basic sizes: single servings and bulk quantity. With the aseptic, or "tetra brik," packaging process, which has been slow to catch on in this country, it is possible to have more shelf-stable products that would otherwise require refrigeration. The system was first designed and used in Sweden in 1961. Ocean Spray Cranberries was one of the first companies to use aseptic packaging in this country. The use of the aseptic packaging has expanded in the 1990s as factories retooled and automated equipment.

KITCHENLESS OR READY-COOKED SYSTEM

With the kitchenless, or ready-cooked, system, fully prepared foods are purchased, stored, assembled, heated, and served. This approach is not new to school foodservices; it has been used by school districts in Detroit (MI), Baltimore City (MD), and St. Louis (MO) for many years.

Today it is possible to purchase high-quality frozen entrees and other food products that require no preparation or cooking until prior to service, when they will be reheated. Many school districts use this system today (most of the time), but may not realize it. The number of fully prepared foods on the menu has increased slowly, and pieces of cooking equipment, e.g., steamers, have become storage cabinets in some schools. Hospitals were among the first to really use this system and to call it a "kitchenless system." Even fine restaurants are beginning to use a form of this system called *sous vide,* a method of preparing individual portions and storing in vacuum packaging.

It is possible for a school district to obtain aseptic-packed, cook-chilled foods, custom-made using the school district's recipes and USDA commodities, at no greater costs than most school districts would realize making the menu items from raw ingredients, e.g., spaghetti and chili sauces. These products have replaced the need for a cook-chill central kitchen to produce six to ten products and without the cost of a multimillion dollar plant to operate.

Some of the advantages to this system are:

- Reduced inventory and better inventory control
- Reduced need for employees, especially skilled employees
- Higher productivity and reduced labor costs
- Consistency in quality and portion size

CENTRAL KITCHEN OR SATELLITE SYSTEM

In the early 1970s, a need developed for producing food at one location and satelliting, when expansion of the school lunch program was at its peak. Central production kitchens may mean one school producing food for three or four other schools, or it may mean a large food production kitchen, resembling a food factory producing for many schools. Central kitchens and commissaries became necessary to meet the needs of some large school districts. The schools receiving the food prepared at the central kitchen are referred to as *satellite schools, receiving kitchens,* or *finishing kitchens*.

There are many terms used referring to satelliting that need to be defined.

Definitions:

BASE OR PRODUCTION KITCHEN—A kitchen where meals are prepared for serving on-site and for one or more other locations.

CENTRAL PRODUCTION OR COMMISSARY (KITCHEN) OR FOOD FACTORY—A large, ideally a centrally located kitchen, where food is prepared for serving at other locations.

SATELLITE FOODSERVICE SYSTEM (SATELLITING)—A system of preparing food at one location for serving at another.

COOK-CHILL/FREEZE SYSTEM—A kitchen that cooks food and chills or freezes it for reheating and serving later.

RECEIVING KITCHEN—School kitchen that receives food ready to serve. The food may be delivered in bulk or in individual servings.

FINISHING KITCHEN—School receiving prepared foods that need heating or finishing off, or reconstituting, before serving.

Many school districts have built central production kitchens and entered into a satellite food system in a big way. Others have used one large school kitchen to prepare foods for other schools. Both works and the latter is the most common primarily because it is cheaper and easier to implement. However, 13 million dollar (more or less) food factories are being built today in a few school districts. The majority of these kitchens being built are for cook-chill preparation, which means the schools receiving the food must be able to reheat or reconstitute the food. "Cook-chill" is best used for soups, sauces, and some casseroles.

Some question the practicality of a large central production kitchen, sometimes referred to as a commissary, producing food for other schools. This is particularly true today when 75% of the popular food items put on menus are convenience foods. School districts considering building a central kitchen in the future need a feasibility study to be done by a knowledgeable team of consultants before spending such a large amount of money and initiating a change in operation. One of the first questions to answer is, "How many items on the menu can be prepared in the cook-chill kitchen?" Many of the cook-chill kitchens in school districts today are idle 50 percent of the time. The next question to answer is, "Would a distribution center connected to the warehouse that would break down cases and assemble meals be the answer?" Several school districts have gone this route.

One of the first school districts to build a central kitchen was the Corpus Christi (TX) Independent School District, where there now stands a new modern complex (see Figures 5.1, 5.2a, and 5.2b). School districts were slow to get into satelliting food because the cost of labor was not an issue in the 1970s and 1980s. At that time, however, the multi-unit commercial foodservice industry, where profit on the bottom line is of great importance, was switching from the true conventional system of producing food to a type of centralized production in the 1970s. The high cost of labor and labor shortages will make the conventional system of preparing and serving on site even less attractive, and in the 2000s centralized preparation of some type more attractive.

A central kitchen may prepare and portion food into individual meals for service (these meals may be hot, ready to serve, or require heating), or prepare the food in bulk for serving on location. Both individual meals and bulk food may be transported hot or cold. Regardless of the type of production and delivery, the basic steps to a successful operation are the same:

- Plan a good cycle menu.
- Forecast the numbers of servings to be prepared.
- Precost and run nutritional analyses.
- Place food orders.
- Plan production of food and schedule delivery of prepared foods.
- Prepare food using standardized recipes/formulas.
- Deliver food to the receiving or finishing kitchen schools in a safe manner.
- Postcost the meals served.

Points to be considered in locating a central kitchen are (1) distances to travel to receiving schools, (2) problems related to plant and vehicle breakdowns and bad weather, (3) expansion needs, and (4) accessibility to primary traffic routes for deliveries.

Some school districts have taken existing high school kitchens and converted them into central kitchens. Using the large kitchen of a senior high school has worked particularly well for small school districts (serving 4,000 or fewer students), when the satellite schools, usually elementary schools, have been within a short distance. The Howard County (MD) School District built its schools with this plan in mind and has realized significant capital outlay savings.

In the 2000s, when solving labor shortages and reducing labor costs will be of increasing importance, the commissary kitchen concept and large central production kitchens will be a solution for more school districts. Productivity can be increased by five to eight times the conventional system production rate. On the average, an on-site production system can produce between 10 to 18 meals per labor hour, whereas the central kitchen can produce 100 to 160 meals per labor hour. The Dayton (OH) School District commissary produces 100 to 110 meals per labor hour. Based on an hourly wage of $14 (including fringe benefits), the on-site kitchen's labor can cost as much as $1.40 per lunch compared to 14 cents per lunch (or less) when produced in a central facility. However, the labor hours and cost at the schools receiving the food must be considered when measuring of productivity and arriving at the cost of a lunch.

Many argue that so much is lost when food is not cooked on site; however, with cook-chill shipped in bulk, the finishing off process takes place on site. The "hominess" of rolls and cookies baking can be obtained.

Figure 5.1. The Corpus Christi Independent School District's Central Kitchen Facility Gertrude B. Applebaum Food Service Center

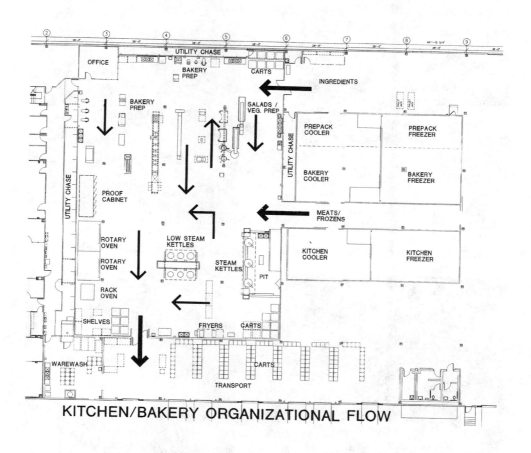

KITCHEN/BAKERY ORGANIZATIONAL FLOW

Architect: Bennett, Martin, and Solka, Inc.

Serves over 35,000 meals daily; 42,000 district enrollment
Average 76,670 sq. ft.
Preparation and delivery of all elementary school meals
Preparation and delivery of sandwiches, salads, and baked goods to the entire system
Receiving and shipping of all warehoused items
Source: Corpus Christi (TX) Independent School District.   Used by permission.

Figure 5.2a. Prepackaging of Meals, Sandwiches, and Salads Are Done Semi-Automatically

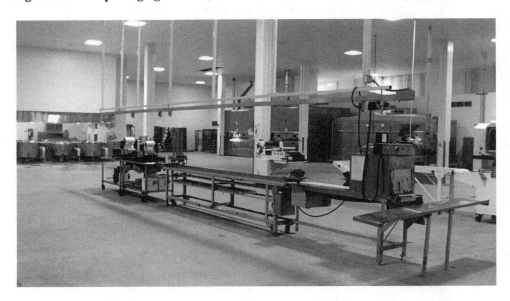

Figure 5.2b. The Bakery Provides Breads, Cakes, and Pies for 35,000 Meals a Day

Source: Corpus Christi (TX) Independent School District. Used by permission.

When and Why the Satellite System Is Used

On-site production kitchens are often converted to "receiving kitchens" or "finishing kitchens" when 300 or fewer meals are served at one location. When building a new school, constructing a receiving or finishing kitchen rather than a traditional on-site preparation kitchen can save $50,000 to $70,000 or more in equipment cost and space needed by 35 percent. The savings in producing a lunch will depend on the method of transporting food and the efficiency of the operation.

Reasons for using a satellite system and advantages that **may be** realized, include the following:

- Reduction in cost of food and supplies as a result of large-volume purchasing
  (The costs of food going into the products can be reduced with better inventory control. With better inventory control, reduction in waste, use of standardized recipes and better planning, some directors report a reduction of 20 percent in costs.)
- Solution to the food and supply delivery problems (not being able to obtain school deliveries from distributors)
  (In areas where distributors won't deliver to many small sites, reducing the number of deliveries from distributors and increasing the volume delivered to one location can decrease prices paid for products by as much as 4 to 7 percent.)
- Reduction in initial cost of building and equipping new school kitchens
  (The school receiving the prepared food needs less space and less production equipment.)
- Better control of quantity and quality (in a good system of operation)
  (If skilled, trained people [the best cooks and bakers in the school district] are preparing the food at the central kitchen, the food quality is usually improved. The menu items and method used to prepare and transport the food will have a bearing on the finished product quality at the time of service.)
- Reduction in need for duplication of labor skills
  (Trained, skilled people are needed to prepare the food in the central kitchen; however, a semiskilled staff member can work alongside a trained, skilled person and produce food. Much-less-skilled employees will be needed in those schools receiving the food from the central kitchen than at the on-site production schools.)
- Increase in productivity and reduction in costs of labor due to reduction in number of employees and labor hours needed
  (Reducing labor costs is a primary reason for centralizing preparation.)
- Standardization of the foodservice operation in all schools.
  (The menu/ food offerings are more alike in the different schools in the district.)

There are also some disadvantages or concerns when a satellite system is used:

- Increased possibility of foodborne illnesses from unsafe food; safe food depends greatly on maintaining the correct temperatures.
- Food distribution problems in congested areas or due to weather conditions.
- High cost of equipment, maintenance, and repair of the more sophisticated and specialized equipment.
- Menu limitations since not all foods will maintain high quality during holding with some systems of satelliting food.
- Loss of cooking smells with some systems of satelliting food.

- Expert management required to operate a "food factory."
- Specialized equipment needed.
- More shorter-hour employees needed and more difficulty in filling the positions.
- Less control by principal over the school foodservice.
  (This could be an advantage, too.)

Staffing guidelines for central production and receiving or finishing kitchens are provided in Chapter 6, "Organizational Structure and Personnel."

Cook-Chill/Freeze Preparation System

The cook-chill preparation system (or cook-freeze) is a time-tested and USDA-approved approach to food production on site or for commissaries. With this system, food products are cooked in a kettle, then pumped (if quantities are large) or poured into flexible casings or special polyethylene bags while still hot (180° F). The bags are closed, then chilled in an ice water bath or tumbler chiller to drop the product temperature from 180° F to 38° F in 30 to 60 minutes. The time required will depend on the food product's viscosity. The USDA requires that the temperature be reduced within two hours and the product can be refrigerated for up to 45 days. Some school districts take the extra precaution of freezing rather than chilling the finished product. Freezing makes transporting the finished product to the service sites safer and easier but may require a change in some recipe formulations to assure product quality.

Groen, a Dover Industries Company, and Cleveland Range, Incorporated, are leaders in the cook-chill field with their cook-chill equipment systems and they are used by most of the school districts using a cook-chill preparation system. Public schools in Montgomery County (MD), Portland (OR), Norfolk (VA), and Los Angeles (CA), as well as Kodak headquarters in Rochester (NY), offer good examples of properly equipped cook-chill systems. Some key pieces of equipment needed in the kitchen are listed below (Humes 1988).

1. **Steam kettle:** Size ranges from 75 to 400 gallons, but the most commonly used is the 100 gallon size.
2. **Pumping station:** Fills 6-9 bags of food per minute; pumps directly from kettle.
3. **Tumbler chiller:** Holds from 75 to 150 gallons of product; recommended with ice builder.
4. **Ice builder:** Makes from 5,000 to 30,000 pounds of ice; can run at night for lower utility rates.

A computer system is desirable for tracking food from purchasing to inventory and doing cost accounting. Kodak's foodservices uses CBORD's computer software program (CBORD, Inc., Ithaca, NY) to produce an internal requisition system, and charges the kitchens receiving the food from the inventory. A computerized system is needed to place orders, track inventory (before and after preparation), extend the recipes or formulas, schedule employees, label products and directions for products, and pre- and postcost. School districts need software that does all the tasks.

A 30,000-square-foot space will house sufficient equipment to process food for 100,000 meals a day. The storage facilities will require as much space or more. See Figure 5.3 for an example of a cook-chill kitchen and warehouse facility that serves Montgomery County (MD) schools.

Figure 5.3. Montgomery County (MD) Schools' Central Kitchen Facility Connected to Their Warehouse

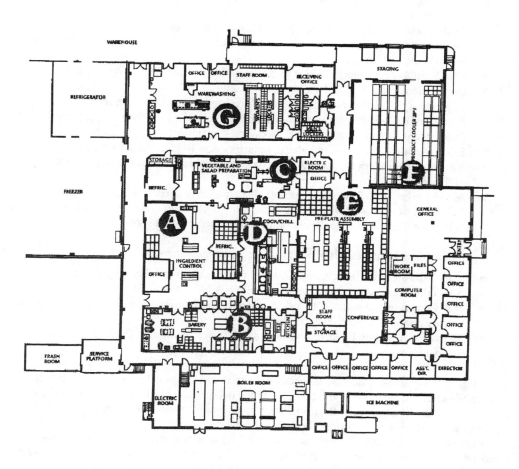

A. Ingredient Control
B. Bakery

C. Salad and Vegetable Preparation
D. Cook/Chill

E. Pre-Plate Assembly
F. Product Cooler
G. Warewashing

30,000 square feet of warehousing
20,000 square feet of cook-chill production
    and preplated-meal assembly area
6,000 square feet of office space

Producing equivalent of 48,000 meals per day
30,000 preplated for all elementary schools
Cook-chill in bulk to support secondary schools
Bakery, catering, and a la carte items the kitchen

Operates eight hours a day, five days a week with 56 employees for a total of 360 hours.
Producing at 133 meals per labor hour. The aisles in the kitchen are 12 foot wide.

Source: Montgomery County (MD) Schools. Used by permission.

Some of the advantages of the cook-chill preparation system are:

- **Flexibility in timing of preparation:** Allows preparation in down-time periods and planning of workload.
- **Cost-effectiveness:** Provides more efficient use of employees' time and equipment (usually can reduce labor hours by 20 percent) and can reduce food costs since only what is needed has to be heated for use.
- **Quality of food:** Captures food at its peak and maintains food quality better than holding food for long periods at hot temperatures.
- **Food safety:** Ensures that food is safe if prepared and handled correctly.
- **Nutritional value:** Maintains the nutritional value of the food for a longer period of time (when the product is transported chilled versus hot).
- **Less pressure:** By preparing ahead, reduces stress level in the kitchen.
- **Ease in preparation for use:** Allows food to be reheated quickly because of the density of the product.
- **More variety possible:** Enables a small staff to offer variety and choices daily.
- **Efficiency of transportation:** Allows food to be transported the day before or whenever is best for the school. The weight of the transported product is manageable.

Some of the disadvantages of the cook-chill preparation system are:

- **Specialized equipment:** Requires special equipment for doing the job properly.
- **Specialized training:** Requires that employees be well trained.
- **Refrigeration:** In addition to an ice source or tumbler chiller, increased refrigeration is usually needed for storage of product.
- **Leftover concept:** Food is considered a leftover even after the first time offered to students.

At the serving school, the food is reheated in the storage bags in hot water, in a compartment steamer, tilting skillet, or on top of the range, or in the oven. Items like macaroni and cheese can be prepared together or separately, then combined in steamtable pans on the day of service. Cheese topping can be added and the product heated in the oven.

It is essential to food safety to minimize the time food spends in the "danger zone" between 40° F and 140°. Techniques of Hazard Analyses and Critical Control Point (HACCP) system should be employed carefully when dealing with high volumes of food. Some tips to ensure that food is safe are: (1) make certain the food is cooked to a safe temperature and reheated to a safe temperature; (2) remember that the density and type of food will affect cooking times and chilling times; (3) package food tightly; (4) use a thermometer and check temperatures frequently; (5) move food from one stage to the next without allowing it to sit at room temperature; and (6) hold hot food at 165 to 175° F.

Methods of Transporting Food

The method of transporting the food—in bulk or preplated—will make a lot of difference in the staff needed at the serving site.

Transporting in Bulk—Transporting food in bulk is one of the oldest and most widely used methods for moving prepared food from the point of preparation to the point of serving. The food is transported in insulated containers—heated food carriers and cold food carriers—to the receiving school where the food is finished to portion and serve. In recent years, the cook-chill method of transporting food in bulk has become very popular in schools as well as in hospitals. Both methods—hot or cold— allow for service at the receiving kitchen resembling on-site preparation. Frequently, the students and parents are not aware that the food was not prepared in their own school's kitchen.

The bulk method may be chosen over the preplated method by a school district for the following reasons:

- Kitchen facilities are available at the receiving school.
- Staff is available for serving.
- The school district wants as little change as possible in the foodservice provided.
- The method can reduce some costs.
- Less equipment is needed than for an on-site production kitchen.

The Cypress-Fairbanks (TX) Independent School District has a very modern, efficient, well-organized central kitchen producing cook-chill food in bulk and preplated components for 47 schools, two meals a day (50,000 meals). Other school districts transporting in bulk include Wichita (KS), Pulaski City (AR), and Jackson (MS).

Transporting in Hot and Cold Carriers —Food may be transported in a hot or cold state. During transportation, cooked, ready-to-serve food is maintained at serving temperature; whereas, the cold food is maintained at a safe temperature. It is usually transported within two to three hours following preparation. Timing is important to maintaining a good-quality product at the proper temperature.

Well-insulated and electrically heated food carriers are necessary for bulk transporting of hot foods. Carriers are available that will hold, for example, five 12 x 20 x 2 ½ inch pans and three 12 x 20 x 4 inch pans. Utility carriers, used with eutectic plates for keeping food cold, are available that hold 12 x 20 inch and 18 x 26 inch pans. The eutectic plate is a type of lid that maintains coldness for hours after chilling in a refrigerator or freezer. The carriers can be obtained with wheels or fitted with dollies for ease in handling. Food is generally transported in the steamtable pans or sheet pans from which food can be served.

At the receiving school, students may be served from a serving line, cafeteria-style, picking up their trays, milk, silverware, and napkins. This method requires little labor and equipment at the receiving school.

Since the proper temperature is crucial to the safety of food as well as to its quality and taste, there is not a lot of flexibility in the time between production and transporting to serving. Before food is sent to satellite schools, the temperature and quantity of each item should be recorded, and the managers at the satellite schools should record the temperature upon arrival and confirm that the quantities sent are correct. A sample record for use with the bulk system is shown in Figure 5.4.

The bulk food system offers the advantage of maintaining a personal atmosphere in the serving of food, characteristic of on-site preparing and serving. Also, portions can be adjusted to the student's need and offer versus serve can be carried out very easily.

Figure 5.4. Sample Satellite School Record for Use with Bulk Transporting System

Components of Meal (1)	Serving Size (2)	PRODUCTION KITCHEN Completes Columns 1 and 2		RECEIVING KITCHEN Completes Columns 3, 4, and 5		
		Number of Servings Transported (3)	Departing Temperature (4)	Receiving Temperature (5)	Number Served (6)	Number of Servings Left Over (7)
Entree						
Vegetables/ Fruit						
Bread or Rolls						
Dessert						
Other:						
		Initial _____		Initial _____		

Examples of cook-chill kitchens in operations transporting food in bulk to finishing kitchens are in the following cities: Corpus Christi (TX), San Bernardino (CA), Riverside (CA), Long Beach (CA), and Norfolk (VA). New cook-chill kitchens being built are for schools in San Diego (CA) and Jefferson County (KY). See Figures 5.1, 5.2a, and 5.2b for layout of Corpus Christi's central kitchen.

Preplated Meals

Preplated meals may be ready to eat or may need reheating. There are several versions of the preplated hot and/or cold meals. Several of the methods used by school districts are described below.

The Los Angeles (CA) Unified School District has operated a central kitchen since 1980, providing preplated meals to more than 98,000 people meals per day for 169 elementary schools and 78 child care centers. The kitchen staff (592 labor hours per day) is scheduled at the production center to prepare one-day in advance of service. An additional 298 labor hours are assigned for warehouse personnel, truck drivers, sanitation, clerical and administrative staff. Their productivity is high at 165.5 meals per labor hour if only production labor is considered. When all necessary to the production, accountability, and delivery are considered, the productivity is 110 meals per labor hour. (See Chapter 6, "Organization Structure and Personnel," for further discussion on meals per labor hour.)

Introducing any one of these systems, other than conventional on-site preparation, will require good communication. Any time a new system for providing food is started in a school—particularly when it is replacing on-site preparation—the school administration, parents, and students have to be receptive for it to work well. Not all of the systems described in this chapter will work for all situations. Each fits a different need.

Preplated Meals—Ready to Eat—In the preplated ready-to-eat method, hot and cold foods are delivered ready to serve, without reheating. A styrofoam, plastic, or aluminum tray may be used. Food will stay hot for up to three hours in these trays, when kept in insulated tote boxes; however, it is recommended that food be served within two hours. Some popular foods do not transport well (e.g., French fries), and menu mixes have to be carefully planned. The biggest complaints are that the heat is not held and the menu is limited.

Service can go rather fast and will require few or no employees at the receiving school. An aide or secretary can record those who eat and distribute the food. Good communication between the preparation kitchen and the receiving school is always essential in any type of satellite system in order to avoid waste or running out.

Preplated Meals—To Be Reheated—Preplated meals usually consist of a cold tray and a hot tray. These may be produced by the school district in a central kitchen or at a large production kitchen, or they may be purchased prepared. The hot tray may be in the frozen or chilled state and require reheating, whereas the cold tray is ready to serve and only needs to be kept cold if containing any perishable foods.

The receiving school will need refrigeration and an oven. This system uses all disposable products, eliminating the need for a dishwashing machine. Preplated meals have the following advantages as compared to an on-site production kitchen:

- Schools with limited kitchen facilities can serve hot lunches.
- Less space and equipment are required.
- Operating costs are cut, productivity is increased, and less labor is used.
- Faster service can be provided.
- Less labor is needed.

An example of a combination cook-chill kitchen and preplated meals is the Montgomery (MD) County's warehouse/central kitchen complex, which is comprised of 56,000 square feet (see Figure 5.3).

An example of preplated meals system is the Archdiocese of Chicago foodservice program with just over a $40 million budget, which has one of the most challenging districts (geographically) to begin with. This archdiocese, made up of 500 parishes, including Cook and Lake Counties, was previously operated by management companies (in at least 50% of the schools). Now it is self-operated and is in the business of serving its own and others from its commissary, or central kitchen. In addition to taking care of the food for its 225 Catholic schools, the district provides food to 40 Chicago city schools and 15 suburban public schools. It serves 100,000 meal equivalents a day. The prepackaged meals are made up of two components: one delivered in a foil container that is heated at the school location before being served and one in a cold pack that contains vegetables, utensils, and other non-heated meal items.

Cold-Pack Lunch System—The bag lunch is the most common example of the cold-pack method. When this method is used to provide lunches to students, the sanitation aspects will limit what can go into the lunch, how long it can be held, and at what temperature it must be held.

INTEAM FOOD SYSTEM

The Olive Garden and Red Lobster Restaurants have a standardized system of operation. Marriott and Aramark have systems of operating school foodservice programs under contract. Self-operated school foodservices now have the option of an operating system, the inTEAM Food System, a standardized approach to managing school foodservice. It is menu-driven, and each process is standardized. Two basic books, the *inTEAM Food System Administrator's Manual* and the *inTEAM Food System Manager's Manual,* provide the instructions for operating the system. In 1999, more than 500 schools in 12 different states were being operated using part to all of the inTEAM Food System procedures and menu concepts. A one-time user fee is charged for the rights to use the System, and the fee is based on the size of the school district, or a state may pay the fee for all the school districts. Six states have purchased the rights to use the system: Georgia, Kentucky, Louisiana, New Jersey, South Carolina, and Tennessee. The results have been increased participation, particularly in high schools, decreased percentage of revenue spent for labor, improved bottom line, and excited managers using a standardized system.

SELECTED REFERENCES

"Berkman Installs 1st "Kitchenless" Kitchen." 1991. *FoodService Director.* 4 (8): 1.

Durocher, J. 1988. "Cook/Chill System." *Restaurant Business 87(9)*: 180, 182.

Humes, S. 1988. "Figuring the Payback on Cook-Chill." *Foodservice Director 1(12)*: 31.

Khan, M. 1987. *Foodservice Operations.* New York: Van Nostrand Reinhold.

King, P. 1988. "Changing with the Times." *Food Management 24(10)*: 63, 66.

_____. 1988. "Cook/Freeze Succeeds in Hawaii." *Food Management 24(9)*: 55-56.

Minor, L., and R. Cichy. 1984. *Foodservice Systems Management.* New York: Van Nostrand Reinhold.

Pannell-Martin, D. 1995, revised 1999. *Cost Control for School Foodservices.* 2nd ed. Alexandria, VA: InTEAM Associates, Inc.

Pannell-Martin, D., and G. Applebaum. 1995. *inTEAM Food System Administrator's Manual.* Alexandria, VA: InTEAM Associates, Inc.

_____. 1995. *inTEAM Food System Manager's Manual.* Alexandria, VA: inTEAM Associates, Inc.

U. S. Department of Agriculture. 1998. *School Food Purchase Study: Final Report.* Washington, DC: Author.

Webster's II New College Dictionary. 1995. Boston, MA: Houghton Mifflin Company.

Winslow, E. 1988. "Has Cook/Chill's Time Come?" *Food Management 24(9)*: 64.

6
ORGANIZATIONAL STRUCTURE
AND PERSONNEL

Organizational Management
Line of Authority
Positions and Job Descriptions
Objectives of Management

Local Foodservice Administration
Director or Supervisor
Span of Control

Staffing at Individual Schools
Determining Meal Equivalents and Measuring Productivity
Staffing for On-Site Production
Other Guidelines for Staffing
Factors to Consider
Staffing Based on Sales
Staffing for Breakfast
Determining Productivity and Comparing with Guidelines

Staffing a Central Kitchen/Receiving School

Distribution and Scheduling of Labor Hours
Planning Work

Labor Shortages and Turnover

Payscales and Labor Costs

Selected References

ORGANIZATIONAL MANAGEMENT

The concept of organizational management is not new, but some new "buzzwords" have come into the picture. Two current terms are "right-sizing" (sometimes referred to as "down-sizing") and "reengineering" in industry as well as in school foodservice. Some major right-sizing is taking place in school districts across the country as costs and shortages of service employees have made it necessary. As school foodservices grew from "soup kitchens" to full-fledged businesses, it became necessary for management to be more aware of organizational structures, personnel matters, staffing and related cost of labor. This growth is illustrated in *I Can Manage: A Practical Approach* (Caton and Nix, 1986).

The basic principles of management are the same for restaurants, hospitals, residence halls, and school foodservices. The larger the operation, the more complex the organization becomes. School foodservices range from those in small, single-unit, decentralized school districts with schools serving less than 100 meals to those in centralized city and county districts with 250 to 1200 schools serving 100,000 to more than half million meals per day.

The purposes of an organization are to deal with managing manpower and meeting goals. According to Payne-Palacio, et al. (1997), "Many of the challenges that managers faced many years ago are the same as those faced by today's managers . . . increasing worker productivity, decreasing production costs, maintaining employee motivation and morale, and meeting the challenges of stiff competition . . . ."

For an organization to function effectively and to grow, it must utilize all resources—people, materials, and facilities—to their fullest. The most challenging resource for many managers is people. To be effective, an organization must provide for maximum utilization of its capabilities in this regard. The organization should follow general principles of good management that call for:

- A clear line of authority established and understood by the employees
- Responsibilities clearly identified for each member of the organization
- Effective leadership
- Objectives and goals set and used as a measurement of success
- Timely provision of necessary materials and equipment

Herman (1998), in his book, *Keeping Good People,* provides 125 strategies used today by successful managers to keep their employees happy and highly productive. They include: working together as a team, insisting on workplace safety, giving people freedom and flexibility, reducing stress, linking performance with rewards, and helping people grow into bigger jobs.

Line of Authority

The responsibility for the National School Lunch Program is given to the U.S. Department of Agriculture, which administrates the program through seven regional offices and individual states.

The delegation of authority from the federal government via the regional offices is shown in Figure 6.1. Administration of the school foodservice programs is the responsibility of the state department of education in all states but one (in New Jersey it is the responsibility of the Department of Agriculture); however, that is about all the different states have in common. At the local level, the school board is usually the overall governing body , and it enters into an agreement (annual contract) with the state agency to carry out federal and state rules and regulations concerning school food programs. The agreement is made in order to receive federal and state reimbursements and USDA-donated commodities.

An organizational chart should show the positions in the organization, the overall responsibilities of the various positions denoted in a general manner, and the relationships among departments and services. Figure 6.2a shows a fairly typical organization chart for a centralized school district with the foodservice director/supervisor reporting to an assistant superintendent. The number of assistants and office staff will depend on the size of the operation and what the central office does for the schools, e.g., handle free and reduced-price meal applications. In the larger school districts area supervisors or area field manager reporting the a director is responsible for 15 or more schools, as shown in Figure 6.2b. Positions with the greatest authority should be shown at the top of the chart, with those with the least authority at the bottom. A chart should make it clear to whom each person in the organization should report. The trend is for 15 to 20 schools assigned to each assistant, e.g., Jefferson County (CO) Schools (guidelines provided later in this chapter).

Positions and Job Descriptions

Once the basic plan of an organizational chart has been established and the line of authority is set, a clear, concise job description is needed for each position. It should provide a general definition of the job to give management and an employee a clear understanding of what a job entails. Examples of job descriptions are shown in Figures 6.3 and 6.4.

In a small school the person responsible for running the kitchen is usually called the *manager* or *cook-manager*. In a satellite school or finishing kitchen, the position may be referred to as the lead person. The trend now is toward less management—not more—and toward giving more responsibility to the staff.

In the 1970s there were head cooks and head bakers, even assistant head cooks and lead bakers. Jobs were very departmentalized; that is no longer the trend. As more convenience foods were used the questions became: Does the "head cook" really cook or does he or she "reconstitute" frozen pre-prepared foods? How many days a week does the baker bake? How much do the products baked really cost? Should staff employees have titles and be paid accordingly, or should all staff be paid at the same level? The answers often pointed toward more general titles—for example, "staff employee" and "foodservice assistant." In a small kitchen (ten or fewer employees), the manager may need the flexibility to cross-train and move employees around to different jobs, in which case the different pay levels can be a problem. Establishing titles for job purposes without pay differences at the staff level gives more flexibility.

142

Figure 6.1. U.S. Department of Agriculture -- Federal Level with Regional Offices

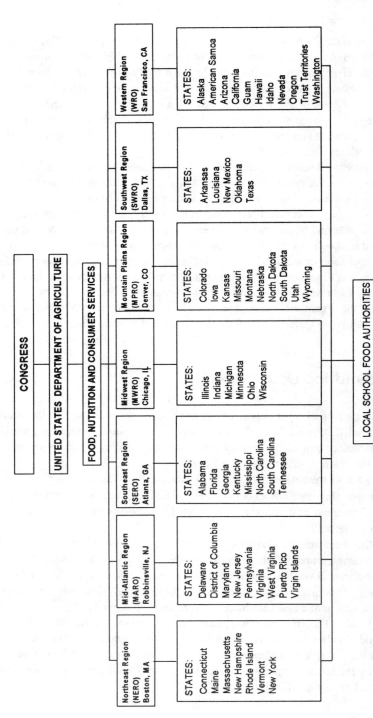

Courtesy of U.S. Department of Agriculture 1999.

Figure 6.2a. A Typical Organizational Chart With Foodservices Reporting to an Assistant Superintendent or Directly to the Superintendent

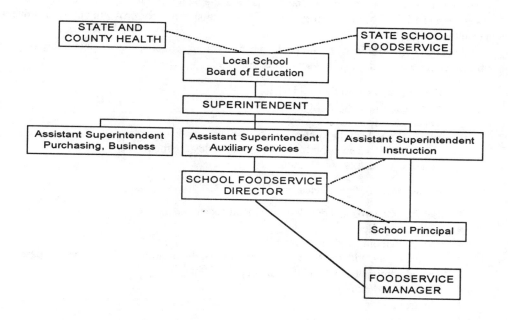

Figure 6.2b. Example of a Large School District With More Than Fifteen Schools

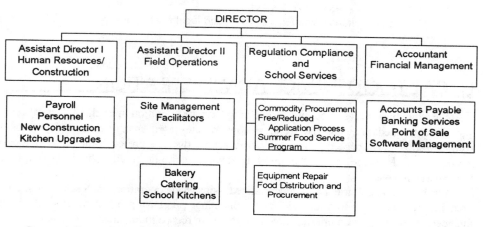

Source: Jefferson County (CO) Public Schools. Used by permission.

Objectives of Management

Management is responsible for planning, directing, and controlling the foodservice in a sound financial manner and for serving good, nutritious food and being an integral a part of the educational system. Some school foodservice programs have the responsibility for providing nutrition education as well as foodservice.

Although specific objectives and goals may differ from school to school, six important general objectives should be adopted by a school foodservice:

1. Operate on a sound financial basis.
2. Serve good-quality, nutritious food.
3. Teach good food habits.
4. Meet the needs of the students in a satisfying way.
5. Give employees an opportunity for personal development.
6. Meeting regulatory requirements.

The management of foodservice should:

- Set the standards and develop the objectives and goals.
- Make the policies.
- Do the planning and organizing.
- Communicate with the foodservice employees, the customers, the public, the parents, the school administration, and the school board.
- Control food quality.
- Control costs.
- Carry out objectives and goals.
- Supervise and direct.
- Evaluate.
- Teach and encourage the growth of the foodservice workers.
- Look out for the foodservice's welfare.
- Monitor compliance with federal, state, and local regulations, policies and procedures.

LOCAL FOODSERVICE ADMINISTRATION

There are two basic ways of administering a foodservice operation in a school district; centralized and decentralized. Though the trend is toward site-based managements (as far as school administration is concerned), more and more school districts are centralizing their foodservice management. In some states the trend is toward merging small school district to reduce administrative costs.

When the school district has a decentralized foodservice operation, each school administers its own foodservice. This may include menu, planning, purchasing, interpretation of regulations, finances, personnel, and preparing state reports. With regard to the latter, many state departments of education require state reports to be combined into one report for the entire school district, and USDA-donated commodities are often distributed to the school district for distribution.

When foodservice administration is centralized, a director or supervisor of foodservices is usually appointed to work under the general direction of the superintendent of schools or the school business administrator. Centralized management means different things to different school districts. In some districts it means little more than doing the accounting work and the monthly state report at one location, whereas in others it may mean centralized planning of menus, purchasing, warehousing, accounting, fiscal control, and hiring personnel.

Centralized administration, with the responsibility for all the various jobs related to the school foodservices' operation, has the following advantages:

- Can afford a qualified person in leadership role. (This saves management time because one person spends time planning menus and purchasing.)
- More purchasing power is possible. (Larger volume usually results in lower prices and a financial savings.)
- Better organization and management are possible.
- Principals have to spend less time on foodservice matters.
- Consistency in services.

Small school districts are frequently staffed with only a director and one or two clerical people, many of which have become very knowledgeable about the school foodservice programs. Most schools are staffed with a manager (a requirement of some states). On the other hand, large school district's foodservice's organization charts may have several levels and be more complex, a more functional structure. The trend is toward fewer levels and more responsibility with authority given the manager.

The most common title for the person in charge of school foodservice is director; however, supervisor and executive director titles are used by some. The person in charge of school foodservice at the school level may be called a manager, an assistant manager, or a lead. Figure 6.3 provides an example of a job description for the manager. One manager may be responsible for two or more schools, which is working effectively for Jefferson County (CO) schools.

Job titles for school-based employees were formerly used to describe what the person did, e.g., cook and baker, but, the title frequently used today is "staff employee" or "foodservice assistant" as illustrated in the job description in Figure 6.4. The philosophy and jobs have changed with the increased use of convenience foods and the reduction in staff and the titles of cook and baker are too specialized/departmentalized to describe the job. An employee may prepare, serve, and clean up breakfast, then start preparing for lunch, set up the serving line, and cashier during the lunch service.

Director or Supervisor

In the large school districts, the head administrator of school foodservice is often given the title of director. According to the American School Food Service Association Certification Committee, "the *director* is one who plans, organizes, directs, administers the foodservice program in a school system according to policies established by the Board of Education."

Figure 6.3. Job Description for a School Foodservice Manager

School Foodservice Manager

Description: Manages foodservice program in an individual school according to school district's policies, procedures, and methods. Cooperates with principal and teachers to promote Child Nutrition programs educational values. Supervises and instructs foodservice personnel. Maintains high standards of food preparation and service with emphasis on appetizing and appealing, maximum nutritive value, and flavor. Maintains high standards of sanitation and safety: records cash receipts, food supplies, and equipment. Salary based on such factors as numbers and types of meals served daily, percent of participation, number of employees manager supervises, and nature of responsibilities.

Education: High school diploma or taking and passing the equivalency test. Specialized education and training in school foodservice management desirable.

Experience: Diversified experience in foodservice production and management with progressively more responsible positions.

Source: Mississippi State Department of Education 1987. Used with permission.

Figure 6.4. Job Description for a Foodservice Staff Employee or Assistant

---

Job Title: Foodservice Staff Employee or Assistant

Grade Step: II

Job Description: Prepares the main dish and vegetables.

General Duties: Is responsible for the preparation of the main dish and cooked vegetables. Prepares food for the serving line and keeps all foods on the serving line at lunchtime. Is responsible for the cleaning and maintaining of the small equipment, and washing pots and pans when needed. Helps with the general preparation and serving of foods and the cleaning.

Requirements: Must be able to read and write English, do simple arithmetic, and follow oral and written directions. Must have the capacity to grasp and adjust to new and changing situations. (Manual dexterity and ability to work under pressure are desirable.) Must be neat in appearance and wear uniform-type clothing, hairnet or cap covering on hair, and comfortable, safe shoes. Must provide a health certificate verifying negative tuberculin test.

Tools and Equipment: Uses scales for weighing ingredients and portion control, mixer, oven range, steam cooker, steam-jacketed kettle, fryer, food chopper and slicer, vertical cutter-mixer, and other related tools and equipment.

Working Conditions: Works an average of 30 hours per week, Monday through Friday with school holidays, for ten months a year, in a well-lighted, ventilated, and comfortable kitchen. Does much standing on feet and some lifting.

Supervision: Is responsible to the school foodservice manager. Supervises an assistant cook in a large school kitchen.

Personal Requirements: High school education or take and pass the equivalency test. At least one year of experience in foodservice preparation.

Source: Mississippi State Department of Education 1987. Used with permission.

In smaller school districts, the person heading a school foodservice may be called a supervisor or assistant director. (In a large school district, the supervisor is someone who works under the director.) A supervisor is responsible for evaluating the foodservice programs in schools, aiding the foodservice manager, and generally directing their individual foodservice programs.

Span of Control

The trend today is toward a broader span of controls and holding each employee responsible for the total job he or she has done. When "right-sizing" occurs, it usually takes place among middle management.

How many schools can one person supervise? When does a supervisor need an assistant or a director need another supervisor? The span of control will depend on what the supervisor/director is responsible for and the training and skills of the managers the person supervises. Table 6.1 provides a guideline for staffing at the supervisory level. The positions are director, supervisor, and assistant supervisor, but the titles may differ—some states/school districts call people in these roles by other titles.

Table 6.1. Administrative Staffing Guide for School Foodservice Based on Number of Schools

Number of School Foodservices	Director	Supervisor[1]	Assistant Supervisor[1]
1-15		1	
16-30		1	1
31-40		1	2
41-60	1	3	
61-80	1	4	
81-100	1	6^2	
101-125	1	7^2	
126-150	1	8^2	
151-175	1	10^2	
176-200	1	12^2	
201-225	1	14^2	

[1]In a foodservice covering more than 40 schools, the supervision may be divided between director and supervisors.
[2]One of these positions could be designated as an assistant director position.

Source: Kentucky Department of Education 1992. Used with permission.

The responsibilities of a central office should influence the number of people needed in the central office. The amount of time that a supervisor spends in the schools is an important consideration in determining the span of control. Meeting the new Dietary Guidelines and being ready for the state reviews (CREs and SMIs), which are discussed in Chapters 1 and 3, may increase the need for training and supervision within the next ten years.

STAFFING AT INDIVIDUAL SCHOOLS

Staffing and productivity should be considered together. The line of authority and span of control have to be considered when staffing a school. Foodservice at the school level will need someone in charge, regardless of how small the unit is. The profile of a school foodservice employee in the 1970s was a person who was 45 to 50 years old, a high school graduate, semiskilled, with 8 years of experience; in the late 1990s these people were 60 to 65. The foodservice director in the 2000s will be younger (35-44 years old) because of the exodus of seasoned directors, which began in the late 1990s (DeMicco, et al, 1997). More part-time employees will be needed in school foodservice. In many cases, the employee will be retired from a job and working only part time at the local school to supplement income and to have something to do. Table 6.2 shows how the labor force is increasing in age and the largest age group is the 35-44 years old group.

An accurate assessment of work to be done is needed to determine the number or labor hours required, or the productivity rate possible, in a foodservice operation. The emphasis has been on increasing productivity in recent years and will continue. Productivity rate is a way of measuring how much an employee-hour produces. Productivity in the United States increased at an overall rate of three percent a year from 1950 through the mid-1960s. During the 1970s the increase slowed to two percent, and in the 1980s was under one percent. School foodservice productivity changed very little in most school districts during the 1960s to 1980s. In the 1990s, the productivity increased in the nation, as well as in school foodservice. Increasing productivity has become a growing concern of school foodservice directors and managers, and they are doing something about it to maintain financial viability. According to a study by the National Foodservice Management Institute (Cater 1999), there is a direct relationship between productivity and labor costs.

Age	1998 (Actual)	2020 (Projected)
16-19	7,926,000	8,800,000
20-24	15,442,000	13,751,000
25-34	34,592,000	31,657,000
35-44	27,233,000	38,571,000
45-54	17,500,000	30,552,000
55-64	11,894,000	12,970,000
65 and over	3,010,000	2,394,000

Table 6.2. Size of Labor Force by Age
Source: Department of Labor, Bureau of Labor Statistics 1998.

Determining Meal Equivalents and Measuring Productivity

"Meal equivalents" and "meals per labor hour" are terms most frequently used to measure productivity in the school foodservice market. The formula for determining the productivity rate of a school foodservice is as follows:

$$\frac{\text{Output}}{\text{Input}} = \text{Productivity}$$

$$\frac{\text{Output} \rightarrow \text{Total meals served}}{\text{Input} \rightarrow \text{Total labor hours}} = \text{Productivity} \rightarrow \text{Meals per labor hour}$$

When staffing it is essential to know the number served for breakfast and lunch and the number of dollars in a la carte sales. These are not equal in amount of work required; thus an equivalency rate is needed. There are a number of equivalency rates used to arrive at "meal equivalents" for breakfast and a la carte (extra food) sales. In this text the following meal equivalents are used:

3 breakfasts	=	1 meal equivalent
1 lunch	=	1 meal equivalent
$3 in a la carte sales	=	1 meal equivalent

"Total meals served" may contain equivalencies for a la carte sales and other programs such as breakfast. This is discussed later in this chapter.

Staffing for On-Site Production

Staffing an on-site production school's foodservices in the past may have been done based on: "We need more labor." There are a number of guidelines for staffing on-site production schools, but the guide in Table 6.3 is widely used (formerly had only figures for "low" productivity). When determining how much staff is needed, the productivity rate desired must be determined; for example, if the productivity is 16 or 18 meals per labor hour, the meal equivalents are divided by the productivity rate. See Table 6.3 for suggested staffing guidelines. This table reflects some changes from the fourth edition of *School Foodservice Management*. The change basically is the addition of a "high" productivity rate, and this is because many school districts are exceeding the "low" productivity rate.

These staffing guidelines are for a conventional system (on-site production using some convenience foods, such as bakery-made hamburgers and hot dog rolls, prepared pizza, and some disposable dishes, but still operating a dish machine) and for a convenience system (discussed in Chapter 5, "Systems of Operating Foodservices"). The number of meals per labor hour should be much greater for a satellite food system.

Another way of determining staff hours needed is by dividing number of meal equivalents by the desired productivity rate.

Table 6.3. Staffing Guidelines for On-Site Production

| Number of Meal Equivalents[1] | Meals Per Labor Hour (MPLH) for Low and High Productivity | | | |
| | Conventional System[2] MPLH | | Convenience System[3] MPLH | |
	Low	High	Low	High
Up to 100	8	10	10	12
101-150	9	11	11	13
151-200	10-11	12	12	14
202-250	12	14	14	15
251-300	13	15	15	16
301-400	14	16	16	18
401-500	14	17	18	19
501-600	15	17	18	19
601-700	16	18	19	20
701-800	17	19	20	22
801-900	18	20	21	23
901 up	19	21	22	23

[1]Meal equivalents include breakfast and a la carte sales. Three breakfasts equate to one lunch. A la carte sales of $3 equate to one lunch.
[2]Conventional system is preparation of some foods from raw ingredients on premises (using some bakery breads and prepared pizza and washing dishes).
[3]Convenience system is using maximum amount of processed foods (for example, using all bakery breads, prefried chicken, and proportioned condiments and washing only trays or using disposable dinnerware).

Other Guidelines for Staffing

The National Food Service Management Institute will be publishing new guidelines and new meal equivalents based more on the federal reimbursement rates for a free lunch. The three breakfasts and $3 in a la carte sales equaling one meal equivalent suggested in this text are easy to remember and will be usable for several years.

Mayo and Olsen (1985) argue that "meals per labor hour" works only when all parts of the lunch are served. With the "offer verses serve" option, Mayo and Olsen recommend allocating labor hours based on portions served. They found that 71 to 73 servings per labor hour were the mean for producing food from raw ingredients. The formula they used follows:

$$\frac{\text{Total food portions}}{\text{Total labor hours}} \quad = \quad \text{Portions produced per labor hour}$$

Since most students take at least four menu items, the "meals per labor hour" still seems to be a fair way of determining labor hours. Figuring the staff based on portions equated to 15 to 18 meals per labor hour. Table 6.3 provides staffing guidelines that take into consideration the smaller operations and those that still produce from raw ingredients. It provides goals for those meeting the low productivity levels to strive for the high productivity levels. School districts that use these guidelines have kept their labor costs under 40% of the revenue and that is the goal.

The Mississippi State Department of Education has set its staffing standards between 14 meals per labor hour (as low productivity) and 18 meals per labor hour (as high). There are many other guidelines for staffing and determining meal equivalents which may result in schools being staffed with more or less labor hours than Table 6.3. Regardless of the guidelines used, the school district's cost of labor (including benefits) should not exceed 50% of the income.

Factors to Consider

Attitude toward work has a lot to do with the productivity level of employees. Many employees do not see school foodservice as a business and are holding on to what they "have always done." Employees need to be involved in the financial picture of operating a self-supporting program, if productivity is to be increased. Across the country the productivity levels vary greatly, from a low of 5 MPLH to 25-26 MPLH for on-site production.

Unless the productivity rate of school foodservices increases, or new payscales are instituted during the early 2000s, labor costs in many school districts will force meal prices up to the point that students will be unable to afford a lunch at school **or** the districts' general funds will be subsidizing the foodservice programs.

Most school foodservices have added a great many convenience foods in the last ten years, discontinuing much of the "from scratch" cooking, which should mean less labor is needed. However, many choices have been added to menus, requiring slightly more labor hours than no-choice menus. The use of disposable dishes has increased, which should reduce the labor hours needed, but the changes have been so gradual that employees have adjusted to making the work last longer.

There are no magic formulas that can be applied to staffing all foodservices. The number of employees needed and the labor hours will be influenced by a number of factors, including the following:

1. **Type of foodservice operation:** On-site production, central kitchen operation, finishing kitchen operation, preplated meals, etc., require different amounts of labor. On-site production will usually have the lowest productivity and preplated meals the highest.
2. **Number of meals to be served at the location:** The smaller operation (serving under 200 meals) will have a higher labor cost percentage than an operation twice the size. The larger the operation, the higher the productivity can be.
3. **Menus:** The no-choice menu will take less labor than the choice menu, particularly in smaller schools.

4. **Type of food used:** Cooking from "scratch" with raw materials, heavy use of convenience foods, or an arrangement somewhere in between must be carefully considered.

5. **Number and length of lunch periods:** The most common and workable schedule in high schools, for example, are three 30-minute lunch periods. Scheduling four or five lunch periods, or lunch over extended time, means more labor needed.

6. **Kinds and arrangement of equipment:** It will make a difference if the equipment is automated or manual. A compact, well-designed, and efficiently planned kitchen can mean increased productivity (versus a too-large, awkward, poorly planned kitchen, which may reduce productivity).

7. **Number of serving lines:** A serving line should be able to handle at least 100 students in 10 minutes. The more serving lines, the more employees needed. How many employees are needed on a serving line? It depends on how much self-service is utilized and how many foods are to be actually served. Good "backup" (keeping food replenished) of serving line is imperative to the speed and efficiency of the line.

8. **Experience and training of employees:** Training in how to do jobs efficiently and correctly, along with experience in doing the jobs, makes a difference in the number of employees needed.

9. **Supervision:** Supervision and direction in what to do and when can mean a better flow of work and more effective staff performance. The value of work schedules cannot be overemphasized—they are a management tool.

10. **Using disposable service items or washing dishes:** The time dish washing takes will depend a great deal on the degree of automation of dish washing and how many dishes are involved. The cost of dish washing, including labor, detergents, utilities, and replacement, should be compared to using disposable eating utensils and trays (Table 6.4). Even when using disposables for students, using a mechanical dish machine for pots and pans may be beneficial to efficiency.

Table 6.4. Cost Comparison of Washing Dishes Versus Using Disposable Dishes

	Cost of Washing	Cost of Disposables
Disposables	$0.009	$0.089
Labor[1]	0.08	0.005
Detergents	0.008	—
Replacement of dishes, equipment[2]	0.042	—
Utilities (estimated)[3]	0.020	—
Total Cost	$0.159	$0.094

[1]$6.91 per labor hour (plus 25 percent fringe benefits).
[2]Replacement of entire set of dishes and silver in the period of one year (trays not replaced) and deprecation on machine over ten-year period was used.
[3]If trash collection costs are assessed by the district, the cost of the disposable option will increase.

Source: Adams 12 School District (Northglenn, CO) 1998. Used by permission.

Staffing Based On Sales

The schools not participating in the National School Lunch Program and those schools where the majority of their service is a la carte sales—not lunches—may prefer using a method employed by commercial foodservices. That method involves determining the percentage of the revenue that will be spent on labor and keeping within that amount. The question will still come back to, "How much time does it take to sell $700 in a la carte?" The factors affecting productivity listed earlier need to be considered, and basically depends on the number of items offered, how much preparation is involved, the time frame in which sales occur, and the type of service involved (for example, selling individually prepared soft-service ice cream will require more time than selling a fresh apple). Many schools bake cookies, pies and cakes for selling a la carte, whereas other schools may purchase all the a la carte items already prepared for sale and adding in recent years bottled water for sale.

Two different methods may be used to arrive at a staffing formula. Twenty-five percent of the revenue from a la carte sales could be designated for labor if most of the food consisted of convenience items and required little preparation. A labor cost of 25 to 30 (up to 40) percent of the revenue from a la carte sales is reasonable for selling most items which are prepared. For example, $300 a la carte sales average per day with labor costing 30 percent is figured as follows:

$$\$300 \times .30\ (30\%) = \$90\ \text{labor cost}$$

To determine how many labor hours can be used, divide $90 by the average wages including fringe benefits:

$$\$90 \div \$15\ \text{per hour (including benefits)} = 6\ \text{labor hours}$$

To sell $300 in a la carte sales will probably require two people —one two-hour and one three-hour shift, leaving the remaining for management time that is involved).

The other method (discussed earlier) involves converting a la carte sales to equivalent meals. Since a la carte items are usually priced to make a profit, the equivalent can be three to one (or $3 in a la carte sales equals one lunch). Using the example above, assuming 17 meals per labor hour, the labor needs would be determined as follows:

$$\$300 \div \$3 = 100\ \text{meals} \qquad \$100 \div 17 = 5.9\ \text{labor hours}$$

The more exact method would be to determine the actual time required for preparing and selling a la carte items at a school with the desired labor costs.

The Clarkstown Central (NY) School District has a goal of at least 18 MPLH and at least $30 in income for every labor hour. The tracking of dollars is by individual food station and the point of sales device.

Staffing for Breakfast

The amount of labor needed for a breakfast program depends on menu, the number of meals served, and how much preparation is involved. In some recent informal surveys of breakfast program menus, it was learned that 70-80 percent of the foods are convenience foods. In some cases there may be only one labor-intense menu a week. Management needs to decide if a less labor-intense menu can be substituted or if flexible staffing will allow for the needed labor on those days. For a simple menu, a formula of 50 breakfasts per labor hour is workable. When the menu consists of a packaged cereal, toast, and portioned juice and milk, very little labor is needed. Labor costs can be kept at a minimum by planning menus with baking that can be done along with the lunch the day before. If the preparation and cleanup of breakfast is worked into the day with the preparation of lunch, income is increased without increases in labor. Using disposables, such as small disposable trays, instead of washing dishes, may be an advantage if the labor is needed for only a short time and is unavailable for that period.

Many foodservices are able to add a breakfast program without increasing labor hours (possibly because they are overstaffed to begin with), but this is an excellent way to increase productivity and revenue. Most on-site production foodservices with a reasonably smooth operation can adjust to the addition of a breakfast program with little difficulty.

The adjustment to breakfast may not be as simple at a satellite school. Satellite foodservices may have a problem obtaining employees who will work for a one-hour period to serve breakfast. It could result in paying labor for more hours than needed to serve breakfast. Many school districts have been able to utilize an aide for another program to serve the breakfast and keep the number of hours down.

Determining Productivity and Comparing with Guidelines

To determine the productivity at a school, the meal equivalents should be divided by the labor hours to obtain the meals per labor hour (MPLH). Those MPLH are compared with the staffing guidelines in Table 6.3. If the existing MPLH are lower than the guidelines, the goal may be to increase productivity by either increasing meal equivalents or by decreasing the labor hours.

STAFFING A CENTRAL KITCHEN/RECEIVING SCHOOL

The growth of the central kitchen/satellite operation, producing food in one location and transporting it to others for service, has presented a need for this section on staffing the central kitchen/production kitchen and the receiving (finishing) school. Tables 6.5 and 6.6 provide some guidelines based on a survey of directors of some successful operations. There are a lot of factors that may affect staffing of schools—the degree of automation is a prime example.

Today many of the school satellite situations involve one kitchen preparing for itself (for the students on-site) and for two or three other schools. The more meals produced at one site, the better productivity can be; thus, reducing production kitchens should be a goal. In addition, little preparation is involved with the number of convenience foods used today, and the production kitchen is often a redistribution point and this controls costs.

When using the guidelines in Tables 6.5 and 6.6, all the meal equivalents are added together (all satellite schools) and the productivity rate is determined. Each school receiving food is staffed based on its meal equivalents and type of satelliting used. For example, if the central kitchen is based on its meal equivalents and type of satelliting used. For example, if the central kitchen is producing 2900 meal equivalents (MEQ) for 10 schools and transporting the food bulk hot, the central kitchen would be staffed at 60-70 MPLH. The ten receiving schools—each serving between 250 and 300—would be staffed at 24-29 MPLH, as shown below.

$$2900 \text{ MEQ} \div 70 \text{ MPLH} = 41.4 \text{ labor hours}$$
$$300 \text{ MEQ} \div 29 \text{ MPLH} = 10.3 \text{ labor hours (includes driver time)}$$

The average MPLH for the schools would be approximately 19-20 (2900 ÷ 144 labor hours = 20.1 MPLH)—relatively good for small schools, but may not be better than would be obtained from on-site production. The more volume from one location, the better the productivity at the central kitchen, as can be seen in Table 6.5.

If one school is producing for itself and only one to three other schools, using the on-site staffing guidelines (Table 6.2) may work best. For example, 1500 meals are produced—500 to serve on-site and 1000 to be divided among the three schools. The production kitchen would be staffed with 21 MPLH, or 71 ½ hours (including the receiving schools)—approximately 10 hours at each of the receiving schools depending upon the type of system being used. See Chapter 5 for more information regarding central production kitchens. *cent + 4 or mor schools*

Table 6.5. Sample Staffing Guidelines for Production of Food for More Than One School

NUMBER OF MEAL EQUIVALENTS (1)	MPLH AND NUMBER OF LABOR HOURS BY TYPE OF PREPARATION SYSTEM[1]				
	BULK COLD[2] MPLH (2)	BULK HOT MPLH (3)	PRE-PLATED COLD (BAG)[3] MPLH (4)	PRE-PLATED FROZEN[1,2] MPLH (5)	PRE-PLATED HOT[2] MPLH (6)
200—500	25-30	27-32	21-26	22-27	20-25
501—1,000	30-35	30-35	30-35	37-42	40-45
1,001—2,000	50-55	45-50	50-55	55-60	60-65
2,001—3,000	65-75	60-70	100-110	120-130	130-140
3,001—5,000	75-85	70-80	110-120	120-130	130-140
5,001—10,000	110-130	110-120	110-120	120-135	130-150
10,001—20,000	150-160	120-130	120-130	120-135	130-150
20,000—30,000	160-175	130-160	130-150	135-150	150-160
30,001 up	175-195	160-175	130-150	150-175	160-190

[1]Transporting of food should be figured. The amount of time will depend on the number of stops, distance, number of meals, and type menus; however, the cost of delivering should be included in total cost.

[2]Requires heating at site before serving.

[3]Highly automated when over 2,000 food items are prepared.

Table 6.6. Sample Staffing Guidelines for Satellite Schools and Finishing Kitchens

NUMBER OF MEAL EQUIVALENTS	MPLH AND NUMBER OF LABOR HOURS BY TYPE OF PREPARATION SYSTEM				
	BULK COLD[1] (FK)	BULK HOT (FK)	PRE-PLATED COLD (BAG)	PRE-PLATED FROZEN[2]	PRE-PLATED HOT
	MPLH	MPLH	MPLH	MPLH	MPLH
Up to 75	16-20	17-22	75-80	30-35	50-55
76—100	18-23	19-23	75-80	30-35	50-55
101—200	20-25	21-26	100-110	50-55	75-80
201—300	22-27	24-29	100-110	60-65	75-80
301—400	26-31	26-31	100-110	60-65	75-80
401—500	26-31	28-33	100-110	60-65	75-80
501—700	28-33	30-35	100-110	60-65	75-80
701 up	30-35	32-37	100-110	60-65	75-80

Definition of terms used in Tables 6.5 and 6.6 are as follows:

Bulk Cold—food cooked, then chilled or frozen (e.g., cook-chill system) and transported for finishing off in the receiving (finishing) school.

Bulk Hot—food cooked and maintained hot through transporting and serving at the receiving (serving) school.

Pre-Plated Cold (Bag)—food prepared and bagged or pre-plated ready for distributing at the receiving (serving) school.

Pre-Plated Frozen—food prepared, portioned and frozen, then transported ready for heating for service.

Pre-Plated Hot—food prepared, portioned, and transported on the day of service, hot, ready-to-eat.

On-site production requires the most labor and has a lower productivity level than efficient satellite systems.

[1]Needs heating, portioning, and serving.
[2]Needs heating and serving.

DISTRIBUTION AND SCHEDULING OF LABOR HOURS

The number of labor hours available should be distributed throughout the work day among the number of people and at the times needed. Scheduling a combination of part-time and full-time employees is usually the most efficient way to staff a foodservice. The one-meal-a-day foodservice does not need cooks and bakers for seven or eight hours each day.

The productivity of foodservice workers is greatest during the first six hours of work and declines after that. When breaking down the labor hours and distributing the hours, the number of employees needed for serving should be decided first. (See examples in Figures 6.5 and 6.6.)

Figure 6.5. Staffing an Elementary School Foodservice

Labor Assigned: 29 hours
Productivity rate: 17 meals per labor hour
Lunches served: 475
A la carte: $40   ($40 ÷ $3 = 13 meal equivalents)
Total of 488 meal equivalents (475 + 13
The 29 labor hours are divided among tasks and the number of employees is determined by the number of jobs that need to be done at lunch time. Three or four employees could cover the spots, e.g., cashier, server, backup/cook, and manager (could be the backup/cook at lunch).

Work	Hours
Preparation/set up	9
Serving	7 ½
Cleaning	5
Preparation	3
Management work/ accountability	4
Breaks	½
TOTAL	29

Figure 6.6. Staffing a High School Foodservice

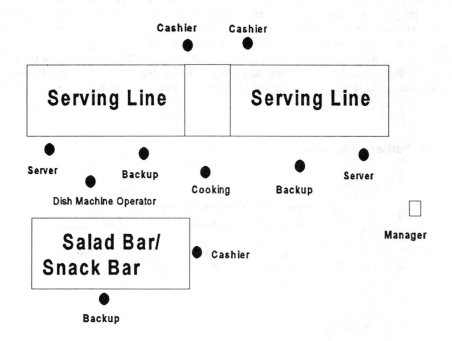

Assigned: 42½ hours
Productivity rate: 20 meals per labor hour
Lunches served: 750
A la carte $320 ($320 ÷ $3 = 106.6 equivalent meals)
Total meal equivalents = 856.6
The hours are divided among the positions and the
number of positions depends on the number needed
at lunch time. The employees are assigned hours
according to when the job needs to be done.

*Employees working five or more hours qualify for
free lunches, but eat the lunches on their time.

Staff	Time	Hours
Manager	7:30-3:00*	7
Cook	8:00-2:30*	6
Assistant/backup	9:00-2:30*	5
Assistant/cashier	8:30-2:00*	5
Cashiers (2)	10:00-1:00	6
Salad/backup	9:00-1:30	4
Dish machine/ clean	10:30-2:00	3½
Servers (2)	10:00-1:00	6
TOTAL		42½

Planning Work

When planning the schedule for the staff, the manager should determine assignments by using job descriptions and keeping each person's abilities in mind. It is necessary to schedule the specific jobs to be done within the time restraints. In order to ensure that all the jobs are completed at the correct time and nothing is omitted, the manager should plan daily work schedules.

Planning a work schedule means assigning workers to do specific jobs at particular times; all jobs and duties should be planned on a daily, weekly, monthly, or yearly basis. The purpose of a work schedule is to inform employees concerning the work to be done, their individual responsibilities, the sequence for each of their duties, and the time it should take to do the job.

Work schedules should be in writing and available to each employee. Some of the advantages of work schedules (Pannell-Martin, et al, 1992) are that they:

- Save time and energy; prevent employees from waiting around for someone to tell them what to do next.
- Distribute the workload evenly and inform the staff as to who is responsible for each job.
- Help the kitchen run more smoothly and more efficiently; help increase employees efficiency by setting deadlines.
- Make the job easier.
- Make it less likely that a job will not be done or will not be completed in time.
- Help the foodservice staff feel more secure, knowing that the job can be done within the time available, and take more pride in their work.
- Make employees more accountable for their assignments.

Parkinson's law which states that, "work expands to fill the time available," is illustrated at an overstaffed workplace without work schedules and time limits. One hour of work can be stretched out to fill two hours. Time needs to be managed. Employees have to be motivated to be efficient and time-conscious.

An example of a work schedule for an elementary school that serves 400 complete lunches a day is shown in Figure 6.7. When planning work schedules, it is important to determine how much time (labor hours) is available to accomplish the work and then how many people are needed (or available) at serving time, which is usually peak time. The labor hours assigned should be divided among the employees according to the assignments. The hours (the number and the times of day) assigned an employee should be based on the job to be done. The earned break(s) can be scheduled into the work day . The starting and ending times for each employee should be scheduled to the benefit of the foodservice program, whereas, food is ready when needed and not before. Batch cooking can be scheduled into the work schedule.

Computerized scheduling of employees and the workday has real merit. No one computer software has yet reached the market that takes into consideration all that is needed to plan a work schedule like the one in Figure 6.7.

Figure 6.7. Sample Work Schedule for a Small Elementary School Offering Three Choices

MENU - BREAKFAST
Cinnamon Rolls - Blueberry Muffins
French Toast (2) - Sausage (2)
Cereal - Toast(2)
Toast (2) - Sausage (2)
Orange Juice-Applesauce - Pineapple-Trail Mix

MENU - LUNCH
Spaghetti/Meat Sauce - Garlic French Bread
Chef Salad/Egg & Cheese - French Bread
Taco with Meat/Bean and Cheese
Tossed Salad/Dressing Applesauce - Fruit
Sherbet

inTeam Food System
WORK SCHEDULE
(To Be Completed for Each Day of Each Menu Cycle)

TUESDAY - WEEK 1

POSITION	Position 1 MANAGER	Position 2	Position 3
NUMBER HOURS	7 Hours	6 Hours	6 Hours
7:00-7:15	Unlock; pickup money; count. Prepare computer for breakfast.	Set out cereal and set up milk in cooler. Put cinnamon rolls and blueberry muffins in heated cabinet.	
7:15-7:30	Set out trays, napkins and sporks.	Prepare sausage and toast. Prepare French toast.	
7:30-7:45	Set out juice, fruit and trail mix.		
7:45-8:00	Setup serving line with hot food.		Prepare lettuce for tossed salad.
8:00-8:15	Cashier	Serve breakfast.	Slice cucumbers and shred carrots for chef salad.
8:15-8:30			Shred cheese for weeks menu.
8:30-8:45	Count breakfast money. Complete breakfast production record.	Put away breakfast. Clean serving line. Clean tables.	Dice tomatoes, chop onions for tacos. Cook eggs for chef salad.
8:45-9:00	*Set up juice, and fruit cup. Label breakfast and refrigerate.	*Pan sliced ham, cover with plastic bag and refrigerate. *Prepare egg mixture for Wednesday.	*Wrap and pan apple cinnamon muffins, coffee cake and English muffins in pan to be served in. Cover with plastic and refrigerate. Label.
9:00-9:15	*Set up 10 cereals.	Portion shredded cheese, onions & tomatoes. Prepare Garlic bread.	
9:15-9:30	Prepare computer and money for cashier.	Prepare spaghetti and meat sauce. Prepare meat and beans for tacos.	Prepare chef salads.
9:30-10:00	Portion applesauce. Mix tossed salad and portion.		
10:00-10:15	EAT LUNCH		Portion croutons. Wash pots and pans.
10:15-10:30		EAT LUNCH	
10:30-10:45	Wash fresh fruit and display. Place utensils and condiments on serving line.	Set up steam table. Check temperatures of food and steam table .	
10:45-11:00			
SERVE LUNCH 11:00 - 1:00			
11:00-11:15	Check line -Batch cook - Keep food on line. Back-up Observe and communicate with customers. Portion more fruits and fixings as needed.	Serving Line (Wash pots and pans during break in service).	Cashier - Spot check line for cleanliness, debris on floor, condiments needing replacement.
11:15-11:30			
11:30-11:45			
11:45-12:00			
12:00-12:15	Supervise money counting. Determine food used for 1st hour.		
12:15-12:30	Backup		
12:30-12:45	Place daily orders.		
12:45-1:00		Count food left/ portions - record.	
1:00-1:15	Supervise money counting. Close out computer.	Clean serving line. Cart canned items to be used following day. Check for following days items.	Count money. Prepare reconciliation form.
1:15-1:30	Determine food used for 2nd hour Check production record for food usage.		EAT LUNCH
1:30-1:45	Adjust next days record for leftovers.		
1:45-2:00	Complete production record.		Wash pots and pans. Wipe tables and seats. Store food in storeroom. Clean storeroom.
2:00-2:15	Check clean up. Final preparation for next day check.		
2:15-2:30			

* Next day's breakfast items.

**Schedule breaks as needed.

LABOR SHORTAGES AND TURNOVER

The shortage of service employees at the low end of the payscale and high turnover will be two of the most challenging personnel problems of the 2000s. Those factors will cause tremendous changes in the traditional kitchen and cause automation to flourish.

To figure the turnover rate, Buchanan (1973) provides the following formula:

$$\frac{\text{Number of separations from job during year} \times 100}{\text{Number of employees at midyear}} = \text{Turnover rate \%}$$

Example:
$$\frac{300 \text{ employees resigned} \times 100}{1075 \text{ employees}} = 28 \text{ percent}$$

The shortage of qualified school foodservice directors will be felt in the early 2000s, especially in California where 50 percent of the directors will reach retirement age in early 2000 (DeMicco, et al 1997). The definition of a "qualified school foodservice director" is so complex it sounds like one is describing a "super" human being. It certainly is desirable to have someone with good communication skills and who speaks more than one language to effectively communicate with the diverse staff and customer of today and the 2000s (Gregoire, Sneed, and Martin, 1993).

PAYSCALES AND LABOR COSTS

Minimum wage rates are discussed by Congress annually. A bill before Congress in 1999 would raise the minimum wage of 1999 from $5.15 to $5.65 in September 1999 and to $6.15 by mid-2000. Some states have established their own minimum rates with higher amounts; e.g., Washington state's minimum wage is $6.50. Herman Cain, president of the National Restaurant Association, debated against the increases in the minimum wage, stating that "146,000 jobs were eliminated in the restaurant industry as a direct result of the last wage hike. . . ." Few school districts start foodservice employees at the minimum wage but for some reason much higher. For example, while Wendy's in the Alexandria (VA) area starts inexperienced people at $5.15, the Alexandria City Schools are starting inexperienced people at $7.42. See Table 6.7 for an example of a payscale.

Unfortunately, the rate of pay per hour worked is not the only cost involved in labor, but included are a number of paid holidays and paid sick leave days, employer's share of taxes (Social Security, 6.2%, Medicare, 1.45%), worker's compensation, unemployment taxes, retirement benefits, health and life insurances, etc. The beginning pay may be $6.50, but the average cost of a labor hour (worked) is $14 or $15. In 1996 the average cost of a labor hour in 17 counties ranged from a low of $9.34 to a high of $17.63. *The Cost Control Manual for School Foodservice* (Pannell-Martin 1995) discusses this in more detail. Chapter 12, "Reducing Costs and Increasing Productivity," discusses reducing labor costs and certainly reducing the amount paid is a possibility.

Table 6.7. Sample Payscale for School Foodservice Employees for 1998-99 School Year

Grade	Number of Hours	Base	Step 1	Step 2	Step 3	Step 4	Step 5	Step 6-7	Step 8-9	Step 10
FOODSERVICE MANAGERS[1]										
3A[2]		$ 11.33	$ 11.80	$ 12.24	$ 12.74	$ 13.26	$ 13.80	$ 14.35	$ 14.91	$ 15.52
4A[3]		$ 11.94	$ 12.39	$ 12.90	$ 13.43	$ 13.95	$ 14.60	$ 15.17	$ 15.74	$ 16.29
5A[4]		$ 13.45	$ 13.99	$ 14.53	$ 15.13	$ 15.76	$ 16.36	$ 17.01	$ 17.69	$ 18.43
6A[5]		$ 14.89	$ 15.51	$ 16.13	$ 6.75	$ 17.44	$ 18.15	$ 18.84	$ 19.60	$ 20.37
7A[6]		$ 15.51	$ 16.13	$ 16.75	$ 17.44	$ 18.15	$ 18.84	$ 19.60	$ 20.37	$ 21.17
Foodservice Workers										
FSW 1-F3	3-6 Hours	$ 7.42	$ 7.76	$ 8.12	$ 8.46	$ 8.86	$ 9.26	$ 9.65	$ 10.08	$ 10.56
Foodservice Hostess										
Hostess	5 Hours	$6,678.00	$6,984.00	$7,308.00	$7,614.00	$7,974.00	$8,334.00	$8,685.00	$9,072.00	$9,504.00
	5.5 Hours	$7,345.80	$7,682.40	$8,038.80	$8,375.40	$8,771.40	$9,167.40	$9,553.50	$9,979.20	$10,454.40
Foodservice Delivery/Warehouse Workers										
F1		$ 8.34	$ 8.70	$ 9.13	$ 9.54	$ 9.93	$ 10.39	$ 10.86	$ 11.34	$ 11.87
F2		$ 8.70	$ 9.13	$ 9.54	$ 9.93	$ 10.39	$ 10.86	$ 11.34	$ 11.87	$ 12.35

Source: Alexandria City (VA) Public Schools. Used by permission.

[1] Grade level of each Foodservice Manager is based on the number of meals/meal equivalents served and is subject to change annually.
[2] Grade 3A—Up to 349 Meals, 6 and 7 hour positions
[3] Grade 4A—350 to 549 Meals, 6 and 7 hour positions
[4] Grade 5A—550 to 749 Meals, 6 and 7 hour positions
[5] Grade 6A—750 to 949 Meals, 6 and 7 hour positions
[6] Grade 7A—950+ Meals, 8 hour position

How many "pay increments" for longevity are reasonable? Some school districts' payscales have 15 to 20 steps whereby a staff employee after 20 years on the job may be at $13.50 per hour plus all the employee benefits. At what point do years of experience make a difference? The answer may be after "the first four or five years" or after the first "15 to 20 years"? The employee may be receiving a 2 to 5 percent longevity raise **and** a 2 to 4 percent cost of living raise annually. These automatic raises have happened in many school districts, and it has resulted in labor costs school districts cannot afford. People are not looking at jobs for the next 25 years, but instead for high wages now, and this has made step raises irrelevant in today's labor market.

For many years, high labor costs were common for larger cities in the East, but the South had low labor costs. Today the cost of labor in the New Orleans (LA) and Atlanta (GA) areas are equal to the cost in many of the large eastern cities, and this is because the labor shortages have force the wages up.

Chapter 2, "Financial Management," discussed how much of the revenue should be used for labor—40 to 45 percent of the revenue. Some school districts cannot afford for labor to take more than 35 to 38 percent of the revenue; however, in many school districts labor costs are consuming 60 percent of the revenue. This does not leave sufficient revenue for food, replacement equipment, and other costs.

SELECTED REFERENCES

Caton, J., and M. Nix. 1986. *I Can Manage: A Practical Approach*. New York: Van Nostrand Reinhold.

Cetron, M., F. DeMicco, and J. Williams. 1996. "Restaurant Renaissance." *The Futurist* (January-February) 8-12.

DeMicco, F., J. Williams, H. Oh, W. Maurice, P. McElwain, and D. Boss. 1997. "In Search of School Food Service Leaders: The Next Millennium." *School Food Service Research Review* 21(1): 2-4.

Gregoire, M., J. Sneed, and J. Williams. 1993. "School Food Service: A Look to the Future." *School Food Service Research Review* 17(1): 175-191.

Herman, R. 1998. *Keeping Good People*. Greensboro, NC: Oakhill Press.

Keiser, J. and F. DeMicco. 1993. *Controlling and Analyzing Costs in Food Service Operations*. 4th ed. New York: Macmillan.

Mayo, C. 1981. "Variables That Affect Productivity in School Food Services." Ph D dissertation. Blacksburg: Virginia Polytechnic Institute and State University.

Mayo, C., and M. Olsen. 1985. "Food Servings per Labor Hour: An Alternative Productivity Measure." *School Food Service Research Review* 11(1): 48-51

Miller, J., and D. Hayes. 1994. *Basic Food and Beverage Cost Control*. New York: John Wiley & Sons, Inc.

Pannell-Martin, D. 1995. *Cost Control Manual for School Foodservice*. 2nd ed. Alexandria, VA: inTEAM Associates, Inc.

_____. 1998. *Controlling Costs in the Foodservice Industry*. Alexandria, VA: inTEAM Associates, Inc.

_____. G. Applebaum, and E. Soares. 1998. *Manager's Food Production Book*. Alexandria, VA: inTEAM Associates, Inc.

Payne-Palacio, J., and M. Theis. 1997. *West and Wood's Introduction to Foodservice*. 8th ed. Upper Saddle River, NJ: Prentice-Hall, Inc.

Rinke, W. 1995. "Total Quality Management: Just Another Management Fad?" *Dietary Manager* 4 (1): 10-13.

Spears, M. 1995. *Foodservice Organizations: A Managerial and Systems Approach*. 3rd ed. Upper Saddle River, NJ: Prentice-Hall, Inc.

VanEgmond-Pannell, D. 1987. *Focus: Management Skills for School Foodservice Managers*. Jackson: Mississippi State Department of Education, Child Nutrition Programs.

White, G., T. Sneed, and J. Martin. 1992. "School Food Service in the Year 2000 and Beyond." *School Food Service Research Review* 10 (2): 103.

Wynn, J. 1973. "Staffing Broward County Style." *School Food Service Journal* 27(1): 44-54.

7
MANAGING HUMAN RESOURCES

Overview of the Labor Market

Labor-Related Laws

Unions

Orientation and Training
> Orientation
> Training
> Employee Dress Code

Performance Appraisals
> Employee Incentives
> Standards for Evaluating Performance
> Importance of Performance Appraisals

Disciplinary Action

Drugs and Alcohol in the Kitchen

Motivating Employees

Management Trends

Selected References

OVERVIEW OF THE LABOR MARKET

In the 1950s this chapter would have been called "Personnel Management." During that period personnel management was little more than seeing that there were sufficient people to do the work and that the paperwork was done so the employees got paid. The 1970s and 1980s were known as "employees' rights" years. The federal government performed the role of protector of the employee. Even if an employee did not perform his or her job especially well, the paychecks continued. School districts seemed to be more susceptible than others to this climate and required management to have "just reasons" for any action, which may have intimidated management. In the 1990s there has been more emphasis on the employee doing the job effectively, and the rights of both the employee and the employer. The 2000s will be driven by efforts to increase productivity, downsize, and find enough short-hour employees to do the job.

During the 1990s "Generation Y", the 18- to 24-year-old group, and the "Generation X" group, ages 25-34, together has made up 56% of the foodservice workforce as a whole. They are described as a group that will work hard, but will be demanding as they enter the middle-age years. Three very different generations—"Generation Y and X," baby boomers, and those over 50—make up the school foodservice workplace, and they have different goals and characteristics. The differences in values of these three or four generations have caused some conflicts; however, employees in general have become more accepting of differences as cultural differences also have become more commonplace. Table 7.1 shows the increases in Hispanics and Asians in the labor force. The attitudes and values of the different generations and cultures will be challenging to management in the future. The older employees, who want to feel that what they are doing is a contribution to society, are retiring. The middle-aged employees will want more meaningful work and will want group involvement and participation. The younger employees may want to move up the ladder of success and be willing to work hard to do so. However, some of the younger group may seem demanding and plugged into their own worlds—wanting to work when they what to work, to do what they want to, and to do no more than they have to. It has been said that the older worker "lives to work" and the younger worker "works to live."

Employees want to be appreciated for the job they do (an expectation not new to this century). Most managers will agree that employees basically want to do a good job. They want to take pride in what they do and in the school district for which they work. The continued success of companies like Federal Express and Apple Computer has been based on employee pride. Employees want to know that they are contributing something good to the community in general and that they are growing. When this happens, the results are happy, motivated employees with good morale and a positive attitude.

The 2000s will see more merit pay, employee accountability for time spent, employee incentives, and a need for increased productivity. "Re-engineering," meaning reorganizing, and "right-sizing" will be common practices as the need for reducing costs become more serious.

Labor shortages will be a leading personnel problem for school foodservice as the need for service employees in general continues to increase in the 2000s. These labor shortages have already been felt in some parts of the country, and recruiting has become necessary to fill many positions. Some school districts have resorted to "temporaries incorporated" for their short-hour employees. "Recruitment" is a new word to some in school foodservice: however it may become more familiar since these labor shortages are expected to continue through 2010. School districts have become more skilled at recruitment as the needs have become greater.

Table 7.1. Labor Force Changes (in millions)

	1986	2000	Annual Growth Rate %
White	101.8	116.7	1.0
Black	12.7	16.3	1.8
Hispanic	8.1	14.1	4.1
Asian and Other	3.4	5.7	3.9

Source: U. S. Bureau of the Census 1998.

LABOR-RELATED LAWS

Anyone who works with recruiting, interviewing, hiring, and, particularly, managing employees needs to be familiar with the Fair Labor Standards laws. Employees have rights by law, and ignorance of the law is not an acceptable excuse in a discrimination suit.

The Fair Labor Standards laws are especially concerned with equality and the rights of the person. These concerns apply not only in the selection process but in the treatment of the person on the job. Lack of knowledge about these laws can result in discrimination charges being brought against a manager/supervisor or a school district. Some of the Fair Labor laws that school foodservice management needs to know date back as far as 1938, with the **Fair Labor Standard Act**. Other more recent laws are discussed briefly below.

The Americans with Disabilities Act (1990) protects disabled Americans who are not covered under existing laws. Two major pieces of legislation regarding handicapped people were the **Discrimination Guidelines of the Revised Code, Chapter 4112**, and **Section 504 of the Rehabilitation Act of 1973**, which make it illegal to exclude disabled applicants as a group on the basis of their disability. If the disability would prevent a person from performing a job, the employer does not have to employ the person; however the employer could have to defend that decision.

The Civil Rights Act of 1964 (Title VII) became effective in 1965 and was revised in 1972, and again in 1991, as the **Equal Employment Opportunity Act**. This law makes it unlawful for employers to refuse to hire, to discharge, or to discriminate with respect to compensation or terms and conditions on the basis of race, color, religion, sex, age, or national origin. It applies to all employers that have 15 or more employees and to public school systems, regardless of how many people are employed. The Civil Rights Act and the Equal Employment Opportunity Act are concerned with more than discrimination. It requires that (1) certain safety regulations be followed, (2) equal rights in selection and transfer of employees be followed, (3) minimum hourly rates be paid, and (4) suitable jobs be found for unemployed minority people who have the skills and meet the qualifications. The Equal Employment Opportunity Commission investigates complaints by applicants and employees when this act has not been carried out.

The **Age Discrimination in Employment Act of 1967** and the amendments of 1978 promote the employment of older persons, 40 to 70 years of age, based on ability, not age. This law prohibits discrimination against people between these ages. It makes it illegal to ask the age or age group of applicants, or to request proof of their ages before hiring. After employing, it is legal to require proof of age, if it is needed. For example, if the position requirement is that a person be 18 years old and the person does not look 18 years old, the employer can ask the person to provide his or her age after the person has been employed. Also, retirement plans will require verification of age.

Title IX of the Educational Amendments of 1972 and the amendments of 1978 ban discrimination on the basis of sex in all federally assisted education programs. They also make it illegal to ask in an interview about marital status, number and ages of children, who takes care of the children while the mother works, and similar matters. Further, they make it illegal to ask if a woman is a "Miss," "Mrs.," or "Ms." or to ask for her maiden name or previous name used.

Other labor legislation that is relevant includes the **Family and Medical Leave Act of 1993, Pregnancy Discrimination Act of 1978**; and **Equal Pay Act of 1963**, which requires employers to provide equal pay for men and women performing similar work. The purpose of these laws is to prevent discriminatory practices. The Equal Employment Opportunity Office is the watchdog and will investigate employers reported as discriminating.

Affirmative Action, which is required nationwide by executive order, requires that an employer make efforts to hire and promote minority groups.

The **overtime pay requirement** became effective in 1986 for public school employees. The employer is required to provide overtime compensation to nonexempt employees who work more than 40 hours per week. Compensation can be in either of two forms: (1) **overtime pay** at a rate of 1½ times the regular rate of pay for all hours worked over 40 hours in a regular work week, or (2) **compensatory time off** at a rate of 1½ hours for each hour worked over 40 hours in a regular work week.

The school district needs to identify those who are nonexempt and exempt. The foodservice manager may or may not be exempt, depending on whether the person is employed to do a job within a certain period of time, as in the case of a principal. If the person is employed to complete a job, then the person is exempt and does not qualify for overtime pay, however, there are specific rules pertaining to this and the employer needs to obtain a copy of these rules.

It is the management's responsibility to see that an employee who is nonexempt does not continue to work past the 40 hours, unless the overtime rate is to be paid. An employee of the school may volunteer, however, to provide services to the school or school district without the hours worked as a volunteer counting toward overtime compensation; the volunteer services provided should not be "the same type services which the individual is employed to perform." For example, a foodservice cook who volunteers to work at a PTA fund raiser should not be assigned to cook, but instead to do something unlike the paid job, such as taking tickets.

There are no federal laws requiring employers to give employees breaks—not even to eat, use the bathroom, or make personal telephone calls. Some states have laws regarding breaks; e.g., California has a law that workers are to be granted a 30-minute break within five hours of starting work or 10 minutes every four hours if they work six hours. A foodservice director needs to check the state laws regarding employees. In New Mexico and Arkansas, laws require breaks for women employees only. It is usually local policies (perhaps union contracts) that decide if and when employees will take a break. Lunch breaks may be given but they do not have to be paid; many school districts provide a free lunch to the employees and pay them to eat the lunch. Policies such as this need to be examined because breaks are expensive, and the trend is for management to tighten up on nonproduction time. However, studies show that productivity begins to fall off after three to four hours, and a break can result in increased productivity. Dayton (OH) Public Schools Nutrition Services has the following break policy:

8-hour employees -------------	two 10-minute breaks
4-hour employees--------------	one 10-minute break
2 to 3 ½-hour employees------	no breaks

The **Immigration Reform and Control Act of 1986** requires that employers verify employees' eligibility to work if hired after November 6, 1986. To be eligible, a person must be (1) a citizen of the United States, (2) an alien lawfully admitted for permanent residence, or (3) an alien with a work permit authorized by the Immigration and Naturalization Service to work in the United States. A form referred to as I-9, provided by the U.S. Department of Justice, Immigration and Naturalization Service, requires that the employer review acceptable documents as verification of eligibility and complete and sign a form stating that the documents have been verified.

The Occupational Safety and Health Act (OSHA) of 1970 has the mission "to assure so far as possible every working man and woman in the Nation safe and healthful working conditions and to preserve our human resources." It is important to provide a safe place for people to work, not only for morale and human considerations but also because of OSHA. If an employee is injured on the job, the employer can be sued if the injury was due to negligence or unsafe working conditions. New regulations are in discussion that would make sweeping changes in the workplace. The new rules would mandate that every employer establish safety training programs.

Many questions management may need answers to are answered in the **Legal Problem Solver for Foodservice Operators** (Griffith et al. 1987). Among these are the following: Does training time have to be considered work time? Can English language proficiency be required and tested? Can an employee be required to wear a uniform?

UNIONS

Many school district foodservice employees belong to unions. In these districts, employees use collective bargaining as a means of acting as a single unit when dealing with management. The areas of common concern are wages and fringe benefits, hours and scheduling, layoffs and firings, days off, rest breaks, and paid holidays.

An important element of good labor-management relations is the bargaining group, which is the group that represents management. They meet with a group of employees and come to an agreement on issues of pay, fringe benefits, and work conditions. In the 1960s, 1970s, and 1980s management was often weak at the bargaining tables and gave what was asked. In the 1990s management began taking back and truly "bargaining."

The U.S. Office of Personnel Management (Biasatti and Martin 1979) identified the elements essential for effective union-management relations:

1. Acceptance of collective bargaining
2. Balance of power between the union and management
3. Respect for each other's goals
4. Recognition of common goals
5. Well-organized labor relations programs set up by management
6. High level of communication
7. Sincere negotiations
8. Effective administration of the labor contract
9. Comprehensive grievance processes
10. Evaluation by both parties of their relationship
11. Sense of participation in their own welfare on the part of employees

Though these elements were identified in 1979, they are good today and need to be practiced.

ORIENTATION AND TRAINING

Orientation

Employee orientation to the workforce should be comprehensive and a requirement for all new employees. Most employees who are new to school foodservices need training. They may or may not have any experience or knowledge of food, particularly regarding preparation of large quantities. Even new, experienced employees need to be taken through orientation to the job, introduced to the principal, told of expectations, and shown how the job assigned is to be done. Also, orientation and making employees aware of the foodservice goals are necessary when the job the person is to do is different from any job he or she has done before, or if the manager wants the job performed in a specific way.

How an employee is oriented can have an impact on how long it takes the new employee to learn the job, how well the person likes the job, the attitudes of fellow staff members toward the new employee, and job turnover. As soon as a person is employed, that person begins to share in forming group morale or group spirit.

An orientation checklist such as that shown in Figure 7.1 can be used for new employees. A checklist will help ensure that the orientation is complete and includes all the areas intended. Others that could be added are who to call to report absence, career ladder, and how foodservice is a business today.

Figure 7.1. Employees Orientation Checklist

_____ **Basic Information**: School name, grades in school, principal's name, manager's name, and general information about the foodservice program, including objectives.

_____ **Welcome:** Greetings to make the employee feel at ease.

_____ **Introduction:** Introduction to the other employees in the kitchen. Tell the new employees something about what each one does.

_____ **Uniform**: Dress code. If uniforms are furnished, make arrangements for employees to obtain them as soon as possible. Discuss good grooming standards, basic cleanliness, hand washing, hair restraints, and policy on jewelry, shoes, stockings, and aprons.

_____ **Payroll:** Payday, length of pay periods, how paychecks are delivered, and how overtime is calculated

_____ **Requirements:** Social Security number, completion of federal and state tax forms, sanitation certification (if applicable) requirements, and verification of eligibility to work.

_____ **Expectations:** What the duties are and what is expected of the employee– "a day's work for a day's pay."

_____ **Policies**: Breaks and mealtimes. Whether the meal is a fringe benefit or the employee must pay for it. Vacation days, personal leave, sick leave, and other types of leave, and when they can be taken. What to do in case the employee is sick or for some other reason cannot be at work.

_____ **Performance Review**: When the employee will be reviewed, by what criteria, and the importance of the performance review.

_____ **Sanitation and Foodservice**: The importance of good personal habits, hand washing, and how the food should be handled.

_____ **Tour of the Kitchen**: Where to park, a tour of the kitchen, and where things are within the school facilities. Where things are located, such as dry storage, detergent closet, locker or place to store purse, coat, etc., and restrooms.

_____ **Training:** Determination of training needed and provision of training for the job to be done.

_____ **Professional Growth Opportunities**: Staff development opportunities, training, and policy regarding promotions.

_____ **Introduction to Job**: Introduction to the particular job the employee will be doing.

Signed by Employee   Date

Signed by Person in Charge of Orientations

Adapted from Mississippi State Department of Education 1987. Used by permission.

Training

Training is the key to a strong, successful school foodservice program today. It is an ongoing process and should never stop. It is the central administration's responsibility to train the manager and a manager's responsibility to train staff. Some of the advantages of a good training program are:

- Low employee turnover
- Low absenteeism
- Few accidents
- Job satisfaction, less complaints and grievances
- High morale
- Low production costs
- High sanitation habits
- Good utilization of commodities
- Increased productivity
- Improve quality of operation

Training should take place when someone is new to a job, when new equipment is purchased, when government regulations or other procedures are changed, and when skills need polishing. Sometimes employees will need to be retrained in order to obtain certain standards desired. In addition, some foodservice directors/managers may need training in the areas of cost-effectiveness, quality food production, or compliance with federal regulations. There appears to be a definite need for more training in the accountability requirements in the School Meals Initiative areas. Unfortunately Nutrition Education and Training monies are no longer as readily available to each state for these purposes.

Because learning is so complex, it is important to use many different approaches to teaching school foodservice employees. Though a person can listen at 700 words per minute, what is remembered the next day is much less. Just "telling" an employee something is a poor method of teaching. It has been said that:

- 20 percent of what is said to a person generally is remembered.
- 30 percent of what a person sees is likely to be remembered.
- 60 percent of what a person sees and hears will be remembered
- 80 percent of what a person does will be remembered.

Some basic principles of learning that are applicable when training foodservice employees are as follows:

- The learner must want to learn before learning can take place.
- The learner must be interested in the subject before he or she will learn.
- The learner remembers things taught that he or she can use right away.
- Absorption of information is more effective if it is based on seeing and doing. The learner remembers things which have made a deep impression.
- The learner remembers things best that are pleasant and tries to forget the unpleasant.

"Hands-on" experiences should be provided as much as possible for maximum retention of learning. On-the-job training can be effective with hands-on experience. For a manager to carry out on-the-job training successfully, he or she will need to know how to operate every piece of equipment in the kitchen. If on-the-job training is delegated, it should be ensured that the person delegated to do the training (1) is using correct methods, (2) knows how to operate the equipment correctly and safely, and (3) can do the job correctly. When proper methods are not taught, poor working practices become inbred.

Employee Dress Code

A uniform dress code policy is needed. The following uniform policy has said it well when describing why the employee dress is important:

> Each Child Nutrition employee is expected to give proper attention to his/her personal appearance. A pleasing appearance in dress and manner influences the reaction of the students to the Child Nutrition employees and to the general school environment. A Child Nutrition employee, also, comes in daily contact with the public, a public which is sometimes very critical of the appropriateness and neatness of a school employee's dress. The Child Nutrition employee who is particular about personal appearances not only contributes to his/her own acceptance by others, but also influences the attitudes of the students and adults toward the Child Nutrition profession. The matter of appropriate dress should be of equal standards of good grooming, as well as promote the safety and well-being of Child Nutrition employees in the performance of their duties. In the interest of enhancing the image of the Child Nutrition profession, at the school and in the community, as well as complying with the requirements of the Louisiana State Department of Education, and applicable local, state, and federal health and safety requirements, it shall be required that each Child Nutrition employee comply with the following uniform policy in the official performance of their duties during the course of the school day.
> Source: Jefferson Parish (LA) Schools 1999. Used by permission.

The image of school foodservices is influenced by how employees look, the cleanliness of uniform, the body appearance, and hair covering. White uniforms and hairnets, which reminds people of surgery, are being replaced with a more contemporary look—bright colored shirts with pants or skirts and a visor or baseball cap. Employees in street clothes should be avoided.

PERFORMANCE APPRAISALS

As teacher performance standards and merit pay are developed and become more commonly used in determining increases in pay, performance appraisals for support service employees, like foodservices staff, will become more meaningful. Performance appraisals should be objective, consistent, and fair. They should identify the quantity and quality of work an employee performs and the areas in which improvement or additional training is needed. When yearly raises are not tied to performance, there may be high labor costs and low efficiency.

Employee Incentives

Schools have not utilized employee incentive plans and merit pay programs to the extent that some commercial companies have. School board policies and lack of need in the past may be responsible. Money can be a good motivator when it is a reward for accomplishment. Under a merit pay program, performance is appraised periodically and salary is adjusted to reflect the individual's output or accomplishments. In order for it to work, it is essential to have (1) a written policy, (2) accurate standards and reporting, (3) a bonus worth earning, and (4) incentive earnings or a visible merit bonus (paid by separate check).

A school foodservice manager's pay raises should be tied to accomplishing goals and operating a successful foodservice. Incentives are needed to provide good food and services, and develop good customer relations. There are some motivators that cost very little—praise and rewards, even in as small a form as a certificate. Rewards need to be obtainable and immediate. Many of today's employees do not respond well to delayed gratification.

The price tag (what it may cost) for incentives may be a stumbling block to some school districts, but there are creative ways of managing the price tag. For example, one foodservice director created a "white elephant" store where employees can shop free as a reward for certain accomplishments. According to *FoodService Director* (1988), the South Washington (MN) Independent School District pays foodservice employees based on performance. The foodservice director believes service to students and the morale of the employees has improved as a results. The bonuses are based on performances in four areas: overall operation, labor efficiency, food cost, and cashier accuracy.

Standards for Evaluating Performance

When standards exist they can be used to evaluate performance. The school foodservice management should establish reasonable goals and quotas each year for the foodservice manager, and the manager, in turn, for the staff employees. Should a goal for the manager be to reduce labor costs, then one of the goals for the staff would be to improve efficiency and serve more meals without increasing labor.

There are very few merit and efficiency standards for evaluating performance one can use at present in foodservice. However, the following indicators can be used:

1. The number of meals per labor hour (used to judge the efficiency of a staff as a whole)
2. A positive balance on the profit and loss statement (used to judge a manager's ability to manage finances)
3. Increases in the number served in a prescribed time (used to judge the efficiency of the staff)
4. Increased participation (an indicator of meeting customer needs)
5. The inventory turnover rate of at least two per month (used to judge the manager's ability to forecast and order)

People are motivated by standards that are realistic and will usually meet them or even surpass them if they are the types of employees management wants in permanent positions.

A part of the job of a director, supervisor, and manager is to evaluate employee work performance. School districts usually have their own criteria and standards to use when evaluating employees. The performance appraisal (evaluation) should be tied to the job description. Employees should be made fully aware of the expectations and be informed on how to reach them.

The profit and loss statements can be used to judge a manager's ability to manage finances (if the prices of food offerings are correctly set). Increases in the number served in a prescribed time can be an indication of efficiency. Increased participation can be an indicator of meeting customer needs.

The formal performance appraisal should be written and it should include documentation (see Figure 7.2). The job performance, not personality traits, should be evaluated.

A system of measuring quantity and quality of work and evaluating performance based on standards may take many different forms, but basically it is based on such benchmarks as the following (based on Nolan, et al. 1980).

> 150 percent: super-skilled level
> 135 percent: expert pace
> 120 percent: incentive pace
> 100 percent: fair day's work pace
> 85 percent: acceptable Level
> 70 percent: minimum tolerable level
> 50 percent: unacceptable level

The rewards for performance need to be carefully thought out and appropriate for the qualities displayed by the employee. The employee evaluations become important when management responds in ways such as the following:

- *Superior performance, exceptional* (150%) = reward and/or promotional opportunity
- *Above average, exceeds requirement or standards* (120-135%) = increment raise
- *Satisfactory, meets all requirements* (85-100%) = cost-of-living raise
- *Below standard, needs improvement* (70%) = maintenance of present pay
- *Unsatisfactory, unable to meet standards* (50%) = removal from position

Importance of Performance Appraisals

The performance appraisal is a motivational tool that can challenge, reward, and provide positive strokes. The appraisal process should help a person determine what to do in order to become a better employee and to grow and be promoted.

The performance appraisal should be tied to pay raises, and raises should not be automatic. In some cases, it is tied to tenure status. The first six months or the first year of employment may be a probationary period. If it is, a person should receive an informal appraisal at intervals during the first year, so that the employee knows how he or she is doing. The probationary period is the time to terminate a new employee's employment if the employee cannot do the job or is not dependable.

Figure 7.2. Employee Appraisal Form/Performance Evaluation Report Form

Employee's Name	Social Security No.	Cost Center Name	Cost Center No.
Position Title	Employee Status	If Unscheduled Report Check Here: ❏	DUE DATE

SECTION A			Immediate supervisor must check each category in appropriate column	SECTION B Superior performance in any category should be described in detail. Check marks in "Unsatisfactory" or "Requires Improvement" must be supported with documentation.
U	RI	MS	FACTOR CHECK LIST	
			1. Observance of Work Hours: Is dependable and punctual in attendance.	U = Unsatisfactory RI = Requires Improvement MS = Meets Standards
			2. Productivity/Quality of Work: Completes an acceptable level of quality work.	
			3. Job Skill Level: Demonstrates required skills.	
			4. Communication Skills: Communicates well orally and in writing; effectively carries out verbal and written instructions.	
			5. Working Relationships: Works with and relates to others effectively.	ATTACHMENTS ADDED YES ❏ NO ❏
			6. Adaptability/Flexibility: Accepts change; works effectively under stress; responds to varying needs.	
			7. Observance of Safety/Health Standards: Demonstrates Knowledge of district safety/ health/sanitary procedures.	

SECTION C
Employee was counseled on noted deficiencies: (Dates)
SUMMARY EVALUATION: Unsatisfactory ❏ Requires Improvement ❏   Meets Standards ❏

IF PROBATIONARY: I do not ❏ I do ❏ RECOMMEND PERMANENT STATUS

SECTION D
Goals and Objectives:
       Continue to accept new learning experiences when offered. Watch for information on various food-related courses offered at local junior colleges and through foodservice department for San Diego City Schools— inservice training classes. (These courses help provide a better understanding of our goals and aims within our own foodservice department.)

RATER:	REVIEWER:
_____ Signature Date	_____ Signature Date

My supervisor has discussed this evaluation report with me and given me a copy of this report. I understand my signature does not necessarily indicate agreement.
Comments:

_____   _____
ATTACHMENTS ADDED   YES ❏ NO ❏   Signature   Date

Figure 7.2. Employee Appraisal Form/Performance Evaluation Report (continued)

INSTRUCTIONS FOR USE OF THE PERFORMANCE EVALUATION REPORT FORM

The Performance Evaluation Report Form is designed to help those being evaluated to achieve and maintain high levels of work performance and behavior. The form can be used by supervisors as an effective counseling device and as a means for establishing performance goals. See the *Performance Evaluation Guide for Classified Employees* for detailed instructions.

General:
1. After marking very lightly with pencil each factor in Section A, the rater shall review the report with her/his principal or department head, if any. Markings and comments shall then be typed or inked in. Either the rater or the reviewer or both shall then review the rating with the employee in a private interview. All signatures shall be in ink. Changes and corrections shall be initialed by the employee.
2. If space for comments is inadequate, attachments (either typewritten or in ink) may be included, but each shall be signed and bear the same date as the Performance Evaluation Report Form.
3. Due dates shall be observed and are particularly important for final probationary reports. Filling dates are flexible; both the first and final reports may be filed at any time between their receipt and the printed due date.
4. All probationers (either new-hires or promotions) shall be evaluated no later than the end of their third full month of probationary service. Probationers may be separated (or demoted, if permanent in a lesser class) at any time such action is deemed necessary by the principal or department head through use of either a scheduled or unscheduled performance evaluation report.
5. All permanent employees (who have completed at least five months of service in permanent status) shall be evaluated every two years as of the printed due date. Permanent employees may be separated or demoted in the same manner as probationary employees, provided that all pertinent merit system rules and district procedures are observed
6. Unscheduled reports may be filed at any time to record progress achieved or specific work performance deficiencies.
7. All performance evaluation reports in an employee's personnel department file are subject to review by principals or department heads whenever the employee is certified to transfer or promotion.

Section A: Check (✓) one column for each factor. N/A may be used when a factor is considered "not applicable" to a particular job. Each check mark "Unsatisfactory" or "Requires Improvement"— must have a specific explanation in Section B.

Section B: Describe outstanding qualities and superior performance. Give specific reasons for check marks in "Unsatisfactory" or "Requires Improvement" columns. Record here any other specific reasons why the employee should not be recommended for permanent status, or–if the employee is already permanent– any specific reasons for required improvement. Attachments, if included, should be indicated in space provided.

Section C: Enter the dates employee was counseled on noted deficiencies. Under SUMMARY EVALUATION, check the appropriate box to indicate overall performance, taking into account all factors and total performance for the full period of service being evaluated.

> **Unsatisfactory:** Performance is clearly inadequate in one or more critical factors as explained or documented in Section B. Employee has demonstrated an inability or unwillingness to improve or to meet standards. Performance is not acceptable for position held. (Note: Such summary evaluation bars the employee form promotional examination for one year.)

> **Requires Improvement:** Total performance periodically or regularly falls short of normal standards. Specific deficiencies should be noted in Section B. This evaluation indicates the supervisor's belief that the employee can and will make the necessary improvements.

> **Meets Standards:** Indicates consistently competent performance, meeting or exceeding standards in all critical factors for the position. Most employees will fall into this category. If margins are narrow and standards are barely met, explained in Section B.

> **If Probationary:** Make a recommendation regarding permanent status.

Section D: Record progress or improvements in performance resulting from employee's efforts to reach previously set goals. Record agreed-upon or prescribed performance goals for the next evaluation period.

Signatures: Both the rater and the employee shall date and sign the report. The employee's signature indicates that the conference has been held and that he or she has had an opportunity to read the report. If he or she refuses to sign for any reason, explain that his or her signature does not necessarily imply or indicate agreement with the report and that space is provided to record any disagreement. Further refusal to sign shall be recorded in the report. Attachments, if included, should be indicated in space provided.

Appeal: Evaluation reports express the judgment and options of the supervisory authority and as such, are not subject to appeal under rules of the merit system unless there has been a resultant action taken to suspend, demote, or dismiss a permanent employee.

Source: San Diego (CA) Unified School District 1999. Used by permission.

After the first year, a yearly appraisal should be adequate, unless the employee is not performing up to standards. In such a case, less formal evaluation can be made more frequently. Documentation should be made on all personnel matters.

The formal appraisal should be in writing. Once the form has been completed, the evaluator should schedule a private meeting with the employee to discuss the appraisal (Figure 7.2).

DISCIPLINARY ACTION

Taking disciplinary action is a necessary part of being a manager. If disciplinary action is not taken for misconduct, or when someone fails to do his or her job, management becomes ineffective and is not respected by other employees. Discipline can be as mild as talking to the employee or as strong as reprimanding and establishing changes that must be made. More stringent discipline includes suspension, demotion, or dismissal. Union contracts may dictate much of the procedures.

The following suggestions regarding reprimand are adapted from Buchanan (1973):

- *Do not ignore.* Impress on each employee the importance of his or her job. Wanting to be liked prevents some managers from functioning at their optimum for the organization.
- *Don't be afraid to praise.* Cash wages are paid by check. Mental wages should be "paid" by expressing appreciation for a job well done.
- *Criticize the work—not the worker.* Praise in the presence of others when possible, criticize in private.
- *Be sympathetic in listening* to an employee's grievance. Hear his or her entire story.
- Make sure that all *reprimands are always constructive.*
- *Begin all reprimands with a question.*
- *Never criticize intentions*—criticize methods.
- *Reprimand publicly only when absolutely necessary*—when an open violation of an important rule is committed, for example.
- *Don't harbor resentment.*
- *Support the school board policy and the superintendent's rules* even if you don't agree with them.
- *Be consistent with your discipline.* Be fair with all employees.
- *Don't be too lenient or too severe.* Set the middle ground.
- *Don't take yourself too seriously.*

All types of reprimands and discipline should be followed up with a written report. This written report does not have to be any more than a handwritten account of what happened for the files with date and what action was taken. For example, if an employee is continually coming to work late, documentation may be a matter of noting this on the calendar with how many minutes late the person arrives and what (if any) excuse is used. This will be essential when more formal action must be taken.

DRUGS AND ALCOHOL IN THE KITCHEN

Unfortunately, for some foodservice employees a day on the job may be negatively affected by several drinks of alcohol or a "tug at the bottle," a "snort of coke," a "break for pot," or a "shooting up." Technical skills and know-how deteriorate when a person is drinking or on drugs. The effects or symptoms the employer may see are poor job performance, high absenteeism, morale problems, irregular behavior, an increased number of accidents, and in some cases, theft. A week's supply of drugs can cost upwards of $350, and where is an employee getting that kind of money? Theft is common when the habit becomes expensive.

An employee may be drinking and consuming drugs on his or her own time and not on the job, with no law broken. However, the effects will be felt on the job. The National Council on Alcoholism reports that workers who abuse alcohol are absent two to four times more frequently than the non-abusers. They also have two to four times more accidents on the job.

Many school districts have employed specialized counselors to deal with problems caused by employees' use of drugs and alcohol. These areas will be important management concerns in the 2000's.

MOTIVATING EMPLOYEES

Managing human resources means understanding human behavior. Just as people's needs are different, it takes different things to motivate different people; however, most people respond to certain motivational factors. Each employee has basic needs, and each is at some level in terms of need fulfillment. Maslow's theory describes the basic needs and the levels of those needs as: physical needs (most basic), safety and security needs, social needs, esteem needs, and self-realization needs (highest level), stacking one on top to the other to form a pyramid-like hierarchy. The basic needs of most people in the workplace can be met in the following ways:

- Work—meets a basic psychological need by providing job satisfaction and security.
- Salary—helps provide for physical needs; an increase in salary and rewards motivates at a high level.
- Working conditions (safe environment)—help meet safety needs; an improvement. in working conditions can motivate at a high level.
- Social environment (relationships with supervisor and fellow employees)—aids in meeting social needs.
- Advancements, achievements, and recognition—help meet esteem and self-realization needs.

Promotions are only one form of recognition for good work. Needed recognition may be as simple as the supervisor's or manager's calling employees by name, showing interest in them, listening to their ideas, praising them on day-to-day accomplishments, and smiling and being pleasant.

Praise is a powerful tool. It is a form of recognition that is easy to provide, and it should be used often. Praise is particularly effective when given around peers, relatives, and others. Just about everyone wants to be praised by others—even "proven employees." Stimulating and motivating employees to want to do their best is an on-going process.

What does the employee want from his or her job? In the 1970s good wages were rated number one by supervisors, and job security number two. Staff employees ranked appreciation of work number one and the feeling involved as number two. Those may still be among the top ranked among workers, but the best way to find this out is to ask employees to rank the following in importance to them:

- Good wages
- Job security
- Good working conditions
- Promotion and growth opportunities
- Interesting work
- Personal loyalty of supervisor to employees
- Appreciation of work
- Feeling involved

Each employee is unique and what is the most important to each employee will reflect that employee's needs and desires.

MANAGEMENT TRENDS

"Quality circles" were replaced with total quality management (TQM) and continuous quality improvement (CQI) in the early 1990s, though all three are still used successfully today. Each had some good points and should not be totally forgotten. Quality circles encouraged management to involve employees—still an excellent motivator and a means of problem solving issues like:

- Improving the quality of school foodservice
- Reducing costs
- Providing better customer service and improving relations with customers (both students and adults)
- Improving the atmosphere/surroundings in the foodservice facility

The "quality circle" approach to management is a form of participatory management that allows employees to be involved in making suggestions and initiating changes. People will support what they have been involved with and will make things work if they have recommended the changes. When an idea comes from the supervisor's office or the manager, however, they may support it but only because they "have to." It is important that employees "buy into" school foodservice's philosophy and believe the work is important. The teamwork approach helps meet social and self-esteem needs of many employees, which are two of the needs identified by Maslow in his "hierarchy of human needs."

Many large companies that have used "quality circles" employed an outside person as the group facilitator (one who keeps the group on track and helps the group determine what the real problems are at the workplace). In a school district, the facilitator may be someone from another department. The people who make up the group may be foodservice employees along with people from other departments, and the group may be selected by all the employees, or they may be the entire staff if the staff is small (no more than six to eight people).

Studies have shown that TQM has worked best for employers who reward employees through non-cash recognition programs and tie raises to quality performance. Technology support can be bought, but employee commitment must be cultivated and shouldn't be taken for granted.

Continuous quality improvement (CQI) is defined in *An Executive's Pocket Guide to QI/TQM Terminology* as "the base theory that quality can be improved on a continuous, or never-ending basis." Though the theory was based in the manufacturing arena it has been moved into the foodservice arena, particularly in health care.

The new style of leadership differs from the old style of leadership in the following ways:

- Power to control distributed among the team instead of with the leader.

- The leader describes the vision or job and the team establishes the goals instead of the leader doing both.

- Each member of the team helps make decisions instead of the leader making the decisions.

- The team is rewarded for achievement instead of individuals.

- The team receives credit for achievement instead of the leader.

Employee empowerment can be effective if the employees are well informed. For many years the foodservice directors kept the financial situation/information to themselves. This is changing as the foodservice budget has become tighter and the help of managers and staff employees is needed.

SELECTED REFERENCES

Altenburg, R. 1984. "Fair Play, Just Cause, and Due Process." *School Food Service Journal* 38(1).

Biasatti, L., and J. Martin. 1979. "A Measure of the Quality of Union-Management Relations." *Journal of Applied Psychology* 64: 387-390.

Bolton, R., and E. Grover. 1984. *Social Style/Management Style: Developing Productive Work Relationships.* New York: American Management Association.

Buchanan, R. 1973. "Personnel." *School Food Service Journal* 27(7): 43.

Bureau of Labor Statistics. 1999. *Occupational Outlook Handbook.* Washington, DC: U.S. Government Printing Office.

Byers, B., C. Shanklin, and L. Hoover. 1994. *Food Service Manual for Health Care Institutions.* American Hospital Publishing, Inc.

Causey, W. 1992. *An Executive's Pocket Guide to QI/TQM Terminology.* Atlanta: American Health Consultants.

Deming, W. 1982. "Improvement of Quality and Productivity through Actions by Management." *National Productivity Review,* 2(1):12-22.

Department of Health, Education, and Welfare. n.d. *Work in America,* Washington, DC: U. S. Government Printing Office.

George, C. 1985, *Supervisors in Action: The Art of Managing Others.* 4th ed. Englewood Cliffs, NJ: Prenctice-Hall.

Griffith, C., R. Johnson, and R. Palmer. 1987. *The Legal Problem Solver for Foodservice Operators.* 3rd ed. Washington, DC: National Restaurant Association.

Herzberg, F. 1966. *Work and the Nature of Man.* Cleveland, OH: World Book.

Long, D. 1985. "Drugbusters." *Restaurant Business* 84(14): 134ff.

Maslow, A. 1954. *Motivation and Personality.* New York: Harper & Row Publishers.

McGregor, D. 1960. *The Human Side of Enterprise.* New York: McGraw-Hill.

McIntosh, R. 1984. *Employee Management Standards.* Vol. 4. The L. J. Minor Foodservice Standards Series. New York: Van Nostrand Reinhold.

McKinsey and Company. 1996. *Foodservice 2005: Satisfying America's Changing Appetite.* Falls Church, VA: Food Distributors International—NAWGA/IFDA, Inc.

Minnesota Department of Education. n.d. *Supervisory Management.* St. Paul: Minnesota Department of Education.

Nolan, R., R. Young, and B. DiSylvester. 1980. *Improving Productivity.* New York: AMACOM, American Management Association.

"Pay and Recognition Are Top Work Concerns." 1988. *FoodService Director* 1(11): 4-17.

Peters, T., and R. Waterman, Jr. 1982. *In Search of Excellence.* New York: Harper & Row, Publishers.

Richie, J., and P. Thompson. 1980. *Organization and People.* St. Paul, MN: West Publishing Co.

Sherer, G. 1984. "Good Intentions Are Not Enough!" *School Food Service Journal* 38(10): 109, 112-13.

Spears, M. 1995. *Foodservice Organizations: A Managerial and Systems Approach.* 3rd ed. Upper Saddle River, NJ: Prentice-Hall, Inc.

U.S. Bureau of the Census. 1998. "United States Population Estimates by Age, Sex, Race, and

Hispanic Origin, 1990-1997." Washington, DC: U. S. Bureau of the Census, Population Division.

VanEgmond-Pannell, D., ed. 1987. *Focus: Management Skills for School Foodservice Managers*. Jackson: Mississippi Department of Education.

Vicary, J., and H. Resnik. 1984. *Preventing Drug Abuse in the Workplace*. Rockville, MD: National Clearinghouse for Drug Abuse Information.

"Watching the Bottom Line Instead of the Clock." 1988. *Business Week*, November 7, 134,136.

8
CONTRACT MANAGEMENT

Management Companies
Why Contract Out School Foodservice?

Management Company Services
Consulting
Providing Food Only
Providing and Serving Food

The Contract
Who Is Responsible?
Competitive Bid Requirements
Non-Performance and Discharge of Contractor

Alternatives for School Districts
Establishing a Foundation
Going off the Child Nutrition Programs
Using the InTEAM Food System

Selected References

MANAGEMENT COMPANIES

Foodservice management companies began managing a few school foodservices in 1959, although they were independent of the National School Lunch Program. They did not have the benefit of federal support—cash reimbursements and USDA-donated foods. In 1969 Congress passed legislation that allowed a commercial management company to contract with a school district to operate the foodservice with the school district still qualifying for National School Lunch Program funding. This legislation was a result of the White House Conference on Nutrition, which brought to light the poverty in the country and made it clear that, even with the National School Lunch Program, school districts were not meeting the needs of all children for a nutritious meal at school. It was thought that not all needy children could be fed without lifting the restrictions on commercial companies. Public Law 95-166 governs the management companies operating school foodservices (see Appendix A for regulations).

According to the USDA's *Study of Food Service Management Companies* (1994), management companies operated 5.6 percent of the school districts participating in the National School Lunch Program in 1990-1991, most of them being on the West Coast, the Northeast, the Midwest, and Texas. *The FoodService Director* reported that slightly over 9 percent of the school districts were contracted out in 1997. USDA (1998) determined that 9.7 percent of the public schools (975 districts) that participate in the National School Lunch Program were using foodservice managment companies serving 3.9 million meals a day. This increase between 1990 and 1998 was in part due to the fears that Nutrient Standard Menu Planning, which is more complicated, requires the use of a computer, and means additional work. Management companies did not make great inroads into the school market until the last five years of the 1990s, when some large school districts turned to privatization, e.g., school districts in Atlanta (GA), Chicago (IL), Duval County (FL), Houston (TX), and Newark (NJ) . Other large school districts are expected to follow course within the next ten years.

Management companies have focused their attention on the school market as other markets have become saturated. According to a USDA study (1994), management companies operated school foodservice programs in 33 states in 1990-91 (since then two other states have been added).

Why Contract Out School Foodservice?

More and more administrators were asking as far back as 1988, "Should we consider contracting out management of foodservice? " The reasons according to Caton (1988) for the question varied, but that administrators were considering management companies primarily because of:

- Red ink on the bottom line
- Boards of education that cannot afford to use general funds to support foodservice programs
- Salary/benefits packages that exceed income
- Problems with personnel negotiations
- Worn-out equipment and not enough money to replace it
- Aggressive sales pitches by competitors, primarily food management companies that promise extra dollars and image improvement with no hassles
- A communication gap between school foodservice administrators and supervisors
- Complacency among rank-and-file school foodservice employees

According to a National School Boards Association survey results which were published in *The American School Board Journal* (March 1997), the factors causing school districts to consider out sourcing (going to commercial companies or privatizing) are: (1) reduction in foodservice costs—45% of those surveyed; (2) efficiency—29%; (3) maintenance—28%; (4) resources—21%; (5) services—19%; (6) additional services they can provide—16%; (7) education—8%; and (8) improvement—4%. The Government Accounting Office report (1996) showed reducing costs and stopping the drain on the general funds as the greater reasons—50-51%—for school districts to use foodservice management companies; reducing the burden on the administrator—35% ; and increasing revenue—30%. The National School Boards Association survey results also stated that only one-third of the school districts using management companies were saving money. Chicago Public Schools began turning some of their schools over to management companies in the late 1990s, but did not realize a cost savings from switching to foodservice management companies—initially the costs were slightly higher.

Labor costs in self-operated school districts are often responsible for driving the costs up, and school administrators/boards don't want to deal with resolving that problem. Wages are too high and productivity too low, and school boards have been too generous with employee benefits; management companies require higher productivity, pay lower salaries, and restrict fringe benefits when they take over the employees. The National School Boards Association survey reported that the biggest obstacle to privatization is employee resistance, which often results in school boards providing salary and employee benefit protection for existing employees in their contracts with the foodservice management companies.

Another big factor, which hasn't come out in the studies, is the inadequate financial reports self-operated program managers have available. The foodservice directors have been at the mercy of finance offices for financial management tools. Many financial officers do not appreciate the needs of the foodservice program managers/directors. Perhaps they do not realize that school foodservice is a business and needs to be treated as such—if it is expected to generate revenue. On the whole, self-operated program managers have poor financial management tools, whereas, foodservice management companies have computerized profit and loss statements by school, which are produced on a timely basis, with analyses to go with them. Many self-operated foodservice directors have established accountant positions on their staff, who will provided the needed financial reports.

H. Kearns, superintendent of the Salem-Keizer School District in Salem, Oregon, was quoted in *School Business Affairs* (May 1997) as follows: "Most school district employees lack the foodservice expertise and the business skills necessary to consistently run a cost-effective lunch program. Working with a contractor can enable educators to devote themselves to matters more directly related to education, and that's the biggest benefit of all."

There are instances when school administrators should consider an alternative to self-operated programs and determine whether it would provide equal or better foodservice at less cost to the community. Some school districts are spending considerable amounts subsidizing the foodservice programs. In some cases the decision to contract out management of a foodservice may be a political decision made by a school board or the result of a philosophical belief that the management of school support services can be handled better by the business world.

The following quiz, used by the Sodexho Marriott Corporation's School Foodservices Department representatives in the early 1990s to promote contract management, illustrates how a management company thinks it can help resolve a school district's problems.

1. Is your precious management time being wasted by foodservice problems?
2. Are you trying to hire another foodservice manager again?
3. Are you and your staff overburdened by foodservice record keeping for state and federal reports?
4. Are student participation and satisfaction in your foodservice programs going down while the lunch-time profits of the surrounding fast-food restaurants and markets are going up?
5. Are you tired of the red ink at the bottom line of your foodservice budget?

If your answer is "yes" to any of these questions, take a close look at a school foodservice management company.

A contract management company might provide a way of resolving high labor costs, of avoiding having the program subsidized, and of giving a facelift to school foodservice in some school districts. Management companies might be able to produce food in a central kitchen or, if the contract requires, provide needed equipment (which remains the property of the management company unless purchased with school foodservice funds). The need for replacement equipment is a rather common problem for school foodservices, because the equipment purchased with federal monies in the 1960s is wearing out and becoming antiquated.

When contracting out foodservice management, labor cost relief is possible only when the employees become the responsibility of the management company. In many situations, school boards are forced to keep employees on their present payscales and protect their retirement and insurance benefits. Thus, there might be two sets of employees—those employed by the school district and those employed by the food management company (this arrangement often causes problems).

MANAGEMENT COMPANY SERVICES

Fifty-four percent of the school districts contracting with foodservice management companies use Sodexho Marriott, Aramark, Canteen, and Service America. Sodexho Marriott was the leader in 1997, serving 354 school districts. A large number of regional management companies are operating in New Jersey, which as a state has the largest number of school districts contracting out their foodservices.

Management companies are involved in school foodservice in three main ways: consulting, providing food only, and providing and serving food. The needs and financial situation of a particular school district determine which type of service is most appropriate.

USDA regulations permit two types of payment, or fee structures:

- Fixed-price, or fee—A unit charge (per-meal equivalent) or annual fee is permitted. Some consider the breakfast a meal equivalent and as little as $1 in a la carte sales a meal equivalent (a bottle of water selling for $1 would be considered a meal equivalent for fee purposes).
- Cost-plus-fixed-fee—Foodservice management companies can pass all foodservice operating costs through to the school district to pay and charge an additional fixed or flat fee that covers management and administrative costs. The fees may be referred to as service fee, a management fee, an administrative fee, or a combination. According to a USDA study (1994), the smaller the school district the higher the fee—e.g., a school district with 10,000 or more students between, 1.8 and 8.8¢ per meal; a school district with 5,000 to

9,999 students, between 4.2 and 15.8¢. School districts serving less than 1,200 students pay annual fees only. The fixed per-meal fees are not used in contracts between the management companies and the school districts with enrollments in excess of 5,000 students. In Chapter 6 of this book, $3 in a la carte sales is considered a meal equivalent, and this is based on the time it takes to do the job (including ordering, inventorying, minor preparation, selling, and cleaning up).

An important issue in pricing is what will be considered a meal equivalent. Many foodservice management companies use $2 in a la carte sales/extra food sales is equal one meal equivalent and two breakfast is equal one meal equivalent or they use the equivalency of what the federal reimbursement is for a free lunch. This is certainly to the foodservice management company's advantage. The meal equivalent should relate to the amount of work involved in providing the service. See Chapter 6, "Organizational Structure and Personnel" for more information on meal equivalents.

Consulting

If a school foodservice has good leadership but has: (1) financial problems, (2) unhappy customer and low participation in the program, or (3) labor problems, the administration should seek a solution. The expertise of a foodservice management company, a consulting company, or a successful foodservice director from another school district could be extremely beneficial. Frequently what the school foodservice needs is the objective outsider's overview or business advice that a consultant may be able to furnish. Oversight or supervision of change seems to be an area where foodservice management companies and consultants can work effectively.

Providing Food Only

When facilities are not available or are inadequate for on-site food preparation, a management company may be equipped to furnish (bring in) good food at a cost per meal that can be afforded. Some big-city systems have turned their larger facilities into central kitchens or bulk central kitchens for preparing thousands of lunches for their own school districts but do not have the expertise to operate them effectively. Other districts do not want to make the large capital outlay necessary for such an operation or do not want to enter the food processing business. Food management companies or other school districts may contract to provide the food in such cases, e.g., Dayton (OH) Public Schools and Archdiocese of Chicago (IL).

Providing and Serving Food

In the arrangement of providing and serving food, the food is procured, prepared, and served by a management company. The preparation may take place in a commissary or central kitchen or on site. Some school districts require the food to be prepared on site: this limitation is costly and defeats some of the purposes for contracting out in the first place. On-site preparation will often reduce the levels of automation and efficiency that are the secret to reducing costs.

THE CONTRACT

Who Is Responsible?

As can be seen with the different types of services provided by management companies, it is important for the school district to spell out what it wants to contract out.

Does contracting out the management (for both food and service) remove all responsibilities for the school foodservice? This may be the hope of some administrators. According to Fran O'Donnell, coordinator of New York's Child Nutrition programs:

> Schools that use the services of a management company incur greater management oversight responsibilities than if they have a self-operated food service program. They fail to recognize that management companies do not provide a magic bullet—they have no management "secrets." Good management is the key and that can occur in self operating schools.

Labor cost is a major issue that should be discussed and included in the contract. It is recommended that every contract include a prevailing wage scale to allow hiring of a quality staff, and a successor clause requiring the new employer to pick up the employees' previous benefits. The state department over the Child Nutrition programs inspects all bid specifications for management of foodservice. Each state has its own restrictions regarding contract management.

Responsibility for costs should be clearly spelled out in the bid specifications (Table 8.1). The school district maintains responsibility for processing free and reduced-price meal applications, verification, and carrying out the requirements of the Child Nutrition programs, as well as doing the paperwork to file claims for federal reimbursement. The management company usually bills the school district for the type service provided, with credit for all income received from sales. The school district is normally responsible for preparing the state report. Federal regulations require that all federal reimbursements for meals served are payable to the school districts and the school district pays the management company. The management company contract may or may not require that the company pay for labor and for the food and supplies used.

According to a USDA study (1994), only 47 percent of the contracts reviewed in the study specified conditions for recovery of financial losses. The two main ways recovery of losses are addressed are these: (1) the food management companies (FSMCs) reimburse the school district for the loss without a limit of how much, and (2) the FSMCs reimburse the school district with limits equal to the management fee or a ceiling.

The guidelines provided by the USDA, FNS in *Guidance for School Food Authorities: Contracting with Food Service Management Companies (1995)*, state that the school district or school food authority is responsible for the following:

- National School Lunch Program agreement—ensuring the foodservice is operated in conformance with the agreement

Table 8.1. Cost Responsibility Summary

Category	School District	Contract Company
FOOD:		
Purchasing of food		X
Processing invoices		X
Payment of invoices		X
Transportation and storage of		
USDA commodities	X	
LABOR:		
Payment of school district		
Employees' payroll	X	
Fringe benefits	X	
Worker's compensation	X	
Unemployment taxes	X	
Payment of contractor		
Employees' payroll		X
Fringe benefits		X
Custodial services for—		
Cleaning dining room	X	
Cleaning kitchen floors	X	
Clerical staff for preparing monthly state	X	
claim report		
Monitoring contractor's performance	X	
ADDITIONAL ITEMS:		
Dishes/silverware/trays–		
Original inventory	X	
Replacement	X	
Telephone—local and long distance	X	
Removal of trash and garbage	X	
Replacement of small equipment		
(pots, pans, etc.)	X	
Replacement of large equipment	X	
Insurance—liability, fire, and theft	X	
Maintenance of equipment	X	
Vehicle for transporting USDA commodities	X	
Operating expenses	X	
Maintenance on vehicle	X	

Category	School District	Contract Company
SUPPLIES AND MISCELLANEOUS COSTS:		
Detergent and cleaning supplies		X
Paper supplies		X
Menu paper and printing	X	
Free/reduced-price meal applications	X	
Meal tickets for free and reduced-price students	X	
Postage	X	
Licenses	X	
Pest control	X	
Utilities	X	

- Control of accounts—retaining overall financial responsibility
- Establishing meal prices
- Signing the reimbursement claim form—and sometimes preparing the monthly claim for reimbursement
- Free and reduced-price meal program policies
- Free and reduced-price meal application process—determining eligibility and verification
- Monitoring meal programs—ensuring that federal regulations are being adhered to
- Control of quality, extent and nature of foodservices
- Assuring that donated commodities are used for the National School Lunch Program— retaining title to USDA-donated foods
- Meals—accountability for them
- Forming advisory boards
- Resolution of review and audit findings
- Maintaining health department certifications
- Menus to be served for pricing of contracts
- Production records—federal requirements that must be carried out

Competitive Bid Requirements

Federal regulations require that a school district contracting out its foodservice operation use a competitive bid system. The specifications need to be complete and carefully written. Many school administrators have experienced difficulty writing into the bid all that is needed for a satisfactory arrangement. It is difficult, for example, to write the "quality" desired into bid specification. Awarding to the lowest bidder is usually required. The contract needs to be monitored, which takes a staff member with foodservice expertise that includes knowing what the contract requires and familiarity with federal and state regulations.

When a school district contracts with a management company, the district is still the legal authority over the foodservice.

The schools' cycle menus to be served should be included in the bid specifications OR the proposal from the bidding companies should be required to contain the proposed menus (see Figure 8.1). Additionally, an advisory board composed of parents, teachers, and students is required. The

Figure 8.1. Sample Management Company 21-Day Cycle School Menu for Elementary and Secondary Schools — "Expressway Concept"

Day One	Fat	Cal	Day Two	Fat	Cal	Day Three	Fat	Cal
Corn Dog ■ ▓	17.4	321	**Ravioli with a**	6.5	241	**Soft Shell Taco** ■ ▓	13.9	350
Hot Turkey & Cheese			**Bread Stick** ■ ▓	4.3	174	**Fish Nuggets with a**	10.5	245
Sandwich ■ ▓	6.7	224	**Hot Ham & Cheese**			**Hot Roll** ■ ▓	4.3	17
Mashed Potatoes/Gravy ■	3.7	108	**Rollup** ■ ▓	11.8	283	Tator Tots ■	6.7	138
Green Beans ■	.0	11	Broccoli ■	.2	18	Refried Beans ■	.4	81
Strawberry Applesauce ■	.1	75	Carrots ■	.1	14	Orange ■	.1	54
Banana ■	.5	84	Peas ■	.1	43	Shape Up ■	.0	80
Jello	.0	93	Apple ■	.4	63	Milk Choice ■		
Milk Choice ■			Million Dollar Cookie	7.0	144			
			Milk Choice ■					

Day Four	Fat	Cal	Day Five	Fat	Cal	Day Six	Fat	Cal
Breaded Chicken			**Cheese Sticks** ■ ▓	15.	364	**Hot Dog** ■ ▓	10.8	229
Sandwich ■ ▓	16.0	339	**Beef Patty on Bun** ■ ▓	6	302	**Spaghetti with a**	9.3	319
Lasagna with a	9.4	258	French Fries ■	14.	125	**Bread Stick** ■ ▓	4.3	174
Bread Stick ■ ▓	4.3	174	Celery with	5	5	Baked Potato Half ■	.0	44
Lettuce Salad ■	1.4	17	Peanut Butter ■ ■	4.8	92	Peas ■	.2	46
Cheesy Potatoes ■	2.2	84	Spiced Apples ■	.0	108	Peaches ■	.0	42
Fruit Cocktail ■	.0	44	Orange ■	7.8	54	Banana ■	.5	84
Apple ■	.4	63	Sugar Cookie	.0	165	Milk Choice ■		
Milk Choice ■			Milk Choice ■	.1				
				7.9				

Day Seven	Fat	Cal	Day Eight	Fat	Cal	Day Nine	Fat	Cal
Burrito ■ ▓	12.7	366	**Pepperoni Pizza** ■ ▓	16.4	384	**Sloppy Joe** ■ ▓	10.5	306
Hot Turkey Sandwich ■ ▓	2.4	193	**Turkey & Noodles** ■ ▓	3.6	211	**Chicken Nuggets with a**	10.6	213
Green Beans ■	.0	11	Lettuce Salad ■	1.4	17	**Hot Roll** ■ ▓	4.3	174
Carrots ■	.1	14	Corn ■	.6	52	Cheesy Potatoes ■	2.2	84
Pears ■	.1	43	Applesauce ■	.1	41	Carrot Sticks ■	.0	12
Apple ■	.4	63	Orange ■	.1	54	Pineapple Tidbits ■	.1	57
Chocolate Fudge Brownie	6.6	137	Milk Choice ■			Apple ■	.4	53
Milk Choice ■						Dream Cookie	4.3	126
						Milk Choice ■		

Day Ten	Fat	Cal	Day Eleven	Fat	Cal	Day Twelve	Fat	Cal
Cheese Pizza ■ ▓	11.1	325	**Ravioli with a**	6.5	241	**Ground Beef Patty**		
Beef Patty on Bun ■ ▓	14.5	302	**Bread Stick** ■ ▓	4.3	174	**with**	16.5	319
Lettuce Salad ■	1.4	17	**Taco Burger** ■ ▓	7.5	226	**Cheese on Bun** ■ ▓	10.8	229
Corn ■	.6	52	Carrot Sticks with	.0	12	**Hot Dog** ■ ▓	4.8	125
Fruit Cocktail ■	.0	44	Ranch Dressing ■	5.3	65	French Fries ■	.5	120
Orange ■	.1	54	Applesauce ■	.1	41	Baked Beans ■	.0	42
Milk Choice ■			Banana ■	.5	84	Peaches ■	.4	63
			Milk Choice ■			Apple ■	9.1	211
						Chocolate Cake		
						Milk Choice ■		

Additional items offered daily are listed on the following page.

Lunch Includes: Choice of ■ **Protein, Two (2)** ■ **Fruits and/or** ■ **Vegetables,** ▓ Bread **&** ■ **Milk.**

Figure 8.1. Sample Management Company 21-Day Cycle School Menu for Elementary and Secondary Schools — "Expressway Concept" (continued)

Day Thirteen	Fat	Cal	Day Fourteen	Fat	Cal	Day Fifteen	Fat	Cal
Corn Dog ■ ▨	17.4	321	Breaded Chicken			Burrito ■ ▨	12.7	366
Hot Ham & Cheese			Sandwich ■ ▨	16.0	339	Fish Nuggets with a	10.5	245
Sandwich ■ ▨	10.3	243	Lasagna with a	9.4	258	Hot Roll ■ ▨	4.3	174
Tator Tots ■	6.7	138	Bread Stick ■ ▨	4.3	174	Tator Tots ■	6.7	138
Mixed Vegetables ■	.1	51	Mashed	3.7	108	Carrots ■	.1	14
Spiced Apples ■	.0	108	Potatoes/Gravy■	.0	5	Orange ■	.1	54
Orange ■	.1	54	Celery with	7.8	92	Shape Up ■	.0	80
Jello	.0	93	Peanut Butter ■ ■	.1	43	Milk Choice ■		
Milk Choice ■			Pears ■	.4	63			
			Apple ■	7.0	144			
			Million Dollar Cookie					
			Milk Choice ■					

Day Sixteen	Fat	Cal	Day Seventeen	Fat	Cal	Day Eighteen	Fat	Cal
Corn Dog ■ ▨	17.4	321	Chicken Nuggets with a	10.6	213	Ravioli with a	6.5	241
Turkey & Noodles ■ ▨	3.6	211	Hot Roll ■ ▨	4.3	174	Bread Stick ■ ▨	4.3	174
Cheesy Potatoes ■	2.3	64	Hot Ham & Cheese			Pig in a Blanket ■ ■ ▨	12.5	274
Broccoli ■	.2	18	Sandwich ■ ▨	10.3	243	Baked Potato Half ■	.0	44
Strawberry Applesauce ■	.1	75	Green Beans ■	.0	11	Peas ■	.2	46
Banana ■	.5	84	Carrot Sticks with	.0	12	Spiced Apples ■	.0	108
Milk Choice ■			Ranch Dressing ■	5.3	65	Orange ■	.1	54
			Pineapple Tidbits ■	.1	57	Milk Choice ■		
			Apple ■	.4	63			
			Chocolate Fudge Brownie	6.6	137			
			Milk Choice ■					

Day Nineteen	Fat	Cal	Day Twenty	Fat	Cal	Day Twenty One	Fat	Cal
Italian Pizza Sandwich ■ ▨	12.3	289	Ground Beef Patty with			Soft Shell Taco ■ ▨	13.9	350
Hot Turkey Sandwich ■ ▨	2.4	193	Cheese on Bun ■ ▨	16.2	319	Hot Sub Sandwich ■	9.2	216
Lettuce Salad ■	1.4	17	Spaghetti with a	9.3	319	▨	.4	81
Corn ■	.6	52	Bread Stick ■ ▨	4.3	174	Refried Beans ■	.1	51
Peaches ■	.0	42	French Fries ■	4.6	125	Mixed Vegetables ■	.5	84
Apple ■	.4	63	Celery with	.0	5	Banana ■	.0	80
Jello	.0	93	Peanut Butter ■ ■	7.8	92	Shape Up ■		
Milk Choice ■			Applesauce ■	.1	41	Milk Choice ■		
			Orange ■	.1	54			
			Milk Choice ■					

Note:
- ◆ Fat Content is listed in grams per serving. Children ages 6-11 average fat intake per day is 67 grams. Fat grams are rounded to the nearest tenth.
- ◆ Calories are listed per serving. Children ages 6-11 average daily caloric intake is 2,000.
- ◆ Some items, such as cookies and fresh fruit, are averaged due to the different choices offered.

Lunch Includes: Choice of ■ Protein,
Two (2) ■ Fruits and/or ■ Vegetables, ▨ Bread & ■ Milk.

Items Offered Daily:		
	Fat	Cal
Deli Sandwich ■ ▨	9.2	216
Peanut Butter & Jelly Sandwich ■ ▨	33.0	548
2% Milk ■	5.0	120
Skim Milk ■	.0	80
1% Chocolate Milk ■	2.5	160

Source: ARAMARK Corporation 1999. Used by permission.
Note these menus are color coded when given to the customer to designate contribution to the menu.

purpose of such a board is to aid in planning menus and evaluating the services of the management company. When a school district includes several schools in the contract, someone on the school district's staff should oversee the contract and visit the schools.

New York's state laws are probably one of the strictest of any state's laws regarding management companies. USDA requires the companies to operate under a fixed-fee contract, but New York requires the district to take the lowest responsive bid. Louisiana's state laws nearly prevent school districts from contracting with management companies at all, by preventing districts that do from receiving federal funds. California's state law allows management companies, but protects the school district foodservice director's job (not necessarily as the director).

A fee based on the number of meals served is probably the most desirable, with all profits going back to the school district for use in the school foodservice program. In the fee charged by some of the major management companies in 1988, costs were between 7 and 10 cents per meal served plus administrative salaries.

Donated commodities should be an important consideration in a contract. The contract should specify that the management company store and use the donated commodities in accordance with USDA regulations and be responsible to reimburse the school district if the donated commodities are allowed to spoil. The school district will be considered ultimately responsible for the commodities in any event.

Listed below are 11 personnel requirements to include in a contract compliance system, adapted from Zaccarelli and Ninemeier (1982).[1]

1. Resumes of all key on-site management personnel provided to facility officials.
2. New management personnel approved in advance by school district officials.
3. Required health examinations passed by all foodservice staff; certificates on file.
4. Training programs conducted for sub-management personnel; records of subjects, names of personnel attending, and training contract hours per month maintained.
5. Foodservice staff (management and sub-management) considered objectionable by facility officials not retained.
6. Foodservice staff paid on a timely basis; fringe benefits paid according to plans in proposal.
7. Foodservice staff policies, to the extent practical, same as those pertaining to non-dietary staff retained by the facility.
8. On-site visit by management company regional and other staff specialists on the basis agreed upon in the contract.
9. Foodservice staff in proper required uniform.
10. Employees' wage rates paid as agreed upon in the proposal.
11. Registered dietitians and other professionally qualified staff employed as outlined in proposal.

Contracts with management companies take many forms and vary greatly across the country.

---

[1]Adapted from *Cost Effective Contract Food Service: An Institutional Guide* by H. E. Zaccarelli and J. D. Ninemeier, pp. 125-26. Used with permission of authors © 1982.

For example, a school district might maintain the employees on its payroll in order to continue the retirement and other fringe benefits and/or present salary scales. In this case, new employees hired would be put on the management company's payscale. This does not relieve the school district of the immediate financial costs.

The Government Accounting Office's survey on foodservice management company contracts reported that Pennsylvania Department of Education has a model contract, which helps the local authority deal with problems inherent in contracting-out foodservice. GAO said the contract (1) ensures that "appropriate" financial controls are in place, (2) provides for optimal use of USDA-donated foods, (3) outlines how local authorities will receive credit from a management company for the value of donated commodities, and (4) ensures that "adequate" procedures are in place for monitoring and evaluation.

School district-managed program staff may suffer from unfair disadvantages related to local school district policies. The salary payscales often are much higher than those of commercial foodservices. As health insurance rates continue to rise, the fringe benefits may be adding more than 30 to 50 percent to labor costs. At the same time, management companies generally pay lower wages and provide fewer benefits. Also, management companies do not have union employees nor are they restricted to the laborious bid system for purchasing as are school districts. They can react quickly and take advantage of "good prices."

The contract agreement should normally contain the answers to these questions:

- Will the foodservice be operated under federal regulations, continue to participate in the National School Lunch Program, and receive reimbursement and USDA-donated commodities? Will breakfast and snacks be offered?
    - If so, who files the claim with the state agency? Who furnishes the data? By what date is the report to be submitted each month?
    - Who is responsible for transporting and storing USDA commodities? Who is responsible if commodities are stored improperly and allowed to spoil or are stolen?
- What quality and quantity (portion sizes) of food will be served? Is the portion sizes similar to what students are accustom to? Will soy be an ingredient in foods be use—at what percentage? Will this be an acceptable level with children?
- What menus will be served? Will they be presented for approval on a regular basis? Will a la carte foods be sold? Will choices be offered on the menus?
- What type of service will be used? Will speed lines, vending machines, self-service, made-to-order service, and/or traditional cafeteria service be provided?
- Where will the food be prepared? Will it be prepared at a commissary (or central kitchen) or on site, and when?
- What are the nutritional standards of the foods to be served? How will the Dietary Guidelines be carried out?
- Who will be responsible for meeting the Dietary Guidelines and who will pay the penalty if the state CRE and/or SMR find non compliance and take back federal reimbursement money?
- Which of the following costs will be borne by which party?
    - Labor, payroll, fringe benefits, personnel records
    - Trash and garbage collection and disposal
    - Accounting system for federal and state claim forms

— Invoices for food and supplies
— Insurance—liability, worker's compensation, fire, theft
— Typing and printing of menus that go home students
— Maintenance and replacement of equipment
— Utilities—electricity, water, gas, oil
— Extermination service
— Cleaning of dining room; kitchen floors, tables, and chairs in the dining area; floors and walls in dining room
— Cleaning of hoods, grease traps
— Storage/warehousing, donated commodity delivery charges
— Sales tax
— Telephone and fax
— Leftovers, over-ordering, meals not eaten because of emergency school dismissal

• Who is responsible for the following?
— Setting lunch periods (how many and how long?)
— Purchasing food and supplies
— Bid process
— Cashiering bank deposits, records, and reports
— Sanitation standards, outbreaks of food poisoning
— Labor negotiations.
— Setting prices charged students for breakfast and lunch and a la carte foods
— Resolving student, parent, faculty, and community complaints
— Training new employees
— Selecting manager
— Nutrition education
— Marketing of program

School districts considering privatizing school foodservices should contact their state department of education (the State Department of Agriculture in New Jersey), child nutrition division for assistance with writing the request for proposal. Also, *Contracting with Food Service Management Companies: Guidance for School Food Authorities* (USDA, Food and Nutrition Services 1995) is a good reference.

Non-Performance and Discharge of Contractor

A 60 to 90-day cancellation clause should be written into any contract between a school district and foodservice management company. It would take at least 90 days to handle a formal bid process to obtain a replacement foodservice management company or to establish a self-operated management staff. Such a clause can be exercised at the discretion of either party without the need for demonstration of non-performance.

In addition, a management company and school district should each have a way out of their contractual obligations at any time during the term of the contract when one or more of the following can be shown to exist: (1) failure of the other party to perform a stipulated condition; (2) fraud and misrepresentation; (3) failure to perform because of actions of the other party; and (4) waiver of performance by the other party.

There are three situations in which the parties to a contract between a school district and management company are released from the duty to perform (Zaccarelli and Ninemeier, 1982): enactment of a new law makes performance illegal; property or material that is required to complete the contract is destroyed; an essential element that the contracting parties assumed to exist is missing (e.g., when a school is closed).

ALTERNATIVES FOR SCHOOL DISTRICTS

Some school district administrators have wanted more flexibility with the school foodservice program in order that they can realize some revenue from the "enterprise" operation. Federal regulations do not curtail a business (corporation) from making profits, but the self-operated programs are restricted as to what they may use their funds for and to a fund balance of three months.

Establishing a Foundation

The Conestoga Valley School District (PA) with a foodservice budget of nearly $1.8 million has privatized its foodservices in a different way from contracting with a foodservice management company—by establishing a foundation and for-profit corporation, which provides a la carte items in vending machines and food at special events, but serves the standard cafeteria lunch at no cost. The school district formed Foundation Management Services, Incorporated, in 1994 and the foundation was successful from the start. In 1994-95, one year after startup, the profits exceeded $130,000. The interrelationship with the school district is shown in Figure 8.2. The foundation raises money through fund raisers and appeals for donations. Twenty-five percent of the corporate dividends go toward endowments and 75 percent to grants and scholarships. The foodservice program at Conestoga Valley has been recognized on both the state and national levels, receiving a Best Practice Award by the USDA. They have published a "how to" book and have made numerous presentations on their concept.

Going Off the Child Nutrition Programs

There is always the alternative of going off the Child Nutrition programs, which means the schools that are off the programs will not receive the federal reimbursement and donated commodities under the National School Lunch and Breakfast Programs. If the schools do not serve many needy children, this is an alternative that might work well for school districts who want more freedom to operate their programs. It is important to know what the state policy and school board policy are about serving meals free to those students who are needy.

A school district may have some schools participating in the Child Nutrition programs and some not. For example, Henrico County and Chesterfield County (VA), have their elementary and middle schools on the Child Nutrition programs and their high schools are off the programs. The foodservice

Figure 8.2 Conestoga Foundation: Systems Interrelationships Model for the Enhancement of School Services

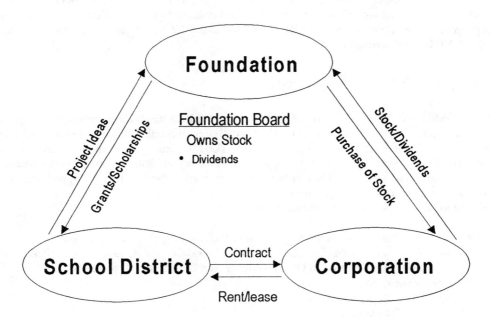

School Board
Owns Contract

- High-quality nutritional lunch
- Schedule
- Maintenance of equity
- Price control
- Menu approval
- Customer focus
- Termination clause
- Rental/lease fees

Executive Board
Owns Service

- Lunch program (nonprofit)
- A la carte service
- Special events
- Vending
- Concessions
- Fund raising
- Take-out sales
- Management services

Objectives:

1. Income for the school district
2. Income for the foundation
3. Marketing a top-quality, high-participatory, nutritional lunch program
4. Impetus and framework for other services
5. Enhancement of foodservices

Source: K. Seldomridge, *Developing Alternative Revenue Sources Through Privatization and Foundations,* Conestoga Valley School District, Lancaster, Pennsylvania. Used by permission.

programs' monies are in separate accounts. The schools off the Child Nutrition programs can sell carbonated beverages and do not have to meet any dietary requirements.

Mountain Brook City (AL) schools and the Glendale (AZ) Union High District are examples of school districts that are off the National Lunch and Breakfast Programs. Some schools were off the program and are back on it because they could not afford the loss of the federal reimbursements and USDA donated commodities.

Using InTEAM Food System

The inTEAM Food System is a public franchise that provides a standardized management system. Six states have licenses to use the inTEAM Food System throughout their states and numerous school districts in other states are using the inTEAM Food System. More than 400 school districts across the United States are using parts of the system. These school districts have realized improved customer satisfaction, 10% to 12% participation increases in their high schools, and increased revenue with no increase in labor costs.

The inTEAM Food System includes the following:

- Required four-day training in operation of the system approach to management
  - The training qualifies for American School Food Service Association Certification (15 credits) and American Dietetic Association Certification (16 credits)
- Two management manuals
  - One for administrators
  - One for managers

The menus and recipes that are a part of the system are available in *Assisted NuMenu Manual with Database on Computer Disk* (for NUTRIKIDS and Snap Systems softwares). A manager's production manual is also available with disk.

SELECTED REFERENCES

Caton, J. 1988. "Sell Some Success for Lunch." *School Food Service Journal* 42(8): 17.

Crimmins, M. 1978. "We Belong in School Foodservice." *Food Management* 13(1): 31-32.

Donovan, S. 1996. "The Benefits of Private Contractors: Four Case Studies." *School Business Affairs* 62 (5): 25-31.

Eyster, J. 1980. *The Negotiation and Administration of Hotel Management Contracts.* 2nd ed. Ithaca, NY: Cornell University Press.

Ganse, R. 1988. "How to Handle Food Management Company Contracts." *School Food Service Journal* 42(8):31.

Jones, R. 1997. "Buyer Beware: Avoiding Privatization's Pitfalls. " *The American School Board Journal* (March), 21-23.

Pannell-Martin, D. 1996. *Assisted NuMenu Manual with Database on Disk.* Alexandria, VA: inTEAM Associates, Inc.

Pannell-Martin, D., and G. Applebaum. 1995. *inTEAM Food System Administrator's Manual.* Alexandria, VA: inTEAM Associates, Inc.

____. 1995. *inTEAM Food System Manager's Manual.* Alexandria, VA: inTEAM Associates, Inc.

Pannell-Martin, D., G. Applebaum, and E. Soares. 1998. *Manager's Production Handbook.* Alexandria, VA: inTEAM Associates, Inc.

Public Law 91-248. [An amendment to the Child Nutrition Act of 1966.] 1970. 91st Congress., 2nd sess. (84 State.107). May 14.

School Food Service Director. 1996. "Incorporation, Subsidies Concern Business Officials." *School Food Service Director* 13 (20), 1-2,5.

Seldomridge, K. n.d. *Developing Alternative Revenue Sources through Privatization and Foundations.* Lancaster, PA: Conestoga Valley School District.

Stevenson, K., and R. Wood. 1997. "What Administrators Are Saying (and Doing) About Privatization." *School Business Affairs* 63(1), 14-21.

St. Pierre, R., et al. 1992. *Child Nutrition Program Operations Study.* Prepared for USDA/FNS.

U. S. Department of Agriculture, Food and Nutrition Service. 1994. *Study of Food Service Management Companies in School Nutrition Programs.* Alexandria, VA: Office of Analysis and Evaluation, USDA Food and Nutrition Service.

____. 1995. *Guidance for School Food Authorities: Contracting with Food Service Management Companies.* Alexandria, VA: Authors.

____. 1998. *School Food Purchase Study: Final Report.* Alexandria, VA: Authors.

VanEgmond-Pannell, D. 1985. "Table Arrangements: When Should a District Opt for Contract Management." *American School and University.* March 64-66, 71.

White House Conference on Food, Nutrition, and Health. 1970. *Final Report.* Washington, DC: U.S. Government Printing Office.

Zaccarelli, Brother H., and J. Ninemeier. 1982. *Cost Effective Contract Food Service.* Gaithersburg, MD: Aspen Publishers, Inc.

9
PROCUREMENT AND CONTROLLING INVENTORY

Overview of Market

Determining What to Purchase
    Factors Influencing Purchasing
    Child Nutrition (CN) Label

Determining the Purchasing Arrangements
    Procurement Methods
    Pricing Methods

Method of Awarding Bids
    Line Item Award of Bids
    Aggregate Award of Bids and Prime Vendor

Who Does the Bid Process
    Individual School
    Centralized Purchasing
    Cooperative Purchasing
    State Purchasing

Centralized Warehousing

Specifications
    Labeling Standards for Processed Foods

Ordering

Inventory Management
    Proper Receiving
    Proper Storing in an Organized Facility
    Accountability for Items in Storage
    Inventory Records
    Value of Inventory
    Inventory Turnover

Selected References

OVERVIEW OF MARKET

This chapter will be devoted to the procurement of food and supplies and controlling that inventory. Purchasing equipment and writing specifications for equipment are addressed in Chapter 13, "Planning Facilities and Selecting Large Equipment."

Purchasing is the process of procuring food, and to most of the school foodservice management it means more than merely buying or ordering. "Purchasing" implies that planning has gone into the ordering. Kotschevar (1994) said the challenge of purchasing is buying the "right product in the amounts needed at the time needed within the price that can be afforded."

Foodservice directors have challenges as buyers today. School districts are no longer in a buyer's market today, though they provide a stable market. Restaurants and other commercial foodservices are 80 percent of the foodservice industry, unlike the 1950s and 1960s when the school foodservice program was considered one of the largest markets in volume. School foodservice is a $14 billion business (in commercial-equivalent dollars), or approximately 10 percent of the foodservice market, employing (according to the USDA) 300,000 people, with purchases amounting to approximately $7 billion. The purchases are primarily food, which use between 30 and 50 percent of the revenue. Paper and disposable products and cleaning supplies use between 3 and 6 percent of the revenue. Large and small equipment generally takes another 2 percent of the revenue. Unfortunately when budgets get tight, equipment replacement suffers and maintenance may be deferred.

Electronic commerce, computerization of the purchasing process, will cause the biggest changes in procurement during the 2000s. The bid process is easy to computerize, and it is being accurately evaluated by computers in many school districts now. The computer can provide the ability to establish the most economical approach to purchasing with accuracy—whether that be the "one-stop" purchasing option (prime vendor) or "cherry picking" (awarding bids by line litem). Shopping through the Internet is a growing trend in the foodservice industry. The director or manager can place an order, pay the bill, arrange delivery, and pull the product from the district's warehouse into a school's inventory through the use of the Internet. Electronic commerce has made ordering, tracking, receiving, and paying invoices easy and will become a way of life within a few years, as more foodservice directors use the computerized process and as distributors push the process.

With the continuing advances in genetic engineering, even the shapes of foods may be modified; for example, flatter watermelons may be developed for easier storage. The Universal Product Code (UPC) has become a standard requirement for products, and the use of computers and scanners will make inventory control and the checking in of products much easier and more accurate and complete. Perpetual inventory when done manually is time-consuming and error-prone, but with computerization it has once again become practical.

Some major changes are being made in the processing of food. Irradiation of food, whereby a low dose a gamma rays is used, kills harmful bacteria, controls sprouting and germination of root vegetables, extends shelf live, and delays ripening and aging of fruits and vegetables. Meat irradiation has just received approval.

Another processing method, which has been slow to catch on the in the United States, is aseptic packaging, which makes food shelf-stable. It has become more widely used in the 1990s. Individual servings of juices were among the first products on the market aseptically packaged. Shelf-stable "TV dinners" were introduced in this country in the 1980s but did not catch on. The "retort pouch" is being used for many items formerly sold only in the can (e.g., applesauce and catsup). The common can and glass jar may not be common by the year 2010. Because these newer processes improve flavor over canned products and are more like the frozen products in flavor, the shelf-stable products will be preferred over canned and most frozen products. The advantages of shelf-stable products are numerous and usually mean financial savings.

DETERMINING WHAT TO PURCHASE

The menu comes first in the purchasing process. Additional menu planning methods resulting from the School Meals Initiative—no longer the simple "Type A" lunch or Meal Pattern—have made school foodservice more difficult for sales representatives. The seller needs to do his or her homework on regulations and understand the peculiarities of the Child Nutrition programs—and that is not easy.

The purchaser should have knowledge of food and have contact with the customer in order to know what is needed, as well as the best sizes, cuts, and grades or quality desired. Specifications should be written by foodservice personnel describing what is desired. According to Gunn (1995), "A school purchaser must be a combination of food technologist, business manager, nutritionist, lawyer, and communication expert."

Factors Influencing Purchasing

The factors that influence what is to be purchased are: student acceptability, menu and nutritional content, food budget, labor costs and skills of personnel, season and availability of foods, storage available, numbers of meals to be served and quantity needed, available equipment, customer likes and dislikes, USDA-donated foods, processing contracts, and federal regulations. These factors are discussed briefly below.

Customer Acceptability—Smart buyers realize that it does not matter what they like; it is what the customers like that really matters. Much can be learned about food preferences by talking with students and watching plate waste. (Methods of obtaining information on student opinions are discussed in Chapter 16, "Marketing and Promoting School Foodservice.")

Menu and Nutritional Content—The menu is the blueprint for purchasing, and a manager should buy for the menu rather than planning the menu around what has been purchased. The menu is planned to meet certain nutritional requirements—the present emphasis is on fat.

Food Budget—The food budget will determine to a large extent what is put on the menu and consequently what is to be purchased. On the average, 30 to 50 percent of the budget is spent on food. In school districts with unusually high labor costs, food costs needs to be closer to 30 percent for the program to break even, although 50 percent may be needed to provide a lot of variety. Food costs rise annually, for example, in 1998 food costs rose 3.2 percent (USDA 1998). Approximately 25 percent of the food dollar may be going to milk and dairy products today (see Figure 9.1). During that same period, USDA donated commodities provided $282 million in protein-rich foods.

Labor Costs and Skills of Personnel—The labor available, the skills of the employees, and the costs of labor should be considered by a foodservice manager, or menu planner and purchaser, when deciding if complicated recipes are to be offered and if raw ingredients will be used or convenience items purchased. Today many school districts are serving breakfasts that are comprised of 80% or more convenience foods. For instance, when school districts compare the true costs of making rolls from raw ingredients, they find they cannot justify the process. Instead, purchased hamburger rolls and hot

Figure 9.1. Distribution of How Schools Used the Food Dollar Based on 1996-97 Data
Source: U. S. Department of Agriculture 1998.

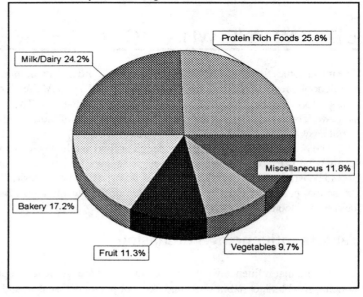

dog rolls will cost less, and students often prefer the bakery products. More and more school districts will be using primarily processed foods as the average cost of a labor hour exceeds $15 (including employee benefits).

Season and Availability of Foods—The price and quality of foods are affected by the season and availability of foods. For instance, purchasing fresh green bell peppers in January will mean higher costs in most parts of the country than purchasing peppers June-August when in season. Drought and other factors can have an impact on availability and prices—particularly produce. Table 9.1 provides the season for a list of selected items. Foods are increasingly acquired on a global food market, especially true for fresh fruits and vegetables, and the seasons do not make as much difference in the price as they once did.

Storage—The type and quantity of storage needed and available should be carefully considered. Many products can be purchased in canned, fresh, and frozen states. The amount of freezer space available may determine how the product will be purchased. Storage capacity will also affect the frequency of delivery.

Numbers of Meals to Be Served—The numbers of meals to be served and other services offered will determine quantities needed. Forecasting with accuracy, especially when choices are offered, is one of the challenges for managers. If cycle menus are used, the food production records kept daily by managers can be used in accurately forecasting the quantities needed.

Available Equipment—The types and amounts of available equipment can affect what foods should be purchased. In some cases, it may be more economical to purchase an item already prepared than to purchase a piece of equipment needed to prepare it.

USDA-Donated Foods and Processing Contracts—The food received by schools from the USDA will continue to make a considerable difference in what is purchased. Donated foods, which account for 12 to 15 percent of the total food used by most school districts, have to be worked into menus, and in some cases immediately (when a product is fresh produce). See Figure 9.2.

Using USDA donated commodities as ingredients in processed foods has become very popular. About four percent of the food used is processed foods containing donated commodities. Nearly 30 percent of the foods issued in 1998 by the USDA for schools went to companies for further processing. State processing contracts are being used in most states, since the National Commodity Processing was phased out during the mid 1990s.

The buyer should be aware that some processing is no bargain. The value of the commodity should be considered and added to the cost of processing to determine if it is a good deal. In some cases, it may

Figure 9.2. Source of Food in 1996-97
Source: U. S. Department of Agriculture 1998.

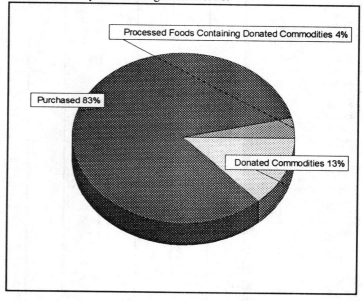

Processed Foods Containing Donated Commodities 4%

Purchased 83%

Donated Commodities 13%

cost more to process raw ingredients than to purchase the product out right when the cost of storage, delivery, backhaul, and state handling fees are included.

Federal Regulations—The federal regulations that affect the school foodservice programs are many. "Buy American products" when possible is a request of schools participating in the National

Table 9.1. Guidelines for Determining Produce Seasons

Produce	Jan	Feb	Mar	Apr	May	June	July	Aug	Sept	Oct	Nov	Dec
FRUIT												
Apples	x	x	x	x					x	x	x	x
Apricots						x	x					
Avocados	x	x	x	x	x	x	x	x			x	x
Bushberries						x	x					
Cantaloupes						x	x	x	x			
Cherries						x						
Dates											x	x
Figs						x		x	x	x		
Grapefruits	x	x	x	x	x		x	x	x			x
Grapes								x	x	x	x	
Honeydew Melons						x	x	x	x			
Kiwi	x	x	x	x	x						x	x
Lemons	x	x	x	x	x	x	x	x	x	x		x
Navel Oranges	x	x	x	x	x							x
Nectarines						x	x	x				
Peaches						x	x	x	x			
Pears							x	x	x	x		
Plums						x	x	x	x			
Prunes									x			
Strawberries				x		x	x					
Valencia Oranges					x	x	x	x				
Walnuts												x
Watermelons						x	x	x				
Winter Pears	x	x	x	x	x							

Table 9.1. Guidelines for Determining Produce Seasons (continued)

Produce	Jan	Feb	Mar	Apr	May	June	Jul	Aug	Sept	Oct	Nov	Dec
VEGETABLES												
Artichokes	x	x	x	x					x	x	x	x
Asparagus						x	x					
Beets	x	x	x	x	x	x	x	x			x	x
Broccoli						x	x					
Brussels Sprouts						x	x	x	x			
Cabbage						x						
Carrots											x	x
Cauliflower						x		x	x	x		
Celery	x	x	x	x	x		x	x	x			x
Cucumbers								x	x	x	x	
Eggplant						x	x	x	x			
Green Beans	x	x	x	x	x	x	x	x	x	x		x
Lettuce	x	x	x	x	x							x
Lima Beans						x	x	x				
Okra						x	x	x	x			
Onions							x	x	x	x		
Peas										x	x	
Peppers						x	x	x	x			
Potatoes	x	x	x		x	x	x	x		x		x
Spinach	x	x		x	x							
Squash						x	x	x	x			
Sweet Corn					x	x		x	x	x	x	x
Sweet Potatoes										x		x
Tomatoes					x	x	x	x		x		
Winter Squash										x		x

Source: United States Department of Agriculture, *Summer Food Service Program for Children, 1998 Nutrition Guidance for Sponsors.*

School Lunch and Breakfast Programs, and it is addressed and encouraged in the National School Lunch Act (see Appendix A) but it is not required. There are federal laws regarding purchasing that schools must be in compliance with, and buyers need to be very familiar with the regulations to receive federal funding for Child Nutrition programs. The Federal Office of Management and Budget Circular (OMB A-102) contains these restrictions. It provides a set of standards related to all public organization receiving Federal funds.

OMB A-102 standards must be carried out for purchases with one vendor of products costing annually more than $10,000. The regulations require competitive bidding by school food authorities at the school district level. The major provisions of the procurement regulations are as follows:

1. All procurement transactions must be conducted in such a way as to provide for maximum open and free competition.
2. Each school food authority must establish written procurement procedures that comply with procurement standards. These include contract administration that ensure the contractor's compliance.
3. Invitations for bids must be based on a clear and accurate description of the material, product, or service to be procured. "Brand name or equal" may be used, but the features of the brand name must be specified. This means that descriptive food specifications should be included in the invitations for bid.
4. Positive efforts should be made to utilize small businesses and minority-owned businesses.
5. School districts cannot use "cost-plus-a-percentage-of-cost" or "cost-plus-a-percentage-of-income" method of contracting.
6. Awards are to be made only to responsible contractors that posses the potential ability to perform successfully under the terms and conditions of the proposed procurement agreement.
7. Each school district must maintain a code of conduct to govern the performance of its officers, employees, and agents in contracting for payment and expending program funds. This means that neither the officers, employees, nor agents will accept any gratuities, favors, or anything of monetary value from contractors. These codes of conduct carry penalties, sanctions, or disciplinary actions for violations.
8. Sufficient records must be maintained to detail the significant history of a procurement for three years.
9. All contracts awarded in excess of $10,000 must contain a provision requiring compliance with Executive Order 11246, entitled 'Equal Employment Opportunity."

These regulations are outlined in detail in Gunn (1995), *First Choice: A Purchasing System Manual for School Food Service,* which can be obtained from the National Food Service Management Institute.

Though most foodservice directors/buyers are not extremely familiar with many of the regulations that affect foodservice programs, there are many that help protect the purchaser. For example, the **Pure Food, Drug, and Cosmetic Act** (enacted in 1938) released the amendments in the form of "**Nutrition Labeling and Education Act of 1990**," which makes some major changes in food product labeling. The **Agricultural Marketing Act of 1953** (amended in 1957) establishes standards and grades for processed fruits and vegetables. The **Meat Inspection Act** and the **Poultry**

Products Inspection Act of 1957 and the **Wholesome Poultry Products Act of 1968** helps ensure that meat and poultry are wholesome. There are many others , such as the Perishable Agricultural laws, anti-trust laws, **Tariff Act of 1930**, and **Fish and Wildlife Act of 1956**, that affect foods purchased.

Child Nutrition (CN) Label

The Child Nutrition (CN) labeling program was put into place in 1984. It is administered by the Food and Nutrition Service of the USDA in conjunction with the Food Safety and Inspection Service and Agricultural Marketing Service of the USDA, and the National Marine Fisheries Service of the United States Department of Commerce. Products that can be CN-labeled include: red meat, poultry, fish, seafood, cheese, eggs, dry beans, peanut butter, hot dogs, corn dogs and other similar sausage products, and juice and juice drink products. The CN label does not guarantee quality, but is some assurance of the quantity of a meal component in a serving of processed food.

The advantages of purchasing a product with a CN label are: (1) the contribution of the product toward meeting the Traditional and Enhanced Food-Based Menu Planning options is known, (2) a warranty against audit claims is provided, and (3) the foodservices are protected from exaggerated claims about a product. The disadvantages are: (1) the CN label could add cost to the product, and (2) there could be some good products not being used because they do not have a CN label. In some cases acceptable products are excluded when states require the local districts to purchase only products with CN labels.

The buyer or foodsevice manager can identify products that are CN-labeled by the CN logo and statement, a six-digit product identification number, a statement of the product's contribution toward meal patterns, a statement that the use of the logo and CN label statement was authorized by the Food and Nutrition Service of the USDA, and the month and year the label was approved. An example of a CN label is shown in Figure 9.3.

Figure 9.3. Child Nutrition (CN) Label
PIZZA WITH GROUND PORK AND VEGETABLE PROTEIN PRODUCT

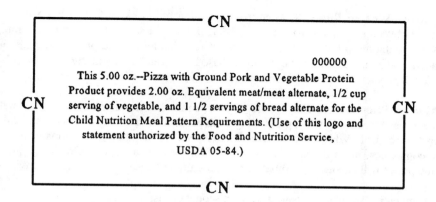

Source: U.S. Department of Agriculture, Food Distribution 1999.

A company may obtain a CN label by contacting Food and Nutrition Service, USDA, and send the required information—including the formula of the product. Food products eligible for CN labels are main dish products and juice and juice drink products.

DETERMINING THE PURCHASING ARRANGEMENTS

Schools may work under different types of purchasing arrangements and directors usually make most of the decisions regarding the purchasing arrangement or process to use. The selection of vendors is made based on three main criteria: (1) price, (2) dependability, and (3) food quality. Some states, e.g., Mississippi and Montana, have statewide purchasing contracts that school districts in the state may use. Because of the federal requirements, most school districts purchase sufficient dollar amounts to require a competitive bid.

Procurement methods

There are basically two procurement methods—formal and informal. The formal method requires specifications be written, issuing of a bid, and awarding of the bid. Whereby, the informal procurement method generally means an order is placed by telephone or with a sales representative that comes to the school.

Bid Buying—Bid buying is the process of requesting prices on products to be purchased. Good, detailed specifications that will describe each product to be purchased are needed. These help ensure that the product bid is the quality product wanted. Some very innovative systems of purchasing are being used today, the most common being: (1) the open-market written bid; (2) the open-market telephone quote; (3) the blanket contract, with discounts off list prices; (4) the formal bid or requirement contract; (5) cost-plus-fixed-fee; (6) market-based bid; and (7) Department of Defense bid.

Open-Market Written Bid—The open-market written bid is like a formal bid and is a legal agreement between a school district and a vendor. In formal bid situations the purchasing agent submits an invitation to bid to all approved vendors. The formal bid process requires written specifications and estimates of quantities to be purchased. The vendor submitting the lowest bid will be awarded the contract. The specification should convey clearly what the buyer wants.

Open-Market Telephone or Fax Quote—The open-market telephone or fax quote system of purchasing is used frequently when purchasing fresh produce, and is used by small school districts for other items as well. When the open market bid is used, prices should be compared among two or three companies, more if time allows and the vendors are available. Obtaining quotes and comparing prices will encourage competition and usually will result in considerable savings.

Blanket Contract—The blanket contract with a discount off list or catalog price is used more often when purchasing office supplies, computers, and equipment than when purchasing food. This method can make the bid process easier and can extend over a large number of items. From studies done by the Texas State Department of Education, however, it was found that the prices paid under the blanket contract were higher than when purchasing under a formal bid, listing exact quantities.

Formal Bid or Requirement Contract—With the formal bid or requirement contract, written specifications and quantities (or estimates of quantities) are needed. An invitation to bid is issued, and the bids are accepted at a designated time. The award is made as an aggregate or by line item to the low bidder who meets specifications. If food products are to be delivered to the schools, the aggregate will probably be necessary to have sufficient volume. Awarding a bid by line item can result in the best prices for large equipment and for truckload quantities for food and paper supplies. Distributors often prefer line-item bidding rather than aggregate for large equipment and truckload quantities of food.

The bid may be for any period of time; however, the firm price can best be used for one year or less. The contract may contain the option to extend a bid contract and maintain the same prices if both parties agree (contractor and school district)—for an equal length of time to the original contract. An escalator clause is often used for milk and ice cream bids where price increases can be tied to the Federal Milk Market prices as published by the Federal Milk Market Administration in the *Market Administration Bulletin*.

Better prices are obtained in most cases with short-term contracts. Monthly contracts are ideal (in terms of price), but bidding monthly may not be feasible to manage. For most school districts, monthly bidding is too time-consuming. The best prices are obtained when quotes are given by telephone and for truckload quantities coming directly from the processors; however, procurement standards may prevent public schools from using this method.

Request for prices may be done as an invitation to bid or as a request for proposal. Below is a definition for the terms.

Definitions:

IFB (Invitation for Bid)—is a formal bid and is usually describes in great detail the services or products required. An IFB has a formal bid opening that can be attended by the public. An IFB requests an exact price and is usually awarded to the lowest responsive, responsible bidder. For example, IFB is used for canned and staple foods.

RFP (Request for Proposal)—is a formal request that describes in a general ways what the needs are. The school district does know what is available and is asking for proposals. It does not have a formal opening and is often subject to negotiation. Terms and prices may not be firm. RFP can be awarded based on what is offered. For example, RFP may be used to obtain a computerized point-of-sale system.

Most school districts use both the formal bid and the informal quotes, particularly on produce. The larger the school district the more that is purchased through a formal bid contract.

PRICING METHODS

There are four pricing methods most frequently used and they are: (1) fixed price, (2) fixed price with escalator (market-based), (3) formula price, and (4) cost-based (often called cost-plus-fixed-fee). Dairy products are usually purchased on a fixed price or fixed price with escalator clause. These two methods of pricing are being used more frequently today than the others. Even produce pricing is moving more toward these methods.

Fixed Price—The price is quoted for a period of time—one time buy, over three months, six months, or a year. It is a contractual agreement.

Most school districts use fixed pricing on the major items, e.g., canned and frozen foods. Companies often have trouble holding prices for long periods of time. A large school district or cooperative bid may involve the distributor obtaining a guaranteed price from the manufacturer or processing company.

Fixed Price with Escalator or Market-Based Bid—Market-based bid pricing is used mostly with produce, milk, poultry, and eggs. This system allows for long-term contracts on items that otherwise would have to bid frequently, such as produce. When using this method source of information from a third-party is important. Some of the sources of this type information can be obtained from:

Urner Barry Publications, Inc.—for poultry, egg, dairy, meat , and seafood
Food Institute Report (weekly) American Institute of Food Distribution, Inc.—for canned fruits and vegetables, frozen fruits and juices
Federal market news reports produced for different parts of the country (referred to as the "terminal markets")—for produce in particular.

For products with frequent price changes, using market-based price lists help to establish vendors that can be purchased from without a fixed-price bid.

Reimbursable Cost-Plus-Fixed-Fee—Reimbursable cost-plus-fixed-fee is a written contract system that is relatively new, but it has grown fast in popularity. Some refer to it as "formula pricing," "fee for service," "contract purchasing," or "one-stop shopping" because the bid contracts are often awarded to one company. In 1987 Marlene Gunn, former Child Nutrition program director for Mississippi, and Etha Bailey, former foodservice director in Florida, were pioneers of this system. Some school districts and cooperative groups use this system of purchasing successfully today, for example, the Archdiocese of Chicago (IL) and the Hillsborough County (FL) School Board. With this system the vendor's reimbursable cost is the price paid plus freight of the product. The fee covers the cost of warehousing, delivery, sales, overhead costs, and profit.

This was a popular way to bid in the 1980s, but the market became more complicated and vendors learned new ways of "sheltering income," and cost-plus-fixed-fee purchasing became more risky. It requires detective work on behalf of the purchaser, and it has become nearly impossible to audit and keep people honest. Sheltered income is in the form of discounts, promotional allowances, etc., which the school district may never see.

Reimbursable cost-plus-fixed-fee usually decreases the number of vendors, means fewer bids, prevents companies from having to take a risk of prices changing, allows bids to cover longer periods of time, and ensures to some degree that a school district will get a product even if the cost has increased. Product lines subject to frequent price changes (like produce and meats) are best bid on this more flexible basis. Table 9.2 provides an example of fixed-fee prices one school district paid for produce. School districts must constantly monitor and audit companies when using cost-plus-fixed- fee. Hillsborough County (FL) Schools audit the invoices monthly on randomly selected items.

Table 9.2. Cost-Plus-Fixed-Fee[1] Prices

Food Item	Fixed Price or Handling Cost
Apples, red delicious, packed, 125/case	$ 3.00/case
Bananas, petite, packed, 150/case	$ 2.50/case
Broccoli, purchase unit, bunch	$ 0.25/bunch
Cabbage, green and white, packed, 50-pound case	$ 2.50/bag
Cabbage, red, purchase unit, head	$ 0.40/head
Cucumbers, packed, 5-pound sack	$ 2.50/sack
Grapes, Thompson green, purchase unit, pound	$ 0.20/pound
Lettuce, iceberg, packed, 24/case	$ 2.00/case
Melons, cantaloupes, packed, 36/crate	$ 3.00/crate
Melons, cantaloupes, packed, each	$ 0.20/each
Oranges. Valencia, packed, 125/case	$ 2.50/case
Parsley, curly, packed, 4-ounce bunch	$ 0.10/bunch
Peppers, green, bell, packed, 5-pound bag	$ 0.15/bag
Pears, Anjou, packed, 120/case	$ 3.00/case
Radishes, red, packed, 6-ounce bags	$ 0.10/bag
Spinach, packed, 10-ounce bags	$ 0.20/bag
Tomatoes, unworked, packed, 25-pound box	$ 2.00/box
Tomatoes, cherry, packed, 12-pint/flat	$ 2.00/flat
Watermelon (in season), packed, each	$ 1.00/each

The success of reimbursable cost-plus-fixed-fee type of bidding depends a great deal on the integrity of the company and how well the school district is kept informed. Purdue University's

---

[1]Current market costs are added to the fixed price.

Restaurant, Hotel, and Institutional Management Department (Stix and Hiemstra, 1989) evaluated the cost-plus-fixed-fee system in the state of Indiana. They found that the school districts using this method of purchasing paid 4.2 percent less than using other system for purchasing their food during the period of study, August-December 1988.

A type of purchasing called "cost-plus-a-percentage-of-cost" is frequently used in commercial foodservices, but is not a legal option for Child Nutrition program purchasers.

Department of Defense Bid—Starting in 1994, the USDA and the Department of Defense (DOD) began testing under a joint project allowing schools to use a portion of their USDA commodity entitlement (money) to purchase fresh fruits and vegetables under the Department of Defense bid contract. Most schools involved are using a "telephonic automated produce information technology" (TAP-IT) to place their orders. Most of the schools in the project have been very pleased with the quality of the produce and appreciate the advantages of having inspectors at the warehouse. Deliveries are arranged by DOD from local produce vendors and should be carefully checked. USDA commodity use of entitlement money to purchase produce from the Department of Defense was expanded in 1996 to include school districts in 32 states and is capped to dollars that can be spent. Some states permit purchase of DOD produce using Sections 4 and 11 reimbursement dollars—yielding a seamless transition from entitlement to purchased. This is an innovative approach for moving fresh fruits and vegetables using USDA commodity money and would work for other foods as well.

Some school foodservice directors have questions the possibility of all USDA commodity entitlement (money) being funneled through DOD. It would take some coordinating and change in procedures but certainly has potential for reducing the cost and dissatisfaction of school districts with the present donated commodities received. The buying power of this agency would be improved, and it should result in savings—both at the federal government level and at the school district level.

METHOD OF AWARDING BIDS

Approximately 90% of the school districts have the "help" of the school board members in awarding bids, according to the National School Boards Association Purchasing Study (1994). The foodservice director may do the recommending the award of a bid to the purchasing department, but the school board members are involved in approving purchase recommendations, and in some school districts the school board reviews the specifications and may become quite involved. For example, if the director has specified a colored napkin, a school board member may question why they need a colored napkin. School boards in other districts do not get involved at all. In Florida only the purchasing department has the authority to recommend bid awards.

It will make a lot of difference to the bidder if the bid will be awarded by low bid on a line item or be awarded as an aggregate or prime vendor.

Line Item Award of Bids

Line item ward of bids usually results in many vendors. The bid is awarded by the lowest price by line item, e.g., on a canned and staple foods bid, applesauce could be awarded to one vendor and sliced apples to another—because of price of each item. A vendor bidding runs the risk that the vendor will be successful on only one item and have to deliver that item to a number of locations weekly. Awarding this way increases the potential of a number of vendors delivering to the schools. Unless a school district is receiving carloads or half carloads of an item, line item awarding is not to the advantage of the school district or to the vendor. Some of the disadvantages to this system are:

- For the school district it may be costly in that it requires time to evaluate bids.
  Manager's time—ordering and receiving products from several companies; interruptions during lunch service, etc.
  Central office's time—dealing with several vendors and trying to enforce the contract with a number of vendors.
  Accounts payable office staff's time—paying multiple invoices which can be time consuming.
- For the distributor it may be costly making the deliveries of a few items.
  Each stop of the truck is costing and many vendors impose a minimum dollar value for each order.
  There is paperwork involved.

Aggregate Award of Bids and Prime Vendor

An aggregate award of bids is used frequently for like items, e.g., canned and staples, frozen foods, milk and other dairy products, and bakery items. There are two types of wholesalers: the "specialty" wholesaler and the "full house" wholesaler. The "specialty" wholesaler carries a limited numbers of products, such as meat, bread, or dairy products. The "full house" wholesaler or distributor today has expanded the products it carries to the point where it supplies all needs.

The prime vendor refers to a formalized "one-stop shopping" policy, that of awarding most products needed to one vendor. It has grown in recently years with schools as time becomes more valuable. Increased volume of products to be delivered usually means better prices, but not necessarily.

WHO DOES THE BID PROCESS

Who does the bid process is a new consideration with many possible solutions for some school districts. Most commonly a school district does its own bid process, but this is changing as more cooperative purchasing groups are being formed.

Individual School

Only a few individual school managers take care of the bid processes. To do it well requires too much time for a manager to handle this process. For the best prices and efficient use of time, it is wise to centralize the bid process. When it is school-by-school, the volume does not warrant a formal bid process; however, an informal bid process is recommended.

Centralized Purchasing

With centralized purchasing, one person in the central office purchases for a number of schools, whereas with decentralized purchasing, each manager meets with sales representatives from the companies and determines the products that will be purchased. The advantages of centralized purchasing include the following: (1) time is saved; (2) buying power is greater, and prices are usually better; (3) the bidding process can be used; (4) the person handling purchasing can specialize; (5) the foodservices in the school district are standardized in terms of the products purchased; (6) better budgetary control is achieved, and (7) federal regulation compliance can be better controlled.

Cooperative Purchasing

By 1996-97 over one-third of the public school districts participate in cooperative buying for nearly 62 percent of their foods compared to less than 10 percent in 1984-85 (USDA 1998). Cooperative purchasing is a form of centralized purchasing in which several school districts within a geographical area combine their purchasing needs. This method of purchasing has become very popular among health care organizations, universities, correctional institutions, and finally, school foodservices. Cooperative purchasing can improve buying power, or "clout," greatly; decrease administrative time spent on purchasing; and result in better service. Small school districts in particular can profit from this method of purchasing. Many school districts in California, Colorado, Kentucky, Michigan, Tennessee, and Texas, for example, are saving considerably on food, paper goods, and supplies with cooperative purchasing. The cost savings can be as much as 20 percent. To arrive at specifications that all the directors/supervisors can agree upon may be the biggest challenge in the process. It requires accepting some change and being flexible for a cooperative to work.

The main reasons for cooperative purchasing are to increase the volume and improve buying power. According to USDA purchasing study (1998) there are price advantages for school districts or groups of school district with 5,000 or more meals. Foodservice management companies are paying 1 ½ percent less than self-operated school districts.

State Purchasing

Many states have a purchasing agent who puts into place a contract for food and supplies for state institutions such as jails, hospitals, and universities. Most states, e.g., Virginia, Tennessee, and Arizona, allow public schools to use the state purchasing service. The state may be purchasing in large enough quantities and have enough clout to obtain better prices than even a large school district can obtain, particularly for such items as sugar, flour, and detergents.

The state agency administering school foodservices in some states, for example, Iowa, Mississippi, Montana, and Texas, are purchasing on a statewide contract. Mississippi's state cooperative prices and services were evaluated, and it was determined there was a saving to school districts in that state. All but nine school districts in the state (140 out of 149) use the state cooperative for purchasing their food and supplies. This makes Mississippi a large volume bidder. The smaller the school districts are the more advantages this will provide, for example, expertise, buying power, better prices, and reduction in workload and paperwork for individual school districts. The school districts do give up some individuality and authority over the food quality and variety.

CENTRALIZED WAREHOUSING

Centralized warehousing and delivery systems may or may not be the most cost-effective approach to obtaining food and supplies. In evaluating this option, several important questions need to be considered.

1. How much does it cost per case to warehouse and deliver? (Gunn [1995] provides a detailed method of self-assessing warehouse costs. How much is too much?)
2. Is the price paid for the products delivered to the warehouse plus warehousing and delivery costs *less or no more than* purchasing the product delivered to the schools?
3. Can satisfactory deliveries to each school by distributors be obtained?
4. Does central warehousing provide better quality control?

Another important concern is whether the volume of the school district's inventory is sufficient to warrant a centralized warehousing and distribution system. If it is not, it may cost four to five times more than having the product delivered by commercial suppliers. Some school district operated warehouses are very cost effective. For example, the Montgomery County (MD) Public School District's foodservice is a cost-effective warehouse system. The school district's volume warrants its operating a 22,000-square-foot foodservice capacity for its 189 schools; however, through contracts they are storing and distributing foods and supplies to other school districts and for the county government.

School districts may need to warehouse for reasons other than cost effectiveness. They may not be able to obtain frequent deliveries, and the food quality may be varying greatly when delivered to the schools versus to the central location.

SPECIFICATIONS

A specification is a precise description of the desired item. It should list particulars precisely and identify the product's characteristics in a manner mutually understandable to the buyer and potential sellers as shown below.

Item name: Beans, green
Description: Canned, 1 to 1½ inch long school cut, dark green, Blue Lake variety, 3 sieves
Grade: Grade A
Pack size: 6/10 cans per case
Net drained weight: 60 ounces
Approved brands: Comstock, Code Red Label, or approved equal
Purchase unit: Case

The specification should communicate to the bidder what is wanted, so when evaluated the bid is the lowest price on the product wanted, not on an inferior product. Many people use brands to identify products; however, the specification should state the approved brands (two to three at minimum) and "approved equal." Some school districts, and especially cooperatives, screen products and restrict bidding to "prior approved brands" or the approved brands only. This requires a lot of time to be fair and for this to be a good system—there is always the need to consider other brands as approved. This means that testing is done before the specifications go out to bid; it is important to select more than one brand in order to obtain competitive bids.

No one should limit competition to the point that the bid process results in higher prices being paid. It is dangerous to get into a situation where only one company provides the product wanted.

Depending on the products, a specification can include the following:

- *Name of item* (When available, the official **Standard of Identity** should be listed for processed food products [such as mayonnaise, ketchup, and peanut butter][1]).
- *Ingredients of processed items* having no standard of identity.
- *Quality or official grade.*
- Class, kind, style, and/or variety. *(Class* may refer to the sex of and type of animal .
  Kind may refer to types of food such as flour [all purpose of whole grain].
  Variety refers to such foods as fruits and vegetables [Red Delicious, Jonathan, and Winesap apples].
  Style generally refers to how a product is processed [canned green beans may be cut, whole or French style].)
- *Size of product* (Refers to weight [18- to 20-pound turkey], number per container [125 per box], can size [Number 10], and count [8 per pound]; see USDA *Food Buying Guide for Child Nutrition Programs* [1984, amended 1990] for yield date to assist in determining sizes desired.)
- *Origin*: Where the product was produced; domestic or imported.
  Congress encourages the purchasing of domestically grown and processed foods. (Public Law 100-237 [H.R. 1340] passed January 1988 states, "The Secretary [of Agriculture] shall require that recipient agencies [any school receiving commodities] purchase, whenever possible, only food products the are produced I the United States.") The law does not require purchasing domestic products, except for the food purchased by the commodity letter of credit sites using CLOCs (discussed in Chapter 1, "Introduction to School Foodservice").
- *Package Unit*: Crate, carton, box, retort pouch, bag barrel, or case.
- *Special instruction*: "Special instruction" may spell out other types of restrictions, for example—on processed canned foods, this year's pack may be required; and for frozen foods, the products must be delivered at 0°F or below.

---

[1]Including equipment for storage may exclude some companies from bidding and result in no competition in bidding process.

Many school districts are now requiring an ingredients list, nutritional analysis from a certified laboratory (Fig. 9.4), and restrict certain ingredients (such as artificial coloring and flavoring, MSG, sulfites, BHT and BHL).

- *Labeling required*: Child Nutrition (CN) label, institutional meat purchase specifications (IMPS), low sodium, and in the case of equipment, National Sanitation Foundation (NFS) label, and so on.

  Some definitions of food label terms appear at the end of this section.

- *Special provisions*: Usually listed in the preface of the invitation to bid.

  It is very important to the bidders to know what is expected of them and what they can expect of the school districts in the following:

  — Quantity needed per delivery ,number of delivery sites and locations
  — Period of time, length of contract
  — Conditions for payment, discounts accepted and considered in award of bid
  — Frequency of deliveries (daily or weekly)
  — Where to be delivered (inside the door, in ice cream cabinet, on dock, etc.)
  — Time of delivery (date and hour)
  — How the bid will be awarded—by line item or aggregate (aggregate means "all or nothing")
  — Conditions for adjusting and canceling orders due to changes in school schedule or other emergencies
  — Display equipment, storage equipment (such as ice cream cabinets), and promotional material required
  — Samples and can cuttings (both are expensive to the company and should be limited to those needed to make a decision on equal items when bid low)
  — Penalty if contract is not complied with
  — Back order provisions

- Specific nutrient composition (e.g., ground beef that is 85% lean)

Some product lines may be difficult to specify in such a way that more than one company can bid on a product. In the case of snack items such as cakes and pies , for example, each company may have its own special products. It may help to bid a product line, giving each company the opportunity to submit prices for a specific number of items that meet some general specifications. Student/adult taste panels can be used to determine acceptable product lines. Then the bid is awarded to the low bidder with an acceptable product line.

Accurate specifications are the secret to obtaining good quality, or the quality desired, in competitive bidding. A director or manager of a foodservice may blame poor quality on having to take a "low bid" when in fact low quality results from inadequately written specifications or a failure to enforce the bid.

When writing specifications, the following criteria should be considered:

1.   Is the bid enforceable?
2.   Is the product tailored to meet menu needs?

Figure 9.4. Example of a Nutritional Analysis

Sample B Pizza ANALYSIS	RESULT AS RECEIVED		LIMIT OF QUANTITATION	LAB CODE
Moisture	41.90	% by wt.	0.010	010101000
Protein (N x 6.25)	12.00	% by wt.	0.100	010401800
Fat (Hydrolysis Method)	17.40	% by wt.	0.100	010802800
Fiber	0.70	% by wt.	0.100	011001700
Ash	2.79	% by wt.	0.010	011201300
Phosphorus	0.23	% by wt.	0.001	011301300
Est. Digestible Carbohydrate	25.90	% by wt.	0.100	011500000
Est. Caloric Value	308.00	cal/100g	0.100	011700000
Vitamin A (HPLC)	200.00	IU/100g	20.000	012407500
Thiamine	0.34	mg/100g	0.001	13104500
Riboflavin	0.29	mg/100g	0.002	013204500
Carotene	920.00	mcg/100g	50.000	013204500
Vitamin C	< 1.00	mg/100g	1.000	013704500
Fatty Acid Profile		attached		
Cholesterol	0.047	% by wt.	0.006	019611000
Calcium	197.00	mg/100g	0.050	039701300
Iron	1.61	mg/100g	0.050	040001300
Potassium	82.80	mg/100g	0.050	040701300
Sodium	736.00	mg/100g	0.050	040801300
Sodium	736.00	mg/100g	0.005	044000000
Sodium	209.00	mg/oz	0.001	044100000
Niacin	2.60	mg/100g	0.100	115904500
Saturated Fat	47.60	%		900100000
This result was calculated from the fatty acid profile for this sample.				
Total Sample Weight	See Below			900200500
Six slices of pizza weighed 813.7 grams.				
Monounsatruated Fat	34.10	%		900300000
This result was calculated from the fatty acid profile for this sample.				
Polyunsaturated Fat	18.20	%		900400000
This result was calculated from the fatty acid profile for this sample.				

3. Is a customized product necessary? Will it add considerably to the cost?
4. Is the language used understandable to companies that may want to bid?

The prices charged in a bid for a school district should cover the company's overhead, and the price is influenced by (1) the cost to the distributor of delivering the product (including hidden costs such as taking directors/managers to dinner, gifts, and other "freebies"), (2) competition and how important the contract is to the company, and (3) the size of a minimum order. Hidden costs should be kept at a minimum, and local purchasing policies often address these issues.

There are several good sources of specifications that are listed in the selected references following this chapter. Two particularly good sources are: *Choice Plus: A Reference Guide for Foods and Ingredients* by The National Food Service Management Institute for USDA/FNS (1996) and Pannell and Applebaum (1995) *inTEAM Food System Administrator's Manual.*

Labeling Standards for Processed Foods

The **Nutrition Labeling Education Act of 1990** mandates new label requirements, which provide specific information on ingredients and nutritional contents of processed foods. The CN label is another aid to purchasers with processed foods. The main features are as follows:

Name of the label: Nutrition facts
Standardized serving size: Based on amounts people can usually eat; food manufacturer no longer determines the serving size
Calories: Total calories and calories from fat
Nutrient listing: Specific nutrients required
Daily values: New label reference number—for both 2,000- and 2,500-calorie diets
Percent daily values: Food's nutrient contribution

Food processors are expected to adhere to Food and Drug Administration ingredient standards in labeling their products. Some of the most current FDA nutritional standards are listed in Table 9. 3.

ORDERING

The process of ordering just enough food and supplies, receiving them at the right time, storing them properly, issuing them, and accounting for them is quite complex. The process is even more challenging for the manager if the menu is to be strictly adhered to and low inventory is desired. Orders should be geared to the menu and include every item needed to produce the recipes that make up the menu, if the item is not in inventory.

The person preparing orders (usually the manager) will need to (1) have a list of all items and quantities needed to serve the planned menus, (2) determine what is in inventory, and (3) determine what will be used between the time the order is placed and the time the menu being ordered for will

Table 9.3. Definition of Terms Used on Labels

Free
Nutritionally insignificant can be labeled as zero. Sodium free...less than 5 mg* Calorie free..less than 5 calories Fat free..less than 0.5 g Cholesterol...less than 2 mg cholesterol   and 2 grams or less of saturated fat* *Also per 50 g for products with small serving size. (Reference amount is 30 g or less or 2 Tbsp. or less)

Low
Low sodium...not more than 140 mg Low calorie...not more than 40 calories Lowfat...not more than 3 g* Low cholesterol....................................no more than 20 mg and   2 grams or less of saturated fat* *Also per 50 grams for products with small serving sizes. (Reference amount is 30 g or less or 2 Tbsp. or less)

Light

Light or lite.. 1/3 fewer calories or
     50% less fat; if more than
     half the calories are from fat,
     fat content must be reduced
     by 50% or more
Light in sodium ....50% reduction in sodium
Light in color.......................................permitted if adequately described

Other Label Words

Reduced, less, fewer ....25% less of the nutrient
     than the reference food
High fiber...5 gm or more per serving
High, rich in, excellent source.............contains 20% or more of the
     daily value per serving
Fresh...raw food that has not been
     frozen, heat processed or
     similarly preserved
  *Also per 50 grams for products with small serving sizes. (Reference
amount is 30 g or less or 2 Tbsp. or less.)

Source: A. Finch 1994. Used by permission.

be served. Regrettably, many managers order by guess. Often they do not have all the ingredients needed and end up borrowing from other schools or changing menus at the last minute; or they over-order and carry a heavy inventory to avoid running short. Ordering just what is needed in the proper quantities is the "ideal" and can best be done using a computerized system. Inventory changes are recorded at the point of sale, when the cashier keys into a programmed cash register what was selected—for example, a hamburger, sliced tomato and lettuce, potato sticks, and one-half pint of lowfat milk. Reordering is thus simplified and can be handled in a timely fashion (see Chapter 14, "Computerization and Automation").

Orders need to be placed in sufficient quantity to make them cost-effective for the company to deliver. Delivery cost is figured into the price paid, and larger deliveries can mean better bid prices. "Emergency" ordering of one or two items can be very costly if it becomes habitual.

In central warehouses or large schools, particularly if a cycle menu is used, an **order point** and **maximum stock level** can be used very effectively. An order point is the minimum stock level needed until the next delivery. **Par stock** is the maximum stock level for an item that should be carried in inventory in order to meet menu requirements. To determine how much to order using order point and par stock, the following formula should be used:

Par stock - reorder point + normal usage = reorder quantity

Cautions should be taken using par stock levels because of the need to reduce inventory every nine months (over the summer months).

A list of ingredients and quantities from the recipe cards and the inventory is needed to determine what to order. The *USDA Food Buying Guide for Child Nutrition Programs* (1984, as amended in 1990[1]) is an excellent source of information on yields and how much is needed.

INVENTORY MANAGEMENT

Though inventory management may not be considered by most managers as one of their hardest jobs, it is a very important one. Knowing the value of the inventory plays an important part in accurately determining the cost of goods sold and maintaining inventory control, which can make or break a foodservice. Proper storage is essential to safe, good-quality food, and product turnover. In moving inventory, it is important to control aging of products by following the "first in first out" (FIFO) principle.

Managing inventory involves (1) proper receiving, (2) proper storing in an organized facility, (3) accountability for items in storage, and (4) proper removal from storage. These topics are discussed below.

[1]New edition will be published in 1999.

Proper Receiving

The individual checking in deliveries needs to be knowledgeable about what has been ordered and the specifications of the products. Before the person receiving the order signs a delivery ticket, the following need to be verified: (1) the items ordered, (2) the quantity ordered, (3) the quality specified, (4) the correct prices and extensions, and (5) the specifications of products. The person receiving a product does not need a detailed specification, but at a minimum—the brand, code number, pack, and price. See Table 9.4, which illustrates the minimum information needed. This information can be used also when precosting and postcosting recipes and/or menus.

If it is determined that the correct quantity has been delivered, the products is undamaged and delivered at the proper temperature and the specifications have been met, the receiving person can safely sign the delivery ticket. Determining all this may require opening cases, crates, and packages,

Table 9.4 Example of the Minimum Information Needed by Receiver of Merchandise

FOOD (1)	BRAND (2)	COUNT (3)	UNIT OF PURCHASE (4)	UNIT COST (5)
Applesauce, Canned	Pocahontas	6/# 10 cans 47.5/1/4 cups	case	$ 13.93
Carrots, Sliced, Canned	Frosty Acres Red Label	6/# 10 cans 47/1/4 cups	case	$ 14.01
Cereal, Dry	General Mills	96 bowls/cs	case	$ 15.58
Corn, Whole Kernel, Canned	Green Giant	6/# 10 cans 48/1/4 cups	case	$ 16.52
Fruit Cocktail, Canned	Sysco Classic	6/# 10 cans 46.5/1/4 cups	case	$ 24.95
Green Beans, Canned	Monarch Heritage	6/# 10 cans 52/1/4 cups	case	$ 12.67
Pineapple, Tidbits, Canned	Sysco Classic	6/# 10 cans	case	$ 22.95
Tuna, Light, Canned	Chicken of the Sea	6/6 ½ oz cans 25.5/2 oz portions	case	$ 40.78
Beef Pattie, Cooked, All Beef, Frozen	Zartic No. 89021F	67/2.4 oz	case	$ 19.02
Chicken Nuggets All White Meat, Frozen	Tyson No. 2377	240 pc/case 5 nuggets = 2 oz cooked meat/meat alternate	case	$ 16.50

weighing and counting to determine if the proper quantity has been delivered, and checking against a "short" version of the product specifications. Before they are stored, the date received should be written on the cases or containers with a heavy magic marker. If there is a shortage of products and it appears on the delivery ticket, a request-for-credit memo should be filled out in triplicate, and copies should be distributed as follows: one with the delivery ticket to accounts payable (within the school district), one with the driver delivering the product, and one to be kept on file at the school. Figure 9.5 shows an example of a request-for-credit memo.

Figure 9.5. Example of a Request-for-Credit Memo

Request-for-Credit Memo				
(prepare in duplicate)			Number: _____	
From: _____		To: _____		
		_____ (supplier)		
		_____		
		_____		
_____		_____		
Credit should be given on the following:				
Invoice Number: _____		Invoice Date: _____		
Product	Unit	Number	Price/Unit	Total Price
Reason:_____			Total: _____	
_____ (delivery person)			_____ (authorizing signature)	

Source: Ninemeier 1995. Used by permission.

Proper Storing in an Organized Facility

The dry storage area should be kept at 50° to 70°F, with the lower temperature preferred. Shelving should provide good air circulation, and products should be kept at least 6 inches off the floor. Refrigerated items should be stored at 32° to 40°F, with good air circulations and at least 6 inch off the floor. Freezers should keep the food below 0°F.

Steps to good storeroom organization are as follows:
- Arrange storeroom areas in assigned grouping.
- Store heavy items at waist height or lower.
- Store light items on the upper shelves.
- Store detergents/chemicals separately from food.
- Store the least-used items in the less accessible areas.
- Label areas with group names and shelves with item names.
- Date all cases before placing them on shelves and rotate stock.
- Store goods in cases with identifiable labels visible.
- Do not store items on the floor (store at least 6 inches off the floor).
- Empty cases as they are opened.
- Schedule cleaning of storage areas.
- Assign one employee the duties of storekeeper.
- Limit the hours during which items can be obtained from the storeroom.
- Record where the food or supply that left the storage area went using food production record or snack bar/a la carte record.
- Lock storerooms

Preventing theft and pilferage is a major concern. A recent study by McGraw-Hill (1996) and the National Food Service Security Council of ten chain restaurants reveals that 44 percent of restaurant employees regularly steal/pilferage something at work each day. Thirty-five percent of workers take supplies for personal use and 17% take merchandise or food. The difference in theft and pilferage is in the amount taken. For example, if someone backs his/her van up and takes out cases of food that is theft; whereas, if someone takes a few granola bars as they leave the store room, that is pilferage. Preventing either from occurring should be the goal of the person in charge.

Accountability for Items in Storage

For an accurate count of items in inventory and accurate payment for what was received, invoices or delivery tickets must be correct when signed, verifying that the items were received. When items are removed from the storeroom in a large operation, an in-house requisition record can be used to record what is removed from inventory. The daily production record and snack bar/a la carte records can provide audit trails that account for how food and supplies were used. This is particularly true for the kitchen where requisition records are not available to provide the audit trail of where the food and supplies were used.

Inventory Records

An important part of inventory management is the inventory records. Most school districts maintain perpetual inventories, particularly of government commodities. A perpetual inventory is often not being used for purchased foods, unless the managers are using computers. All managers should be taking a physical inventory, at a minimum monthly. Unfortunately not all are doing a physical inventory, which is essential to determining the costs of food used.

Perpetual Inventory—A perpetual inventory system is an up-to-date, running record of each item on hand in the storeroom. It provides ready information to a manager for placing orders. Many managers discontinued this control measure in the mid-1970s because they could no longer justify the cost. Small school foodservices may still find it not feasible to keep a perpetual inventory. It is time-consuming; however, with the use of computers, scanners, and Universal Codes, it can easily be maintained. Perpetual inventory is desirable and recommended when automated for keeping track of food and supplies. The USDA has a requirement regarding perpetual inventorying of commodities, but it is carried out in different ways in the states.

Physical Inventory—A physical inventory is an actual count of goods in stock—at a minimum a physical inventory should be taken monthly. If a perpetual inventory is not being kept, a "mini" physical inventory will have to be taken before placing orders—if ordering is going to be done accurately. An accurate physical inventory should be taken monthly, at the end of the month. The philosophies of different state agencies about the need for inventory differ, as do their requirements. If a perpetual inventory is maintained, the physical inventory should be compared and reconciled. Any difference should be evaluated by management.

Following are some general rules for taking inventory:

1. Inventory is taken by two people, one to count and the other to record. It should not be taken by the storekeeper, since it is a check on what is in inventory.
2. Items should be inventoried by location, in the order that they are stored. Jumping around may cause an item to be overlooked.
3. Cans should be left in cases or boxes until needed and removed from cases once they have been opened.
4. Consistency should be observed. If broken cases, opened containers, or parts of containers, are counted—a procedure that should always be followed. If food in process is counted, this should be done consistently (particularly at large production sites).

The quantity of food and supplies in inventory should be lowered considerably at the end of the school year.

Value of Inventory

To obtain the value of inventory, the current price paid per purchased unit should be multiplied by the quantity on hand. Some in the profession will maintain that the value is the price paid, others use the price of the item at the time inventory is taken, and still others use an average price. There is a case for each approach. The main consideration in obtaining a meaningful cost of goods sold is consistency in how inventory is figured. Foodservice management needs to determine its policy and stick with it.

A beginning inventory (at the start of a month) and an ending inventory (at the end of a month) are needed in order to accurately determine food costs. The process of determining the cost of food and supplies used for a period of time is as follows:

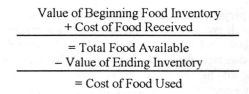

The same approach is used to determine the value of USDA donated commodities used. This should be done for purchased foods and USDA donated commodities monthly (at a minimum) to determine the true food cost.

Inventory Turnover

What is a reasonable inventory? How much should a manager have on hand at any one time? No more should be on hand than can be used between one delivery and the next. For fear a delivery will be late or participation will increase, there are few who keep "just enough."

If weekly deliveries are being made, a good gauge for determining a reasonable inventory is to have inventory turnover once every seven days. The method for determining inventory turnover is shown below in Figure 9.6 with an example.

Figure 9.6. Steps to Determining Inventory Turnover

Divide month's food cost by number of serving days in month, to determine **daily food cost**.

Food Cost $ _____ ÷ No. Days _____ = **Daily Food Cost $** _____

Divide ending inventory by daily food cost——the answer is **number of days of inventory** in stock.

Ending Inventory $ _____ ÷ Daily Food Cost $ _____ = **No. Days** _____

Example:

If 10 is the answer, the **inventory turnover rate** is twice a month (if 20 serving days in the month) or every 10 days; or use the following formula:

20 ÷ No. Days _____ = **Inventory Turnover Rate** _____

Steps to Determining Inventory Turnover Example:

$ 3,225	Beginning of Month Inventory
+ 9,200	Food Purchased During Month
$12,425	Total Food Available
− 2,950	End of Month Inventory
$ 9,475	Cost of Food Used

$ 9,475 Food Cost ÷ 20 Serving Days = $474 Daily Food Cost

$ 2,950 End of Month Inventory ÷ $474 Daily Food Cost = 6.2 Number of Days in Inventory

20 Average Number of Serving Days in Month ÷ 6.2 Number of Days Inventory =
3.2 Turnovers of Inventory

SELECTED REFERENCES

Blake, K. 1987. "Centered in Diversity." *Food Management* 22(6): 132-37, 192-99.

Dittmer, P., and G. Griffin. 1989. *Principles of Food, Beverage, and Labor Cost Controls for Hotels and Restaurants*. 3rd ed. New York: Van Nostrand Reinhold.

Gallup Organization. 1994. *National School Boards Association Purchasing Study*. Alexandria, VA: National School Boards Association.

Gunn, M. 1995. *First Choice: A Purchasing System Manual for School Food Service*. University, MS: National Food Service Management Institute.

Kaiser, J., and F. DeMicco. 1993. *Controlling and Analyzing Costs in Food Service Operations*. 3rd ed. New York: Macmillan Publishing Co.

Kotschevar, L., and R. Donnelly. 1995. *Quantity Food Purchasing*. 4th ed. New York: Macmillan Publishing.

McGraw Hill/London House and National F/S Security Council. 1996. *Study of What Food Service Workers Steal*. New York: McGraw Hill.

National Association of Meat Purveyors. 1992. *The Meat Buyers Guide*. McLean, VA: National Association of Meat Purveyors.

National Association of Purchasing Management. 1992. *Principles & Standards of Purchasing Practice*.

National Frozen Food Association. 1995. *Frozen Food Book of Knowledge*. Harrisburg, PA: National Frozen Food Association, Inc.

Ninemeier, J. 1995. *Management of Food and Beverage Operations*. 2nd ed. East Lansing, MI: The Educational Institute of the American Hotel and Motel Association.

Pannell-Martin, D. 1995. *Cost Control Manual for School Foodservice*. 2nd ed. Alexandria, VA: inTEAM Associates, Inc.

Pannell-Martin, D., and G. Applebaum. 1992. *inTEAM Food System: Administrator's Manual*. Alexandria, VA: inTEAM Associates, Inc.

Pavesic, D. 1998. *Fundamental Principles of Restaurant Cost Control*. Upper Saddle River, NJ: Prentice-Hall, Inc.

Shugart, G., and M. Molt. 1989. *Food for Fifty*. 8th ed. New York: Macmillian.

Spears, M. 1995. *Foodservice Organizations*. 3d ed. Upper Saddle River, NJ: Prentice Hall.

Stefanelli, J. 1992. *Purchasing, Selection, and Procurement for the Hospitality Industry*. 3rd ed., New York: John Wiley & Sons.

Stix, C., and S. Hiemstra. 1989. *Analysis of Cost-Plus-Fixed-Fee Purchasing System in Indiana Schools*. West Lafayette, IN: Purdue University, Restaurant, Hotel and Institutional Management Department.

U. S. Department of Agriculture (USDA). 1983. *Menu Planning Guide for Child Nutrition Programs*. PA 1260. Washington, DC: U.S. Government Printing Office.

USDA/Food and Consumer Service. 1984 (Revised 1990). *Food Buying Guide for Child Nutrition Programs*. Washington, DC: U.S. Government Printing Office.

_____. 1988. *Child Nutrition Label*. Washington, DC: U. S. Government Printing Office.

_____. 1990. *Commodity Description*. USDA FNS Instruction 716.1, USDA, Food and Consumer Service. Washington, DC: U.S. Government Printing Office.

_____. 1992. *Catalog of Food Specifications: A Technical Assistance Manual*. Vol. I, 5th ed. Dunnellon, FL: Food Industry Services Group in cooperation with the U.S. Department of Agriculture, Food & Nutrition Service.

_____. 1992. *Contract Purchasing: A Technical Assistance Manual*. Vol.II. Dunnellon, FL; Food and Industry Service Group in cooperation with the U.S. Department of Agriculture, Food & Nutrition Service.

_____. 1992. *Food Facts for Food Service Supervisors: A technical assistance manual*. Vol.III, 2d ed. Dunnellon, FL: Food Industry Services Group in cooperation with the U.S. Department of Agriculture, Food and Nutrition Service.

_____. 1992. *Guidelines for the Storage and Care of Food Products: A Technical Assistance Manual*, Vol. IV, 3d. ed. Dunnellon, FL: Food Industry Services Group in cooperation with the U.S. Department of Agriculture, Food and Nutrition Service.

_____. 1995. *The Almanac of the Canning and Freezing Industry*. Westminster, MD: Edward F. Judges, Co.

_____. 1995. *Choice Plus: A Reference Guide for Foods and Ingredients* (1996), Publication Number FCS-297. Washington, DC: U. S. Department of Agriculture, Food and Consumer Service.

_____. 1995. *The Packer 1995 Produce Availability and Merchandising Guide*. Lenexa, KS: The Packer.

_____. 1996. *USDA, Food and Consumer Service Food Distribution Program: Facts About USDA Commodities*. Washington, DC: U.S. Government Printing Office.

_____. 1998. *Summer Food Service Program for Children*. Washington, DC: U.S. Government Printing Office.

VanEgmond-Pannell, D. et al. 1987. *The School Foodservice Handbook: A Guide for School Administrators*. Reston, VA.: Association of School Business Officials International.

10
MANAGING PRODUCTION
AND SERVICE

Preparation
    Standardized Recipes
    Format for Quantity Recipes
    Adjusting Recipes
    Quality Control

Managing Production
    Production Records
    Production Board
    Scheduling "Just in Time" or Batch Cooking
    Portion Control
    Food Presentation and Garnishing

Managing Service
    Time Required to Serve
    Attitude of Employees
    Temperature of Food
    How Food Is Served

Uses for Leftovers

Selected References

PREPARATION

Some say foodservice is an exact science and others argue that it is a "love affair." Perhaps it is a little of both—which is the approach used in this chapter. The exact science part starts with standardized preparation procedures and the control aspect of the business; the "love affair" is with the beautifully presented finished products.

The greatest changes in the last ten years in school food preparation have come as a result of the emphasis on reducing fat and the continued increase in the use of convenience foods. The preparation of food in school foodservices, as in many other segments of the food industry, no longer requires a "chef" or "good cook" per se. It is with this in mind that this chapter is written. Even when food is prepared from raw ingredients, the standardized recipes and controlled equipment available today make it possible—even easy—for the novice to turn out good products. The manager and cook must be able to read and understand directions; the manager must be skilled in scheduling the cooking; and the person portioning/serving must be creative enough to present the food in an attractive, appetizing, and interesting way.

Convenience foods have improved and have become more commonly used, better accepted, and more reasonably priced. As labor costs have increased and labor shortages have grown in the 1990s, it has become hard to rationalize preparing certain foods from raw ingredients. In the 1970s pizza took days to prepare. Today most school districts purchase prepared, frozen pizza that requires only 10 minutes in the oven before serving, or components that turn out excellent pizza with two minutes' preparation time. Throughout the country a few school districts have clung to baking—even hamburger rolls. The breads they produce look and smell great to adults, but frankly, even the adults have to admit the hamburger made with a school-made roll tastes different—from what McDonald's serves. The cost of the roll may be twice what a purchased roll would have cost, and food waste may be staggering on the day served as the children eat the pattie and leave the unfamiliar bun. Many school districts have failed to check the cost of producing from raw ingredients because they have convinced themselves that such foods are always better and less expensive. The important questions to consider are what the customer prefers, whether the cost is affordable, and whether the item is priced correctly when sold a la carte.

Whether foodservice is using raw ingredients or convenience foods, its primary functions are to (1) improve the digestibility of the food, (2) conserve the food's nutritive value, (3) improve flavor and appearance, (4) provide the quality food the customer wants and (5) make the food safe for consumption. All of these goals can be achieved only when preparation starts with a good-quality ingredient.

Creativity and skill are required to make food attractive, appetizing, and interesting. Probably the area that school foodservices need to improve the most is how the food is presented and how it looks and smells to the customer. Many smaller children will smell food before they eat it—and if the aroma penetrating the building before lunch is that of ground turkey, ground beef, reconstituted onions, broccoli, or cabbage cooking, they may be turned off before they get to the cafeteria. Contrast that to the appetizing smells of chocolate chip cookies or cinnamon rolls permeating the halls which attract students and school staff alike.

Standardized Recipes

Even convenience foods and components that are combined need recipes or directions—even if it is just heating and assembling. School foodservices cannot afford to prepare food without following directions and prescribed portions. This can be done best with standardized recipes. In recent years, the emphasis on nutritional analysis has done more to encourage the use of standardized recipes than anything else. A standardized recipe is like a blueprint to a builder—exact and tested for quality and yield. Using standardized recipes and standard weights and measures accomplishes the following:

- Ensures uniform quality and eliminates "trial and error'
- Helps to ensure planned yields and prevent waste
- Saves time and money
- Facilitates more accurate precosting of menus
- Simplifies the job for employees
- Helps in determining what to order and how much
- Helps ensure compliance with meal requirements
- Helps maintain customer confidence

The recipes should be selected (developed) while planning the menus, and there should be a recipe for every item on the menu. There are numerous published sources of standardized recipes available. The standardized school foodservice recipes published by the U.S. Department of Agriculture in *Quantity Recipes for School Food Services (PA-1371)* have the advantage of calculating the contribution of each recipe to the school lunch and breakfast menus. When using recipes from other sources, it is necessary to use the U.S. Department of Agriculture *Food Buying Guide for Child Nutrition Programs* (1984, revised in 1990) to determine the contribution the recipe makes toward the menu. When there is no standardized recipe available or when the recipe used is not standardized, the manager needs to develop a standardized the recipe.

Some abbreviations that are commonly used in recipes are as follows:

tsp	= teaspoon	No.	= number
Tbsp	= tablespoon	cyl	= cylinder
cup	= cup	ml	= milliliter
pt	= pint	gm	= gram
qt	= quart	kg	= kilogram
gal.	= gallon	wt	= weight
oz	= ounce	°F	= degrees Fahrenheit
lb	= pound	°C	= degrees Celsius
fl oz	= fluid ounce	AP	= as purchased
pkg	= package	EP	= edible portion

Periods may or may not be needed after abbreviations for clarity—but if abbreviations are used, it is important to be consistent.

Format for Quantity Recipes

Figure 10.1 gives an example of a standardized recipe for pizza made with components. The format used was adapted from (Morgan, 1993) *On the Road to Professional Food Preparation*. Each school district should have a set of recipes to accompany menus—the set may be made up of recipes from several sources. It is suggested that the recipes be typed using a large-size print (12-14 size font), with the original recipe laminated. The following format is suggested:

Name of Recipe. Use chief food in name of recipe or a name that is readily understood. Simple, descriptive terms such as "Fruited Gelatin," "Grilled Cheese Sandwich," and "Deli Sandwich" are examples of good recipe names.

Ingredients. List ingredients in the order they are used in preparing the recipe. Use a descriptive term after the ingredient name to indicate the type or style to be purchased or the cooking needed before its use (for example, "tomatoes, canned," "rice, cooked," "broccoli, florets" "apple, fresh, slices").

Weights and Measures. Give weights and measures when practical, the weight alone when the item is not easily measured. Use measure alone for liquids, such as water, broth, and milk, and for small quantities too small to weigh accurately. " Part One: General Information" in (Shugart and Mott 1989) *Food for Fifty, 8th ed.,* and (Morgan, 1993) *On the Road to Professional Food Preparation* are useful when developing recipes.

Directions or Procedures. Make sure recipe directions or procedures are simply written and easy to understand and follow. Eliminate or combine as many steps as possible to reduce the time required to prepare the recipe. Use as few words as possible in describing procedures, **and** the directions or procedures should appear in the same order as the ingredients are listed. The number and size of pans should be indicated along with the cooking method, baking temperature, and time required.

Serving and Yield. Give portion sizes in common measures (e.g., ½ cup), numbers (e.g., 5 chicken nuggets), or weight units (e.g., 1 ½ ounce portion) and indicate the total number of servings the recipe will yield (e.g., 100 ½-cup servings). Adjusting a recipe is extremely easy if the original recipe will yield 100 portions. It might be helpful if quantity of ingredients is listed for 25 portions as well as 100 portions.

Nutritional Information and Contributions. Provide the nutritional content for the size portion for the same nutrients being required in the nutrient analysis of the menus. If Food-Based Menu Planning method (Traditional or Enhanced) is being used, list the recipe's contribution to the menu, e.g., one slice of pizza may contribute 1 ½ grain/bread, 2 ounces meat alternate, and 1/8 cup vegetable.

Additional Information. Include other information that is helpful in menu planning and in ordering, such as:
1. Variations that can be obtained by changing or replacing an ingredient, by changing the method of cooking, or by changing the method of combining ingredients, etc.

Figure 10.1. Pizza Recipe
CHEESE PIZZA (16" = 8 SLICES) SETUP

Yields: 104 slices
Portion Size: 1 slice (1/8)

M101

Cooking Pan: 18" x 26" x 1 ½"

INGREDIENTS/SUPPLIES	104 SERVINGS OR 13 PIZZAS	PIZZAS	DIRECTIONS
Pan Rack Rubber Spatula Scales Cup Measurer Cutting Board Pans[1], 18" x 26" x 1 ½" Pizza Cutter Knife Pot Holders Bowl, Small	1 1 1 1 1 13 1 1 2 1		1. Arrange station set up as shown below.
Pan Liners Pizza Crust, 16" Pizza Sauce, No. 10 can Cheese Mix, 5 lb bag	13 13 1 1/4 can 13 lb		2. Put pan liner on pan; add 1 crust per pan, allow to rise. 3. Spread evenly 1 cup of sauce on crust. 4. Distribute evenly 1 lb of cheese on pizza.
Deli Paper or 6-inch Paper Plate	100 sheets/plates		5. Bake pizza at 400° F for 7-9 minutes. 6. Cut pizza into 8 equal slices and serve hot on deli paper or plate.

1 slice of pizza = 2 oz of meat alternate, 1 ½ grain/bread servings, and 1/8 cup vegetable.
[1]Reuse pans and pan liner, if possible.
TIPS:
1. Thaw all ingredients in refrigerator the day before use.
2. Roll pan liners (in bulk) and stand up in stock pot; remove liners from center.
3. Prepare pizza 1 to 2 hours before cooking off for them to completely proof.
4. Spread sauce and cheese to 1/4 inch of crust edge. Do not allow either to get onto the 1/4 inch edge of crust.
5. Use bottom of measuring cup or an 8 ounce spoodle to measure and spread sauce.
6. Weigh cheese into a lunch tray/bowl; 16 ounces to each tray/bowl.
7. Bake pizza until golden brown and crust is crisp.
8. Allow to set 4 to 5 minutes after cooking before cutting.
9. Transfer the cooked, cut pizza onto a 16 inch pizza pan for service.

Pan Liners	Pizza Sauce	8 oz Ladle	Scales	Pan Rack
Pizza Crust	18" x 26"		Cheese Measuring Cup	

■ Employee

2. Marketing guide for selected items
3. Space for cost per portion (to be updated frequently)
4. Appropriate garnish
5. What the item is to be served on or in (if this is standardized in the school district)
6. Altitude adjustments, if necessary

Adjusting Recipes

When increasing or decreasing a recipe, the conversion factor method can be used. It is explained in detail in the information section of the USDA *Quantity Recipes for School Food Services* (1988). Simply stated, it is done by dividing the number of servings needed by the base yield of the recipe (using decimals). This will determine the conversion factor. The quantity of each ingredient is multiplied by the conversion factor. The factor will be greater than 1.0 when increasing the number of servings and less than 1.0 when decreasing the base yield. For example: If 475 portions are needed (1) divide 475 by the yield of the recipe (50 portions); 475 ÷ 50 = 9.5 factor or if the recipe is for 100 portions, the factor is 4.75; (2) convert measures to weights (see Shugart and Mott's *Food for Fifty* or the USDA *Food Buying Guide* [1984, Revised 1990] for conversion tables); (3) multiply the weight of each ingredient by the factor to obtain the amount to be used for the number of servings desired (see Figure 10.2). The formula is:

$$\frac{\text{New Yield}}{\text{Base Yield}} = \text{Conversion Factor}$$

Figure 10.2. Adjusting a Recipe for Grilled Cheese Sandwich

Ingredients	Base Yield 100 Portions Weights	Measures	For 475 X Conversion Factor =	New Yield 475 Portions Weights	Measures
Cheese, Sliced Lowfat, 2 oz	12 lb 8 oz		X 4.75 =	60 lb 8 oz	
Margarine, Light, Melted	8 oz		X 4.75 =	2 lb 6 oz	
or	or		or	or	
Butter, Melted	8 oz		X 4.75 =	2 lb 6 oz	
Bread, Sliced (20/loaf)		200 slices or 10 loaves	X 4.75 =		950 slices or 48 loaves

There is computer software, like SNAP, NUTRIKIDS, BOSS, and CBORD's Menu Management, that provides for precosting recipes/menus and increasing yield of recipes easily. The advantages of the computer calculation are more accurate extensions of quantities, the convenience of determining exact quantities (the number of portions) in seconds, and the conversion of quantities to the largest measurable units. Leftovers are costly and are being "made" every day by not correctly adjusting recipes when the need changes. The attitude of the cook may be, "I've always made this recipe for 350" (even though they will serve 275 at most) and creating 75 servings of leftovers.

Quality Control

Quality control starts with the quality of the product or the ingredients that make up the product, storage and handling in the process of delivery, handling during preparation, storage and handling on site up to the point of service, and storage, handling and reuse of leftovers. Using a standardized recipe, using standardized measures, and following the directions in the recipe or on the package are necessary to obtain a good-quality safe product. Regrettably, the quality of a product is often damaged after the cooking or heating, while it is being kept hot. For fear the food will not be ready on time or because the employees want to eat together before lunch is served, rather than in shifts, food is often cooked too long before it is to be served.

A quality assurance program is needed for checking the food receiving, for checking food-handling practices at the school-level, and for determining if the customer is satisfied with the quality served. Large operations (with four or more employees) may find it will save time and quantity of food ingredients to have one person weighing and measuring and setting up the work center for the other employees. This process is called "Quality and Quantity Control" (Q&QC), which is a modified ingredient room approach to controlling quality and quantity.

MANAGING PRODUCTION

Managing or supervising production of food is an important role, and in most small to average size schools it is the role of the manager. Many managers are in their offices doing paperwork when their supervision is needed in the kitchen. There are many good sources of information put out by the USDA and others on the details of producing food. It is important for the manager or the person supervising to know what a good-quality product is; otherwise, the lasagna may not look like lasagna or the spaghetti and meat sauce may be unfit to eat. Recipes may be standardized and seem complete with enough detail in directions and still not communicate to the person preparing the recipe how the product should look—and certainly not how it should taste. If an employee who is preparing a recipe has no idea what lasagna should look like, the employee may produce an entirely different product than the recipe intends.

Production Records

Production records are required by federal regulations to demonstrate meal requirements have been met, as well as being necessary for good management of inventory. The records should provide an audit trail to determine whether enough food was planned and prepared to serve the appropriate portion size. With the introduction of "offer versus serve" into the school lunch and breakfast programs, it became very difficult, indeed nearly impossible, to determine by auditing production records if enough food was available for each student to be served required components of the meal pattern. The information on the production record is valuable to the manager as well.

The information on a completed production record, such as the one shown in Figure 10.3, not only meets federal requirements but also provides very useful information. This information can be a valuable guide the next time the menu is served. The information on this record should be completed in stages; and in a centralized foodservice operation some parts can be completed by the central office (as shown in Figure 10.3). Forecasting is done by managers and takes place before orders are placed for the menu and with Nutrient Standard may form the bases for nutrient analyses. How much was prepared can be recorded in the kitchen directly on the production record by one or more employees and the leftovers and their planned use can be recorded after service of the meal.

Production Board

A production board is different from a production record, though both show how much to prepare. Production boards come in the form of chalkboards or the white wipe-off boards (40" x 60") where special pens are used in various sizes. If short menu cycles are used, this production board is easier to maintain than if a long menu cycle is used. Figure 10.4 illustrates the use of the production board for the manager or production supervisor to record the number of portions to prepare and even assign the persons responsible. At the end of the day, the board can be used to record the number served. This becomes the forecasted number for the next week when a one-week cycle menu is used. Brownsville (TX) Independent School District high school managers use a one-week menu cycle for breakfast and lunch. A production board controls their production and is easy for everyone to see and follow.

Scheduling "Just in Time" or Batch Cooking

Scheduling "just in time" to match what is needed for service is a skill that has to be learned. Unfortunately, not many school foodservice cooks practice "just in time" or "batch cooking." The advantages are many. Most foods deteriorate in quality if held at hot or cold temperatures for long periods of time. Hot foods in particular need to be cooked by batch (in quantities needed for a short period of time), as close to serving time as possible. Most students complaints about quality will be due to cooking too far ahead, not about the quality of the ingredients that go into the product.

Chapter 6, Figure 6.7, provides an example of a work schedule that plans work over the workday. Information on time should be added to each recipe for future reference and to motivate employees.

To schedule cooking close to service, the cook needs to know how long it will take for the product to be cooked and be prepared for service. Regrettably, there are very few time studies for one to use and many recipes do not provide information on preparation time. There may be variables to consider; therefore, it may be necessary for standards to be set locally or within the state. (An example of a time study is shown in Figure 10.5). All recipes should indicate how many minutes preparation will take. If work scheduling is to be done by computer, the time required must be calculated.

Figure 10.3. Example of a Daily Production Record with Portions Filled in by Central Office to Use with Cycle Menus

InTeam Food System
DAILY FOOD PRODUCTION and POSTCOSTING RECORD

1) DAY OF WEEK: TUESDAY-WK 1   MEAL (BREAKFAST/LUNCH):   LUNCH   SCHOOL: DATE:

2) NUMBER OF MEALS SERVED (From Cashier Report):   STUDENTS: ADULTS/STAFF: TOTAL:

3) A LA CARTE SALE OF MENU ITEMS (Number of Portions):

4) WEATHER CONDITIONS: (5) UNUSUAL CONDITIONS:

(6)	(7)	(8)	(9)	(10)	(11)	(12)			(13)	(14)	(15)	(16)	(17a)	(17b)	(18a)	(18b)	(19)	(20)
RECIPE #	MENU		FORECAST-100		QUANTITY FOOD PLANNED	TEMPERATURE			SERVING INFORMATION				PURCHASED		COMMODITIES			COST PER PORTION (19+18a+20)
															COST FACTOR			
CODE	MEAL COMPONENT	PORTION SIZES	SERVINGS PER UNIT	PORTIONS PLANNED		BEGIN-NING	ENDING	QUANTITIES OF FOOD PREPARED	LEFTOVERS TO BE USED	QUANTITY USED AND WASTED (13+14-15)	NUMBER PORTIONS SERVED		$ UNIT COST	$ TOTAL COST	$ UNIT COST	$ TOTAL COST/ VALUE	POSTCOST (17b+18b+19)	
INTM312B	Spaghetti Sauce/Meat	1 serving	100/rec.		1/2 rec								.1004					
INTM301	Taco w/Beef &Cheese	1 taco(2.5oz.)	100/rec.		1/2 rec								.2805		.2169			
INTL013A	Chef Salad "D"	1 serving	100/rec.		1/8 rec.								.4084					
INTV001	Salad, Tossed, no dressing	½ cup	100/rec.		1/2 rec.								.122					
09020	Applesauce, cn, sw., wolva	½ cup	16.6/#10		2/3 cn								0		.056			
19097	Sherbet, orange	1 cup	72/cs		3/4 cs.								.1562					
01982	Milk; lowfat, 1%	½ pint	50/cs.		10 es.								.1428					
01104	Milk; chocolate, lowfat, 1%	½ pint	50/cs.		1 1/2 cs.								.1352					
01077	Milk; whole, 3.3% fat	½ pint	50/cs.		1/2 cs.								.1466					
INTB020	Bread, French Garlic	1 slice	100/rec		1 rec.								.079					
06164	Salsa, commercial, variety	.25 cup	250/cs		40 ea.								.1055					
04021	Salad Dress., fat, diet	.25 cup	100/cs.		20 ea.								.0314					
04021	Salad Dress., fat, diet	2 tbl	100/cs.		20 ea.								.0314					
04023	Salad dressing, 1000 isl, diet	.25 cup	100/cs.		20 ea.								.032					
04023	Salad dressing, 1000 isl, diet	2 tbl	100/cs.		5 es.								.032					

	Total Cost - Portion Cost	
	Average Meal Cost	
	1.8964	0.68094	0.272	0.1140

**Servings per unit may be recipe (rec), pounds (#), case (cs) and can (cn).
*Menu portions are for NuMenus and meeting nutritional requirements of 5 - 11 year old.

21. COMMENTS:

22. NOTES TO MANAGER: Attach copy of today's menu to production record or the month's menu to the front of the production records for the month and all recipes used.

Manager or designee

Source: Pannell-Martin, et al. 1995.

Figure 10.3. Sample Production Record and Instructions (continued)
DIRECTIONS:

ITEM	INSTRUCTIONS
1.	Complete with school name.
2.	Record reimbursable breakfasts **or** lunches; number of students should include free, reduced-price and paid students. Add paying adults and staff breakfasts or lunches together. Total both students and adults/staff together. If more than one menu is available, and on different serving lines or areas, you may want to complete a production record for each menu; however, keep all of the production records for a day's meal (e.g., lunch) together.
3.	Record the number of servings or portions sold a la carte (separate from the lunch or breakfast) for those items that make up the meal patterns. For example: If you prepare 400 portions of pizza, sell 75 a la carte and 325 with lunch, you would record 75 pizzas under a la carte.
4.	Date the meal was served. Weather conditions often influence the number you serve. Since the production record from the last time a menu was served provides helpful information when forecasting, knowing the weather condition may also be helpful.
5.	Unusual conditions (complete for the same reasons as weather conditions); include information such as 50 out on field trip, flu epidemic, pep rally, early dismissal, etc.
6.	Put **recipe** number and indicate source. For example, USDA D-20. **If no recipe was used**, leave blank.
7.	Breakfast and menu components for lunch are: (1) meat/meat alternate, (2) fruit and vegetable, (3) grain/bread, and (4) milk. List menu items under each component that contributed to meeting the meal pattern requirements. For example: under bread/bread alternate may be **pizza crust** on a day when **pizza** is on the menu.
8.	Portion sizes; examples for bread may be one roll; for meat may be one (2 ½ oz.) patty; for vegetable may be ½ cup; milk, ½ pint.
9.	Servings per unit—refers to number of servings per pound, per can, etc. Refer to *Food Buying Guide* (USDA) and the product information in the *inTEAM Food System Administrator's Manual*.
10.	Portions planned—refers to how many you think you will serve based on previous times this menu was served or based on number you have been serving.
11.	Quantity of food planned—refers to pounds, number of cans, number of dozens, etc.
12.	Temperature of food is critical to food safety. Cold food should be at 45° F or below and hot food should be at 150° F or higher. Check temperature before service begins and again at end of service to see that equipment is holding food at safe temperatures.
13.	Quantity of food prepared is the amount of food cooked, prepared in pounds, dozen, cans, etc.
14.	Leftovers used is the quantity left over that will be served at a later time. Leftovers that are dumped should not be included.
15.	Quantity used and/or wasted is the difference between what was prepared and what is left over that will be used. Show in cans, quarts, pounds, etc.
16.	Number portions served are the portions shown on cashier report (if item is entered at point of sale).
17a.	Purchased unit cost may be obtained from delivery tickets or from the "Product Information" in the *inTEAM Food System Administrator's Manual*.
17b.	Multiply 17a (cost) by number of units (item 15).
18a.	Commodity unit cost is generally provided by USDA. If no other cost figure is available, use the price you pay when purchasing the item (value).
18b.	Multiply 18a (cost or value) by number of units used and wasted.
19.	Add 17b and 18b "Purchased Cost" and "Commodity Cost."
20.	Divide total in column 19 by number portions served (column 16).
21.	Use this space to make yourself notes for use the next time this menu is served.

Figure 10. 4. Example of a Production Board

MENU ITEM	MONDAY	TUESDAY	WEDNESDAY	THURSDAY	FRIDAY
BREAKFAST 1	Cereal with Toast 45	Cereal with Toast 25	Cereal with English Muffin 25	Cereal with Bagel 25	Cereal with Biscuit 25
2	Toast 'n' Sausage 20	Toast 'n' Sausage 20	Toast with Ham 25	Bagel 'n' Cream Cheese 25	Ham 'n' Biscuit 35
3	Cinnamon Roll 35	Cinnamon Roll 35	Hot Coffee Cake 30	Breakfast Sausage Pizza 50	Sausage 'n' Biscuit 35
4	Waffle 'n' Sausage 25	French Toast 25	Egg 'n' Ham on English Muffin 35	Hot Cinnamon Roll 30	Whole Wheat Donut 30
5	Bran Muffin 20	Blueberry Muffin 20	Apple-Cinnamon Muffin 25	Bran Muffin 20	Blueberry Muffin 25
TOTAL					
LUNCH Mama's Kitchen	Crispy Chicken 50	Hot Wings/ Roll 45	Chicken Nuggets 75	Baked Potato 50	Country Fried Steak 75
	BBQ Ribs 35	Hot Ham 'n' Cheese 40	Roast Beef 25	Local Special 35	Macaroni Ham 'n' Cheese 25
Fiesta Fare	Beefy Burrito 40	Enchiladas 45	Chicken Fajita 50	Beefy Bean Burrito 50	Crunchy Tacos with Meat 50
	Taco Basket 35	Red Beans 'n' Rice 40	Nachos and Cheese 100	Frito Pie 50	Jumbo Tostad 60
Pizzeria					
COMBO I	Double Cheese Pizza 325	Cheese/Sausage Pizza 300	Cheese/Pepperoni Pizza 325	Double Cheese Pizza 325	Cheese/Pepperoni Pizza 350
COMBO II	Chicken Parmesan/ Roll 50	Spaghetti/Meat Sauce/French Bread 100	Cheese Ravioli/ French Bread 50	Lasagna/French Bread 75	Macaroni Ham 'n' Cheese 50
Grille Works					
COMBO I	Hamburger 50 Cheeseburger 250	Hamburger 50 Cheeseburger 250	Hamburger 50 Cheeseburger 250	Hamburger 40 Cheeseburger 230	Hamburger 50 Cheeseburger 250
COMBO II	Hot Dog 50	BBQ Ribs 60	Chicken Fillet 60	Steak Sub 100	Fishburger 50
Sub Shop					
COMBO I	Tuna Salad 50	Italian Sub 30	Roast Beef Sub 40	Ham and Cheese 50	Chicken Salad Sub 30
COMBO II	Turkey 30	Ham and Cheese 50	Italian Deli 40	Grilled Chicken 35	Sliced Turkey and Cheese Sub 50
Chef Salads	Turkey 25	Ham and Cheese 25	Egg (½) Cheese (1 oz) 23	Ham and Cheese 25	Sliced Turkey 25
Bag Lunch	Tuna 10 Turkey 15	Ham and Cheese 25	Roast Beef 25	Ham and Cheese 25	Sliced Turkey 15 Chicken Salad 10
Fresh-Made Cookies	Choc. Chip 200 Peanut Butter 100	Choc. Chip 200 Oatmeal and Raisin 100	Choc. Chip 200 M & M Cookie 150	Choc. Chip 200 Peanut Butter 100	Choc. Chip 200 Choc. 100

Source: Pannell-Martin, et al. 1995

Figure 10.5. Example of a Time Study on How Long Different Jobs Take (in Minutes)

1. Cut watermelon into portions (100 6 oz portions)---------------------------- 20 minutes
2. Butter toast for browning in oven
    Use four 18" x 26" pans with 24 portions in each, 96 portions----------------- 3 minutes
3. Prepare cinnamon toast for browning in oven
    Use four 18" x 26" pans with 24 portions in each, 96 portions----------------- 5 minutes
4. Fill and roll 96 burritos --6 ½ minutes
5. Assemble 100 hamburgers in buns-- 10 minutes
6. Make 100 mini ham and cheese submarine sandwiches ---------------------- 17 minutes
    (Using hot dog size rolls, 2 oz of ham and ½ oz of cheese)
7. Make and cut 100 peanut butter and jelly sandwiches------------------------ 25 minutes
    (Applying peanut butter and jelly separately)
8. Fill tortillas and roll into 120 quesadillas-- 18 minutes
9. Fill and roll 120 tacos with meat and cheese------------------------------------ 20 minutes
10. Assemble 96 grilled (toasted) cheese sandwiches----------------------------- 8 minutes
11. Ice (frost) and cut an 18" x 26" cake into 50 pieces ---------------------------- 1 minute
12. Pan cookies for baking off --96 portions-- 7 ½ minutes
13. Portion 96 lettuce and tomato cups (servings)--------------------------------- 12 minutes
14. Pack 100 bag lunches with fruit, vegetable, cookies,
    sandwich, napkin, and straw--- 20 minutes
15. Bag 96 portions of French fries -- 12 minutes

Source: Y. Major, 1996, *Work Methods: "Work Smarter Not Harder."* San Diego (CA) School District.
Used by permission.

Portion Control

Portion control means giving a specific quantity of food for a definite price and obtaining the number of servings planned from a given recipe. Portion control plays an important part in cost control and in meeting the dietary guidelines. For example, if a roll recipe for 100 portions yields only 90 rolls, the cost per roll goes up. When food cost is high, one of the reasons may be the lack of portion control—serving portions that are too large are frequently the case.

Some of the essential tools needed to achieve portion control are slicers, scales, scoops/spoodles or dishers, ladles, and other measurers. Scoops /spoodles or dishers and ladles come in different sizes. Menu planners usually determine portion sizes, and should make certain the tools are available. Charts like the ones in Tables 10.1, 10.2, and 10.3 can be posted near the serving line. These charts will save time and can mean the difference in whether the correct portion size is served.

Table 10.1. Common Abbreviations, Equivalents and Scoop (Dipper) Equivalent Chart

COMMON WEIGHTS AND EQUIVALENTS:

1 ounce	= 2 tablespoons	= 1/8 cup
8 ounces	= 1 cup	
1 pound	= 1 pint	
	= 16 ounces	

COMMON MEASUREMENTS AND EQUIVALENTS:

3 teaspoons	=	1 tablespoon
4 tablespoons	=	1/4 cup
8 tablespoons	=	½ cup
16 tablespoons	=	1 cup
1 cup	=	½ pint
2 cups	=	1 pint
2 pints	=	1 quart
4 quarts	=	1 gallon
1 gallon	=	16 1-cup servings
	=	32 ½-cup servings
	=	40 3/8-cup servings
	=	48 1/3-cup servings
	=	64 1/4-cup servings
1 quart	=	4 1-cup servings
	=	8 ½-cup servings
	=	10 3/8-cup servings
	=	12 1/3-cup servings
	=	16 1/4-cup servings

PORTIONING TOOLS AND EQUIVALENTS:

Scoop/Spoodle Size		Measure
No. 6	=	2/3 cup
No. 8	=	½ cup
No. 10	=	3/8 cup
No. 12	=	1/3 cup
No. 16	=	1/4 cup
No. 24	=	2 2/3 Tbsp
No. 30	=	2 1/5 Tbsp

Ladle Size		Measure
1 ounce	=	1/8 cup
2 ounce	=	1/4 cup
4 ounce	=	½ cup
8 ounce	=	1 cup

Establishing the number of servings that should be obtained before the portioning begins will help in obtaining the proper yield. This information should be put on the recipe, and if the recipe does not yield the number of portions planned, this needs to be noted on the recipe. Precosting of the recipe will need to be changed to reflect the actual number of portions. Many foods are purchased today by portion, making it easier to control yield. Proportioning items like chilled fruit cups, tossed salad, and sliced meats before service can also help with speeding service and reducing number of employees needed at serving time, as well as control portions. The portioning/weighing out of meats ahead is a good "down time" job (when there is free time). An inexperienced person can be taught to do this job quite well.

Table 10.2. Pan Capacity and Portion Chart

SERVING PAN SIZE (1)	CAPACITY (2)	CUP MEASURE (3)	SCOOP NUMBER (4)	NUMBER PORTIONS PER PAN[1] (5)
Full Size 12" x 20" x 2 1/4"	7 ½ quarts or 30 cups	1/4 1/3 3/8 ½	16 12 10 8	120 90 80 60
Full Size 12" x 20" x 4"	13 quarts or 52 cups	1/4 1/3 3/8 ½	16 12 10 8	208 156 138 104
Full Size 12" x 20" x 6"	19 ½ quarts or 78 cups	1/4 1/3 3/8 ½ 1	16 12 10 8 8 ounce ladle	312 234 208 156 78
Half Size 12" x 10" x 2 ½"	3 3/4 quarts or 15 cups	1/4 1/3 3/8 ½	16 12 10 8	60 45 40 30
Half Size 12" x 10" x 4"	6 ½ quarts or 26 cups	1/4 1/3 3/8 ½	16 12 10 8	104 78 69 52
Half Size 12" x 10" x 6"	9 3/4 quarts or 39 cups	1/4 1/3 3/8 ½ 1	16 12 10 8 8 ounce ladle	156 117 104 78 39
Third Size 12" x 6 7/8" x 2 ½"	2 2/5 quarts or 9 cups + 9 tablespoons	1/8 1/4 1/3 3/8	2 tablespoons 16 12 10	76 38 28 25
Third Size 12" x 6 7/8" x 4"	3 7/8 quarts or 15 ½ cups	1/8 1/4 1/3 3/8	2 tablespoons 16 12 10	124 62 46 41

[1]Rounded off to lower full portion.

Table 10.3. Scoop Equivalent Chart With Measures and Weights

SCOOP SIZE	MEASURE	WEIGHT
#6	= 2/3 cup	or 5 ounce
Tuna, Chicken and Turkey Salad for Sub		
#8	= ½ cup	or 4 ounce
Fruit, Mashed Potatoes, Hot Green Vegetables, Tuna, Chicken, and Turkey Salad; Meat Sauce for Spaghetti		
#10	= 6 tablespoon	or 3 ounce
#12	= 1/3 cup	or 2 ½ ounce
Chili for Nachos		
#16	= 1/4 cup	or 2 ounce
Cheese Sauce for Nachos; Egg (Scrambled) = 1 Large Egg		
#20	= 3 tablespoon	or ½ ounce
#24	= 2 2/3 tablespoon	or 1 1/3 ounce
#30	= 2 1/5 tablespoon	or 1 ounce
Cream Cheese or Peanut Butter for Bagel		
#40	= 1 3/5 tablespoon	or 4/5 ounce

Source: Pannell-Martin, 1995, *inTEAM Food System Manager's Manual.*

Food Presentation and Garnishing

The preparation of good food is an important step to customer satisfaction, but how the food is presented and garnished can make a difference to the overall customer satisfaction. Food may be of excellent quality but be dull and uninteresting in appearance, so the customer won't try it because of how it looks. Does the food have that "cafeteria look" or does it look so good that customers can't resist it? A high school boy 's comment about the school cafeteria food was, "I wish it showed you cared." Garnishing refers to the serving and decorating of food in such a way as to make the food more appealing. People tend to select food based on its appearance, and students notice the difference. A meal of excellent quality may be perceived as dull and uninteresting as a result of presentation—or it can be mouth-watering and interesting-looking.

Eye appeal is influenced by the color and shape of food, dishes/containers in which it is served, portion size, neatness, expectations it caused by its appearance. Garnishing is the finishing touch that makes food look better and increases its eye appeal. A garnish can be as simple as a sprinkle of paprika or as elaborate as a radish rose. The following guidelines to garnishing and the use of color in presentation come from the filmstrip "The Art of Getting Kids to Eat" produced by Chiquita Brands many years ago, but usable today:

- *Choose garnishes that fit the budget.*
- *Make sure the garnishes can be accomplished by the average worker* (not everyone is an artist).
- *Use seasonal garnishes and decorations when appropriate.*
- *Use garnishes that are natural.*
- *Add color to fruit dishes, salads, etc., with red apples. Leave the peel on; it adds texture, color, and freshness.*
- *Use raw carrots chopped, grated, or cut into sticks or circles.*
- *Use a small amount of fresh spinach to bring an iceberg lettuce salad to life with color and texture. Spinach also adds nutritional value.*
- *Use onions (green, white, or red) for color, flavor contrast, and crispness. Chop them or cut them into rings or strips.*
- *Use small amounts of beets, though they are not usually a favorite vegetable, as an effective garnish, particularly cut in julienne strips.*
- *Add cabbage, grated or shredded, in all its varieties (red, green, or white) for color and chewiness.*
- *Make beautiful garnishes with oranges, lemons, limes, and kiwi fruit. Cut them into wedges or thin slices, or– if time permits– shape them into twists.*
- *Add snap and interest with cucumbers sliced thinly–unpeeled or peeled. Run the tines of a fork down the side of an unpeeled cucumber for a fluted effect.*

A pastry bag (with decorative tips) is a useful garnishing tool. Whipped topping available in disposable bags, for example, dispenses topping much more attractively and efficiently than when dropped by the spoonful. A twig of parsley or a mint leaf can add the fresh look desired. The addition of red and green bell peppers to corn can create a colorful Mexican-type dish. Cutting French bread on an angle not only makes it look like a larger piece, but makes it look good. The extra touch is what food presentation and effective garnishing are all about, and this should become a standard part of the recipe and , in turn, the food order. The Mississippi State Department of Education's *School Recipe Portfolio: A Merchandising Manual* (1984) and the USDA's *A Menu Planner for Healthy School Meals* (1998) provide excellent ideas on food presentation.

Garnishes have to be planned because they won't "just" happen. Each week's produce order should contain some materials for garnishing. In addition to planning the garnishes, how the food will be presented, the container or dish, and what condiments go with it, need to be planned. Disposable products allow more flexibility in container, but the cost has to be considered.

MANAGING SERVICE

Generally food in schools is served cafeteria style. The world around us is changing; however, and today very few colleges, universities, and commercial foodservices still serve cafeteria style—it is an outdated style of service. Self-service for vegetables, as well as salad/ deli bars, are popular in schools, but hard to control. Family style is used in very few instances in schools. Setting up the serving area/line or the self-service bar correctly is essential to efficient service and needs to be planned. California has probably led the way in schools with food courts and window-type service, particularly in high schools.

A diagram of where food will be put on the line or on a cart can reduce the possibility of leaving something off or placing it in an inappropriate place. Figure 10.6 provides an example of a typical line setup using a form with directions to the employees. Figure 10.7 shows an example of another type setup— window service for secondary schools with hot and cold units. This particular setup has considered every movement of the server/cashier necessary, in order to reduce wasted motion and increase speed of service.

Time Required to Serve

Elementary children are usually scheduled by the principal to eat by class and come to the cafeteria at specific times, which can work well these schedules encourage "just in time" or "batch" cooking. But, ordinarily, middle and high school students go in larger groups and have fewer lunch periods, e.g., 11:30 a.m.-12:00 noon, 12:00 noon-12:30 p.m.. Secondary school students are not willing to stand in line more than 10 minutes. If the rate of service is 10-12 meals per minute, then a line of more than 100 students will cause discontent.

Running out of food slows a line. Not having the advertised menu items and having to make students wait while more food is prepared delays a line and makes for unhappy customers. Students may be forgiving the first time (usually), but not after repeated occurrences.

In recent years, block scheduling in the high schools in some school districts has meant one lunch period and an entire student body to serve. Additional serving areas and people, proportioning and packaging food, will be needed to provide the speed in service when all the students are to be served during the same lunch period. Figure 10.7 illustrates the use of window-type service for a secondary school, where timing is very important. The San Diego (CA) Unified School District, as do many other school districts, employs students to serve/sell, which is quite successful in San Diego with the window-type service. The students are paid and trained—the result is a very efficient operation.

Attitude of Employees

The attitude of employees toward their jobs and the customer makes a lot of difference in how customers feel about the school's food. Too often when students are questioned about their school foodservice, they complain that those serving the food are "mean," "always grumpy," or "always yelling." It is important to be friendly, patient, and nurturing to the first graders and kindergarten children, who at the first of the school year may be frightened and uncertain. Those students will be the customers for the next six years.

Temperature of Food

It does not matter how pretty food looks, if it is not good, or if hot food is served cold or cold food is served warm. The serving temperature should be appropriate to each food. Hot food should be served hot–140°F. This is discussed in more detail in Chapter 11, "Serving Safe Food." There is

Figure 10.6. Example of a Serving Line Set Up to be Used by the Person Setting Up for Service In TEAM FOOD SYSTEM

SERVING LINE SETUP (WITH 4 WELLS)

MENU NO. CYCLE 1 WK. 2   LINE NO. 1   Breakfast ☐   LUNCH ☒   DATE _____   DAY MONDAY

	1	2	3	4	COLD SECTION	BEVERAGES
SERVING COUNTER WITH 4 WELLS	BARBEQUE RIB ON BUN	BEEF AND BEAN BURRITO	CORN / PEAS	TEXAS TOAST	CHEF SALAD / TOSSED SALAD / APPLE / GRAPES	Ice; ✓ Milk, 1%; ✓ Choc, 1%; 2%; ✓ Whole; Lemonade; Iced Tea; Fountain

CONTAINER FOR ITEM TO BE SERVED IN

Option	1	2	3	4
6 inch Plate	✓	✓		✓
Oval Bowl				
Hot Dog Boat				
Pizza Tray				
Plaid Boat #25				
Plaid Boat #50				
Styrocup, 4 oz			✓ (Styrobowl, 4 oz)	
Styrocup, 8 oz				
Sandwich Wrap				
Deli Paper			✓	✓
Gloved Hand	✓			

SERVING UTENSILS

Utensil	1	2	3	4	COLD SECTION
Tongs					
Spatula		☒			
Scoop					
Ladle					
Spoodle,slot#			☒ #4 OZ		
Spoodle,sol.#					

SALAD DRESSING: Ranch; ☒ Italian; French; ☒ 1000 Island

CUPS: 8 oz; 12 oz; 16 oz; 20 oz   Scoop ☐   Tong ☐

CONDIMENTS: Margarine; Butter; Salt &; Pepper; Sugar; Creamer; Lemon; Catsup; Mustard; Tartar Sauce; ✓ BBQ Sauce; Taco Sauce; Honey; Mayonnaise; Relish; Jelly; Syrup

TEMPERATURE RECOMMENDED / HEAT

	1	2	3	4
HEAT:	Off / ☒ Medium / Low / High	Off / ☒ Medium / Low / High	Off / ☒ Medium / Low / High	☒ Off / Medium / Low / High

Special Instructions:

☒ Sanitizing Solution with Cloth   ☒ Plastic Gloves   ☒ Hot Pads

DIRECTIONS: Use this form for planning line setup and to direct someone in setting up a line. Fill in those containers designated with quantity expected to be needed.

Source: Pannell-Martin, et al. 1998.

Figure 10.7. Secondary Window Service with Hot & Cold Food

Arrange all merchandise in hot and cold units within easy reach; place most popular items closest to the cashiers.

Keep serving areas attractively set up and uncluttered.

Place all fruit and vegetable selections in a wirebasket for cashiers to share.

Position merchandising racks on serving area in front of stationary window for easy reach and visible display—two cashiers share one merchandising rack.

Never leave the serving window during service. Let assigned "floater" replenish supply as needed.

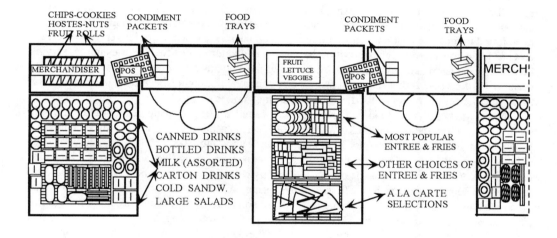

Source: Y. Major, 1996, *Work Methods: "Work Smarter, Not Harder,"* San Diego (CA) School District. Used by permission.

very little written on "how" best to hold cooked foods at the appropriate temperature; however, more damage occurs to quality during the holding period, after the food is cooked, than at any other stage of the process. The newer temperature and humidity controlled heated holding cabinets help hold a high quality product, but they do not take the place of "just in time" cooking.

"Just in time," or cooking in batches according to need, should be encouraged when feasible to prevent food from having to be held for long periods of time(discussed above). Hot- and cold-holding equipment placed near the serving line can help provide proper temperatures, which are necessary to safe and good-quality food.

How Food Is Served

How food is served, as well as on what it is served, can make a difference. For example, serving hamburgers and other sandwiches in aluminum or paper wraps as used by fast-food restaurants has been found to increase customer satisfaction and keep the sandwiches warm longer. However, the cost has to be considered. Can the cost of the serving container be justified? For example, serving French fries in bags makes portion control easier, and the students feel content with the serving size because it is the same as that served in fast-food restaurants. For some, this makes the portion look much like the commercial fast food, which may or may not be desirable.

Novel ways of serving food will spark interest; for example, preparing peanut butter and jelly sandwiches, calling them "lunchables" or "biteables". This is done by putting the ingredients for a peanut butter and jelly sandwich (No. 30 scoop of peanut butter, No. 30 scoop of jelly, and two slices of bread cut in half with a disposable small knife) in a disposable tray (like a nacho tray). This idea of making your own sandwich can be fun for elementary children and often increases the popularity of this menu item. Serving lunch on a frisbee in the spring, in a bag when lunch can be eaten outside on a nice day, or in a basket for a picnic or field trip adds interest to eating the school's food. For example, serving a sandwich lunch at Halloween in a "trick-or-treat" bag, imprinted with safety tips can make a hit with students (and parents). Using the outdoors when weather permits can make eating at school more fun.

USES FOR LEFTOVERS

A key to controlling or reducing food costs is to forecast, order, and prepare **just enough** food for the number of customers served. It is impossible to always meet this goal because of unexpected events that may occur. Restaurants that stay in business and school foodservices that have low food costs usually are the ones that (among other good practices) utilize their leftovers. Planning the use of leftovers is a job that should be assigned to someone. Leftovers should be documented on the production record when left over and on the production record on the day they will be used. With Nutrient Standard Menu planning, the leftovers need to be used within the week.

The USDA has sponsored a "National Summit on Food Recovery and Gleaning," with the purpose of encouraging foodservices to utilize food leftovers to serve people in need. While helping the hungry is commendable, the goal of the foodservice manager should be that there is not enough food left over on a typical day to make it worth picking up for distribution elsewhere.

SELECTED REFERENCES

Freeland-Graves, J., and G. Peckham. 1987. *Foundations of Food Preparation.* 5th ed. New York: Macmillian Publishing. Co.

London, R., and S. Stallings. 1986. *Food Preparation and Service.* Columbia, SC: State Department of Education.

Major, Y. 1996. *Work Methods: "Work Smarter Not Harder."* San Diego, CA: San Diego Unified School District, Food Services Department.

Mississippi State Department of Education. 1993. *High Time for Low Fat.* Jackson, MS: State Department of Education, Bureau of Child Nutrition.

_____. 1984. *School Recipe Portfolio: A Merchandising Manual.* Jackson, MS: State Department of Education, Bureau of Child Nutrition.

Morgan, E. 1993. *On the Road to Professional Food Preparation.* Publication Number NFSMI ET5-03. University, MS: The National Food Service Management Institute.

Ninemeier, J. 1995. *Management of Food and Beverage Operations.* 2d ed. East Lansing, MI: The Educational Institute of the American Hotel and Motel Association.

Pannell-Martin, D., and G. Applebaum. 1992. *inTEAM Food System Administrator's Manual.* Alexandria, VA: inTEAM Associates, Inc.

_____. 1995. *inTEAM Food System Manager's Manual.* Alexandria, VA: inTEAM Associates, Inc.

Pannell-Martin, D., G. Applebaum, and E. Soares. 1998. *inTEAM Manager's Production Manual.* Alexandria, VA: inTEAM Associates, Inc.

Payne-Palacio, J., and M. Theis. 1997. *West and Wood's Introduction to Foodservice,* 8th ed. Upper Saddle River, NJ: Prentice-Hall, Inc.

Shugart, G., and M. Molt. 1989. *Food for Fifty.* 8th ed. New York: Macmillan Publishing   Co.

U. S. Department of Agriculture. 1998. *A Menu Planner for Healthy School Meals.* Washington, DC: U. S. Government Printing Office.

_____ . 1984 (revised 1990). *Food Buying Guide for Child Nutrition Programs.* Washington, DC: U.S. Government Printing Office.

_____. 1988. *Quantity Recipes for School Food Services.* Washington, DC: U.S. Government Printing Office.

11
SERVING SAFE FOOD

Foodborne Illnesses

Hazard Analysis and Critical Control Point (HACCP)

Purchasing Safe Food
    Food Allergies
    Concerns About Ingredients
    Foreign Substances

Preventing Bacterial Growth
    Temperature
    The pH of Food

Storing Food Safely

Food Handlers

Sanitary Preparation and Serving Conditions
    Potentially Hazardous Foods
    Thermometers
    Sanitizing of Work Surfaces and Utensils

Employee and Customer Safety
    AIDS Risk
    Hazardous Substances
    Emergency Situations

Selected References

FOODBORNE ILLNESSES

Good food is safe food. Safe food is free of microorganisms, chemicals, and foreign substances. To be safe, food must be purchased clean and kept wholesome and free from spoilage. It must be properly stored under sanitary conditions and be prepared by people who have sanitary habits and who are free from communicable diseases. To keep prepared food safe, it must be held at the proper temperature and be served by people with sanitary habits who are free from communicable diseases.

One of the greatest fears of most foodservice managers is foodborne illnesses, particularly an outbreak of food poisoning resulting from food served in their facilities. Symptoms of foodborne illnesses include abdominal pain, nausea, vomiting, and/or diarrhea. Death can result from foodborne illness. (Chapter 16 addresses responses to the media in case of such emergencies.)

New bacteria have appeared in foods and situations one would never have expected, for example, contaminated frozen strawberries from the USDA. During the 1980s, the overall public health risk from foodborne organisms, such as salmonella, and in the 1990s the appearance of E. coli 0157:H7, a rare but particularly virulent strain of bacteria, and Cyclospora on fresh produce caused concern. When hamburgers are juicy and pink, there is the risk of E. coli, as Jack in the Box learned in 1994, when four children died and approximately 700 adults and children became ill as a result of their serving under-cooked hamburger contaminated by E. coli bacteria. Bacterial organisms in meat and poultry are frequently the cause of illnesses. The Centers for Disease Control estimated the annual death toll from E. coli 0157:H7 in 1994 was 500. Young children and elderly people that are more susceptible to the effects of these bacteria.

An outbreak of typhoid in suburban Washington, DC, in 1988 was traced to a local McDonald's. Shrimp salad was contaminated by an infected employee and transmitted typhoid to the customers. Typhoid had been rare in the United States in recent years.

Campylobacter, as well as salmonella, organisms should not be forgotten because they are responsible for many of the outbreaks of food poisoning. They cause a "flu"-type illness. *Campylobacter Jejuni*, a recently identified pathogen, is most common in poultry and is transmitted when poultry is served raw or insufficiently cooked. The FDA and USDA have in place a nationwide program of testing poultry to track down sources of salmonella contamination. Eggs are an unusually high source of salmonella poisoning. It is believed that the bacteria enter the eggs during ovulation. Originally, it was thought that only cracked and uncooked eggs transmitted salmonella, but research has shown that this is not the case.

It is important in food preparation to cook poultry, ground beef, and pork until done. Meats like deli turkey and chicken slices for sandwiches should be purchased only from processing plants with good quality-control measures and high sanitation standards. According to the Center for Disease Control and Prevention in Atlanta, when foodborne illnesses occur the contributing factors have confirmed that improper holding temperatures were partially responsible for about 59% of the cases and poor personal hygiene for about 35%.

The FDA has a comprehensive food code which calls for lowering the required refrigeration temperature for potentially hazardous food to 40°F. or lower. Fast-food chains are requiring processors and suppliers to provide hamburger, poultry, and other fresh or frozen protein foods with low pathogen levels, essentially free of bacterial contamination. School foodservice directors may want to add these requirements to meat, poultry, and fish specifications.

There have been a few instances when USDA-donated commodities were contaminated, e.g., ground beef. The USDA has since taken corrective action and stepped up its inspection of plants. The department has also tightened up regulations on the storage of raw ingredients and the processing of precooked foods as far as time and temperature requirements are concerned. The labels on precooked foods now warn the users: "For Safety, Cook Until Well Done (Internal Meat Temperature of 160° F.)." In some parts of the country the temperature must be 165° F.

The Food Safety and Inspection Service of the Department of Agriculture has pressured the poultry industry to "clean up" its products. In the 1980s, poultry was the largest single source of salmonella and other foodborne organisms that cause food poisoning. There are excellent training packages, that contain videotapes, posters, and trainer's guides available from the National Food Service Management Institute (University, MS). One such package called "Food Safety Is No Mystery," was developed in 1987. This training package can be obtained at a nominal sum from the Food Safety Poultry Hotline (1-800-535-4555) in Washington, DC.

The three basic rules for keeping food safe and preventing food-related diseases are (1) buy safe food, (2) keep food safe, and (3) when in doubt, throw it out.

HAZARD ANALYSIS AND CRITICAL CONTROL POINT

Hazard Analyses and Critical Control Point (HACCP), a procedural method of keeping food safe, was developed by the Pillsbury Company for the space program. It was a revolutionary method, but it did not gain wide acceptance right away. M. Sanson, managing editor of *Restaurant Hospitality*, describes HACCP as "a space-age food safety idea whose time has come." Legal mandates regarding safe food are now becoming a reality with the cooperative efforts of the Food and Drug Administration (FDA) and the USDA. It serves two functions: monitoring of food and controlling food-borne illness. For example, it is a mandatory inspection for the seafood industry and for the meat and poultry industry. It is slowly becoming the required system of inspection for all foodservice operations.

The USDA has expanded the HACCP system beyond the nation's largest meat and poultry processors and it now is including 3,000 smaller plants across the country. The federal budget for fiscal year 2000 contains increased spending for food safety, particularly in the form of food-handling educational efforts.

HACCP focuses on preventive controls rather than emphasizing monitoring and corrective action. The way employees handle food from the time food enters the back door until it is served is stressed. Many restaurant chains, school district foodservices, and other foodservice operations are requiring the HACCP procedures for keeping food safe.

The seven steps in HACCP procedures are:

1.   Complete a hazard analysis checklist that includes the critical control points where or when foods may become contaminated.

2. Identify the controls necessary for avoiding contamination.
3. Establish the danger zone and limits at each critical point.
4. Identify procedures for monitoring each critical point.
5. Determine corrective action to be taken when a critical control point limit has been exceeded.
6. Establish a record-keeping system that is checked daily and whereby action taken is recorded.
7. Determine through verification procedures that the HACCP plan is working.

These seven steps were adapted from "Food Safety I.Q.: Understanding HACCP" by M. Sanson in the *Restaurant Hospitality Magazine* (1997).

There are critical control points in every recipe and preparation procedure, and they need to be identified. It is often wise to insert in recipes ways of avoiding contamination. For example, when preparing chicken salad:

- Refrigerate cooked chicken immediately after it has completed cooking, cooled to a temperature of 40°F, or lower within four hours, under refrigeration.
- Refrigerate all ingredients and tools (e.g., mixing bowl) prior to combining salad ingredients.
- Keep preparation time to a minimum; refrigerate between steps if much time will elapse.
- Maintain a safe temperature after preparation and during serving time.
- Check temperature of product frequently.

A frequently overlooked part of the HACCP process in school foodservices is processes whereby products are partially prepared one day and finished another day and in the handling of leftovers. Some managers, for example, precook the ground beef for taco filling, spaghetti sauce, or lasagna the day before service. The following day the meat is used. Each time a product is heated and cooled it passes through the unsafe (danger) zone and is increasing the risk of contamination. It is far safer to prepare and serve foods on the same day whenever possible.

The procedures are detailed but most school kitchens are already doing most of the proper things. There is an HACCP-certification program that many foodservice operations have instituted. Local health departments in many parts of the country require all foodservices to have a certified operator on duty at all times during the preparation and service of food.

The FDA and the Educational Foundation of the National Restaurant Association have teamed up and sponsor SERVSAFE "Serving Safe Food" seminars across the country. The training program will test and certify attendees who successfully complete the course. The National Science Foundation (NSF) has a specialized food and beverage safety and quality-control program for the foodservice industry that is based on the Recommended International Code of Practices/ Iso9000/ HACCP and Food Hygiene Practices.

Two excellent sources of training information and courses for school foodservice managers can be obtained from the USDA, "Serving It Safe: A Manager's Tool Kit" (FCS-295), available through the National Food Management Institute, and the HACCP training, available through the National Restaurant Association, Education Foundation.

PURCHASING SAFE FOOD

Purchasing safe food is not difficult in the United States. A National Academy of Sciences report states that the food supply in the United States is the "safest in the world." There is still need for concern, however, and this is illustrated by Congress' budget for the year 2000, which earmarks money for improving food safety. Presently, there are ten or more major federal laws protecting the public against contaminated foods.

Food Allergies

Food allergies are concerns for school foodservice management. Some schools have banned certain foods because some people may be allergic to them, such as peanuts. Most agree that banning some foods could set a dangerous precedent because there are children allergic to many other foods. The Food Allergy Network recommends that children learn how to eat safely while surrounded by foods that could harm them. Foodservice management should make available to parents upon request the ingredient lists for foods, so the child will know what he or she can and cannot eat. Information regarding food allergies can be obtained from the American Academy of Allergy and Immunology (Milwaukee, WI), the Food Allergy Network (Fairfax, VA), and USDA, Food and Nutrition Services (Alexandria, VA).

Concerns About Ingredients

Public awareness and increased sensitivity to certain chemicals in food have brought attention to the various chemicals found in processed foods. There are more than 2,000 chemicals used as direct additives to food. These have to be designated as "generally recognized as safe" (**GRAS**) under the Food, Drug, and Cosmetic Act. The **Delaney clause** is a provision of the U.S. Food, Drug, and Cosmetic Act that prohibits the use of additives that have been shown to be carcinogenic in animals or humans. Color additives amendments mandate to the Delaney clause that public safety be the primary consideration of any food.

Artificial coloring, such as yellow dye, Number 5, is associated with allergic reactions. Feingold (1974) has brought attention to this substance.

BHA and BHT are chemicals that are added to fat-containing foods to prevent oxidation and to delay rancidity. **Butylate hydroxy anisole** (BHA) is in processed foods such as potato chips, pre-sweetened cereals, and bouillon cubes. **Butylate hydroxy toluene** (BHT) is used in frying oils.

Monosodium glutamate (MSG) enhances the flavor primarily of protein-containing foods, but is used in everything from soup to nuts. Some people are allergic to it and experience headaches, tightness in the chest, and a burning sensation in the forearms and back or neck.

Sodium nitrite and sodium nitrate are used to preserve meat, maintain red colors, contribute to flavor, and prevent the growth of bacteria. The levels used have been lowered in recent years, and these chemicals have been eliminated in some foods where previously used. Whenever they are eliminated, however, the products become very perishable, particularly in the case of pork.

Sulfite is used to prolong the shelf like of fresh fruits and vegetables. Because of the chemical reactions some people experience, particularly asthmatic children, the federal government banned sulfites in July 1986 in most fresh fruits and vegetables. The ban did not cover processed potatoes. The FDA requires that the ingredient label indicate if sulfites have been used in the products.

Alar, a trade name for the chemical daminozide, is used on fruit and vegetable crops to increase firmness, enhance color, and extend storage life. It is currently thought to be used on as much as 20 to 30 percent of the apple crop in the United States. The Environmental Protection Agency (**EPA**) says it is used on as little as 5 percent of all crops. However, as a result of animal studies showing the potential carcinogenicity of Alar, the EPA halted the use of the product.

The EPA tolerance for daminozide is 20 parts per million (ppm) for apples and apple products and 55 ppm for canned cherries. *Tolerance* means the maximum safe level of pesticide, and that anything over the tolerance is not safe (*FDA, Consumer Report*, 1988)

Washing or peeling an apple will not remove daminozide if it has been used on the crop. School districts are requiring of distributors lists of pesticides used, lab analyses, and/or certification from the food processor or orchard that Alar and other unsafe pesticides have not been used on a product.

Insecticides, if ingested (depending on the amount), can cause a person to experience the following symptoms within five minutes if particularly allergic: headache, nausea, vomiting, diarrhea, salivation, blurred vision, cyanosis, nervousness, sweating, and chest and abdominal pains (Taetakow and Vorperian 1981). One way of preventing harm from most insecticides is to wash all fresh fruit and vegetables carefully before using or serving. However, some residues cannot be removed by washing.

It is nearly impossible to eliminate (or avoid) all added chemicals from foods. Even processed American cheese has artificial coloring added. Ben Feingold's book, *Why Your Child Is Hyperactive*, led to the organization of Feingold parent groups in the late 1970s. These groups brought pressure on school foodservice directors in several parts of the country. Studies done by school foodservice programs show that it is possible to eliminate some to the additives, preservatives, and artificial flavorings and colorings; but the costs of the food products were higher when this was done and acceptance by consumers is mixed. The concerns of the 1970s subsided during the 1990s, but will probably reappear in the future.

Foreign Substances

Foodservice managers have to be alert to foreign substances that might find their way into foods—before reaching the kitchen as well as during preparation and service. The most common substance is hair, which can turn a customer off and also carry bacteria. Other substances that occasionally make their way into food are nuts or bolts from equipment, wire ties, metal shavings, and broken glass. If consumed, these substances can damage teeth or the intestinal tract. Manufacturers carry product liability insurance that will pay for damage or injury, but foodservice specifications should include this as a requirement.

Pests, such as rats, mice, flies, worms, and roaches, may sometimes be found in any foodservice operation. When they are present all the time, however, it is a sign of poor sanitation standards. These insects and rodents can spread disease organisms and filth and should be controlled using methods approved by the local health department.

Periodic visits by an exterminator can help control pests in foodservice operations, but good housekeeping practices, as described below, are the basic means of controlling pests:

- Inspect food supplies before storing for signs of insects and rodents.

- Keep stocks of food as fresh as possible by rotating stock.
- Store foods in a dry place at the correct temperature.
- Do not store food or supplies directly on the floor.
- Remove and destroy infested foods.
- Clean up spillage immediately.
- Do not use shelf paper.
- Screen all windows, doors, and outer openings.
- Make sure that all doors are self-closing (and open outward for safety reasons).
- Keep all food covered.
- Place all garbage promptly into nonabsorbent, easily cleaned garbage cans with tight-fitting lids.
- Scald and air garbage cans daily.
- Clean up all piles of rubbish, boxes, rags, and so on.
- Seal all openings around pipes.

PREVENTING BACTERIAL GROWTH

Foodborne illnesses are a major health problem in the United States today. There are five major types of food poisoning today, which are shown in Table 11.1. Foodservice management can prevent unwanted bacterial growth by eliminating the conditions under which bacteria reproduce. Bacteria need suitable temperature, food, moisture, pH, and in some cases, oxygen. Temperature and pH are discussed below.

Temperature

There are many critical points in preventing bacteria from growing. A very important step in preventing bacterial growth is to keep food cold or hot. (See Figure 11.1 for guidelines on safe temperatures for foods.) The Education Foundation of the National Restaurant Association has numerous training manuals and textbooks on HACCP that are recommended.

A food thermometer should be used by the manager and cook several times a day to determine if foods are at the correct temperature. Harmful bacteria multiply extremely rapidly when the temperature is between 40° and 140°F. When most perishable foods are refrigerated, most harmful bacteria will be in a dormant stage. Cooking at temperatures at 165°F kills most bacteria.

The temperature of food should be taken at several points in the process, as follows:

- When fresh meats/fish/poultry or frozen foods are received to determine if it is at refrigerator temperatures or at freezing temperatures
- In storage the temperatures of the cooler and freezer checked and recorded daily
- During preparation temperatures are checked at several points
- Just prior to service and at the end of service (when on a serving line or in a holding cabinet)

Figure 11.1.   Critical Temperatures for Keeping Food Safe

Temperatures
for
Food Safeness

TABLEWARE
AND UTENSIL
SANITATION

FOOD HANDLING
AND STORAGE

	F.	C.	
Maximum temperature for mechanical rinse	195°	91°	
Mechanical rinse at nozzle	180°	82°	Food cooked to this temperature-- harmful bacteria killed
Minimum rinse temperature at dish (mechanical or drip rinse)	170°	77°	
	165°	74°	Minimum safe temperature of cooked food (store or display hot cooked food above this temperature after cooking)
Temperature for mechanical dishwashing	150°	66°	
	140°	60°	
Water temperature for hand dishwashing	130° TO 120°	54° TO 49°	**Rapid Bacterial Growth**
Temperature for scraping dishes	110° TO 100°	43° TO 38°	**DANGER ZONE FOR FOOD SAFENESS**
	90° TO 65°	32° TO 18°	Normal room temperature
	50°	10°	
	40° TO 32°	4° TO 0°	Cold or chilled food storage (slow bacterial growth)
	0° TO -10°	-18° TO -23°	Frozen food storage

Source: Hatco Corporation 1999.

Table 11.1. Five Major Types of Food Poisoning

Type of Food Poisoning	Description and Characteristics
Salmonellosis	Bacteria borne illness caused by *Salmonella*. Grows in intestinal tracts of humans and animals. **Transmitted by:** salads, custards, poultry, raw eggs, red meats, dairy products, and infected persons. **Symptoms:** nausea, severe headache, diarrhea, abdominal pain, and fever. **Characteristics:** onset 6-12 hours (as long as 72 hours); lasts 1-3 days. **Preventive measures:** thoroughly cook poultry; heat food to 165° for 15 seconds.
Clostridium Perfringens Enteritis	The spore-forming bacteria, *Clostridium perfringens*, can grow with oxygen. **Transmitted by:** eating foods containing the toxin; human (intestinal tract), animals, soil. **Symptoms:** abdominal pain, nausea, diarrhea, and acute inflammation of stomach and intestines. **Characteristics:** onset 6-24 hours; lasts 24 hours. **Preventive measures:** for cooked meats, gravies, and meat casseroles that are to be stored, cool rapidly and refrigerate at 40°F or below.
Staphylococcus	This bacterium produces a toxin that is very difficult to destroy even with heat; caused by *Staphylococcus aureus*. **Transmitted by:** food-handler to food, usually high-protein foods, e.g., egg custard, egg salad, casseroles. **Symptoms:** vomiting, headaches, diarrhea, and abdominal cramps. **Characteristics:** onset 2-8 hours; sometimes within 30 minutes; lasts 1-2 days. **Preventive measures:** control growth by keeping hot foods hot and cold foods cold.
Botulism	Caused by *Clostridium botulinum*, a spore-forming organism and produces toxin; fatality rate is high (about 50 percent). **Transmitted by:** canned, low-acid foods, and smoked fish. **Symptoms:** nervous symptoms, weakness, double vision, difficulty swallowing, speech difficulty, vomiting. **Characteristics:** onset 4 hours to several days; lasts several days to a year. **Preventive measures:** proper canning procedures; the toxin is destroyed by boiling for 10 minutes.
Escherichia coli or E. coli 0157:H7	Lives in the intestines of animals and humans. **Transmitted:** meats (especially undercooked meats), deli meats, apple cider, unpasteurized dairy products and commercial mayonnaise. **Symptoms:** watery diarrhea, blood in urine, jaundice, fever, and severe abdominal pain. **Characteristics:** onset 3-8 days up to 10 days. **Preventive measures:** good personal hygiene, clean meat processing, irradiation of meats, and avoidance of raw, rare, or undercooked ground beef.

Once food is cooked, the cooling-down period is crucial. Improper cooling can be the reason for food poisoning outbreaks. The food may take hours to cool if stored in too deep a pan. Food should not be left at room temperature but refrigerated immediately. Warm or hot food should be stored in shallow pans. If stored in deep pans, it may take five to six hours to reach a safe temperature; during that time bacteria can grow rapidly.

The pH of Food

The pH is a measure of the acidity or alkalinity of a medium. A pH of 7 is neutral, neither acidic or alkaline. A food with a pH below 7 is acid, and above 7 is alkaline. The pH range of food will determine to some degree the potential of food poisoning developing. The normal pH range of food is from 0 to 14— 0 being the level of high-acid foods. A pH of 4.5 or lower inhibits growth, so the lower the pH, the less likely bacteria will grow.

The pH of meats, for example, occurs is favorable to bacterial growth, as shown in Figure 11.2. Bacteria grow best in foods that have a neutral pH or are slightly acidic or slightly alkaline (a range between 5 and 9). The growth of bacteria is greatly inhibited by a very acidic medium. Table 11.2 shows the approximate pH of selected foods.

Figure 11. 2. Effect of pH on Bacterial Growth

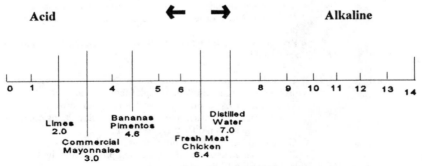

Adapted from the Educational Foundation of the National Restaurant Association 1992. Used by permission.

Table 11.2. Approximate pH of Selected Foods

Food	pH Range	Food	pH Range	Food	pH Range
Egg white	7.6-9.5	Celery	5.7-6.0	Dry sausages	4.4-5.6
Shrimp	6.8-8.2	Peas	5.6-6.8	Pimentos	4.3-5.2
Crab	6.8-8.0	Turkey	5.6-6.0	Tomato juice	3.9-4.7
Scallops	6.8-7.1	Chicken	5.5-6.4	Mayonnaise	3.8-4.0
Cod, small	6.7-7.1	Halibut	5.5-5.8	Tomatoes	3.7-4.9
Cod, large	6.5-6.9	Beans, lima	5.4-6.5	Jams	3.5-4.0
Catfish	6.6-7.0	Potatoes, Irish	5.4-6.3	Apricots	3.5-4.0
Soda crackers	6.5-8.5	Walnuts	5.5-57	Applesauce	3.4-3.5
Maple syrup	6.5-7.0	Pork	5.3-6.4	Pears	3.4-4.7
Milk	6.3-6.8	Beef	5.3-6.2	Grapes	3.3-4.5
Brussels sprouts	6.3-6.6	Onions	5/3-5.8	Cherries	3.2-4.1
Whiting	6.2-7.1	Sweet potatoes	5.3-5.6	Pineapple	3.2-4.1
Haddock	6.2-6.7	Cabbage	5.2-6.3	Peaches	3.1-4.2
Cantaloupe	6.2-6.5	Turnips	5.2-5.6	Rhubarb	3.1-3.2
Dates	6.2-6.4	Spinach	5.1-6.8	Strawberries	3.0-4.2
Herring	6.1-6.6	Asparagus	5.0-6.1	Grapefruit	2.9-4.0
Butter	6.1-6.4	Cheese, most	5.0-6.1	Raspberries	2.9-3.7
Honey	6.0-6.8	Camembert	6.1-7.0	Apples	2.9-3.5
Mushrooms	6.0-6.5	Cottage	4.1-5.4	Plums	2.8-4.6
Cauliflower	6.0-6.7	Gouda	4.7	Oranges	2.8-4.0
Lettuce	6.0-6.4	Bread	5.0-6.0	Cranberries	2.5-2.8
Egg, yolk	6/0-6.3	Carrots	4.9-6.3	Lemons	2.2-2.4
Corn, sweet	5.9-6.5	Beets	4.9-5.8	Limes	1.8-2.0
Oysters	5.9-6.6	Bananas	4.5-5.2		

Source: Banwart 1981.

KatchAll Industries International (Cincinnati, OH) provides cost-effective HACCP products, such as Kolor-Cut™ cutting boards, Rapi-Kool™ for cooling food, and BladeRunner™ cleaner of slicers.

STORING FOOD SAFELY

Food should be stored in a safe environment and always be checked for spoilage before using. Canned foods should be checked for containers with swollen tops and bottoms, dents along the side seam, and foam or "off" odors when the can is opened. Fresh fish and seafood are usually spoiled if there is an off odor similar to ammonia and the eyes are sunken and off color around the gills. Meat will usually have an off odor if spoiled. Regrettably, many prepared salads do not show telltale signs until the foods are totally spoiled. Purchasing prepared chicken salad, tuna and other fish salads, non-acid potato salad (made without vinegar), and any custard-filled pastry is risky. It is important to purchase only from a reputable processor and distributor.

FOOD HANDLERS

Many of the bacteria that cause food poisoning are transmitted to the food by food handlers. Many of these viruses/diseases are caused by human respiratory bacteria. Respiratory illnesses are often transmitted through (1) discharges from the mouth and/or nose, (2) spoons used for tasting more than once without cleaning, and (3) sneezing and coughing on displayed food. The other main source of bacteria causing foodborne illness is the intestinal tract. The bacteria that cause these illnesses are transmitted to food by the food handler who does not throughly wash his or her hands after visiting the toilet. Hand washing cannot be overemphasized for workers in the kitchen.

Some undesirable hand habits that should be avoided are:

- Failure to wash hands after using the restroom or smoking
- Scratching one's head
- Arranging one's hair
- Touching one's mouth or nose
- Protecting a sneeze or blowing one's nose without washing hands afterward
- Touching one's moustache or beard
- Touching pimples or infected cuts or burns
- Working with hand cuts or sores uncovered

SANITARY PREPARATION AND SERVING CONDITIONS

Food needs to be handled in a sanitary manner during preparation and serving. Keeping food at a safe temperature at all times is the most crucial and the most controllable aspect of handling food. The cook can assume that most foods have the potential to become contaminated with sufficient bacteria to cause foodborne illness. To prevent bacterial growth, food should be held below 40°F or above 140°F at all times. To ensure bacterial destruction in the cooking process, foods should be cooked to 165°F or above.

Cross-contamination of foods is a factor in about 20% of the foodborne illnesses and can be a problem in the school foodservice kitchen where a lot of poultry and ground meat products are used. This may occur when preparing different meats and using the same cutting board, slicer, and/or knives without washing and sanitizing between products. Many schools are using the "Kolor-Cut" cutting boards, which come in six colors, specific colors used for specific type foods.

The Industry Council on Food Safety provides the following recipe for safe food handling:

Ingredient #1: Time and Temperature
- Refrigerate or freeze perishables, prepared food, and leftovers immediately.
- Never defrost (or marinate) food on the kitchen counter; use the refrigerator, running cold water with drain open, or microwave method.
- Cook food to the proper internal temperature; look for visual signs of doneness and use a thermometer to be sure.

Ingredient #2: Personal Hygiene
- Wash hands with hot soapy water before and after handling food.
- Avoid handling food when ill, or if cuts and sores are on hands.

Ingredient #3: No Cross-Contamination
- Separate raw meat, poultry, and seafood from other food on storage cart; thaw or store on the bottom shelf of refrigerator .
- Wash and sanitize cutting boards and knives before and after food preparation, and especially after preparing raw meat, poultry, or seafood.
- Never place cooked food on a plate that previously held raw meat, poultry, or seafood.

Potentially Hazardous Foods

Moist, non-acid protein foods are the most hazardous because bacteria grow faster in them. These foods include most meats, poultry, seafood, eggs, milk and other dairy products, and, to a lesser extent, cooked cereal grains and vegetables, sauces, and gravies. The safe preparation steps and hazards of beef stew, shown in Table 11.3, illustrate how foods can become contaminated in the cooking process.

Thermometers

How do you measure the temperature of food? What should that temperature be? These are important questions to answer. All cooks and managers should have properly calibrated thermometers accessible at all times when cooking and serving food and should use them. Thermometers need to be calibrated frequently using ice water to ensure accurate readings. The better-quality food thermometers have a calibration nut near the dial that allows for adjustment. Temperatures of 212°F (190°F -195°F at high altitudes) for boiling and 32°F temperatures for beginning-to-freeze are temperatures that should be used as reference points in making the adjustment to or in checking the reliability of a thermometer. See Figure 11.1 for critical temperatures.

An infrared thermometer, which determines the temperature quickly, has advantages over the traditional thermometers. It makes it easier and faster to take food temperatures because it requires no contact with the food. It particularly effective with taking the temperature of food on a steamtable or salad bar, where sticking a thermometer into a product may be distasteful to the customer. There are disadvantages too, such as, the accuracy may vary .

Sanitizing of Work Surfaces and Utensils

Two basic sanitizing techniques should be taught all employees:

1. How to correctly prepare a sanitizing solution. Use enough chlorine (unscented) bleach in water to reach 100-200 ppm. Test this with a chlorine test kit to make sure it is at the correct strength. (These test kits can be purchased from a small equipment company.) Start with one tablespoon of chlorine bleach per gallon of water and gradually add bleach (or

water) until the correct concentration has been reached. Use this solution for sanitizing work tables, serving counter areas and dining tables.

2. How to set up three-compartment sinks correctly for washing pots and pans. Establish the first compartment for hot soapy water, the second for rinsing, and the third for sterilization. Sterilization can be done by two means: water at 180°F or sanitizing solution (approximately one tablespoon of chlorine bleach per gallon of water and test to assure accurate concentration is reached).

Table 11. 3. Potential of Contamination During Cooking Process: Safe Flow Chart for Beef Stew

	Preparation Step[1]	Hazards	Controls and Alternatives
A.	Cube and sear beef (1:00 p.m.)	Cross-contamination to other foods	Clean and sanitize utensils; wash hands; handle separately from other foods.
B.	Wash, peel, and cut vegetables (1:10 p.m.)	Natural and cross contamination	Wash vegetables throughly and handle separately from other foods. Use clean/sanitized utensils. Wash hands.
C.	Combine ingredients and seasonings (1:30 p.m.)	Chemical contamination: if seasoned to taste, "bacterial contamination"	Read labels. Store and use chemicals away from foods. Measure seasonings in advance or use clean tasting spoon each time.
D.	Simmer, cook (4:30 p.m.)	Survival of bacteria	Cook until parts reach an internal temperature of 165°F.
E.	Hold on hot table (7:30 p.m.)	Recontamination growth or bacteria	Use clean/sanitized utensils. Keep food covered. Keep internal temperature above 140°F, reheat to 165°F.
F.	Cool for storage (11:30 p.m.)	Growth of bacteria (extremely critical)	Cool rapidly to 45° within four hours. Use shallow pans 4" deep or less and ice baths and stir food to facilitate cooling or rapid-cool™ stirrer. Check temperature every 30 to 60 minutes. If food has not reached 45°F within four hours, reheat to 165°F and cool again. Discard after second reheating.
G.	Store	Recontamination	Keep covered. Store away from contaminants.
H.	Reheat for service (4:00 p.m., following day)	Recontamination, bacterial growth	Use clean, sanitized utensils. Do not "top off" with new product. Heat rapidly on stove to 165°F. Do not hold. Serve immediately.

Adapted from Harrington 1986.

---

[1]Times indicated when the step is completed.

EMPLOYEE AND CUSTOMER SAFETY

AIDS Risk

The chance of a school foodservice employee who has AIDS spreading it through casual contact or food is almost nonexistent. AIDS is transferable mostly through sexual contact, shared needles, or blood transfusions, or possibly from an infected mother to her child at birth. Employees who have AIDS cannot be discriminated against or fired for that reason. Legally, a supervisor cannot violate the confidentiality of an employee with AIDS by telling other employees. People who have infectious diseases, including AIDS, are considered to have a disability and legally cannot be dismissed any more than any other person with any other disabilities.

To minimize the risk of spreading any infectious disease, it should be the policy to wash hands routinely and wear gloves to clean up with a household bleach, especially if there is a cut and bleeding.

Hazardous Substances

Concern surrounding hazardous substances relates to the potential effects of such substances on both employee and customers. The employer has an obligation to provide a safe place for people to work as well as for people to be served. (This is discussed further in Chapter 10.)

In 1971, the Occupational Safety and Health Administration (OSHA) adopted regulations regarding hazardous chemicals or substances and the employer's responsibilities in the work location. These regulations are referred to as the **Federal Hazard Communication Standard**. Many states have responded in this area, probably more because of the hazardous substances used in school chemistry laboratories than because of employees at risk.

A hazardous substance is defined as any substance that is capable of producing adverse effects on the health or safety of human beings. Any product that has a health or safety warning on its label is considered hazardous. A problem may arrive when the product is removed from the original container. Labeling a secondary container (if the product has been removed from the original container to another container) is very essential to safety.

The Federal Hazard Communication Standard, sometimes referred to as the "Right-To-Know Law," requires that employees be protected against harm, requires inservice training for all employees who handle or use potentially hazardous chemicals and requires that the employer have a "material safety data sheet" (MSDS) on each hazardous chemical known to be used by a particular group of employees in the workplace. The MSDS is provided by the manufacturer (an example is shown in Figure 11.3) and must contain the following information:

- Product identity (used on the container label)
- Physical and chemical characteristics of hazardous chemical or chemicals
- Physical hazards (potential for explosion, fire, and so on)
- Known acute and chronic health effects and related health information
- Primary routes of entry into the body

Figure 11.3. Sample Material Safety Data Sheet

Section 1—Product Name

Manufacture's Name: Address: Emergency Telephone No.:

Section 2—Hazardous Information

Components	C.A.S. Number	CERCLE RQ Spill labs.	RCRA Waste	AGGIH TLV	OSHA TWA	%, Wt.

Carcinogens (As defined in 29CFR 1910-1200)	NTP	IARC	OSHA

Proper Shipping Name:	Hazard Class:	Hazard I.D. No:

Section 3—Physical Data

Boiling Point, °F:	Specific Gravity:
Vapor Pressure (mmHc):	Volatile, % by vol.:
Vapor Density (air = 1):	Evaporation Rate (Bu. Ac. = 1):
Appearance and Odor:	Solubility in Water: pH:

Section 4—Fire and Explosion Hazards

Flash Point and Method Used:
Extinguishing Media:
Special Fire Fighting Procedure and Precautions
Unusual Fire and Explosion Hazards:

Section 5—Health, Emergency, and First Aid Information

Effects of Over-Exposure: Eyes:	
Skin:	
Inhalation:	
Ingestion:	
Medical Conditions Which May Be Aggravated	
First Aid: Eyes:	

Figure 11.3. Sample Material Safety Data Sheet (continued)

Skin:
Inhalation:
Primary Route of Entry: Inhalation _____   Skin Contact_____   Other_____

Section 6—Reactivity Date

Stability: Stable _____   Unstable _____
Conditions to Avoid:
Hazardous Decomposition Products:

Section 7—Spill, Leak, and Disposal Procedures

Spill or Release Procedure: Concentrate: Use Solution:
Disposal Information: Concentrate: Spent Solution and Rinses:

Section 8—Special Protection Information

Respiratory Protection:
Ventilation:
Protective Equipment: Chemical Face Shield or Goggles ❑   Gloves ❑   Boots ❑   Apron ❑   Protective Suit ❑ Gloves, Boots, Apron, and Suit Made From:
Recommended Personal Hygiene:

Section 9—Other Information

Special Precautions—Storage and Handling:
Mixing:
Repair and Maintenance of Contaminated Equipment:
Date Prepared: Date Reviewed: Approved:

- Information on exposure limits
- Whether the chemical is considered a carcinogen by OSHA, the International Agency for Research on Cancer, or the National Toxicology Program
- Precautions for safe handling
- Generally acceptable control measures (engineering controls, work practices, and personal protective equipment)
- Emergency and first aid procedures
- Date of MSDS preparation or last revision
- Name, address, and phone number of party responsible for preparing and distributing the MSDS

Some of the hazardous substances found in most school kitchens are household ammonia and bleach, institutional cleansers with bleach, detergents, oven and grill cleaners, rinse agents used in dishwashing machines, lime-cutting agents, and stainless steel cleaners.

Managers should ensure that all of these chemicals are in the original labeled container or in a secondary container that has been properly labeled. If the employees do not read and understand English, the labeling should be in their languages or at least bear a danger sign on the label.

Emergency Situations

Emergency situations may occur and the foodservice manager should have training in basic first aid and what to do in case of an emergency. There are many pieces of potentially hazardous equipment in any institutional kitchen. It is important to know what to do if an employee receives an electrical shock or is seriously cut or burned. It is also important to be trained in what to do if a person is choking on food, or an employee or customer is having a heart attack or stroke on the job. These are emergencies that may occur that have to be reacted to within minutes for the victim to survive. Figure 11.4 provides a safety checklist to be used in the work location.

It is not uncommon in a foodservice dining room for a customer to choke on food. The most acceptable technique to use in such a case is the abdominal thrust maneuver. Minutes count in this emergency situation, but it is important that the person performing emergency treatment be trained in proper procedures. The American Red Cross teaches first aid courses that include the abdominal thrust maneuver.

If a person's heart stops beating, action is needed immediately. Cardiopulmonary resuscitation (CPR) is the technique used to keep the person alive until medical help can be obtained.

The foodservice manager needs a personal profile card on file for each employee. These cards should include information on who to contact in case of an emergency, any allergies or health problems that the manager may need to know about, the doctor and/or hospital where the employee should be taken in case of an emergency, and other pertinent information. These cards contain confidential information, have to be optional, and should be kept in a safe, but accessible location. The telephone numbers to call in case of an emergency and the street address of the school/office/central kitchen should be posted right over the telephone.

Figure 11.4 Safety Checklist for a Foodservice

A checklist for a foodservice operation should include the following:

1. Is an OSHA poster posted in a prominent place where employees report to work?
2. Is a properly filled first-aid kit readily accessible to employees? _____
3. Is there ongoing safety training? _____
4. Are aisle ways clear of obstructions? _____
5. Are extension cords used with caution and are they safe? _____
6. Are there hand rails or railings on stairways? _____
7. Do employees know where the nearest fire extinguisher is? _____
8. Are fire extinguishers tested (hydrostatic test every five years)? _____
9. Have foodservice employees participated in fire drills and do they know procedures?
10. Are emergency exits marked and illuminated? _____
11. Is the electrical wiring system grounded? _____
12. Are food mixers, grinders, slicers, dish machines, and other pieces of electric equipment grounded?
13. Is cutting, chopping, and grinding equipment guarded? _____
14. Are all hazardous chemicals (substances), e.g., bleaches, detergents, labeled properly?
15. Are all hazardous chemicals stored in places separated from food? _____
16. Are ventilation and illumination adequate in the kitchen and storage areas? _____
17. Is instruction given on the proper use of steam equipment? _____
18. Is there a safety latch on walk-in freezer and refrigerator door? _____
19. Are all fixed machines securely anchored to prevent "walking" or moving? _____
20. Is someone on duty within the school (and readily available to the foodservice area) who knows basic first aid?
21. Is the emergency telephone numbers and street address of school/office/central kitchen posted near the telephone? _____
22. Does the manager have personal profiles on each employee accessible in case of allergies and other health problems? _____

SELECTED REFERENCES

"Bad Apples." 1989. *Consumer Reports*. (May) pp. 288-291.

Banwart, G. 1981. *Basic Food Microbiology*. New York: Van Nostrand Reinhold.

Chenault, A. 1984. *Nutrition and Health*. New York: Holt, Rinehart & Winston.

The Educational Foundation. 1992. *Applied Foodservice Sanitation: A Certification Coursebook*. 4th ed. Chicago, IL: The Educational Foundation of the National Restaurant Association.

_____. 1995. *ServSafe Training, A practical Approach to HACCP Coursebook*. Chicago, IL: The Educational Foundation of The National Restaurant Association.

_____.1998. *HACCP Reference Book*. Chicago, IL: The Educational Foundation of The National Restaurant Association.

Fairfax County Public Schools. 1998. *Material Safety Data Sheets*. Fairfax, VA: Fairfax County Public Schools, General Services Department.

Feingold, B. 1974. *Why Your Child Is Hyperactive*. New York: Random House.

Harrington, R. 1986. "How to Implement a SAFE Program." *Restaurant USA* 6(7): 31-33. Washington, DC: National Restaurant Association.

Loken, J. 1995. *HACCP Food Safety Manual*. New York: John Wiley & Sons.

Longree, K., and G. Armbruster. 1987. *Sanitary Techniques in Foodservice*. 4th ed. New York: John Wiley & Sons.

Marriott, N. 1994. *Principles of Food Sanitation*. New York: Chapman and Hall.

Minor, L. 1983. *Sanitation, Safety & Environmental Standards*. The L. J. Minor Foodservice Standards Series, vol. 2. New York; Van Nostrand Reinhold.

Nash, G. 1987. "Applied Food Sanitation Course Offered to Members." *School Food Service Journal* 4 (4): 117

"New Bacteria in the News: A Special Symposium." 1986. *Food Technology* 40(8): 16-26.

Sanson, M. 1996. "A Blueprint for Safety." *Restaurant Hospitality*, (August) 65-67.

_____. 1996. "How Do You Spell Food Safety." *Restaurant Hospitality, (March) 109-110*.

"Setting Safe Limits on Pesticide Residues." 1988. *Food and Drug Consumer Report*: 41-45.

Tarakow, I., and J. Vorperian. 1981. *Foodborne and Waterborne Diseases*. New York: Van Nostrand Reinhold.

United States Department of Agriculture. 1987. "Food Safety Is No Mystery." A training package in VHS and BETA. Washington, DC: Food Safety and Inspection Service, USDA

_____. 1996. Serving It Safe: A Manager's Tool Kit (FCS-295), Washington, DC: Government Printing Office.

United States Department of Health and Human Services. 1993 and 1997. *Food Code*. Washington, DC: Government Printing Office.

12
REDUCING COSTS AND
INCREASING EFFICIENCY

Experiencing Financial Problems

Reducing Labor Costs
　　Increasing Efficiency
　　Training to Improving Job Efficiency
　　Applying Work Simplification Methods
　　Arranging the Kitchen for an Efficient Flow of Work
　　Scheduling Work Effectively
　　Establishing Time Standards
　　Utilizing Automation
　　Utilizing Convenience Foods and Disposable Supplies
　　Changing the Type of Foodservice System Used
　　Using Volunteers, Paid Student Labor and Other Labor
　　Reducing the Cost of a Labor Hour

Reducing Food Costs
　　Obtaining More Competitive Food Prices
　　Reducing Waste
　　Utilizing Leftovers
　　Purchasing Less Expensive Products
　　Planning Less Expensive Menus
　　Reducing Portion Sizes
　　Carrying Out "Offer Versus Serve"
　　Utilizing USDA-Donated Commodities Better
　　Ordering Only What Is Needed
　　Checking In Orders and Storing Properly
　　Eliminating Theft

Selected References

EXPERIENCING FINANCIAL PROBLEMS

Many school districts have been experiencing financial trouble in the 1990s. Those years have been the first time their foodservices have had a difficult time breaking even. Financial problems develop mainly because the increase in revenue (price charged students plus federal reimbursement) has not kept pace with the increase in expenditures. Labor costs have been and will continue to be a major factor in the financial picture..

Foodservice employees often receive the same raises and fringe benefits as employees in other school district departments. The average labor hour with fringe benefits may be costing in excess of $15. The other departments are probably being funded by tax monies and do not have to be as concerned with productivity and costs and are actually not as accountable as foodservice operations. Unfortunately, those departments are not the competitors that school foodservice management has to deal with. The competitors, the fast-food restaurants, commercial management companies, and the foodservice industry in general, are often paying much less per labor hour than a school district-managed foodservice. The fast-food industry is built around turnover and has little to offer for longevity, whereas many school districts' payscales have a number of step raises, based on years of service (and often not on performance).

Fringe benefits, especially health insurance, have undergone steep increases in the last ten years. In some cases the fringe benefits exceed 50 percent of the pay an employee receives. During the 1970s, some of the fringe benefits began for foodservice employees and little thought given to costs. For instance, the 15-minute break may be a part of a union contract agreement for all employees, including part-time employees, and it is a costly benefit. If a kitchen has four employees and the average labor hour with fringe benefits is costing $12.50, a 15-minute break would cost $2,312.50 a school year, or $12.50 a day.

Food costs are just as much the financial problem as is labor—the school district may have financial problems because either or both. For example, food costs have increased as USDA-donated foods have added processing and delivery fees. Between 1991 and 1999, the value of entitlement commodities has increased only three-quarters of a cent—falling far short of inflation. Weather conditions have caused shortages and price increases, and the mergers of food companies have reduced competition in some cases, and all this has influenced food costs. School districts no longer have the buying power they once had as restaurants have multiplied, and eating out has doubled the amount of money spent in restaurants today over the last ten years.

The costs of producing and serving a school lunch vary across the nation, as do the prices charged students for lunch. In many cases not all costs are being identified, and the subsidy by the school district is considerable. A study done by the National Food Service Management Institute (1998) showed that the average cost of a lunch in four school districts ranged between $1.74 and $2.40. A breakdown of the costs appears in Chapter 2, "Financial Management."

At the same time that school foodservices are needing some financial relief, school district general budgets are also under pressure. As a result, foodservice programs are being charged for services they have never had to pay for in the past. More and more school districts are charging the foodservice program for utilities, for example. Some school districts are looking to the food service budget for revenue for the general fund's budget (the general fund is the education money budgeted for operating a school district).

When revenue does not cover food services' costs, the first impulse is to increase prices charged. This is certainly one approach, but the customers and community may resist. School boards are telling foodservice directors to reduce costs, and most foodservice programs can cut costs by reducing food waste and increasing employee productivity/efficiency. These are the two areas covered in this chapter; however, there are other costs that may need to be reduced.

Although some school districts are turning to outside management companies to resolve their financial problems, these problems often can be resolved by the school foodservice director/supervisor with the support of the school administration. If the school district decides to take on the challenge of solving a financial problem, it will usually mean a combination of raising prices and reducing costs. (Meal pricing is discussed in Chapter 2, "Financial Management.")

One of the main qualifications for a director or supervisor for the 2000s should be a good financial management background. It will be necessary for management to "control costs," which means direct, regulate, and carry out controls to achieve a financial goal and increase revenue.

Since labor and food costs often consume 80 to 90 percent the foodservice budget, this chapter will concentrate on reducing the costs in these two areas.

REDUCING LABOR COSTS

When labor costs exceed 40 to 45 percent of the revenue, steps need to be taken to reduce these costs. Personnel is an area most administrators don't want to touch because of community politics involved but they have to for the financial success of the program and for job security reasons. When the costs of foodservice labor result in the general funds having to be used to subsidize the program, administrators have to face the problem.

How labor costs have gotten out of hand can usually be determined by looking at past history. During the 1960s, labor costs consumed between 28 and 32 percent of the school foodservice revenue—foodservice employees were the lowest paid in the school districts with no fringe benefits. During the 1970s, with the addition of fringe benefits and a popular annual cost-of-living raise and step raise, the percentage of the revenue used for labor inched up. Studies on "equal pay for equal work" in the 1980s resulted in foodservice employees in some school districts receiving large raises. For example, all the school districts in Minnesota are required to adjust the pay of certain employees (including foodservice employees) to meet the "equal pay for equal work" requirement. During the 1990s the competition for employees and the continued school board actions of increasing employee pay have resulted in financial problems for school district foodservice programs that is difficult to solve.

Even though a school district's starting pay for foodservice workers may be only $6.34 (cost of $8.37 per hour with employer's share of the fringe benefits), the average cost per labor hour may be as high as $14. This is due to employee longevity, different position guidelines, and high managers' salaries. Unfortunately, many school districts have starting salaries over $8 an hour and fringe benefits available to three- and four-hour employees—with the average costs of labor (including employee benefits) when prorated over the days of service averaging nearly $20 an hour.

Today the labor costs in many school districts exceed 60 percent of the revenue. This may be because (1) revenues are not high enough, (2) payscales are out of line with the industry, (3) productivity is low and schools are overstaffed, or (4) there is no control on use of overtime and substitutes. High labor costs may be caused by one or a combination of these factors.

Some school districts need to do a thorough salary study, reclassify employees, and establish new payscales that more closely resemble the competitors' payscales. Step raises need to be tied to performance. If possible, restrictions may need to be placed on fringe benefits—that is, either staff employees are eligible for the retirement program **after one year of employment**, or only managers are eligible for this program—and the employer may need to be paying less of the costs of health insurance for part-time than for full-time employees.

There are some trade-offs that can be considered. When a school district begins reducing wages and fringe benefits for foodservice employees, the results are often higher turnover, lower morale, and employees who are less dedicated, motivated, and qualified. This usually means negative changes in the quality of the school foodservice. However, many of the fast-food restaurants function successfully with high turnover and employees with no pervious foodservice experience. Their secrets are a very limited menu, standardized recipes and procedures, and a good training program. See Chapter 4 for suggested menu changes that can aid in standardizing the school foodservices and increasing revenue.

An excellent study done by the National Food Service Management Institute (1998) provides an example of the kinds of labor costs found in four school districts. This information (Table 12.1) illustrates the problem with low productivity .

Management can reduce labor costs by (1) realigning the salary scale and reducing the starting salary, (2) eliminating the need for some positions, e.g., eliminate the need for dish machine operator by discontinued to wash dishes, (3) increasing co-payments for health insurance, (4) making retirement and health insurance benefits available to management only or to full-time employees only (may have to grandfather existing employees), (5) monitoring use of substitutes and eliminating use when overstaffed, (6) reducing the number of hours full-time employees work from 7 or 8 hours to six hours, and (7) eliminating many of the full-time positions (replace with part time employees who will not qualify for many of the expensive fringe benefits).

Increasing Efficiency

One of the main reasons for high labor costs, as mentioned above, may be low productivity. To determine why this is, productivity rates need to be evaluated. They are usually based on meals per labor hour or productivity rates(see the guidelines discussed in Chapter 5).

Increasing productivity means increasing speed, or efficiency. It means producing more meals with the present number of labor hours or producing the same with fewer labor hours. Preparing work schedules is essential to an efficient operation (see Chapter 5).

Management can increase the productivity of the staff by (1) staffing the school properly, (2) providing training in time and motion and efficiency, (3) scheduling employees to work the hours needed to do the job, (4) reducing the number of hours full-time employees work (to six hours or less), (5) planning the work day for each employee (breaking it down into 15 minute intervals), (6) eliminating breaks of employees who work four or fewer hours, (7) discontinuing the use of "paid time" for employees to eat their lunch, (8) having a good manager manage more than one school, and (9) converting small schools to satellites (see Chapter 5, "Systems of Operating Foodservices").

Table 12.1. Comparison of Labor Information for School Districts in Different Parts of the Country
(Based on 1995-96 Data—No Employee Benefits Included)

Category	District A	District B	District C	District D
% Labor Expenditure[1] to Revenue	42.83%	26.95%	30.7%	38%
Labor Turnover Rate	5%	11%	8%	16%
Average Meals/ Labor Hour[2]	12.50 MPLH	14.71 MPLH	18.75 MPLH	14.70 MPLH
Staffing Formula[3]	1 cook/100 meals; 1 manager; with consideration for extra serving line or special meals	Different formulas; depending on if employees clean dining room; length of serving times	Elementary 20-23 MPLH., middle schools 14-15 MPLH, high schools 12-13 MPLH	12 MPLH for elementary and middle schools; 11 MPLH high schools
Pay Increase Basis	Longevity	Longevity plus cost of living	Longevity; % determined by state; ASFSA certification premium	Longevity
Full-Time Employees (Kitchen/Serving	$ 9.48/hour (7 hours)	$ 5.37/hour (6 ½ hours)	$ 9.43/ hour (6 hours)	$ 6.89/hour (7 hours)
Part-Time Employees (Work daily, but less hours than full time)	$ 5.00	None	$ 7.31	$ 5.95
Substitute Help	$ 5.00	$ 5.00	$ 5.98	$ 5.75
School Site Manager	$15.37	$ 8.13	No managers	$ 8.50
Cost/Hour of Benefits[4]	$ 4.08	$ 1.48	$ 4.37	$ 2.20

Source: National Food Service Management Institute, n.d. Used by permission.

---

[1]Includes administration.

[2]Average meals per labor hour (MPLH) is a way of judging productivity of staff. The higher the productivity the better.

[3]See Chapter 6 of this text for a staffing formula.

[4]Divide total cost of employee benefits for year by number of serving days= benefits per day; divide benefits per day by number of daily labors = benefits per hour.

The following steps may be used to improve efficiency and productivity of a staff:

- Training to improve job efficiency
- Applying work simplification methods
- Arranging the kitchen for an efficient flow of work
- Scheduling work effectively
- Establishing time standards
- Utilizing automation (see Chapter 14)
- Changing the type of foodservice system used (see Chapter 5 for more details)
- Motivating employees to improve productivity (see discussion in Chapter 7)
- Paying for performance (see discussion in Chapter 7)
- Using volunteers, paid student labor, or other labor
- Reducing the cost of a labor hour

Management costs can be reduced by increasing the span of control, for example, giving one good manager responsibility for two or more schools.

Training to Improving Job Efficiency

The school foodservice manager should be trained in the basic principles of motion economy, to improve productivity. The manager will need to use the principles of motion economy in training and motivating employees to increase productivity. If the manager knows these steps and principles, he or she can use them in on-the-job training as well as in the kitchen to improve jobs.

The principles of motion economy as described by Barnes (1968) and Kazarian (1979) can be used in school foodservices to increase productivity. Motion economy can be divided into three principal segments: (1) hand and body motions, (2) work process or sequence, and (3) design of tools, equipment, and the workplace.

Observation is one of the main ways of determining if a job can be improved. The six steps toward improving productivity are as follows:

1. Select the job to be improved and define the situation (problem).
2. Break down the job into parts by using a flow chart.
3. Question each step and each process to determine: Is there a better way? Can steps be eliminated? Can steps be simplified?
4. Arrive at a new method.
5. Put the new method into action.
6. Follow up and evaluate

Applying Work Simplification Methods

Motion economy principles can be applied to school foodservices in the form of work simplification methods, as follows:

- Use both hands at the same time to do useful work whenever possible. Examples:
  — Panning rolls: pick up a roll in each hand and put onto the pan.
  — Racking dishes: pick up a plate in each hand to put into the dishwashing racks. Use both hands to take dishes out of the racks and stack.
  — Serving food: pick a plate up with one hand and bring midway to meet the food that has been dipped or picked up by the other hand.
- Perform work in a rhythmic way. Examples:
  — Using a French knife: place the knife point on the cutting board and with other hand move the food under the knife; rock the knife up and down, cutting the food and developing a rhythm.
  — Developing a natural rhythm: practice with motions such as stirring, racking dishes, rolling, or cutting rolls and biscuits.
- Use smooth, continuous, curved motions when possible rather than straight-line motions with sharp changes in direction. This can increase productivity by 25 percent. Examples:
  — Wiping tables: use a wide arch-like motion rather that a straight-line one.
  — Spreading sandwich filling on bread: spread with circular motion without lifting the tool.
- Use the fewest, shortest, and simplest motions. Examples:
  — Brushing and spreading: use a 2-, 3-, or 4-inch pastry brush instead of the hand or a 1-inch brush for greasing pans, or a spatula for spreading mayonnaise and butter on bread; reduce strokes by using the largest brush feasible.
  — Measuring: use the largest measure practical, not multiples of a smaller one (e.g.,a cup measure instead of 16 tablespoons, a 2-ounce ladle to obtain a 2-ounce quantity).
- Combine operations and eliminate all unnecessary parts of the job. Examples:
  — Cooking in serving pans.
  — Adding dry milk to dry ingredients, then adding water, eliminating reconstitution of milk.
  — Congealing gelatin in the portion cup or dish in which it is to be served.
  — Combining peanut butter and jelly before spreading on bread for sandwiches.
- Eliminate unnecessary walking, reaching, stretching, and bending. Examples:
  — Using a cart to carry supplies needed from the storeroom to the work center.
  — Using food pedal controls and knee levers when possible.
  — Arranging work where reaching or stretching will be kept to a minimum. (The normal reach of most people is 12 to 14 inches, and the maximum reach without stretching is 22 to 24 inches.)
- Develop standardized procedures. Examples:
  — Eliminating "to taste" directions in recipes by determining how much salt, sugar, or other flavoring is needed and adding the information to the recipe.
  — Putting the same number of items (hamburger patties, cookies, and so on) on a pan each time.
  — Using short menu cycles and standardizing all procedures.

Several of the above principles of motion economy are illustrated in Figure 12.1, "Assembling Sandwiches."

bling Sandwiches

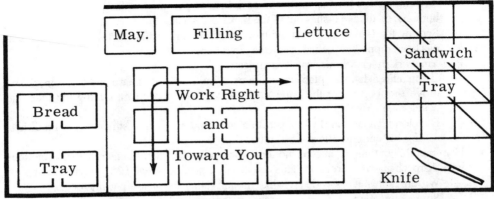

OPERATOR

Steps to sandwich assembly:

1. Pull sandwich recipe and read thoroughly.
2. Collect all ingredients and supplies ready for assembly. Use cart.
3. Set up work center with all ingredients, pans, utensils, and supplies needed.
   Supplies should include:
   Cutting board
   Sharp knife
   Scoop or other measurer for filling
   Spatulas for spreading mayonnaise and mustard (consider combining)
   Selected wrap to be used (should merchandise sandwich)
   Pans or containers to hold finished sandwiches; cart or rack for holding pans
4. Place all ingredients and supplies within easy reach of the assembler.
5. Work in sequence; avoid backtracking; finish process first two layers of sandwiches before start-
   ing others.
6. For tuna fish salad sandwiches:
   Have opened loaves of bread to left. Cover cutting board with one layer of bread.
   Spread mayonnaise on bread if a part of recipe,
      scoop appropriate amount of tuna salad on each slice of bread, with spatula and using a
      circular motion spread filling to edges/corners of bread .
   Top with lettuce (if in recipe) and place two slices of bread, which begins the process for
      the second layer of sandwiches.
7. Cut through two layers/sandwiches and wrap the two halves to show the filling/sandwich off.
8. Place in serving pan.

Henry Ford II is given credit for saying, "Productivity is a measure not of how hard we work but of how well we use our intelligence and imagination...." and this can be applied to providing school breakfasts and lunches at the lowest prices possible.

According to a training manual of the South Carolina Office of School Food Services, the objectives of increasing productivity and work simplification are to (1) reduce the costs of operation, (2) eliminate all unnecessary or nonessential activities, (3) increase the effectiveness of each necessary activity, (4) eliminate duplication of activities, (5) make work safer and less fatiguing, (6) eliminate waste of time, energy, and material, (7) improve customer relations, and (8) develop an attitude of receptiveness to change.

Arranging the Kitchen for an Efficient Flow of Work

The kitchen should be divided into work centers—separate areas for baking, preparing salads and fresh produce, and cooking. Equipment should be arranged within each center according to the sequence of its use, to avoid crisscrossing, backtracking, and unnecessary walking and reaching. Food and supplies should flow from receiving of food through the kitchen to service. Foods such as French fries, which are batch-cooked and served hot, should be prepared as close as possible to the serving line. Equipment that needs to be used by more than one work center should be put on wheels if possible, and it should be located close to the point of use and in a definite place.

If work centers are color-coded, the coding can be used on the equipment and tools assigned to a center so that they are easily returned to the center. Refrigerator doors that contain each center's supplies should be color coded to reduce time spent locating ingredients.

The arrangement of the storeroom should be planned carefully, and the physical facility should be set up in the same order as the inventory form.

Scheduling Work Effectively

Ideally the work would be scheduled before the employees' scheduled times to work are established. The tradition of all full-time employees and all part-time employees come and leave at the same time is not effective scheduling of employees' time. The time an employee works should be governed by the job he or she does and what time the job needs to be done. Instead, many managers establish the time an employee works and then schedules the work to be done. This often results in food being prepared too early and waiting for time to service. In Chapter 7, "Managing Human Resources," appears a discussion on preparing work schedules.

Establishing Time Standards

Since there are so many variables in accomplishing a job, each individual district (or region or state) needs to determine what is a reasonable amount of time for doing each job. For example, how long should it take an employee to portion 250 fruit cups and tossed salads or make 50 chef salads? (See Chapter 10, Figure 10.5, which provides an example of establishing time requirements.)

Knowing how long a job should take (1) acts as a motivator to the employee, (2) provides a goal, (3) gives a standard for evaluating the productivity of an individual, and (4) provides information needed for work scheduling. It would be useful to have the time it takes to do certain jobs, such as those established by San Diego (CA) Unified School District Food Service Department, which has developed excellent training materials on work efficiency.

Utilizing Automation

Computerization and automation have been slow to take hold in the foodservice industry. However, the next ten years will see unbelievable progress in this area. When it becomes necessary to purchase a new piece of equipment, an automated version should be considered. Among the types of automated equipment presently available are deep fat fryers with automated lift baskets that will remove the product from the fat when it is done , automatically filtering the fat. These convenient features save time and make the processes almost foolproof.

It may not be practical for each individual kitchen to have automated portioning machines and similar equipment. However, in a central kitchen, computerized automation can be better utilized and reduce labor cost substantially. (See Chapters 13 and 14 for discussions of other automated equipment and the use of robotics and computers in school foodservice.)

Utilizing Convenience Foods and Disposable Supplies

The use of convenience foods and disposable supplies instead of cooking from raw ingredients and washing dishes can reduce the number of employees and labor hours needed. The cost of food, however, will increase. Will the labor cost be lowered more than the cost of the food will increase? It should, if hours are reduced as convenience foods are added. Will the finished products be the foods the majority of customers prefer? A taste test is probably the best way to determine acceptability to trying a new item for the menu. Will the nutritional value of foods be comparable or improved? Some convenience foods are higher in sodium and may have hidden fat. Specifications and looking for products with lower sodium and fat may be the only way around these concerns.

Using more convenience foods and disposable supplies are rather major steps and should be carefully weighed to determine the real cost per meal as compared to making the items from raw ingredients. A study done in three Southern school districts showed the breakfast menus contain 70 to 80 percent convenience foods, which meant two labor hours should be able to handle 100 breakfast meals. In these school districts several employees were coming to work by 6:30 a.m. to serve breakfast at 7:45 a.m., because they had always come to work at that time. This much labor with nothing to do often resulted in lunch being ready to serve by the time breakfast was ready or shortly thereafter.

It is important that the addition of convenience foods and disposable dishes be matched by a cutback in staff or hours. Otherwise, according to Parkinson's Law— *"Work expands to fill the time available"*— the staff will simply slow down and adjust to the lesser workload.

Using disposable supplies, which can be good merchandisers, if it is cost-effective. In a small rural school district, where labor costs are low and paper supplies are high, washing dishes may cost less than using disposables. In most school districts, however, the use of disposables can reduce costs, particularly at breakfast when a small disposable type tray or paper food boat may be all that is needed. Many of the popular convenience foods being used at breakfast are finger foods and do not require eating utensils. (See Table 6.4 for a comparison of the costs of washing dishes with the costs of using disposable supplies.)

Changing the Type of Foodservice System Used

To reduce labor sufficiently, it may be necessary for a school district to change the type of food service system used. On-site production and service is generally the most labor-intensive type. The highest productivity can be obtained with preplated meals prepared in a central kitchen that serve 20,000 or more. Bulk satellite food for portioning on location can obtain higher productivity than on-site production in most situations. The larger the central kitchen and the more automated it is, the higher the productivity will be.

The Corpus Christi, (TX), Independent School District has been able to maintain one of the lowest labor costs (28 percent including fringe benefits) in the industry. With a central kitchen preparing 18,000 meals for bulk transporting to satellite schools, this foodservice has been able to maintain very high productivity. Staffed with 16 employees, a total of 120.5 labor hours, the central kitchen produces at a rate of 149 meals per labor hour. At the satellite schools the employees heat, portion, and serve. The schools are staffed on the average at 24.3 meals per labor hour. See Chapter 5 for the layout of the new Corpus Christi, (TX), kitchen facility.

Other examples of high productivity are in the automated, high-volume central kitchens of the Dayton (OH) Public Schools and the Los Angeles Unified Public Schools.

Reducing the need for employees is one of the solutions to high labor costs. Having on-site production kitchens in every school, for example, requires more employees than when food is prepared at a central kitchen and delivered to finishing kitchens. By making all but one kitchen—the production kitchen—"finishing kitchens," labor hours can be reduced substantially in most cases. With the finishing kitchen concept, food is prepared for finishing on site (heating or maintaining at cold temperature, portioning, and serving). The Fairfax County (VA) Public Schools foodservice program has excellent productivity using six large high schools as the production/distribution sites serving more than 200 schools/centers plus contracts every school day. The Adams 12 School District in Colorado has achieved excellent productivity without the centralized production, but has concentrated on training in efficiency.

Using Volunteers, Paid Student Labor and Other Labor

School districts have had to become creative in their efforts to attract volunteers, student labor, and other labor. Many schools in California, e.g., San Diego City Schools, and in other states utilize student labor quite effectively at service time. In the San Diego City Schools the high school students work for short periods of time, but are paid well, and are taught to be quite efficient. One of the reasons for their efficiency is the service area, which the Food Service Department has designed using the concepts of time and motion to their fullest. See Figure 10.7 in Chapter 10, which shows an example of the service areas.

Using volunteer labor to reduce labor costs is frequently used . Many school districts use parent volunteers. However, working in a kitchen may not be the most popular job among volunteers unless there are incentives. At the peak hours, especially lunch periods, if the motivation is provided, a volunteer or group of students can provide needed "hands" at the snack bar. For example, one school district contributes the hourly wages for every hour worked to a school computer fund, and it limits the jobs the parents do to cashiering and running snack bars.

A good means of adding labor in high schools where so many labor hours are needed at service time is to contract with a club or class to run a snack bar. Clubs and classes are always looking for ways to raise money. An hourly rate, a percentage of profits, or a flat sum, which is much lower than the cost of an employee labor hour, can be paid to a club, class, parent-teacher association, or school. Tight inventory and cash controls have to be in place when a student group operates a snack bar and definite procedures followed particularly to account for the inventory. This arrangement can work to the advantage of both the club and foodservices.

Reducing the Cost of a Labor Hour

The first step to reducing the cost of a labor hour is to lower the payscale and secondly to reduce the costs of fringe benefits. These ways to reduce the costs of a labor hour are discussed below, plus others.

Lowering the Payscale—by establishing a new, lower payscale. Lowering a payscale is out of the norm and isn't easy to do. School districts have successfully done this, but often it was by "grandfathering" the pay of the existing employees.

Decrease the Number of Absences—by motivating employees to come to work and not use sick leave days unless really needed. Employee absenteeism in the work world jumped 25 percent from 1997 to 1998 according to a recent survey by CCH, a provider of human resources information. Incentives have worked for some school districts in their efforts to reduce the number of absences, e.g., bonuses, certificates of merit, and recognition. Other school districts have let unused sick leave days apply toward number of years of service for retirement purposes.

Decrease the Costs of Fringe Benefits—by requiring employees to pay a small premium for their insurance (if none is being charged); or requiring them to pay more if already paying a portion. One school district started requiring employees to pay $6 per month for a single person's basic health insurance coverage, and more than 700 employees dropped the insurance (they were already covered on a spouses' policy). The savings to the school district was approximately $1 million per year.

The Wallingford (CT) School District reduced the cost of health insurance by paying employees 40 percent of the premium for not taking insurance as an employee benefit, and it saved them $500,000. There was a savings to foodservices as well.

Decrease the Cost of Worker's Compensation—by finding out how the rates are set in your location, and improving the safety record. Worker's Compensation costs are usually based on accident rates for three years. Sponsoring a comprehensive accident and injury prevention program resulted in a "best safety" award for the Lake Central School Corporation in St. John, Indiana. They also realized a savings of $48,000 in 1996 and $12,500 in 1998 through their concerted efforts to reduce accidents.

REDUCING FOOD COSTS

High food costs are the cause of more financial problems than once thought. Labor costs were thought to be the big problem—and they usually are a big part of the problem, but not all of it. When food costs (including the value of commodities used) exceed 40 percent, steps need to be taken to reduce these costs.

Food costs can be reduced in a number of ways, including the following:

- Obtaining more competitive food prices
- Reducing waste—in preparation, on students' plates, and from overcooking
- Utilizing leftovers
- Purchasing a less expensive product
- Planning less expensive menus
- Implementing Nutrient Standard Menu Planning option
- Reducing portion sizes
- Carrying out "offer versus serve"
- Utilizing USDA-donated commodities better
- Ordering only what is needed
- Checking in orders and storing properly
- Eliminating theft of employees, distributors, and students/customers
  - Placing all a la carte items behind the serving counter
  - Locking storerooms during the day
  - Moving employee lockers away from back doors

Also to be considered is the cost of employees' lunches if it is considered a fringe benefit. Some school districts charge employees for their lunches. If a meal is costing $2 to prepare and serve, it would cost approximately $364 per year to feed each employee a free lunch.

Obtaining More Competitive Food Prices

School foodservice programs are having problems obtaining competitive food prices. The lack of competition among distributors and dairy monopolies (only one dairy bidding on the school business in many areas) has resulted in a new problem that will become worse in the early 2000s. Some school districts are keeping prices they pay lower by awarding their food bids to a prime vendor (where most foods and supplies are purchased from one or two distributors). Hospitals and colleges have done an excellent job of forming cooperatives, and it may be possible for school districts to join a cooperative or start one. Mississippi, Montana, and Texas, for example, have a state school foodservice cooperative handled by the states' departments of education.

Milk bid prices have increased in some markets tremendously in recent years. Dairy prices vary greatly across the mainland United States (as was discovered recently in a random survey) from as low as 14 cents per half pint to as high as 22 cents per half pint. It is not likely that the cost of producing and distributing milk varies that much across the country. Instead, it is usually the lack of competition that causes high prices. Some school districts have formed cooperatives for diary products, improving their prices. Reducing the number of deliveries needed per week and reducing the number of types of milk can help make dairies more interested in the business. Some schools have added more milk coolers to store two days of milk and accept/expect every-other-day milk deliveries.

It may be necessary for a school district to reduce the vendors' costs of doing business with their schools in the future to obtain better prices. Many school districts have established warehouses, which may or may not achieve a savings. The costs of storing and distributing may be costing the school district more than is saved.

Reducing Waste

Allowing waste creates an unnecessary cost that is desirable to control. The following should be considered in reducing waste and by controlling production:

- Produce just what is needed by better forecasting
- Institute "offer versus serve" at all grade levels
- Put someone in charge of planning the use of leftovers and byproducts
- Practice "just in time" cooking, reducing holding time and loss
- Practice portion control
- Preportion food for service when possible
- Provide close supervision during preparation and service
- Overcooking or cooking more than is needed

Miller (1987) recommends auditing waste. First, returning plates should be watched for plate waste and kitchen waste (checking garbage cans). There are two concerns: (1) waste in preparation and (2) the food students are throwing away. Waste in preparation usually results from:

- Cooking too far ahead
- Burning or overcooking a product and having to throw it away
- Failure to obtain all the product from a can or bowl with the use of a spatula
- Throwing away less-than-perfect products such as broken cookies and ends of breads that could be utilized
- Excessive paring and cleaning vegetables and fruits
- Improperly storing items not used
- Failing to utilize products before they spoil

If the plate waste is heavy, why? Is it because the students do no like the food? Is it because the portions are too large? Is it because recess is after lunch and students' attention is focused on play rather than eating. It may be a combination of these that are causing heavy waste. "Offer versus serve" and offering choices (discussed below) are recommended ways of reducing plate waste. Instituting offer versus serve will reduce costs by 10 to 12 cents per meal.

Utilizing Leftovers

Overproduction of food is common, particularly in schools that offer choices. The answer to this problem is not discontinuing choice, but instead cooking "just in time" and better forecasting using the production record information from the last time the menu was served. Overproduction results in leftovers, which often become food waste. The use of leftovers has to be planned—used as a choice the next day, or made a part of another dish. Working leftovers into already planned menus is an art; the returns are lower food costs.

No food, such as leftovers, should go home with employees. Allowing leftovers to be taken home can encourage employees to cook more than is needed.

Purchasing Less Expensive Products

Purchasing the grade product actually needed is the goal. For example, using Grade A fruits and vegetables may not be necessary. For instance, Grade A sliced peaches are not needed for fruit cobbler. It is desirable to use seasonal foods in season and planned menus accordingly. Purchasing beef products that contain soybean products will reduce the cost per pound. In some cases, the product will be improved in flavor by adding soy, moisture content, and nutritional value. Adding soy to extend ground beef, particularly for highly seasoned dishes such as spaghetti and meat tacos, will reduce costs. According to the United Soybean Board, a mix of 70 percent lean ground beef and 30 percent hydrated soy protein will reduce the average cost of a pound of meat 28 cents per pound. If a school district uses 40,000 pounds of beef a year, a beef-soy mixture could save as much as $11,200 a year. A Gallup research study shows that more than half of the school districts are using soy protein as a way to reduce fat (and costs) in their lunch menus. Using a different piece of chicken or cut of meat may reduce costs.

Using a less expensive ingredient that will do the job is desirable. Using refried beans and kidney beans in Mexican-type dishes will reduce the costs of many of these popular lunches. Salad dressing, for example, may be satisfactory substitute for mayonnaise and may cost less. Other imitation or substitutes should be considered: for example, imitation cheese (there is a maximum substitution level under Traditional Food-Based/Enhanced Food-Based), whipping topping, and sour cream.

Planning Less Expensive Menus

By precosting menus, the planner should be able to tell if menus need to be planned with less expensive menu items. For example, if the average revenue for lunch is $2.09 (see Chapter 2,

"Financial Management") and the goal is to keep food cost at 40 percent of the revenue, the planner needs to determine how much money is available for food.

$$\begin{array}{ll} \$ \ 2.09 & \text{Total revenue} \\ \underline{\text{X} \ .40} & \text{(40\% of revenue) for food} \\ \$ \quad .836 & \text{Amount for food} \end{array}$$

The menus should be planned to meet basic USDA meal requirements. Any additional foods may consist of the condiments needed with the foods. However, extras may be limited or eliminated from the menu in order to reduce waste and costs. Examples of additional foods are potato chips and some desserts, which, in any case, may be sold a la carte for those who need or want the additional calories. Providing more items on the menu than are needed is nice, if one can afford the extra cost.

There may be some menu items that can no longer be afforded, or must be sold a la carte or as part of a higher lunch price. If 80 percent or more of the students pay for their lunches (20 percent or less free and reduced-price), two differently priced lunches may be a solution. This approach works particularly well in high schools, where the needs of students with widely different appetites—from athletes to weight-conscious girls—must be met. The higher-priced lunch menu can include a quarter pounder, eight-inch French bread pizza, chicken breast, and so on. It should be noted that the students eligible for free and reduced-price lunches must have the option of the higher-priced lunch if the lunch is to be claimed for reimbursement.

Reducing Portion Sizes

Correct portion sizes are critical to meeting the menu planning guidelines. The new menu planning options (e.g., Nutrient Standard or Assisted Nutrient Standard Menu Planning) can be used to help reduce costs. There are different-size portions for different grade levels, and if students are coming by class to the cafeteria, it may be possible to vary the portions slightly and reduce the costs.

Serving too large a portion is often a problem. Managers should always be aware that portion control needs supervision. Preportioning can help ensure that a standard portion is being given. Overportioning adds up and can be costly.

Carrying Out "Offer Versus Serve"

"Offer versus serve" is the regulation that allows foodservices to offer a complete meal and the students the option of taking less. Though "offer versus serve" is required by regulation at the high school level, the local school district can decide whether it will be carried out at other levels. Carrying out "offer versus serve" at all school levels can reduce plate waste by 10 to 20 percent, particularly in elementary school and reduce the food cost by 10 to 12 cents.

Utilizing USDA-Donated Commodities Better

Considering commodities at their purchased value rather than as "freebies" is important to the attitude toward and the use of USDA-donated foods. The fact that a food is donated does not justify giving very large portions or serving the food simply to "use up." This is a philosophy that was taught in the early days of commodities. Then the commodities became "entitlements," and a specific dollar amount had to be provided each year.

If a commodity can be used to take the place of an item having to be purchased, it adds real value to the foodservice program. Some commodities are not easy to use, and some should be refused. Refusing a commodity that requires preparation of a product that has poor acceptance will save money in the long run, since it may save time and the cost of other ingredients needed to use the commodity, and in addition prevent lowered participation.

Many states' commodity distribution agencies, e.g., Colorado, Georgia, Texas, and Maryland, do excellent jobs of processing USDA commodities into more usable products. In California, a group of foodservice directors have organized state cooperatives that handle the commodity processing and distribution. Local school district foodservice directors can get involved in state processing contracts and better utilize commodities.

Ordering Only What Is Needed

Ordering only what is needed is a skill that can be learned. Forecasting and ordering are discussed in Chapter 9. To place an order correctly, it requires having a planned menu, pulling recipes, forecasting the number of portions, listing all ingredients needed, determining what is on order for delivery, taking a "mini" inventory, and then determining what needs to be ordered. The goal should be having just enough to last until the next delivery and maintaining a low inventory (no more than seven days of inventory).

Aramark, a management company , requires schools to take an inventory weekly before placing their orders and is strict on the number of days of inventory a school can have.

The saying is that "the more one has in inventory the more one uses." Managers fear running out and often overorder to ensure that doesn't happen. Overordering can result in waste, particularly with produce. Well-stocked storerooms may encourage theft. It takes careful planning to order just enough for delivery at the right time.

Checking in Orders and Storing Properly

A manager (or a manager's designee) should check in deliveries carefully against what was actually ordered. When a manager does not carefully check in deliveries, the foodservice may be shortchanged, may be given an inferior product, or may not receive what was ordered.

As soon as possible after delivery , foods and supplies should be stored at the proper temperature, with good air circulation. Improper storage can result in food waste.

Eliminating Theft

High food costs can be caused by theft—either of food or revenue (either will cause food cost percentages to increase). The most important safeguard against theft is a good system of accountability. Such a system accounts for every item received and used, and will bring shortages or losses to the attention of the manager. Perpetual inventory is an excellent accountability tool, particularly when computerized and tied to the food rung up on the cash registers.

Customer theft is a major problem for some schools, particularly high schools. Unfortunately, displaying easy-to-pocket items is asking for problems. It has become necessary for schools' foodservice staff to hand students a la carte items from behind the serving counter rather than allow students to pick them up. Likewise, locking back doors can prevent robbers from coming in and stealing the day's receipts. It is not unusual for a large high school to have between $1500 and $3000 per day , and that is an attractive sum to steal.

Embezzlement by cashiers is a widespread problem in the foodservice business, as well as in stores, and is probably a bigger problem for school foodservices than is realized. Strict internal controls are needed to prevent theft of money and food. Moving employees' lockers away from the back door will make it harder for employees to store money or items in their locker during the day and take them home at the end of the work day.

SELECTED REFERENCES

Barnes, R. 1968. *Motion and Time Study: Design and Measurement of Work.* 6th ed. New York: John Wiley & Sons.

Boehrer, J. 1993. "Managing to Meet the Bottom Line." *School Business Affairs 59 (10), 3-8.*

Bureau of Business Practice. 1986. *Quick-Action Productivity Ideas for the Supervisor.* Waterford, CT.; Bureau of Business Practice.

Dittmer, P., and G. Griffin. 1989. *Principles of Food, Beverage, and Labor Costs Controls for Hotels and Restaurants.* New York: Van Nostrand Reinhold.

Kazarian, E. 1979. *Work Analysis & Design for Hotels, Restaurants & Institutions.* 2nd ed. New York, Van Nostrand Reinhold.

Miller, J., and D. Hayes. 1994. *Basic Food and Beverage Cost Control.* New York: John Wiley & Sons, Inc.

Miller, S. 1987. "Improving Production Standards—Reducing Waste." Presentation at National Restaurant Association Convention in Chicago.

Minor, L., and R. Cichy, 1984. *Foodservice Systems Management.* New York: Van Nostrand Reinhold.

National Food Service Management Institute. n.d. *Revenue Generation and Cost Control Measures Currently Used in Financially Successful Child Nutrition Programs.* University, MS: Author.

____. 1998. *Revenue Generation and Cost Control Measures Currently Used in Financially Successful CNPs.* University, MS: Author.

Pannell-Martin, D. 1995. *Cost Control Manual for School Foodservice.* Alexandria, VA: inTEAM Associates, Inc.

____. 1998. *Controlling Costs in the Foodservice Industry.* Alexandria, VA: inTEAM Associates, Inc.

Rinke, W. 1989. *The Winning Foodservice Manager: Strategies for Doing More with Less.* Rockville, MD: Aspen Publishers.

VanEgmond-Pannell, D. 1986. "Labor Costs Are Overcoming Food Costs." *School Business Affairs* 52(2):38-39.

____ 1987. *Management Skills for School Foodservice Managers.* Jackson, MS.: State Department of Education, Child Nutrition Division.

13
PLANNING FACILITIES AND
SELECTING LARGE EQUIPMENT

Trends in Foodservice Facility Planning

Facility Planning
　　Basic Physical Considerations
　　Serving Area and Dining Room Atmosphere

Large Equipment
　　Using Technology
　　Writing Specifications
　　Equipment Design

Preventive Maintenance

Selected References

TRENDS IN FOODSERVICE FACILITY PLANNING

School foodservice directors today may not be planning a lot of new facilities, but planning facilities is one of their responsibilities and requires a lot of knowledge. Keeping up with what is new in the industry may be one of the biggest challenges, particularly for directors of small school districts. One of the best ways to keep up with the trends and see what is new is to attend the National Restaurant Association annual May meeting in Chicago (IL) and the North America Food Equipment Manufacturers' (NAFEM) conference held every two years (on odd years) . There are a few school districts that are converting to central kitchens and satellite foodservices. This concept of centralizing food preparation can mean a savings when building additional schools and in day-to-day labor costs. Even rural school kitchens are being built to provide food for other schools in the district. If the distances between schools is reasonable, the centralizing of food production can be a means of reducing the costs of producing and serving meals and equipping a kitchen.

The South has been very slow to centralize preparation and satellite operations and continues to build schools with self-contained kitchens; whereas, many school districts in California have central kitchens. There are pros and cons to both approaches. The challenge is to plan flexible foodservice facilities that can be adapted to the needs of the future, which may include more summer meal programs, serving the elderly, and providing other special activities and adapting to new student meal trends.

Food courts and nontraditional serving areas are the biggest trends in schools today. Make-overs and re-imaging efforts are turning dull, institutional serving areas into beautiful new food courts or "mock food courts," resulting in increased participation in school foodservice programs.

FACILITY PLANNING

Knowledgeable people who know the foodservice operation and the menu that will be served should be involved in the planning of facilities. Good planning of facilities is necessary for the highest productivity and the greatest efficiency. When working in an old building with construction faults and a poor layout, the waste of time and motion is costly but often unavoidable. However, when a new facility is being planned and constructed, it would be expected that these faults could be avoided. Frequently, however the same mistakes are made.

Foodservice management must insist on being a part of the planning team for a new school. The local and state health departments should also be consulted during the early planning stages because the new emphasis on Hazard Analysis Critical Control Point (HACCP) is influencing enforcement of policies by local and state health departments. The factors to be considered in facility planning include (1) the capacity of the school and its potential for future expansion, (2) how many lunch periods the school is likely to have in the future, (3) the number of meals to be served, (4) the age of the children, (5) the type of foodservice system to be used , (6) menu and food offerings to be provided, (7) the type of equipment needed, and (8) the type of utilities to be used. Table 13.1

Table 13. 1. Guide to Space Planning of a School Foodservice Facility

Area	Meals			
	Up to 350	315-500	501-700	701-1000
Receiving area				
Loading platform	60	80	100	100
Receiving area inside building	48	48	60	80
Storage				
Dry storage (⅓-½ sq ft per meal)	175	250	325	450
Nonfood storage	30	50	70	90
Office space	40-48	48	60	80
Lockers and toilet for employees	45	60	75	85
Kitchen				
Preparation including refrigeration (1.1-1.5 sq ft per meal)	500	650	800	980
Serving	200	300	400	600
Dishwasing	150	150	180	210
Maintenance area				
Mop area	25	25	30	30
Garbage area	30	48	60	75
Total kitchen and serving areas	1303	1709	2135	2780
Dining area (based on two seating)				
Elementary (10 sq ft/meal)	1750	1750-2500	2500-3500	3500-50000
Secondary (12 sq ft/meal)	2100	2100-3000	3000-4200	4200-6000
Total dining, kitchen, and serving area				
Elementary	3053	3459-4209	4635-5635	6280-7780
Secondary	4303	3809-4709	5135-6335	6980-8780

provides a guide to space planning for a conventional on-site production kitchen; however, it is generous in space, and if funds are limited one could reduce the space. Architects and kitchen planners may tend to over-equip a kitchen, particularly if they are paid based on the dollars spent.

"Bigger is not necessarily better" when planning kitchen space. Enough space, but not too much, is the first requirement for an efficient kitchen; the second essential element is good layout. A few school districts have built schools with "kitchenless cafeterias" and are using a satellite approach or resorted to using all convenience foods. The menu that will be served should determine what equipment is needed. Some school kitchens today do not need a mixer, compartment steamer, or steam kettle, because they no longer produce foods that require their use.

General requirements and considerations that should be provided to the architect for the foodservice area are the following:

- Menu to be served
- Type food system to be used
- Enrollment anticipated
- Number of lunch periods
- Age of students
- Kitchen location desired
  - Near a back loading dock
  - On the first floor or ground floor
  - Adjoining the dining room
  - In the center of the classroom area
- Dining room seating capacity
  - Ability to seat a third to a half of the student body at one time (or all students at one lunch period?)
  - A combination of round and rectangular tables (or booths)
- Physical conditions desired
  - Adequate lighting (type)
  - Bright-colored accents to be included in the decor
  - Good air circulation
  - Air conditioning (kitchen included)
  - Adequate hot water supply (140°F all year round, with booster heaters to raise the temperature to 180°F, if needed)
  - Electrical outlets where needed on plan
- Kitchen layout
  - Planned around work centers
  - Manger's office enclosed with glass panels three to four feet above floor level
  - A secure place for counting money
  - Restroom with employees' lockers off kitchen
- Serving area
  - Scramble, straight line, food court, etc.
  - Located near kitchen
  - Number lines, serving points

The work center of a kitchen should be planned so the that the flow of work is natural and logical, and follows the sequence of food processing (Figure 13. 1). The emphasis needs to be on (1) using as little space as needed, (2) having efficiencies built in, and (3) consideration of possible labor shortage and the need for convenience. Normally, the flow of food is from receiving to storage, to prep area, to preparation, to service, and to cleanup without criss-crossing or back-tracking.

The California Department of Education's *School Nutrition Facility Planning Guide* (Pannell, 1992) has an useful checklist for the director who is not too familiar with the opportunity to get corrections made in a new facility.

Figure 13.1. Flow of Work

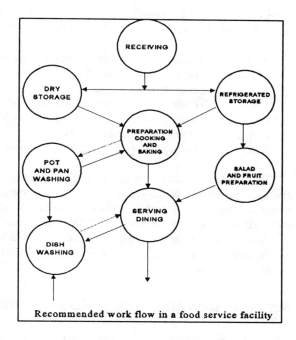

Recommended work flow in a food service facility

Basic Physical Considerations

The following physical conditions are most conducive to foodservice work:

Light:	35 foot candles on equipment; 50-75 foot candles on work surfaces and food display; 50 -75 at the cashier's stand; 50-75 in the serving area; 80-100 in the office; warm white florescent lights in the serving areas

Temperature:	68° to 78°F
Relative humidity:	40 to 45 percent
Ventilation:	change of air every 5 minutes
Height of work surfaces:	35-37 inches
Wall and ceiling color:	light without producing glare

When selecting wall colors, an institutional look should be avoided. Among the physical features and conditions that affect customers' perceptions and well-being are the colors; illumination; noise levels; temperature and relative humidity; odors; the type of seating; furnishings, including floor and wall coverings and drapes; the shapes and sizes of rooms; the layout of tables; the appearance and dress of employees; and sanitation (Kazarian, 1983).

Colors can have a significant impact on foodservice customers. Different colors promote different feelings, moods, and mental associations:

Yellow:	Sunny, warm, cheerful, inspiring, high-spirted; boosts morale and enhances food.
Orange:	Bright, warm, jovial, lively, forceful, energetic; enhances food; most stimulating color to the appetite.
Green:	Clear, cool, quieting, refreshing, low spirted; sells more salads.
Blue:	Transparent, cold, subduing, melancholy; the least stimulating to the appetite.
Purple:	Deep, cool, dignified, mournful.
Red:	Brilliant, hot, exciting, active, intense.

Bright accent colors should be used to enliven the decor. In a Maryland company the management changed the colors of carts from bright orange to battleship gray and the flowered cups orange and yellow to plain white at the recommendation of a consultant. It was reported that within six weeks the food sales had dropped 40%. Color makes a difference.

Sound also is a consideration and can be used to a foodservice's advantage. Fast music piped into the cafeteria is said to increase the speed with which the students eat, and slow, peaceful music to cause the opposite effect.

Serving Area and Dining Room Atmosphere

A few of the older school dining rooms do not show any indication that the person drawing the plan considered atmosphere. Atmosphere is identified as one of the prime inducements for people to want to dine out, as can be seen from the importance fast-food restaurants place on decor and from the incidents described above with the Maryland company. Though students may not be "dining out," the school dining room serves as the scene for many a meal. It should be pleasant and attractive to the age group it serves, and a fun place to eat. Such an atmosphere does not have to add much cost to the building.

The atmosphere has an effect—negative or positive—on the students' behavior in the dining room, as well as on the degree of participation. The atmosphere can create a fun place to be or an unpleasant place to be. Six schools in the Laconia (NH) School District converted to "mock food courts" in 1995, and participation at the high schools jumped 153%, and in the elementary schools, 120%. Colquitt County (Moultrie, GA) Schools have had a similar experience at their high schools, which have converted to "mock food courts." They expanded the menu choices using the inTEAM Food System and received excellent media coverage as a result of students' comments. School districts in Indianapolis (IN), Brownsville (TX), and Albuquerque (NM) have had similar experiences.

The design for the Stephen F. Austin High School in Texas, which has a beautiful food court arrangement, won the 1997 Foodservice Consultants Society International Annual Award for Excellence in Design. It features the openness of a food court , designed to allow students to make their own food choices with each line serving its own specialty. The food court uses bright colors and neon lights and resembles a food court you might find in a mall.

LARGE EQUIPMENT

In many school districts large equipment has not been replaced as it should have been—before it died. Much of the equipment in schools today was purchased during the 1960s, when the number of schools being built was at a peak and when federal monies were available for equipment. Much of the equipment bought in the 1960s that had a "life" of 25 to 30 years has worn out, is outdated, and labor-intense equipment, and needs to be replaced.

Large equipment specified and purchased should be based on the following: (1) the menu and number of meals served, (2) skills of the personnel, (3) location of the kitchen, (4) safety, health, and sanitary standards, (5) equipment and installation costs and utilities, (6) available space, (7) maintenance service available within a reasonable distance, (8) ease in operating, and (9) money available.

When determining equipment capacities needed, the requirements, the menu items, and quantities to be processed should be considered. For example, what is the maximum number of pans that can be put in the ovens at one time? What quantity of French fries will be needed over a lunch period, and what size and how many fryers will be needed?

Equipment is generally purchased for one or more of the following reasons: (1) to improve sanitation, (2) to reduce labor costs, (3) to maintain the nutritional value of foods, (4) to lower food costs, (5) to add appeal and variety to menus, (6) to increase productivity to make the work easier, or (7) to replace ineffective, malfunctioning, high maintenance cost equipment.

When money is available to replace or purchase a new piece of equipment, it is important for the foodservice director to look at what is new, and try to upgrade and use technology where available. The cook's advice may be, "Just like what I have." Hopefully, the director will not take that advice, but will evaluate what is out there. For instance, the combi-oven, which is a combination steamer and oven is not exactly new, but is being more accepted today than when it first appeared in this country. The multi-uses for this piece of equipment is its strongest feature. It can defrost, warm, cook, roast, bake, steam, and braise; however, it takes a lot of room and it is expensive.

Table 13.2 may be of some help in determining equipment needs; however, equipment should not be chosen on the basis of a chart in a book, but determined by the operation's needs. A variety of questions need to be considered. How often will each piece of equipment be used—daily, weekly, or monthly? How many work tables will be needed? Will the foodservice need more work tables than workers? Does the equipment allow for changes in or expansion of services? When determining quantities and items of equipment needed for a new school, one should anticipate needs for a reasonable period into the future. It is unwise, however, to buy oversized equipment in anticipation of future growth many years away. Over-equipping and over-designing a kitchen wastes funds and will hamper efficiency.

The Maryland State Department of Education's (School Food and Nutrition Service) *Design Manual* (1996) provides an equipment schedule and layouts for a highschool kitchen with a food court arrangement. This manual describes the serving area in all schools as the "Retail Activity Zone," where students are presented with the foodservice products. The manual points out that this

Table 13.2. Sample List of Large Equipment Needed for a Centralized Base School Shipping Food to Finishing Kitchens for Heating and Serving

Item	Finishing Kitchen Elementary* (quantity)	Finishing Kitchen Intermediate* (quantity)	Production Kitchen High School* (quantity)
SERVICE			
Milk cooler, drop front	2	3	6
Serving Line:			
Hot table	2	2	4
Cold/display table	2	2	4
Cash register	2	3	6
Solid top portion	4	4	8
Ice cream cabinet	2	3	6
Ice machine, large	—	1	1
Ice machine, small	1	—	—
Refrigerator, pass-through two-door**	—	1	2
Heated cabinet pass-through two-door**	—	1	2
Salad bar with table and cashier stand**	1	1	1
Soup pot (if soup is on the menu)	1	1	1-2
Vending machine**	—	1	2
Milkshake machine (if labor is available)	—	—	2
Heated Cabinet	2	1	2
PREPARATION			
Oven, convection, double	2	3	4
Oven, microwave**	1	1	1
French fryer, double	—	1	—
French fryer, triple	—	—	1
Slicer, automatic with table**	—	—	1
Steamer-jet trunion combo	1	1	1
Braiser	—	—	1
Trunion kettle, sized per unit	—	—	1
Mixer and parts 30-quart**	—	—	1
Qualheim or other cutting equipment	—	—	1
Table, work, stainless steel with wheels	2	4	6
Table, work, stainless steel enclosed, with shelf and wheels	—	—	2
Sink, three-compartment with booster heater	1	1	1
Sink, food prep with disposal	—	1	1

Table 13.2. Sample List of Large Equipment Needed for a Centralized Base School Shipping Food to Finishing Kitchens for Heating and Serving (continued)

Item	Finishing Kitchen Elementary* (quantity)	Finishing Kitchen Intermediate* (quantity)	Production Kitchen High School* (quantity)
Hand Sink	1	2	2
STORAGE			
Cart, Rubbermaid	2	3	4
Pan rack without doors	2	3	6
Receiving scale with stand*	—	—	1
Mobile wire shelf, 4 ft (storeroom)	6	8	15
Utility carrier truck	1	2	3
Dunnage rack*	2	3	4
Fans*	1	2	4
Freezer, reach-in			
Single	—	1	—
Two-door	—	—	—
Three-door	1	1	1
Refrigerator, reach-in			
Two-door	—	—	—
Three-door	1	1	1
Freezer, walk-in	—	—	1
Refrigerator, walk-in	—	—	1

*The elementary and intermediate finishing kitchens serve between 400 and 600 meals and the production kitchen at the high school has on-site service as well as transporting to four or more other schools.
**These are pieces of equipment that should be examined and questioned. Are they needed for the menu that will be served and for the way food is received (how much of the food is convenience—ready-to-heat and serve)? How often will the piece of equipment be used?

"Retail Activity Zone" should be exciting and appealing. It should do the following:

- Provide lighting levels appropriate to commercial food product display
- Provide colorful, durable, and easily cleanable finishes appropriate to commercial food product displays
- Provide clear, colorful signage that is suited to the educational level of the reader
- Provide a bright, attractive atmosphere that enhances the presentation of the food products
- Clearly identify degree of self-service available

Using Technology

The National Restaurant Association survey in 1988 (a Delphi study) predicted the following for the 1990s, but will need be extended to the 2000s as school foodservice operations replace equipment and the use of technology reaches more kitchens:

- Computerization of kitchen equipment will cut energy costs.
- Microwave technology will be put to greater use.
- Automation will help in food ordering and in fund transfers.
- Dishwashing will be robotized.
- Equipment manufacturers will make little response to industry's need for labor-saving equipment.

Unfortunately, the latter statement is correct because equipment manufacturers are not responding to the need for labor-saving equipment at the present time. Not many of these predictions for the 1990s have materialized. For example, computerization of kitchen equipment hasn't done much for energy cost yet. The use for microwave ovens is limited, particularly in school kitchens, because of the volume needed in a short period of time. Computerized temperature controls and timers are found on many ovens today but they have not always achieved satisfactory results. The digital panels have computer chips that may require frequent service.

The greatest uses of automation are in food ordering and with point-of-sale devices. Robotics have not found their way to school kitchens though there are ideal jobs for a robot to do. For example, consider the potential of robotics handling the cooking and backing of service areas for fryers.

Writing Specifications

Written specifications for equipment should describe to the potential bidder or company filling the order exactly what is wanted. See Figure 13.2 for a sample specification. There are a number of guidelines that can be used when writing equipment specifications. Besides experience with the particular type of equipment, the best aids are printed literature from equipment manufacturers' representatives or salespeople, U. S. government bid specifications, and National Sanitation Foundation standards. Specifications can be broad or detailed; they may specify manufacturers and models as standards. Usually when brands and models are specified, the specification will include the phrase "or the equivalent" to allow for a range of similar brands qualifying. However, when a school district is standardizing the equipment to reduce "expertise" and repair parts needed, a single brand may be desirable.

Specifications should include special features that are not standard for a particular piece of equipment, such as additional attachments for a mixer. A mandatory demonstration of the equipment, such as, and how the calibration of ovens works following installation, should be specified. At least two operating manuals should be obtained—one for the foodservice operator and one for the

Figure 13.2. Sample Equipment Specifications

ITEMS TO BE AWARDED AS AN AGGREGATE
3587009011—Refrigerator
STANDARD: Beverage-Air Model ER-48, Hobard Model QV-2 or equal
DESCRIPTION: Self-contained, tow full doors, front opening-unit. Automatic defrosting and evaporation system. Refrigeration system located on top of cabinet.
MATERIAL: Exterior— all carbon steel with front, doors, and sides faced with scratch-resistant vinyl or acrylic enamel.
　　Interior—Scratch-resistant interior with ⅜" radius bends. Automatic interior lighting
　　Legs—6-inch stainless steel, adjustable.
　　Insulation—minimum of 2-inch polyurethane foam insulation, poured into place, bonded to shell and liner.
　　Shelves—to be adjustable at one-inch intervals.
CAPACITY/SIZE: 46-50 cubic feet of storage space. 52"-55" wide; 32"-34" deep; and 82"-84½" high (including legs)
COLOR: Exterior to be bright yellow or lemon yellow (gold or avocado not acceptable).
ELECTRICAL: 115 volts; 60 cycles; 7-11 amps; single phase; ⅓ HP; 90° Ambient Temperature; 20°F Evaporated Temperature.
PLUMBING: none
APPROVAL AND LABELS REQUIRED : NSF and UL
ACCESSORIES:
　1.　Dial thermometer on exterior of unit, very visible. Calibrated adjustment. Power "on" Indicator.
　2.　Heavy-duty wire shelves that are rust-resistant and will withstand heavy use. QUANTITY: 12 shelves.
　3.　Heavy-duty, chromium-plated handles, with positive action hinge mechanism, magnetic gaskets, and cylinder locks on all doors.
WARRANTY: One-year, including labor and parts
SERVICE: Must be a service representative in metropolitan Washington area.
DELIVERY: See special provision 11.

---

maintenance department. The specifications should indicate whether the equipment is to be installed by the company, the method of delivery, the type of warranty or guarantee expected, and when delivery is expected or required.

Also, the following questions should be considered when writing a specification:

- Is there a service representative within 50 to 70 miles?
- Is a demonstration on site needed?
- Are the certification requirements met? (Underwriters' Laboratories, for electrical; American Gas Association, for gas; National Sanitation Foundation, for sanitary design requirements.)

- Is there a minimum of a one-year warranty for parts and labor?
- Is delivery to be within the building or on the dock?
- Should installation be included in price?
- Should the old equipment removal be included in the price?

Federal regulations do not require public bidding for purchases of $10,000 or less, although this may be required by state or local governments. Competitive bidding will usually result in considerable savings, particularly if more than one brand is acceptable. When bidding equipment, requesting price by line item or group of similar products (two different sizes of refrigerators, for example) will probably yield the best prices.

Equipment Design

The trend in design of equipment is toward modular and movable, providing flexibility. Modules allow for changing the facility design according to changing conditions. For example, when serving lines are purchased by sections and on wheels, it is easy to change the location or length of the line. The equipment can be moved easily where wanted and the modular design will accommodate the 12" x 20" or 18" x 26" x 2" pans.

Steam cooking has increased in use with the emphasis on low fat. Probably more improvement has been made in the last 20 years in steam-related equipment than in any other area with the pressureless convection steamers, tilting braising pan or tilting skillets, and combination ovens (see Figure 13.3). The combination oven, sometimes referred to as a combi or combo, is a combination of convection oven and convection steamer with optional features of "cook and hold/proof." It has proven to be popular but expensive.

Foodservice employees often like the tilting braising pan or tilting skillet (see example in Figure 13.4) because of the numerous tasks it can handle: thawing, reheating, braising, roasting, pan frying, kettle cooking, griddle cooking, sauteing, steaming, poaching, and boiling. Many schools still rely heavily on the traditional convection oven as the standby in the kitchen (see example in Figure 13.5).

A nice change in kitchens and serving equipment is the trend toward bright colors, versus only black, white, and shiny stainless steel. A kitchen can be brightened up with the addition of a colorful piece of equipment.

The materials used in kitchen equipment now allow not only the free use of color but have also reduced costs and increased durability in some cases. As a matter of fact, the plastics being used are often more durable, more lasting , more attractive, and easier to keep clean than more conventional materials.

Considerations to be addressed when planning to purchase new equipment are: (1)"How efficient is the equipment?" and (2) "Will it help employees work more efficiently?" One of the first features to consider is the height of work surfaces. Stress may be caused by surfaces that are either too high or too low. A person is most productive when the trunk of the body is vertical, the lower arms are at a right angle to the upper arms, and the work surface is one to three inches below elbow height. The following heights may be needed: 33 to 36 inches for women and 36 to 38 inches for

Figure 13.3. Example of a Convection Combo™ Steamer-Oven

Photo courtesy of Groen, A Dover Industries Company, Elk Grove Village, Illinois.

Figure 13.4. Example of a Tilting Braising Pan or Tilting Skillet

Photo courtesy of Groen, A Dover Industries Company, Elk Grove Village, Illinois.

Figure 13.5. Example of the Popular Convection Oven

Photo courtesy of Vulcan-Hart Corporation, Louisville, Kentucky.

men. Tables with adjustable feet are recommended as a way to provide for differences in height needs.

An important need of school foodservices is good food-holding equipment. The new holding cabinets with temperature and humidity controls by Winston and Carter Hoffman are excellent for controlling temperature and not damaging quality. The manufacturing industry needs to continue to pay more attention to temperature and humidity control in food-holding cabinets, and the effects of holding temperature on food quality. One of the main complaints of students about school food is that it is often cold by the time it is served.

Although technology and automation have been slow to come to the foodservice industry, labor costs will provide the needed impetus in the 1990s. Labor-saving equipment and robots of all types will hit the market, and computerization will be a standard feature of the new equipment.

PREVENTIVE MAINTENANCE

Preventive maintenance is thought of by some as being a luxury. The saying, "Pay now or pay **more** later," is very true with foodservice equipment and facilities. The results of regular, scheduled service of equipment can make emergency calls rare and can save money. Summer in school districts with traditional calendars provides an opportunity to perform preventive maintenance. See Figure 13.6 for an example of a preventive maintenance checklist. A service contract for preventive maintenance,

Figure 13.6. Example of Preventive Maintenance

EQUIPMENT	✓	N/A	COMMENTS
MIXER			
Adjust Belt Check Gear Box Cut Rubber Pads Grease/Oil All Movable Parts			
SLICER			
Oil All Moveable Parts Sharpen Blade			
CHOPPER			
Oil All Moveable Parts Sharpen Blade			
PROCESSOR			
Oil All Moveable Parts Remove Top/Clean Interior			
WARMER(s)			
Check Temperature Setting Calibrate Temperature If Necessary Check Element(s) Replace Element(s) If Necessary			
CAN OPENER			
Change Gear Blades Lubricate			
UPRIGHT COOLER (s)/FREEZER(s)			
Clean Condensers Check Temperature Gauge Calibrate Temperature If Necessary Check Refrigeration System			
WALK-IN COOLER(s)/FREEZER(s)			
Clean Condensers Wash Evaporators If Necessary Check Refrigeration System Check Temperature Gauge Calibrate Temperature If Necessary			
STEAMERS			

Open Boilers
  Replace De-scaler
  Replace Hand-Hole Gasket
  Check Timers for Operation
Remove Door Covers
Check Door Lock Mechanism
Oil/Grease Doors			

OVENS			
Remove Racks Check Blower Wheels Clean Blower Wheels If Necessary Replace Light Bulbs If Necessary Check Main Burner Valve Grease Valve If Necessary Oil Motor(s) Light/Calibrate Temperature			
STOVE (2-Burner)			
Adjust Pilot Grease Valves If Necessary			
FRYER			
Check for Leakage in Fryer Pot Check Thermostat Calibrate Thermostat If Necessary			
KETTLE			
Grease Check Operation			
BRAISING PAN			
Grease Crank Mechanism (manual) Clean Pilot Check Thermostat Calibrate Thermostat If Necessary			
SERVING LINES			
Check That All Burns Are Operating Check Thermostat Change Out Thermostat If Necessary			
HOODS			
Wash Interior Wash Exterior Paint If Necessary Power Wash Duck System/Blowers			
OTHERS			

Figure 13.6. Example of Preventive Maintenance (continued)
Source: St. Tammany (LA) Parish Food Service. Used by permission.

or school district provided maintenance service, should include exhaust systems, cooking equipment, hot water, grease removal, refrigeration, and sanitation equipment.

A record should be kept on each piece of equipment that will track the service calls, the costs of maintenance, and the overall condition of the equipment. Sometimes the cost of maintenance on a piece equipment is greater than the remaining value of the piece of equipment indicating it should be replaced. Many school districts have set up computerized records on each piece of equipment which provides the repair history, in addition to the basic information on each piece of equipment. Some school districts keep this information on 5 inch x 8 inch cards.

SELECTED REFERENCES

Birchfield, J. 1988. *Design & Layout of Foodservice Facilities*. New York: Van Nostrand Reinhold.
"Foodservice Equipment 2000: The Shape of Things to Come." 1996. *A Supplement to Restaurant Business*.
Kazarian, E. 1983. *Foodservice Facilities Planning*. 2nd ed. New York: Van Nostrand Reinhold
_____. 1983. *Work Analysis and Design for Hotels, Restaurants and Institutions*. 2nd ed. New York: Van Nostrand Reinhold.
Kotschevar, L., and M. Terrell. 1986. *Foodservice Planning: Layout and Equipment*. 3rd ed. New York: Macmillan Publishing Company
Maryland State Department of Education. 1996. *Design Manual*. Baltimore, MD: Mississippi State Department of Education, Nutrition and Transportation Services Branch.
Nettles, M., and D. Carr. 1996. *Guidelines for Equipment to Prepare Healthy Meals*. University, MS: National Food Service Management Institute.
Pannell, D. 1992. *School Nutrition Facility Planning Guide*. Sacramento, CA: California Department of Education, Child Nutrition and Food Distribution Division.
Payne-Palacio, J., and M. Theis. 1997. *West and Wood's Introduction to Foodservice*. 8th ed. Upper Saddle River, NJ: Prentice-Hall, Inc.
Scriven, C., and J. Stevens. 1999. *Food Equipment Facts: A Handbook for the Foodservice Industry*. New York: Van Nostrand Reinhold
Silberberg, S. 1997. *The New Design Handbook*. University, MS: National Food Service Management Institute.

14
COMPUTERIZATION AND AUTOMATION

Progress in Computerization Through the 1990s

Advantages of Computerization

What Can Be Computerized
Point-of-Sale/Point-of-Service
Electronic Spreadsheet
Procurement/Electronic Commerce
Inventory Control
Free and Reduced-Price Meals
Employee Time and Scheduling

Computer System

Preparing for Computerization

Software
Nutrient Standard

Automation

Selected References

PROGRESS IN COMPUTERIZATION THROUGH THE 1990s

Technology has had a noticeable impact on most centralized school foodservice program in this decade and will accelerate in the 2000s. Today many school foodservice programs—large and small—depend on computer systems in many ways. If the school district's mainframe goes down it can delay the issuance of paychecks, updating of enrollment data, affect in-house developed programs, and other functions; however, most school foodservice computer functions are being done on a stand-alone system.

In the early 1980s, computer mania was seen in all industries, including school foodservice. Many directors/supervisors became computer-literate, and some became slaves to the computer as they spent long hours feeding data into their microcomputers. The prices of microcomputers were affordable and could be covered by most school foodservice budgets. For some, the computer became a status symbol, and then in the late 1980s came the slow-down in computer interest, which was rather dramatic.

Some of the most successful users of the computer are not the large school districts but the small to middle-size districts. Many are self-taught and begin early with computers in the central school foodservice office. As far back as the 1980s over 72 percent of all school districts were using computers in foodservice. Software systems designed strictly for the school foodservice market and those that were altered to include this market began to mushroom. Nutrient Standard Menu Planning requirements made it essential to computerize in some school districts. Today there are several companies to choose from, and software to do all the jobs. A directory of school foodservice software is included later in this chapter.

Administrations in school districts have been slow to computerize foodservice programs, perhaps not realizing that foodservice may have more need for computerization than most departments. School foodservice directors have purchased different programs and, regrettably, have ended up with piecemeal situations, with numerous small programs that do not interface with one another. As a result of so many brands of software, it is not uncommon for a school district to enter the same data into more than one database. For example, recipes and the food file may be entered into one software package to precost, into another for nutrient analysis, inventory control, and production records, and on another for detailed profit and loss analysis. For some, the controls, the management information, and time savings that are possible to obtain are not realized.

The importance of computerization has been realized by large foodservice management companies, such as Sodexho Marriott Services and Aramark. They have made considerable progress with computerization, as have the giants in the fast food industry. McDonald's has put millions into the development of an integrated service, digital network, which is the ultimate in computerization.

With computerization entered a new vocabulary and the use of some common words, like menu, meaning something new. Communication has changed rapidly with the introduction of E-mail, the Intranet and Internet, and world-wide web. These are defined as follows:

Definitions:

E-MAIL—Electronic mail, sent and received through the Internet.

INTRANET—An electronic system that communicates within a given school district.

INTERNET—An electronic system that connects a computer to many other computers around the world.

MODEM—Hardware that converts digital computer information into audible telephone transmission.

WORLD-WIDE WEB—A part of the Internet that makes the information easier to get to.

ADVANTAGES OF COMPUTERIZATION

There is probably no department in a school district with as much need for computerization as the foodservice department, which must meet strict standards of accountability and requires various types of reports and detailed technical analyses for efficient management. The information needed to run a successful school foodservice program is extensive and varied.

Some of the benefits of a well-thought-out computerized system with "checks and balances" and accurate data entry are: (1) increased efficiency and greater speed of data handling, (2) more reliable, accurate information, (3) more timely report processing, (4) improved inventory control, (5) comprehensive management reports and analyses, (6) nutritional analysis of meals served, (7) reduced food and labor costs, and (8) improved standardization. School districts that are computerized realize many pluses to obtaining information on a more timely basis.

Self-audit capabilities should be built into the foodservice database, such as the school calendar and enrollments for each school, so that large data entry errors will be caught in "exception reports" and meals won't be claimed for non-school days. Computerized reports can be incorrect and thus always need to be proofed to see if the data looks right. Here are some of the problems identified by federal auditors in test audits done in 1987 (*Foodservice Director*, 1988):

- **Incorrect data were transmitted over the computer terminal** from the schools to the central office.
- **The automated data on student's eligibility were inaccurate** because schools did not keep the system updated. (For example, students were listed as eligible for free or reduced-price meals though their parents had not applied for benefits.)
- **School districts did not reconcile meal claims** against either the number of eligible children in attendance—or, on the other hand, school districts replaced school counts with the maximum number eligible.

Since 1987 federal regulations have required school districts to do edit checks, that today are often done by computer. The edit checks involve checking the numbers meals served by category against the numbers of students present and qualified in each category.

The Internet has become an indispensable on-the-job tool for many school foodservice people. They use it to keep up-to-date on federal legislation, to take a class at a university, and to communicate quickly and inexpensively. Penn State University offers courses in dietetics and controlling costs for the foodservice industry on the World Wide Web, and other courses are being added.

Competing with the fast-food industry and management companies in the 2000s will be nearly impossible for any foodservice without both the savings and improved information provided thorough computerization. The advantages will go to the "knows" rather than the "know-nots," or guessers. Savings will vary depending on the type of school operation and the scope of computer used. Some of the potential savings as a result of computers include:

- Reduced inventory because of better projections and more accurate ordering
- Error-free recipe calculations when altering batch sizes, which helps prevent overproduction
- Electronic commerce—just-in-time purchasing and placing orders using computers
- More rapid payment of bills and processing of federal and state monthly claims for reimbursement
- Fewer over claims found during state and federal audits
- Use of the power of the Internet, the World Wide Web, and E-mail
- Precosting and postcosting of foods on a timely basis, providing management with the information to make better decisions
- Reduction of time spent preparing reports manually
- Faster service (for example, reduced time between ordering and delivery of goods)
- Reduction in overproduction and waste from leftovers if recipes are extended properly
- Commodity management in the 2000s

WHAT CAN BE COMPUTERIZED

The list of activities that can be computerized is almost endless. In general, the activities of foodservices that are best suited for computerization include the following:

Point-of-sale functions
Payroll checks and time and attendance reports
Accounts payable and accounts receivable reports
Profit and loss statements by schools
Staffing using meal equivalents
Free and reduced-price meal application processing
      (Certification and verification)
Inventory—perpetual and physical

Procurement, including bid evaluation
Informal bid process
Payment of invoices and billing for services
Recipe extensions
Production records and planning
Scheduling of employees
Participation and revenue reporting
Precosting and postcosting of recipes and menus
Forecasting and ordering
Recording leftovers
Nutritional evaluation of menus (analysis)
Menu planning with preference data
Menu planning within cost restraints and meeting nutritional requirements
Meal accountability
Equipment inventory and preventive maintenance records and depreciation
Correspondence

Many of the functions listed above are being done in school foodservice offices. See Figure 14.1 for the parts to be computerized and the flow of data.

It should be noted that with computerization the reams of paper can mount and still not provide the information a manager/supervisor needs to manage, or the information may be in an unusable form or too massive. The manager/supervisor may need to have the information analyzed and interpreted. Groups of figures may need to be compared with prior years, prior months, or other schools to become meaningful. Percentages are usually more meaningful than lists of dollar amounts. In the final analysis, the real success of computerization may be determined by how useful the reports generated are to management.

Point-of-Sale/Point-of-Service

Many dream of a point-of-sale (POS), or point-of-service (POS), device that would recognize the student and the food on the tray, automatically provide the nutritive analyses of what the student selected, determine if the tray has a reimbursable breakfast and lunch on it, charge the right price, and order the replacement food to make those food items. The ideal is for the POS to push the "back of the house"—a meal sold reorders and establishes the size of production needed the next time the menu is repeated. Such a system could track history, customer count by day and by menu, the number of customers served by each station (line or server), and sales by lunch period, and do many more functions.

One of the best descriptions of a POS computer system is that it is "a computer that thinks it's a cash register." POS registers provide a lot more than just record-keeping and breakfast and lunch counts by category. All kinds of valuable information can be obtained from the communicating POS that is connected to a central computer.

At the school level the POS is usually the first function to be computerized—and should be. Over 30 percent of school foodservice operations are using some form of computerized POS. That's not many, and there are certainly many more schools to be computerized.

Figure 14.1 Sample Foodservice Information System Configuration

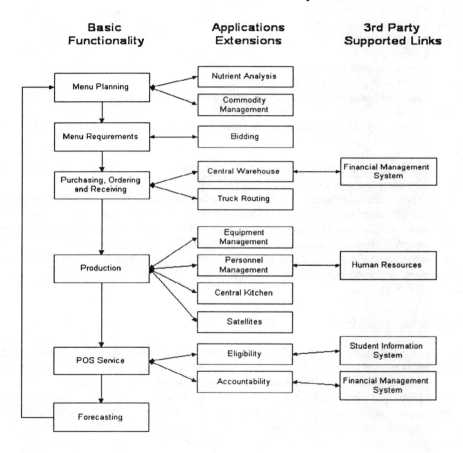

Source: Snap Systems, Inc. 1999. Used copyright material by permission.

Speed, accuracy, and "small footprint" (space required) should be three important features of the point-of-sale system a school foodservice purchases. Features of computerization to look for are:

- Speed in getting students through the line—speed of looking up a student's account, accepting a transaction
- Accuracy in maintaining data
- Small footprint—not requiring much space
- Touch screens with icons
- Online-photo IDs
- Wireless remote
- Biometric or bar code readers
- Multi-tasking computing
- Minimum number of key strokes to do the task
- Keypads and personal information numbers (PINs)

Using a bar code reader or magnetic strip scanner to access a student's record is pretty neat, but consider, "would you rather scan a student's eyes, thumbprint, voice, or handwriting?" The University of Georgia foodservice uses a biometrics access system for the contract dining halls that uses a three-dimensional handprint and gets students through the POS in less than three seconds. The system is so sensitive that a change in the ring the student is wearing will make a difference in recognition.

No one POS system fits the needs of everyone and there is no need for features that will never be used. Some school districts prefer using the key pads and personal identification numbers (PINs) rather than cards, but there are drawbacks to each. Forgotten PINs and long ones can slow the service down. Others like the photo-IDs and this positive identifier in order to prevent fraud, but there may be problems with lost cards. Some school districts have controlled this by charging for replacement cards (fee of $5).

Debit cards are like a bank card for students; they access a student's information and keep a record of money paid up front. These cards can increase cashier speed by as much as 50 percent—a cashier/POS device can process from 10 to 12 customers per minute, which is the speed a high school serving line should strive for. The ID cards improve accuracy in processing and security. Debit cards, which draw from funds deposited by the customers, are frequently used in high schools. The "Smart Card" is a type of debit card that has many uses, including using in vending machines, getting into a ballgame or school dance, and checking out books. It provides convenience to parents, who can transfer money via their bank account or from a credit cards. The terminals can be conveniently placed for students and teachers to add on card value.

Some promotions can help in getting the debit card system started. Students don't trust it at first, but once they do, they like the idea. The card can be started with a credit of $2, which can be accessed with the first $10 or more the customer adds on. An "advantage program" can be offered with special discounts for customers using debit cards, or "frequent user," points can be allowed to accumulate which can be redeemed for prizes. A group of students in Boston said they liked "mystery," freebies, premiums, or prizes. The university environment has found that customers with the debit card purchase on an average of 20 to 30 cents more in the cafeteria.

Touch screen displays are something to consider although they are not for everyone. If the school sells a limited number of a la carte items and have a limited number of menu items, the programmable keys on the POS may be adequate temporarily. Either the touch screen or programmable keys can have icons (instead of words) and, as more and more employees are hired who speak English as a second language, the icons on the keyboard are a good feature to consider. Trainers say the touch screen is easier to train on than the programmable key board.

A portable, wireless POS terminal makes it possible to sell food in a different place every day. School districts in the warm states use the portable POS terminals (battery-run) frequently to allow collection of data from mobile carts. They function well indoors and out, up to a mile away from the main computer. They come small enough to fit into the palm and are light in weight.

Because of labor shortages in schools and all industries the trend is to provide service requiring fewer employees. For example, Shell Oil is testing gasoline stations with no attendants in Houston, Texas, and Dayton, Ohio. Shell calls them "satellite" facilities; detractors call them "ghost stations." Perhaps a vending machine in the school dining room and other areas is the equivalent for foodservices.

Electronic Spreadsheet

The area least (and often last) to be computerized in school foodservices is financial management tools. Software companies have failed the school foodservice industry in this area. The biggest obstacle has been the computer hardware and software in the school dining room and other areas used by financial service departments. There are a number of systems being used—many are using in-house developed programs. Unfortunately, not many financial service departments have realized that school foodservice is a business and needs to operate like one. Instead they wait until the foodservice fund gets into trouble and then the administration's response may be to privatize.

Every software company that has a POS program should have an electronic spreadsheet with financial records built right in, so the information can be used to produce a profit and loss statement each day. The software should evaluate the day's expenditures—where the costs are out of line, what corrections are needed.

Most foodservice departments that have good financial management tools have created them within the foodservice office—often using software such as Lotus 1-2-3 or Excel. Figure 14.2 is an example of how one foodservice director is using Excel to help evaluate the profit and loss statement for the district and school by school. Even a novice can set up a financial analysis using templates like those provided by Warren Sackler and Samuel Trapani, *Foodservice Cost Control Using Microsoft Excel for Windows (*and another for Lotus 1-2-3), and run the following:

- Profit and loss statement (or income statement) with percentage of sales or revenue for month and year-to-date (see Figure 14.3)
- A budget—with percentage comparison with previous year's budget ready for evaluating variance from month to month to ensure the targets are met
- Bank deposit and bank statement reconciliation
- Inventory evaluation, number of days in inventory
- Prorated overhead costs

Figure 14.2. An Example of the Financial Analyses Created Monthly for a Foodservice Director Using Excel

1997 - 1998 REVENUE			% of Revenue
Cash Income from Meals Served	$	297,467	18%
Cash Income from Extra Sales	$	27,052	2%
State Funds - MFP	$	259,156	15%
Bank Account Interest	$	3,429	0%
Miscellaneous Income	$	4,053	0%
Commodities Received	$	116,709	7%
Federal Reimbursement from Meals Served	$	972,521	58%
	$	1,680,387	100%

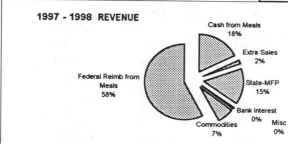

1997 - 1998 EXPENSES			% of Revenue
Labor - Salaries and Benefits	$	741,757	43%
Food - Purchased	$	531,108	32%
Food - Commodity	$	91,782	5%
Paper and Chemical Supplies	$	76,786	5%
Equipment - Kitchens. Cafeterias, Offices	$	28,960	2%
Other Costs - Indirect and Direct	$	129,766	8%
	$	1,600,159	95%

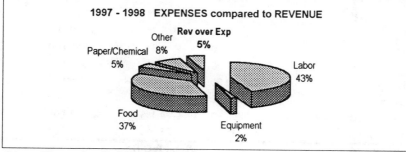

Source: Plaquemines Parish (LA) Schools 1999. Used by permission.

Figure 14.3. Example of a Computerized Financial Management Analysis

PROFIT AND LOSS REPORT

Site: Central Office	July Through December ———PERIOD———		—YEAR-TO-DATE—	
REVENUE Reimbursements	$2,677.00	25.2%	$9,655.00	24.8%
Local Revenues Student Lunches	$5,945.00	56.0%	$22,453.00	57.6%
Student Breakfasts	$429.00	4.0%	$1,454.00	3.7%
Adult Sales	$315.00	3.0%	$1,132.00	2.9%
A La Carte	$687.00	6.5%	$2,218.00	5.7%
Other	$219.00	2.1%	$619.00	2.1%
Total Local Revenue	$7,595.00	71.6%	$28,076.00	72.1%
E.O.Y. State Supplement	$143.00		$644.00	
E.O.Y. Earned Interest	$193.00		$585.00	
Grand Total Revenue	$10,608.00	100.0%	$38,960.00	100.0%
EXPENDITURES				
Labor Salaries	$2,045.00	19.3%	$8,244.00	21.2%
Temporary Services	$815.00	7.7%	$1,880.00	4.8%
Fringe	$423.00	4.0%	$1,875.00	4.8%
Total Labor	$3,283.00	30.9%	$11,999.00	30.8%
Food Costs Beginning Inventory	$1,488.00		$6,550.00	
Plus Purchases	$2,977.00		$9,807.00	
Less Ending Inventory	$568.00		$2,309.00	
Total Food Cost	$3,897.00	36.7%	$14,048.00	36.1%
Supply Costs Beginning Inventory	$254.00		$398.00	
Plus Purchases	$118.00		$566.00	
Less Ending Inventory	$189.00		$176.00	
Total Supply Cost	$183.00	1.7%	$788.00	2.0%
Direct Cost	$350.00	3.3%	$2,203.00	5.7%
Indirect Cost	$125.00	1.2%	$400.00	1.0%
Travel	$0.00	0.0%	$200.00	0.5%
Wares Replacement	$0.00	0.0%	$0.00	0.0%
Contracted Services	$25.00	0.2%	$75.00	0.2%
Grand Total Expenditures	$7,863.00	74.1%	$29,713.00	76.3%
PROFIT (LOSS)	$2,745.00	25.9%	$9,247.00	23.7%
01/04/99 10:29 AM		Visual B.O.S.S.		Page 1

Source: Horizon Software International, Inc.

Procurement/Electronic Commerce

Computerization by distributors has resulted in a sophisticated approach to procurement—sometimes referred to as electronic commerce. In many school districts automation in foodservice is coming through the back door. Distributors are computerizing their operations and are using the computer for "scientific buying." More and more foodservice companies and manufacturers are utilizing the Uniform Communications Standard (UCS) and telecommunications. This enables buyers and sellers of products to communicate through computer links with the school district or individual school foodservice manager. With an order entry system, which is designed to provide on-line communications between foodservice managers and their vendors, managers transmit their orders to the vendors' central warehouse computers. Current prices can be down-streamed, or sent from the host to the manager.

Electronic commerce has made ordering, tracking, receiving, and paying invoices easy. With the click of a computer mouse and the use of electronic commerce, a foodservice director can place orders, pay for products, reduce inventory, arrange delivery, and have inventory replaced without any human interaction. This is an area of computerization that large and small school districts will have to use in the future with the larger distributors.

The bid process is easy to computerize and can be more accurately evaluated with the use of computers. It can also provide the ability to establish the most economical approach to purchasing—whether that be the "one-stop" purchasing option (purchasing all from one vendor) or "cherry picking" (purchasing by line item from several vendors based on the best price).

Shopping through the Internet is a growing trend in the foodservice industry. Schools have been slow to use this means, which has merit when looking for specific items that may not have to be bid. On-line catalogs enable managers to find small equipment and gadgets and product information. The foodservice director can shop around for the best price, place an order, pay for the order, arrange delivery, pull the product from the company's inventory, and add it to the foodservice's inventory through the use of the Internet.

Many school districts do not bid produce, yet there is much to be gained from competitive prices—weekly bids. With the use of computers and the Internet (or the FAX machine) obtaining price quotes weekly for produce and analyzing the quotes can be done in a fraction of the time it took in the past. Checking out the produce market prices can be done as well. Obtaining prices quickly has been improved through the use of E-mail.

The grocery industry was the first in the food industry to utilize the UCS system successfully. UCS was developed by the Uniform Code Council in Dayton, Ohio. It allows a school foodservice manager/supervisor with a computer and a modem to talk to a distributor for ordering and billing purposes. It eliminates a great deal of paperwork and manager/clerical bookkeeping time. Orders can be processed more quickly.

With the Universal Product Code (UPC) and a bar code reader, the school's perpetual inventory can be updated while checking in the vendor order. At the same time, products that do not meet specifications will show up with a "buzz." The UPC is a national system of product identification consisting of small blocks of parallel lines and numbers unique to each product. The UPC symbols are printed or applied on many food packages. These symbols can be read by moving a bar code scanner over the code. With a laser beam device the code can be read at a greater distance. The use of a scanning devise and portable hand-held computer can reduce the taking of inventory to a few minutes.

Inventory Control

Perpetual inventory, as well as physical inventory, can become paperless with the use of bar code readers and a hand-held terminal unit that is connected to an integrated system. The perpetual inventory process that became too expensive in the late 1970s to maintain manually can be maintained by computer efficiently and accurately today. The need for maintaining a perpetual inventory is certainly present. For instance, tracking food and supplies can help deter theft, which is a major problem for some school districts.

With computerization it makes more sense to adopt the "just-in-time" philosophy rather than that "too much because I'd rather be safe" philosophy. The menu to be served next week and what is in stock the week before should determine what is ordered. No foodservice manager should have to place an order for food five weeks ahead of use in order to give the vendor time to obtain the products on the school's order.

Free and Reduced-Price Meals

With a computer program, free and reduced-price meal applications can be acted upon, parents and schools notified, and meal tickets or rosters generated. If the action on an application taken for free and reduced-price meals becomes a part of the student roster, it moves with the student when he or she transfers from one school to another in the same school district. Preprinted applications containing students' names, grades, and schools, and Social Security numbers of family members in five different languages (or more) can be provided for parents to update yearly. Information from the social services department in the county can be loaded into the database for direct certification, and those who qualify for the social services can be qualified within a short time.

Computer programs, like Snap Systems, that contain the names of those qualifying for free and reduced-price meals in the school's computer system can interface with the POS device. Then, when a student who does not qualify is served, the system will tell the cashier. Charging and draw downs can also be handled with systems like this. These systems can prevent a number of irregularities, including over-claiming, from occurring. See Figure 14.4 which shows a sample school list. This may be a districtwide list first, then sorted by school and by classroom.

Employee Time and Scheduling

Some commercial foodservices have taken advantage of computerization and use it to schedule their employees to work when they need the employees. In most school districts foodservice employees work the same hours each day when school is in session and sometimes when school is not in session because the days are in the "contract" with the employees. In some school districts, there is abuse of work time—employees are sometimes being paid for six hours but they finish work in five hours. When a labor hour is costing $17 or $18 (including all the many employee benefits), this becomes a serious matter. This is discussed further in Chapter 6, " Organizational Structure and Personnel," and is not an issue for this chapter. The computerized time clock, which uses software to track employees' hours as the employee punches in and out can be valuable—if employees do not punch in for others. The biometric system has some merit here—it recognizes thumbprint or voice, etc. The time clock can be used to track how much time is spent on certain jobs, e.g., catering, vending, breakfast, and lunch. By 2010 this type of tracking will be commonplace. Micros System has a

Figure 14.4. Sample School List Coded With Students Approved for Free and Reduced-Price Meals

School Site 10
Customer Group: All (Active)
Homeroom: AAAAAAAA to ddddddd   Sort By: Site, Last Name, First Name

Id	Site Name	Customer Id	Bar Code	Customer Name			Status		Status Type	Gr	Home-room
E10	Site 10	47766	30001	Alcala	Michelle	A	X		Directly Certified	11	Blanco
		51986	30002	Anderson	Jami	A	Z		Not applicable	12	Arthur
		47526	30003	Anselmo	Leslie	A	Z		Denied App	11	Blanco
		40486	30004	Arndt	Matthew	A	X		Application	12	Arthur
		46946	30020	Arthur	Tonya	A	T		Not Applicable	AD	Arthur
		48071	30005	Basenberg	Jessica	A	Z		Not Applicable	12	Arthur
		48539	30006	Baxter	Teri	A	X		Application	11	Blanco
		46999	46999	Bell	Sherry	A	Z		Not Applicable	11	Blanco
		46916	30008	Bell	Valerie	A	X		Application	12	Arthur
		53750	30009	Benavides	Maribel	A	X		Application	12	Arthur
		47229	30010	Blum	Nicholas	A	Y		Application	12	Arthur
		46923	30011	Borre	Richard	A	Y		Application	12	Arthur
		47394	30012	Brown	Kristy	A	Y		Application	11	Blanco
		46928	30013	Brown	Rachel	A	X		Application	11	Blanco
		48175	30015	Calabrese	Adam	A	Y		Application	11	Blanco
		46932	30016	Callahan	Keagan	A	Z		Not Applicable	12	Arthur
		47867	30017	Campbell	Zacharey	A	Z		Denied App	12	Arthur
		48457	30018	Chacon	Diana	A	Z		Not Applicable	12	Arthur
		47264	30019	Chibe	Mark	A	X		Application	12	Arthur
		50199	50199	Du Pree	Tricia	A	X		Temporary App	11	Blanco
		10000	9090	Fisher	Susan	A	Z		Not Applicable	11	Blanco
		49024	49024	Fisher	Timothy	A	Z		Not Applicable	11	Blanco
		52878	52878	Frye	Brandon	A	Z		Not Applicable	12	Arthur
		48623	46999	Galarza	Angela	A	X		Application	11	Blanco
		49769	49769	Gimbut	Erin	A	Z		Not Applicable	11	Blanco
		46940	46940	Gimbut	Steven	A	X		Application	12	Arthur
		50030	50030	Gomez	Silvester	A	X		Application	11	Blanco
		49781	49781	Goreczny	Ryan	A	X		Application	12	Arthur

Figure 14.4. Sample School List Coded With Students Approved for Free and Reduced-Price Meals (continued)

Id	Site Name	Customer Id	Bar Code	Customer Name			Status	Status Type	Gr	Home-room
		49773	49773	Harvey	Stephanie	A	Y	Application	11	Blanco
		49030	49030	Helgren	Robyn	A	Y	Application	11	Blanco
		49031	49031	Henson	Lincoln	A	Y	Application	11	Blanco
		49032	49032	Herbst	Brian	A	X	Application	12	Arthur
		55045	55045	Herzog	Amy	A	Z	Not Applicable	11	Blanco
		49033	49033	Hinton	Karli	A	T	Not Applicable	AD	Blanco
		92099	92099	Smith	Angela	A	Z	Not Applicable	12	Arthur
		20922	20922	Wilson	Stephanie	A	X	Application	12	Arthur

Total Free:	14	Directly Certified: 1	Expired: 0
Total Reduced:	7		
Total Paid:	13	Denied:	2
Total Adult:	2		
Total Customers Printed:	36		

Id = Identification number   **GR = grade**

Source: WinSNAP, Snap Systems, Santa Monica, CA, 1998. Used by permission.

computer program, "Labor Management," that has potential for use by school foodservice managers when scheduling work.

Sodexho Marriott Management Services has been using computer software (for windows [operating system]) to schedule employees, and it has increased their productivity by 8.3 percent in one service division. They have cut labor costs by $2 million in two years in that service division in just one part of the country.

COMPUTER SYSTEM

Determining the best type of computer system for a school foodservice is made more difficult by rapid changes in the electronics industry. The decision requires technical knowledge in both the computer field and school foodservice. One of the recommended ways to start is to conduct a feasibility study. According to Pug (1989), a feasibility study should define "the specific needs [and] requirements that the computer software must satisfy." It starts with determining the answers to a number of questions, such as "what are the purposes?" and "what should be computerized first?" Once questions like these are answered, a list of what is to be computerized initially or later on should be drawn up. The list can then be turned into a flow chart such as that shown in Figure 14.1.

One of the first decisions to make is how data will be entered and at what level. There are three basic methods:

- **Batch:** Information is collected and sent by courier or taken to a central location for data entry.
- **On Line:** Data are entered into a terminal at the school and warehouse level.
- **Networking:** Microcomputers with memory are located at each of the schools (in the managers's office) and used to transmit date electronically to a central location. The communication can be in all directions.

Networking is the most progressive approach to transferring data and using a database and is being commonly used in the 1990s. For example, the Tennessee State Department of Education has encouraged school district to use the Internet by putting frequent important messages on it. Telecommunications have added an entire dimension to the ECR industry. With a network, schools in a centralized system can be polled at a specific time for daily participation and revenue data. It is possible to have the POS programmed so that when one hamburger is sold the perpetual inventory shows one less hamburger bun, one less hamburger patty, and one less portion of ketchup; this daily information triggers the placement of orders for these items.

PREPARING FOR COMPUTERIZATION

Computerization will not transform a poorly organized foodservice with high costs into a well-organized, profitable operation. Management is still responsible for good organization and decision making. As a matter of fact, the foodservice has to become well-organized and standardized to computerize the entire operation successfully.

When preparing for computerization, the following suggestions may be useful:

- Prepare the staff by making them computer-literate.
- Begin standardizing recipes. Inaccurate, ballpark figures on yield and ingredients will not work.
- Design forms for collecting data to fit the computer programs. Highlighting of shaded blocks with data that are used frequently will help.
- Plan to run dual systems (manual and computerized) for two to three months until any problems ("bugs") have been worked out.
- Consider the consequences if the computer system is down for a day or more. Be sure the foodservice office maintains a backup so that it can continue to operate.
- Have someone who is familiar with recipes and foods input or proof the data when setting up files in these areas.

SOFTWARE

Many school districts have chosen to write their own software programs. In order to do this, or to determine if a commercial package will meet the facility's needs, the list of what is to be computerized should be determined. One entire aspect unique to school foodservice is the free and reduced-price meals accountability requirement.

Software needs to be considered before selecting computer hardware. Software can be more of a limiting factor and more costly than the hardware. Some of the popular software programs generally used are Excel, Lotus 1-2-3, Multiplan for spreadsheet, Word, WordPerfect, and Writing Assistant for word processing, and a variety of graphics programs. See Figure 14.2 for an example of using Excel to analyze the profit and loss statement. Figure 14.3 provides an example of a commercial software that is designed for school foodservices. It is important to have software program that not only provides good point-of-sale accountability, but also one that does the accounting function.

Although commercial software companies were slow to enter the school foodservice market, a number of software packages have been designed for school foodservice or altered to fit the industry. Table 14.1 lists software with five or more applications for the school foodservice market that has been adapted from *School Foodservice & Nutrition*'s January 1999 issue.

NutriKids and Snap are widely used software programs for nutritional analysis and are approved by the USDA, Food and Nutrition Services. NutriKids is available through LunchByte Systems, Inc. (Phone: 800-724-9853). Their software is not listed in Table 14.1 because it does not have five or more applications. *Assisted NuMenu Manual with Database on Disk* (Pannell, 1996, updated, 1998) published by inTEAM Associates, is a source of assistance with Nutrient Standard Menu Planning. It contains popular menus, a set of standardized recipes, and an enhanced database for Snap Systems and Lunch Byte's NutriKids.

Nutrient Standard Menu Planning

California has led the way in computerizing the menus and using nutrient standards to plan menus. SHAPE California (Shaping Health as Partners in Education) is a network of school districts and child care agencies working together to promote nutritious meals. The group found that basing menus solely on Recommended Dietary Allowances (RDAs) ignored the role of healthful eating habits.

The USDA's administration in the early 1990s has pushed the use of computers and nutrients for planning menus; 35 school districts nationwide participated in a three-year test of the Nutrient Standard Menu Planning (NSMP), based on nutrients instead of just food groups, which ended in January 1994. Some of their results are reported in Chapter 4, "Planning Menus and Food Offerings."

The National Food Service Management Institute sponsored a conference in 1992 on "'Trends' School Food Service in the Year 2000 and Beyond," wherein excellent speakers pointed out some of the areas that self-operated school foodservice programs were lagging in and the use of computerization was one of them. John Alexandria, president of CBORD computer software company, said school foodservice "needs to simplify the operation—the simpler but effective operations tend to be in place in contract operations. Self-operators often do not have a good financial system, good purchasing and receiving controls." Many school districts have taken on the challenge and are converting to a simpler, effective operation that is highly computerized.

Table 14.1. List of Software Packages with Five or More Applications for the School Foodservice Market[1]

Company	Function	Name of Software Packages
ACCU-SCAN® 1818 W. 2nd Street Wichita, KS 67203 Phone: 888-880-8278	F/R, POS, FPRO, INV, BID, PER	Meal Tracker®
BON APPETIT SOFTWARE 9215 Youree Drive Shreveport, LA 71115 Phone: 800-347-4681	F/R, NUT[2], POS, FPRO. INV, BID	Each function by name
CAFS, INC. 1084 Judge Sekal Avenue Biloxi, MS 39530 Phone: 800-748-9631	F/R, NUT[1], POS, FPRO. INV, BID, PER, FIN	CAFS
COMALEX, INC. 2367 Trade Center Way Naples, FL 34109 Phone: 800-643-2762	F/R, NUT[1], POS, FPRO. INV, BID, PER, E-M, FIN, WP	FARMA, Cafe Terminal, B.O.S.S., Quickbooks
COMPUHELP 5205 Airport Blvd. Austin, TX 78751 Phone: 800-266-7843	F/R, NUT, POS, FPR, . INV, BID, PER, FIN, Other	Nutrition Plus™
EDUCATION MANAGEMENT SYSTEMS 1638 Military Cutoff Road Wilmington, NC 28403 Phone: 800-541-8999	F/R, POS, INV, BID, FIN, Other	Meals Plus
KYRUS CORPORATION 113 Regional Park Drive Kingsport, TN 37660 Phone: 800-932-6737	F/R, NUT, POS, FPRO. INV, BID, FIN, Other	LunchBox™
MICROCHECK SYSTEMS, INC. 6300 Rothway Street, Suite 190 Houston, TX 77040 Phone: 800-647-4524	F/R, NUT, POS, FPRO. INV, BID	Win-Master, Win-Ear Inventory Express, Win-Mem Recipe Express
NUTRI-COMP SOFTWARE, INC. 1012 NW 51st Street Vancouver, WA 98663 Phone: 800-699-4589	NUT[1], FPRO, INV, BID, PER, FIN	Recipe Express, Inventory Express, Bid Analysis, Scheduler Pro

[1]These companies are constantly updating their software and adding new programs.

[2]Indicates the software system has been approved by USDA's Food and Nutrition Service for implementing Nutrient Standard.

Table 14.1. List of Software Packages with Five or More applications for the School Foodservice Market (continued)

Company	Function	Name of Software Packages
NUTRITION DATA SYSTEMS 5315 Victoria Place Westminster, CA 92683 Phone: 714-894-6131	F/R, NUT, POS, FPRO, INV, BID, PER, E-M, FIN, WP	Food Trak
PACIFIC TRIANGLE SOFTWARE 23861 El Toro Road, Suite 700 Lake Forest, CA 92630 Phone: 800-567-2632	F/R, NUT, POS, FPRO. INV, FIN, WP, Other	Panda
SCHOOLHOUSE SOFTWARE, INC. 3009 Douglas Blvd., Suite 200 Roseville, CA 95661 Phone: 800-683-2234	F/R, NUT, POS, FPRO. INV, FIN, WP, Other	CafTRAC
SNAP SYSTEMS/CAFS P. O. Box 2410 Santa Monica, CA 90407 Phone: 800-423-2113	F/R, NUT[1], POS, FPRO. INV, BID, PER, FIN, Other	WinSNAP, CAFS
UNISOFT SYSTEMS ASSOCIATES 1441 King Avenue, Suite 212 Columbus, OH 43212 Phone: 800-448-1574	NUT, FPRO, INV, BID, Other	Food System 4/Windows
WORDWARE, INC. 26616 CSA, Hwy 24 Dassel, MN 55325 Phone: 800-955-2649	F/R, POS, INV, BID, FIN, Other	Lunch Cashier System, Food Inventory System

Source: American School Food Service Association, *School Foodservice & Nutrition 1999*. Used by permission.

Abbreviations used for functions above are as follows:

F/R = Free and reduced-price processing   BID = Bidding and procurement
NUT = Nutrition analysis   PER = Personnel management
POS= Point-of-sale   E-M = E-mail
FPRO= Food production   FIN = Financial management
INV= Inventory control   WP = Word processing

---

[1]Indicates the software system has been approved by USDA's Food and Nutrition Service for implementing Nutrient Standard Meal Planning. For a current list call USDA, Food and Nutrition Services.

Chapter 4, "Planning Menus and Food Offerings" provides a comparison in using four of the leading software packages done by the National Food Service Management Institute. Table 14.2 provides a comparison of nutrient analysis software for schools provided by the USDA in 1994. Food and Nutrition Services, USDA, can provide an up-to-date list of software approved for nutrient analysis.

AUTOMATION

Kitchen equipment companies have been slow to automate equipment, but the 1999 National Restaurant Exhibition did show more use of automation than in the past. Computer chips are controlling many pieces of equipment today. There are many routine jobs in the school foodservice kitchen to be automated, particularly in the cleanup, and robotics are bound to flourish in the near future.

Automation and robotics are making vending good food a winning way of reducing labor costs in college dorms, hospitals, schools, and business and industry foodservices. Vending of food is a convenient way to provide food where and when the customer wants it. Many foods are being provided packaged and ready-to-heat-and-eat. Food being vended no longer means "junk food," but "convenience food." Vending can make food available 24 hours a day, and labor costs can be kept under control.

Table 14.2. Nutrient Analysis Software for NuMenus Comparison Guide

NSMP Programs	CAFS	Compuirition	B.O.S.S./ Horizons	NutriKids LunchByte	PCS Revenue Control System	NSMP SNAP
USDA-approved Nutrient Standard Menu Planning Program	Yes	Yes	Yes	Yes	Yes	Yes
Precosts recipes and menus	Only with purchasing/ Inventory Program	Yes	Yes	Yes	Yes	No
# of items	Items in USDA database plus branded products CNP nutrients	18,000+ items	3,500+ items	7,000+ items	Items in USDA database	3,500+ items
# of nutrients		30 nutrients	CNP nutrients	CNP nutrients	CNP nutrients	12 nutrients
Allow adding to or modifying nutrient profiles	Yes	Not currently; will add local items not already in database free of charge	USDA items - no Others - yes	Yes	USDA items - no Others - yes	USDA items - no Others - Yes
Updates (monthly/ annually/irregularly)	As needed	3/year	As needed	2-3/year	Annually or as needed	Annuallly or more frequently if warranted
Maintenance costs	Complete Maintenance and Support Agreement $195/year	Annual subscription membership	1% of cost of software/mo ($150/year minimum)	$150/year	$598.50/district $59.85/school	Free for 6 months $270/yr after first 6 month
Commercial products included in database (other than USDA items)	Yes	5,000+	Yes	5,000+	No	No
Current version	1.3	95-2	3.0	6.0	1.217	4.16
Other NSMP information	● Data entry and analysis service ● On-screen help ● Dietitian on staff	● Hs provided NSMP software for over decade	● Context sensitive on-line help ● User friendly documentation ● Dietitian on staff	● On-line help ● Dietitian on staff	● User-friendly interface ● Training documentation	● Training Guide ● Keyboard Template ● Dietician on staff ● On-line help

Hardware	CAFS	Compuirition	B.O.S.S./ Horizons	NutriKids LunchByte	PCS Revenue Control System	NSMP SNAP
IBM/IBM comparable	Yes	Yes	Yes	Yes	Yes	Yes
Macintosh comparable	Yes with MS-DOS emulation	Yes with MS-Dos emulation	Yes with MS-Dos emulation	Yes	No	Powe Mac only
DOS/Windows/Windows 95/ Network	DOS/UNIX/ Network/ Novell	DOS/UNIX/ AIX	DOS/UNIX/ Windows 95/ Network	Yes	DOS/Windows/ Windows 95/ Network	DOS 5.0+/ Windows/ Windows 95/ Network
Requires mouse	No	No	No	No	No	No
Other hardware information	Also runs on RS6000 1 MB RAM 20 MB disk space	Also runs on RS6000 640 K RAM 25 MB disk space	1 MB RAM 50 MB disk space	640 K RAM 15 MB disk space	585 K RAM 40 MB disk space	1 MB RAM 600 K available memory 15 MB disk space

Table 14.2. Nutrient Analysis Software for NuMenus Comparison Guide (continued)

Support	CAFS	Compuirition	B.O.S.S./ Horizons	NutriKids LunchByte	PCS Revenue Control System	NSMP SNAP
Provides Training	Yes ● Training tape included with software ● On-site - $350/day plus expenses ● Regional group training available	Yes	Yes ● On-site ● Step by step training video with every module ● Context sensitive help ● Regional workshops	● Regional workshops	Yes ● Over the phone training ● 3 days at $365/day	Yes: toStates - cost of travel, expenses ● Schools - $350/day plus expenses ● Regional workshops
Provides on-line support	Yes	Yes	Yes	Yes	Yes	Yes
Provides toll-free phone support	Yes	Yes	Yes	Yes	Yes	Yes
Provides list of districts using the system	Yes	References available	Yes	Yes	References available	References available
# School districts using this system	Hundreds	30+	Hundreds	2,700+	Available upon request	800+
Any support costs	Yes, various options to be determined	To be determined	Indluded in maintenance cost	No	Included in maintenance cost	Included in maintenance cost
Other support services	●Extensive help screens ● Rds on staff	● Newsletters ● Users meetings ● Help screen ● Rds on staff	● Newsletters ● Users group meetings	● Newsletters	● Newsletters ● Users group meetings	● Rds on staff
Point of sale accountability	Yes	No, but have point of sale interface	Yes	No	Yes	Yes
Free and reduced-price application processing program	Yes	Yes	Yes	No	Yes	Yes
Food production/inventory program	Yes	Yes	Yes	Yes	Included in NSMP	Yes
Bidding and procurement program	Yes	Yes	Yes	No	Yes	Yes
Personnel management/financial management program	Yes	Yes	Yes	No	Yes	Yes
Other program	● Central kitchen production and management ● Warehousing and distribution ● Fixed asset management	● Warehouse inventory and distribution management ● Menu mix analysis and forecasting module ● Color/ texture menu planning and evaluation module ● Recipe and menu costing	●Asset management ● USDA commodity allocation ● Inventory management ● Purchasing ● Central warehouse ● Central kitchen		●Inventory & vendor bidding ● District meal accountability ● Labor scheduling & management ● Interface to inventory ● Interface to point of sale history	● 2 versions of integrated software - menu based and windows based ● Central kitchen
Company Name Address and Telephone Number	Computer Assisted Food Service, Inc. 1050 Rutherford Road Waxahachie, TX 75165 TEL:(214) 845-2260 FAX:(214) 845-2260 John Trojacek, Director of Marketing	Compuitrition, Inc. 9121 Oakdale Ave. Chatsworth, CA 91311 TEL:(800) 222-4488 TEL:(818)701-5544 FAX:(818)701-1702 Kim Goldberg	Horizon Software 2230 Scenic Hwy Suite 300 Snellville, GA 30278 TEL:(800)741-7100 FAX:(770)736-7376 Teresa Williamson	LunchByte Sys., Inc. 1800 English Road Rochester, NY 14616 TEL:(800)724-9853 FAX:(716)227-8594 Sales Department	PCS Revenue Control Systems, Inc. 360 Sylvan Avenue Englwood, NJ 07632 TEL:(800)247-3061 FAX:(201)568-8381 David Smith	SNAP Systems, Inc. P.O.Box 2410 Santa Monica, CA 90407-2410 TEL:(800)423-2113 FAX:(310)829-1936 Sandy DeSantis (x8947)

Source: USDA, Food and Nutrition Services 1994.

SELECTED REFERENCES

Begalle, M. 1997. "Technology for Today & Tomorrow: The Future Is Now for School Foodservice Operations." *School Foodservice & Nutrition* 51 (1): 25-32.

Corrigan, K. And M. Aumann. 1993. " But Is It Nutritious? Computer Analysis Creates Healthier Meals at School." *School Business Affairs* 11: 9-12.

Gordon Food Service. 1995. "Is the Year 2000 at Davison High School Today?" *Impact* (April/May). MI: Gordon Food Service.

Harris, J. 1999. "Getting to the Point (of Sale)." *School Foodservice &Nutrition* 53 (1): 38-43.

Kaud, F. Editor. *Effective Computer Management in Food and Nutrition Services*. Rockville, MD: Aspen Publishers, Inc.

McGraw-Hill School Systems. 1996. Monterey, CA: Educational and Professional Publishing Group of the McGraw-Hill Companies, Inc.

McKinsey & Company. 1996. *Foodservice 2005: Satisfying America's Changing Appetite*. Falls Church, VA: Food Distributors International-NAWGA/IFDA.

McLaren, P. 1999. "Are You Cyber-Savvy?" *School Foodservice & Nutrition* 53 (1): 30-37.

Morrison, S. 1997. "Lost in Cyberspace?" *School Foodservice & Nutrition*. 51(1): 35-41.

National Food Service Management Institute. 1992. *Trends: School Food Service in the Year 2000 and Beyond*. University, MS: Author.

_____. 1996. *Using Computer Simulation to Solve School Foodservice Problems*. University, MS: Author.

Pappas, M. 1996. *Eat Food, Not Profits! How Computers Can Save Your Restaurant*. New York: Van Nostrand and Reinhold, Inc.

Rubinstein, E. 1998. "Integration Nirvana: Foodservice Operators Embrace ERP Application Suites," *Nations Restaurant News (Oct. 19, 1998): 42, 50*

_____. 1998. "Curtailing Labor Costs: Softwares Let Operators Optimize Scheduling."*Nations Restaurant News* (Oct. 19, 1998): 42, 50.

Sackler, W., and S. Trapani. 1996. *Foodservice Cost Control Using Microslft® Excell for Windows®*. New York: John Wiley & Sons, Inc.

Schmidt, D. 1997. "POS FYI." *School Foodservice & Nutrition* 51(1): 70,72.

_____. 1999. "1999 Software Buying Guide." *School Foodservice & Nutrition* 53 (1): 44-5.

_____. 1999. "The Clock Is Ticking: Understanding the Implications of Y2K." *School Foodservice & Nutrition* 53 (1): 22-29.

Society for Foodservice Management. 1994. *Second Annual Benchmarking Study*. Prepared by Consumer Metrics.

15
OTHER SOURCES OF REVENUE
AND
SERVING THE COMMUNITY

Other Sources of Revenue

Catering

Vending

Contracts With Other School Districts

Community Nutrition Services

Child and Adult Care Food Program

Senior Citizen Food Programs
    Home-Delivered Meals
    Congregate Dining

Summer Foodservice Program

Contracts With Other Agencies

Head Start

Home-Meal Replacement

Lost Revenue Opportunities

Selected References

OTHER SOURCES OF REVENUE

There are two types of foodservice directors when it comes to taking advantage of increasing business and other sources of revenue. One type sees school foodservice as a business and wants it to grow, and if a group needs food, that director wants to offer it. The other type sees the job as that of providing school-age children with lunch and maybe breakfast, and doesn't want any more responsibility. Also, some school boards and administrators don't want foodservices to get involved with other programs or provide other services.

Most school districts that do provide other services to boost revenue usually do it for profits that will help subsidize the school breakfast and lunch programs and will utilize the facilities that the schools provide.

Labor costs of school foodservice may be too high for school foodservice to compete with outside businesses for some services. For example, if a local restaurant can cater an event at a school for less, the school foodservice cannot expect to be the caterer selected. Unless the school foodservice employees are efficient (achieve high productivity) and employees receive salaries comparable (discussed later in this chapter) to that of commercial foodservice employees, the other sources of revenue may **not be sources of profit**. A director may rationalize that the labor was on the employee's regular time and won't cost any more, in which case the director has over-staffed the schools. If labor cannot be cut because of a contract, providing the additional service will increase revenue, if fixed costs do not increase.

The foodservice staff should never lose sight of its main purposes, and if additional services would negatively affect the school breakfast and lunch programs, they should not be provided. Many school districts' foodservice staffs have the expertise, the desire, and the requests sufficient to warrant their taking on additional business.

There are many child care centers, senior citizen groups, etc., located in remote areas that need service, but are too small to be of interest to management companies. Often schools are located where people are and can produce another 40 or so meals for a child care center or senior citizen group with little effort and meet a need.

CATERING

A survey done by Carnation Foodservice Company and reported in the *School Food Service Journal (1991)* showed that nearly two-thirds of the school districts in the country were providing some catering services. Such an effort is a source of additional revenue but it may or may not be a source of profit. It was for certain catering should not be taken on without a financial system that will capture the revenue and expense related to catering; nor should catering be taken on if management is having trouble managing or staffing the school foodservice programs. Many school districts have started catering on a big-time scale but discontinued it when financial data showed catering was costing, not making, money for the district foodservice program.

Catering, as discussed in this section, is limited to special meals, banquets, receptions, teas, coffees, and other activities requiring food and beverages.

If a school foodservice program caters, it should do it well—creating a positive image of school foodservice (considering it a marketing tool). The skills of the staff have a good chance to "shine," with attractive table settings, ice sculptures, and fancy foods. Details should be concentrated on, such as making the food look good, providing music (using CDS), decorating with centerpieces to go with a theme, and creating a pleasant atmosphere.

Pricing is one of the most difficult aspects of catering. Many directors rely on costing out the food and supplies and doubling that cost to arrive at the price to charge. However, labor costs are such a big part of the costs that it is recommended that the price of labor be determined and added to the food and supply costs before arriving at a sale price. While one school district may under-price a dinner with roast beef au jus at $8, another may price it at $18. The $18 is probably more realistic if all costs are captured. Pricing catered meals is much like pricing items to be sold a la carte, and the same criteria can be used. See Chapter 2, "Financial Management," for pricing information.

To avoid paying employees time and half for catering jobs, a contract labor rate can be established. For example, a manager could be paid $10 per hour for catering after the normal work day, regardless of her/his years of experience, and the staff employees could be paid $7 or $8 per hour, regardless of their years of experience. Employees can decide if they want to work. If sit-down service is desired, student servers can be used, and their pay might be less than using foodservice staff for a particular catering event. Sometimes students will be unpaid volunteers, in turn reducing the price the organization would be charged for the catered meal.

If equipment has been purchased just for catering, the cost of that equipment should be charged against catering—depreciating over three to five years. Rental companies offer all catering needs, and renting may be advisable over purchasing an item—the potential frequency of use in the future should help make this decision.

Some safeguards are needed, such as a contract with the group and a guaranteed number that will attend an event. The cutoff date should give time for ordering exact numbers of meals to be served. A guaranteed number is important if all the planned profit can be lost with a "no show" of 10 to 25 people.

The Hillsborough County (FL) Public Schools is focusing on catering to groups inhouse. They have adopted the "Campus Catering" logo, have formalized service, standardized menus, set prices, set up mobile catering station, and have specific ordering and production procedures. The program is already yielding a profit of over $150,000 a year, which subsidizes the school breakfast and lunch programs. It takes a well-organized foodservice operation to expand its services this much, and the results for this school district are commendable.

VENDING

School foodservices have expanded their services into vending in many states and find it quite profitable (and puts school foodservices in charge), and this usually is a good solution to having vending machine open selling competitive foods at undesirable times (right during lunch). If school foodservices comply with federal or state guidelines and satisfy other groups vying for this revenue, vending can operate in the dining room (in most states) all during the day. There is also the potential of school foodservice handling all the vending in the teachers' lounges, the administration building, and many other places within a high school building. The foodservice director in Chesterfield County (VA) schools was notified after some school audit problems that foodservices would be in charge of vending (250 machines). After the director got over the shock and after the initial adjustments were made, the program has been working well for all. The profits are being shared, and more profits are being realized by principals than when others were handling the machines. Some foodservice directors frown on such ideas, but vending (or selling) is going on and competing with the foodservice programs in schools across the country.

Fairfax County (VA) Public Schools started operating vending machines in 1989, and the operation has grown from 50 fruit-based drinks in the high school dining rooms to more than 500 machines in 1992 and over 800 in 1999. They are serving the county recreation department's vending machines as well as those in schools. The total sales are $3 million. Fairfax considers it a "robot" that increases employees' productivity. Teacher lounges generate $175,000 profits for the school foodservice programs. The machines in the dining rooms dispense bagels, sandwiches, chef salads, snack items, juices, cereal, and milk. The teachers' lounges and other machines may contain those items, plus carbonated beverages and candy. The machines in schools dispensing carbonated beverages and candy are not allowed to open for service until after the last class period of the school day.

School foodservice programs in other public school systems—Philadelphia (PA), Jefferson County (KY), Charlotte-Mecklenburg (NC), Denver (CO), and Dayton (OH) have successful vending programs. As the Dayton foodservice director pointed out, " they make good money and run after school hours." The foodservice director in Jefferson County said, "Our goal is to speed up serving lines. . . ." The profit margin from the machines is generally 50% to 60%. Chesterfield County (VA) splits the profits with the schools 50-50.

There are three ways of administering a vending program: (1) lease the machines and have foodservice employees fill them, (2) contract out the service with the outside company providing the machines and filling them, and (3) have the school foodservice own the machines and fill them. The latter yields the most money—owning the machine and filling it. The second most desirable way is leasing the machines with the cost figured in the price of the product and having foodservice employees fill them. Filling the vending machine can be an early morning and late afternoon job for employees. Eugene (OR) Public Schools and Waterbury (CT) Public Schools, for example, choose to contract the machines out. The Burbank (CA) Independent School District and the Fairfax County (VA) Public Schools owns the machines and fill them. Most school districts are leasing and filling the machines.

Vending machines can be used to dispense food in alternative schools where the costs of providing service can be high because of low participation (number served). Many directors have found this reduces the number of foodservice employees needed. Students/adults in after-school programs and athletes find vending machines a convenient way to obtain food when they want it. Nutritious foods can be dispensed—and having them available may reduce the consumption of high-calorie foods and carbonated beverages.

The attractive, dramatically new kinds of vending machines help to market the sale of products. "Lucky cans" (so many drink cans in the machine are marked as lucky), with the winners going to the foodservice manager to collect their prizes, can provide excitement and yield increased sales. According to *FoodService Director* (July 1998), the average machine in schools generates $8,600 in food/beverage volume.

Accountability is an important aspect to vending. Management needs to have controls in place and have "checks and balances" to provide information on inventory going into a machine and money coming out of the machine in revenue. Upkeep, breakdowns, and security are also concerns that must be addressed with a maintenance contract or a trained staff member who can repair the machines. Someone within the school district should be trained in minor repairs, so that a breakdown does not last long. Management will need to make certain the locking system is customized (not one key fits all) and that a policy is in place regarding lost coins. The new machines with electronic components have less problems in all of these areas than some of the older machines had.

The "smart card" has been used by colleges and universities for a while in vending machines, as well as the many other places where payment is due, but has just caught on in schools. Smart cards can contain a prepaid cash account for use in vending machines and in a la carte lines and regular serving lines, and be programmed with meal subsidy verification information. Prepayments allow schools to get cash up front. Paying up front by putting money into an account can be easier for parents, and make sure the "lunch money" is used for what it is intended.

The smart card can have restrictions on it, and the accountability is excellent. Snap Systems, Inc., a computer software company, has been promoting the use of a card for years. Jefferson County (KY) School Food and Community Nutrition Services tested using the debit and credit cards for students to purchase school meals and items from vending, but they have discontinued it. The concept has possibilities, particularly for a high income school district. The built-in computer debit subtracts value from the debit card and records receipts from the purchases. Parents can replenish debit cards' cash values for their children by telephone using their credit cards or other electronic means or by check, and students can add cash to their accounts at school.

At the National Automatic Merchandising Association Expo in Chicago (fall 1998) exhibited a new vending machine with a door that opened after inserting the "smart card" was exhibited. Its sensor records what was taken and automatically charges the card. The door closes when the card is removed. School meals can easily be dispensed and the account charged accordingly, with the student paying the student prices and the federal subsidy being verified and applied. The potential is there and will be realized more in the near future—a way of serving small operations, adding service/points-of-sales in large schools, and keeping labor costs down.

CONTRACTS WITH OTHER SCHOOL DISTRICTS

Contracts with other school districts—meals served outside of their schools—should all be governed by a legal contract with a clear understanding of the responsibilities and expectations of both parties. These contracts with other school districts must meet federal regulations for meeting meal requirements. Also, the cost of providing this service should be known by the school district; the prices to be charged the receiving school district established; and providing the school districts bill the recipients monthly. If meals are being served under federally subsidized programs, the school district producing the meals must provide the production records of what goes into the meals. The school district receiving the meals is responsible for submitting monthly claims to the state for federal and state reimbursement.

The Dayton (OH) City Schools have a central kitchen that produces preplated meals with high efficiency. They serve not only their 51 schools but several other school districts and some private schools in the area. Also, the Archdiocese of Chicago (IL) has a central kitchen that is quite efficient and contracts to serve others. The capacity of their kitchen is greater than needed by their schools and has resulted in contracts to provide some meals to Chicago Public Schools, adult care community centers, convalescent homes (three meals a day seven days a week), and to small school districts nearby.

Though public school districts aren't likely to go out of business, it is wise to have a written contract in place and require an initial deposit from the contractor (school district receiving the food) equal to costs for one month's meals. This is certainly recommended for private schools and centers that may want the meal services. Again, pricing is a challenge. All costs should be included—food, supplies, labor, overhead, depreciation of equipment, etc. Being efficient is the key to being able to be a contractor and to being able to provide services at a reasonable price and yet make a profit for the school district's foodservices.

COMMUNITY NUTRITION SERVICES

The number of people in need is increasing, and more and more communities are finding it necessary to provide nutritious food for larger numbers than ever before, including senior citizens, day cares, and homeless people. The categories of those in need of food are expanding from the very young to the very old, and from the poor family to the middle-income family.

By the year 2000, 34.7 million people in this country will be 65 years old or older. This figure will continue to grow as the baby boom generation reaches its "golden years" in 2030, when it will be nearly doubled today's elderly population and the needs will increase accordingly for Meals on Wheels and congregate meals for senior citizens (see Figure 15.1). Over 60 percent of the mothers of small children will be working outside the home full time, which will mean an increasing need for day care, extended day care (for those in school), and other types of organized care.

In many urban areas the government has already become involved in providing care for children of working mothers. As a result, public schools are being used to house extended day-care programs. Congress is being forced to deal with the need for child care. A logical approach would be extend the Child Nutrition programs in schools to include a snack and perhaps a dinner meal for children who have an extended day after the school day.

Working mothers are using the schools' breakfast programs to help meet the needs of working mothers and their children. The breakfast program, which had been mainly for the poor, showed a large increase in 1998, as the USDA administration has placed more emphasis on the program for all students.

Figure 15.1. Elderly Population, 1990-2050 (in millions)

	65 and Older	75 and Older	85 and older
1990	31.3	13.5	315
2000	34.7	16.6	4.1
2010	39.4	18.3	5.7
2020	53.2	21.8	6.5
2030	69.4	31.9	8.4
2040	75.1	42.2	13.5
2050	78.7	44.1	18.2

Source: Based on data from the U.S. Bureau of the Census 1990 and 1998 updates from the Population Division, PPL-91, "United States Population Estimates, by Age, Sex, Race, and Hispanic Origin, 1990-1997.

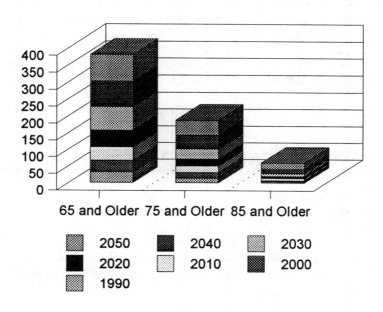

With labor shortages in the child-care field, working mothers are having a difficult time finding full-time child care in the summer months. The summer meal program, sponsored by the USDA, which has provided lunch and/or snacks for mainly the needy, needs to serve those who can pay as well.

Feeding the homeless became a recognized need beginning in the 1980s. Washington was the first state to complete a review of the Community Childhood Hunger Intervention Project, a survey developed by the Food Research and Action Center that measured the extent of hunger in poor communities ("Survey Finds Hunger" 1998).

Many school districts' foodservice programs have served their communities when emergencies have occurred. For example, in 1992, when Hurricane Andrew hit Dade County (FL), it left 250,000 people homeless. Twenty-six schools served as Red Cross shelters providing three meals a day and shelter. Los Angeles (CA) Unified School foodservice department has formalized plans for reacting in emergency situations.

School foodservice has the opportunity to become a community nutrition center in many communities. This would mean providing foodservices all year round to a variety of federally funded programs and to different age groups.

A few school districts have discovered these opportunities. Dayton (OH) City Schools and Montgomery County (MD) Schools' foodservice programs are providing their communities with services that generate revenue. Both school districts operate an efficient central kitchen that is capable of producing more than enough to supply their own school districts. As a result, in 1989 Dayton's school foodservice program was providing preplated meals to more than 62 other sites (parochial and private schools, schools in other districts, day-care centers, and recreation sites).

School districts such as that in Montgomery County (MD) provide for the elderly and for summer food programs for their own and two different counties. The school district runs a central warehousing and delivery system that stores food and distributes it to the needy in cooperation with the social services department. Under a contract with the school district, the social services department is charged for storage and distribution of inventory and for any meals received.

CHILD AND ADULT CARE FOOD PROGRAM

The federally subsidized Child and Adult Care Food Program is open to all children up to the age of 12 who are enrolled in a licensed public or private nonprofit day-care center, family day-care home, or similar organization providing nonresidential care, and to adults enrolled in adult day-care centers. The federally subsidized Child Care Food Program was created under the Child Nutrition Act of 1966. In 1987, the National School Lunch Act was amended to allow adult day-care centers to participate in the Child Care Food Program. Generally, the federal regulations and funding are the same as for the school foodservice programs as for federally funded child-care centers with a few exceptions.

1. Federal commodities and cash reimbursements are available to nonprofit centers that provide specialized care services to functionally impaired adults over age 60 for less than

24 hours a day. These can include victims of Alzheimer's disease and other neurological and organic brain dysfunctions.

2. The criteria for determining who is eligible for adult care free or reduced-price meals are different from those of Child Nutrition programs. The only income that has to be considered is the income of the adult and his or her spouse, not the income of anyone else in the household.

    Eligibility guidelines for free and reduced-priced meals and supplements are the same for the Child Care Food as for the National School Lunch and Breakfast programs. The federal FY 2000 budget proposes to cut the budget for these programs and it will reduce congregate and home-delivered meals funding.

3. The meal requirements for the Child Nutrition programs are the same as for the Child Care Food Program for ages 6 to 12, with the exception that yogurt or cheese can be substituted for milk. The USDA is expected to develop a meal pattern for the older children in the Child Care Food Program with larger portions and more flexibility.

The reimbursement rates for Child and Adult Care Food Programs are the same as for the National School Lunch and Breakfast Programs. Since the state may or may not provide subsidies, it is important to determine who will pay the difference between the federal reimbursements and the total costs of providing the services. For schools to provide these meals under contract a subsidy will be needed, unless the school district will settle for a contract that break evens.

State regulations for child care vary from state to state. At least 14 states mandate foodservices at child care centers. Child care participation increased the first half of 1990s and decreased during the latter half. Over the next ten years, a decrease in population of day care-age children is projected, the child care needs are expected to continue at an increasing level. This is because of the increase in percentage of mothers working.

As stated earlier, the Child and Adult Care Programs are similar to the National School Lunch, Breakfast, and After-School Snack Programs. The cash reimbursement and entitlement commodities are the same also, which were as follows for July 1, 1998-June 30, 1999:

Category	Breakfast	Lunch or Supper	Supplement
Free	$1.0725	$ 1.9425	$ .5325
Reduced-Price	$ .7725	$ 1.5425	$ .2675
Paid	$ .2000	$ .1800	$ .0400
Commodities	NA	$ .1475	NA

The Traditional Food-Based Menu Planning method meal is designed to cover the Child Nutrition programs, including the Child Care Food Program. The school lunch requirement for Group I (ages 1-2) and Group II (ages 3-4) prescribe the portion sizes to be used generally. In some states where kindergarten is not a part of the public schools and in being served under the Child Care Food Program, and Group III category (ages 5-8) will be used as well. The snack must contain a fruit or vegetable and bread or bread alternate. Figure 15.2 provides a sample day-care lunch and snack for Groups I and II.

Figure 15.2. Sample Day Care Lunch and Snack Menu

	Group I Ages 1-2	Group II Preschool
Lunch		
Crispy Chicken	1 piece	2 pieces
Whipped Potatoes	¼ cup	¼ cup
Steamed Green Peas	¼ cup	¼ cup
Dinner Roll	1 piece[1]	1 piece[2]
Fresh Orange Sections	¼ fruit	¼ fruit
Milk	¾ cup	¾ cup
Snack		
Cheese	½ ounce	1 ounce
Saltine Crackers	2	4
Juice	½ cup	½ cup

[1]Group I   5 servings of bread per week
[2]Group II   8 servings of bread per week

SENIOR CITIZEN FOOD PROGRAMS

It is estimated by the National Council on the Aging that 6.7 million people over the age of 65 in 1998 needed some form of assistance. That number is expected to reach 9 million by the year 2000. The needs of the aging will have to be met by a combination of means. Corporate-managed retirement communities are for those who can afford the cost; group living is a popular solution when income is tight. It is the people in the group homes, living alone in "granny apartments," and living with relatives who need foodservice.

There are a number of federally funded programs for the elderly authorized under the Older Americans Act of 1965 (as amended), and the Elderly Nutrition Program (Titles III and VI), signed into law in 1972. These programs provide grants to support nutrition services to older people throughout the country. They target older people with the greatest economic or social needs, with special attention given to low-income minorities.

The Administration on Aging (in the U. S. Department of Health and Human Services—see Figure 15.3) provides meals free or for a contribution of a nominal amount to persons age 60 or older and supports the delivery of hot meals to the homebound elderly. The "congregate meal program," which serves those who are able to meet at designated places, was authorized in 1972, and the home

Figure 15.3. The National Aging Service Network

The federal organization that makes the Older Americans Act
a reality is the Administration on Aging (AOA). AOA is currently
placed in the Office of Human Development Services within
the Department of Health and Human Services (OHDS/DHHS).
The administrative network reaches through the ten regional
offices of DHHS to the 57 State Units on Aging (SUAs) and
some 664 Area Agencies on Aging (AAAs).

PRESIDENCY

DEPARTMENT OF HEALTH AND HUMAN SERVICES

OFFICE OF HUMAN DEVELOPMENT SERVICES

ADMINISTRATION ON AGING

Recommends policy, develops regulations to
implement the older Americans Act, allocates
and administers OAF budget, grants for research,
training, model projects, etc.

REGIONAL OFFICE ON AGING

(10 Regions)

Provide technical assistance to state and monitor state aging programs

STATE UNITS ON AGING

(57 Jurisdictions)

Coordinate state-level activities on behalf of older
people, develop and administer the state plans on
aging, serve as advocates, provide technical
assistance to Area Agencies on Aging

AREA AGENCIES ON AGING

(664)

Develop and implement the area plans on aging, serve
as advocates for older people, coordinate with other
agencies and organizations in planning and
service areas to develop comprehensive aging service
systems, administer Older Americans Act programs
within their jurisdictions

Source: United States Department of Health and Human Resources 1999.

delivered meals in 1982. The funding for the congregate meals in 1999 is nearly $400 million and for home-delivered meals, nearly $100 million. For every $1 of federal funds for congregate meals, $1.70 additional funding is leveraged, and for every $1 of federal home-delivered funds, $3.55 additional funding is leveraged. These leveraged funds come from other sources including state, tribal and local, as well as other federal moneys and services.

The USDA provides cash in lieu of donated commodities for use in preparing the meals. Each menu for these programs is designed to provide one-third of the Recommended Dietary Allowance (RDA), which are established by the Food and Nutrition Board of the National Research Council of the National Academy of Science. Therapeutic meals or special diets may also be needed.

The cost of a meal in 1997 was estimated to be as high as $5.17 for a group meal and $5.31 for a home-delivered meal. The bulk of the meal costs now are either for labor and food, but there are some transportation costs included. Many elderly people eat in local restaurants, and cafeterias are favorites. These meals eaten out can be expensive if Social Security is the only source of revenue. According to the National Restaurant Association, the national average per-person cost of eating lunch was $4.86 at cafeterias and $5.29 at "family-style" restaurants in 1995. A school district entering into a contract for providing these meals should enter into an agreement with the group on prices.

The federal budget for food for the elderly was set at around $1.5 billion for 1998. Unfortunately there are no requirements placed on states for "matching funds." In 1998, federal funding provided approximately 41 percent of the revenue available for elderly meals. The food programs available for senior citizens depend heavily on private donations and client contributions (the expected levels of gratuities are posted at serving lines). The federally funded programs provide approximately 300 million meals per year—69 percent congregate meals and 31 percent home-delivered meals.

The federally subsidized meals served should:

- Comply with the Dietary Guidelines for Americans
- Provide each person a minimum of 1/3 the recommended dietary allowances

A major study, "Serving Elders at Risk the Older Americans Act Nutrition Programs: National Evaluation of the Elderly Nutrition Program 1993-1995" by Mathematica Policy Research, Inc., was completed in 1996. The major findings produced were that elderly nutrition programs improve nutritional intake; decrease social isolation; serve at-risk, vulnerable populations; provide high-quality services and increasingly are connected to both acute care and home and community-based care services.

Home-Delivered Meals

Home delivery of meals, often referred to as "meals on wheels," is primarily a volunteer delivery program. The meals are provided by churches, schools, hospitals, and commercial restaurants. Often the meals delivered include a hot lunch and in a few cases a cold evening meal. In some cases, a weekend meal is included. With the increase in the number of elderly persons and the costs of nursing homes, there are more and more needing home-delivered meals on a regular basis. The study by Mathematica (1996) found that 41 percent of home-delivered nutrition service programs have waiting lists and that the demand for home-delivered meals is expected to grow. See Figure 15.4, for an example of Union County's (NJ) menu for April 1999.

Congregate Dining

Congregate (group) dining takes place in stand-alone buildings, in churches, in rooms in local libraries or schools, and in other available public spaces. The congregate elderly program provides some activities and a socialization component as a part of the services, as well as a nutritious meal. Many of the programs provide breakfast as well as lunch. Regulations require that at least one hot meal be served five days out of the week. There are few other guidelines for operating the program. These programs need the services of schools.

Union County, New Jersey, and Greenville, South Carolina, are examples of well-organized senior citizen foodservice programs operated by groups other than school foodservices. Union County's meals are planned on a six-week cycle, prepared in a central kitchen, and transported in insulated boxes throughout the county within two to three hours. One of the weekly menus is shown in Figure 15.4. The people served are referred to as "clients" and they may request a nutritional analysis if they desire. Schools do provide these services quite effectively, for example, in Montgomery County (MD) and Knox County (TN). These services can be a source of revenue for school foodservice programs as well as providing a service for the growing number of senior citizens.

SUMMER FOODSERVICE PROGRAM

The Summer Foodservice Program was started by Congress and in 1968 was administered by USDA as a pilot program. It became a separate program in 1975. It was established to ensure that during school vacation, needy children would be able to receive the same nutritious meals provided during the school year. The local school foodservice program often provides food for the Summer Foodservice Program. In fiscal year 1997, more than 2.3 million meals were served a day under the program at 28,000 sites, and in 1998 the sites had increased to 30,000 and there was a 10 percent increase in the number of children participating—a 45 percent increase since 1989. The programs, which include breakfasts, lunches, suppers, and supplements, have continued to increase annually.

In most states, Summer Foodservice Programs are administered by the state departments of education. Where states do not administer the program, the regional office of the USDA does. The programs are operated at "open" or "enrolled" sites. Open sites operate in low-income areas where half or more of the children are from households with incomes at or below 185 percent of the federal poverty guidelines are provided meals free. Children who participate in the program must be under 18 years old, unless determined by a state educational agency to be mentally or physically handicapped.

The program must have a local sponsor that contracts for foodservices or prepare their own food. The sponsor is responsible for submitting claims for reimbursement. Usually, school districts that provide summer foodservice program meals are responsible only for the food, not the distribution or the determination of who qualifies to receive the food. In some cases the foodservice

Figure 15.4. Meals On Wheels, Union County, New Jersey

APRIL 1999

MONDAY	TUESDAY	WEDNESDAY	THURSDAY	FRIDAY
			1 Baked Virginia Ham, Mixed Vegetables, Potato Au Gratin, Coconut Cake, Chicken Gumbo Soup, Dinner Roll, Milk — **EASTER DINNER**	**2** **GOOD FRIDAY**
5 Knockwurst with Mustard and Sauerkraut, Peas, Sweet Potatoes with Apples, Sliced Peaches, Pineapple Juice, Bread, Milk	**6** Hawaiian Chicken, Sliced Carrots, Rice, Pound Cake, Orange/Grapefruit Juice, Bread, Milk	**7** Spaghetti with Meatballs, Mixed Vegetables, Tossed Salad, Chocolate Pudding, Minestrone Soup, Italian Bread, Milk	**8** Chef's Salad with Lettuce and Tomato, Egg Wedge and Russian Dressing, Macaroni Salad, Tropical Fruit Salad, Pea Soup, Bread, Milk	**9** Breaded Fish, Summer Blend, Au Gratin Potatoes, Fruit Cocktail, Clam Chowder, Bread, Milk
12 Salisbury Steak with Mushroom Gravy, Chopped Spinach, Bow Tie Pasta, Tapioca Pudding, Tomato Juice, Bread, Milk	**13** Crab Cake, Diced Beets, Macaroni and Cheese, Gingerbread Cake with Topping, Orange Juice, Bread, Milk	**14** Baked Chicken, Broccoli Spears, Mashed Potatoes, Pound Cake, Tomato Soup, Dinner Roll, Milk	**15** Pepper Steak, Mixed Vegetables, Rice, Pear Halves, Pineapple Juice, Bread, Milk	**16** Vegetable Lasagna, Stewed Tomatoes and Zucchini, Tossed Salad, Sliced Peaches, Minestrone Soup, Italian Bread, Milk
19 BBQ Pork Rib, Winter Blend, Baked Potato, Chocolate Pudding, Apple Juice, Bread, Milk	**20** Meatloaf with Gravy, Chopped Spinach, Mashed Potatoes, Pear Halves, Vegetable Soup, Dinner Roll, Milk	**21** Eggplant Parmigiana, Tossed Salad with Dressing, Mixed Vegetables, Orange Sherbet, Grape Juice, Italian Bread, Milk	**22** Chicken Cutlet with Gravy, Peas and Carrots, Rice Pilaf, Apricot Halves, Chicken Gumbo Soup, Bread, Milk	**23** Tuna Salad with Lettuce and Tomato, Pickled Beets, Pasta Salad, Fruited Jell-O, Beef Barley Soup, Bread, Milk
26 Grilled Chicken Sandwich with Honey Mustard, Carrot Raisin Salad, Potato Wedges, Fresh Fruit, Beef Noodle Soup, Bread, Milk	**27** Veal Parmigiana, Spaghetti with Sauce, Italian Green Beans, Sliced Peaches, Pineapple Juice, Bread, Milk	**28** Pork Chop with Gravy, Mixed Vegetables, Sweet Potatoes, Vanilla Pudding, Vegetable Soup, Bread, Milk	**29** Baked Fish with Lemon Butter, Green Peas, Scalloped Potatoes, Banana Cake, New England Clam Chowder, Bread, Milk	**30** Baked Manicotti, Italian Blend, Tossed Salad, Sugar Cookies, Cranberry Juice, Italian Bread, Milk

Source: Union County (NJ) School District. Used by permission.

program is the sponsor as well as the provider. Montgomery County (MD) serves not only their own county needs but contracts and serve two other counties' summer food programs. It is a natural for school foodservice program, because it provides summer jobs for those employees who need or want to work and the revenue from the Summer Foodservice Program will help pay some of the administrative costs during the summer months.

The prices of the meals, like those for the other programs listed earlier, should be carefully arrived at, so that all costs are covered. The accountability described earlier for the Child Care Food Program is applicable for the Summer Foodservice Program also. The federal reimbursement rates for summer 1999 are shown in Table 15.1.

The Summer Foodservice Program needs a sponsor that does the paperwork and organizes the service. A lack of sponsors for the program and making people aware of the availability of meals have been the biggest hurdles. In the FY 1999 plan, the USDA has removed some restrictions to encourage more sponsors. The projections are that 32,000 sites will be approved and the number participating will reach 2.6 million by year 2000.

The food requirements are the same for the Summer Foodservice Program as for the National School Lunch and National School Breakfast Programs. Often bag lunches are provided. A typical menu is shown in Figure 15.5.

Figure 15.5. Sample Menu for Summer Foodservice Program

Bag or Box Lunch	
Ham and Cheese Sandwich with Salad Dressing Lettuce and Tomato Salad Sliced Peaches Oatmeal Cookie Milk	Thinly Sliced Turkey on Bun with Salad Dressing Chilled Orange Juice Fresh Grapes Graham Crackers Milk

CONTRACTS WITH OTHER AGENCIES

Should outside groups be provided foodservices by the public or the private school sector? Will school foodservice be unfairly competing with commercial foodservices? Will sales tax need to be paid? These are some of the questions to be answered when considering an extension of school foodservice to other segments of the community.

In some cases, foodservice programs in public schools are providing meals for private, for profit schools. The menus for the school district and for private and parochial schools can be basically the same. In most cases, a school foodservice that provides meals to another school district and to private and parochial schools will do so under contract. The contact may stipulate the furnishing of just the

Table 15.1. Federal Reimbursement Rates for Summer Foodservice Program for 1999*

Contiguous United States Administrative Costs for Meals Served			
Type of Meal Served	Operating Costs	Self-Preparation or Rural Sites	Vended or Urban Sites
Breakfast	$1.22	$0.1200	$0.0950
Lunch or Supper	$2.13	$0.2225	$0.1850
Supplement	$0.49	$0.6000	$0.0475
Alaska Administrative Costs for Meals Served			
Administrative costs for meals served are rural or self preparation sites			
Type of Meal Served	Operating Costs	Self-Preparation or Rural Sites	Vended or Urban Sites
Breakfast	$1.98	$0.1950	$0.1550
Lunch or Supper	$3.45	$0.3600	$0.3000
Supplement	$0.80	$0.0975	$0.0775
Hawaii Administrative Costs for Meals Served			
Type of Meal Served	Operating Costs	Self-Preparation or Rural Sites	Vended or Urban Sites
Breakfast	$1.43	$0.1425	$0.1125
Lunch or Supper	$2.49	$0.2600	$0.2150
Supplement	$0.58	$0.0700	$0.0550

*These rates change annually.

food or for the management of the foodservice program at the school (including service and food). Generally, the school foodservice would bill the group with whom they contracted, they would be responsible for any claims for reimbursement from federal, state, and /or local sources.

When a school district's foodservice provides meals for any group —federally subsidized day care, senior nutrition program, or other school district—a contract should be drawn up with advice from a lawyer. It should address the prices to be charged, the menu pattern, when the bills should be paid, and how both parties can dissolve the contract. A contract may be with an individual day care provider, a senior nutrition site, a school district, a local government agency, or other sponsoring group that administers the program.

Pricing these services should be considered carefully. The prices for the services should re-elect the total costs (all costs, even an appropriate share of indirect cost/depreciation or those paid by a school district). These types of contracts should not be operated at any cost to the regular school foodservice programs. The price may also reflect a fee for services (or a profit). For example, if the cost of producing a lunch for a day-care program is $2, the fee for service could be an added 25 cents, bringing the price of the meal to $2.25. This price may exceed the federal reimbursement, in which case the local government or sponsoring group would be subsidizing the program.

Good accountability for all programs is essential. If federal funds are involved, audits can be expected. Also to be remembered are the federal regulations that a "contractor" (school district) would have to follow federal guidelines in providing the meals and snacks.

The billing at the end of the month or pay period should list the number of meals/snacks by category and the prices charged. The number of meals/snacks received daily should be verified by each of the contracted agents receiving services. A form similar to the one in Figure 15.6 should be used to avoid controversy over the charges.

When providing any contracted services, there is always the possibility that a group or agency will go out of business. This should be addressed in the contact. A deposit equivalent to the cost of services for one month or more may be required. Billing should be done as soon after the first of the month as possible, and the due date should be watched carefully. The discontinuing of service if payment has not been received should be adhered to rather strictly, since the sponsoring group may be having financial trouble. It may be necessary to involve an attorney in the collection of outstanding bills.

Figure 15.6. Sample Delivery Form for Contracted Services

Office of Food Services
Jasper-Smith Public Schools
RECEIPT FOR MEALS

_____ acknowledges receipt of _____
(Day-care center/private school)   (Number of student meals)

and _____ from _____
(Number of adult meals)   (Production school)

Temperature _____°F when food arrived

Supplies:_____   Signature: _____ _____
                                                     Production School   Date

_____   Signature: _____ _____
                                                     Day-Care Center/Head Start   Date

_____

Distribution: White copy to day-care center, Head Start/senior citizens group —yellow copy to production school file.

HEAD START

The **Head Start Act Amendments of 1994** established the Early Head Start program, which expands the benefits for children to low-income families with children under three and to pregnant women. The program is administered by the U. S. Department of Health and Human Services, which provides technical assistance and support to the Head Start programs.

There is a new initiative for helping the parents on welfare move into jobs. The initiative is attempting to build a partnership with child-care providers to deliver full-day and full-year Head Start services.

HOME-MEAL REPLACEMENT

Home-meal replacement (HMR) is a new trend, but hasn't been utilized by the school market. These are meals that are partially or completely ready to serve—for dinner. According to a study done in 1995 by the Food Marketing Institute, 35% of HMRs are coming from the supermarket. The school foodservice director should have the superintendent and school board's approval before getting into a market like this. It is doubtful that this will ever become much of a source of revenue for school foodservices.

LOST REVENUE OPPORTUNITIES

There are obviously a lot of ways to increase revenue in a school district foodservice program and one that should be overlooked is the students in the school not participating in the school foodservice breakfast and/or lunch programs. Adams 12 School (Northglenn, CO) foodservice director has made each manager aware of the lost revenue opportunities using the form in Figure 15.7. When managers realize how many dollars are lost from students not participating in the school breakfast or school lunch program, often they are motivate to try to do something about it.

One manager was able to increase the number of free and reduced-price students participating in the school lunch program by writing personal notes to each student on the list telling the students they were missed. Lunch cards (good for one month) were enclosed with the notes, which were delivered to the student by the guidance counselor.

Another manager renotified students about qualifying for free or reduced-price meals. The first notification letter may have been lost or did not get attention. The number participating increased by 10 percent.

A high school manager discovered that the number participating at breakfast time doubled when the breakfast was made more assessable—near where buses unloaded. Also, it helped to make the breakfast foods available in a bag.

Figure 15.7. Form for Determining Lost Revenue Opportunities

FREE LUNCHES		
Number free approved: _____		
Number free eating: _____		
Number not eating: _____		
Cash revenue per lunch: $1.89 x _____ Number not eating =	$_____	Lost/day
USDA entitlement commodities $.1475 x_____ Number not eating =	$_____	Lost/day
TOTAL	$_____	Lost/day
Revenue lost per day $_____ X 180 serving days =	$_____	Lost/year

REDUCED- PRICE LUNCHES		
Number reduced-price approved: _____		
Number reduced-price eating: _____		
Number not eating: _____		
Cash revenue per lunch: $1.49 x _____ Number not eating =	$_____	Lost/day
USDA entitlement commodities $.1475 x_____ Number not eating =	$_____	Lost/day
TOTAL	$_____	Lost/day
Revenue lost per day $_____ X 180 serving days =	$_____	Lost/year

PAID LUNCHES		
Number paid student: _____		
Number paid eating: _____		
Number not eating: _____		
Cash revenue per lunch: $.18 x _____ Number not eating =	$_____	Lost/day
USDA entitlement commodities $.1475 x_____ Number not eating =	$_____	Lost/day
TOTAL	$_____	Lost/day
Revenue lost per day $_____ X 180 serving days =	$_____	Lost/year

TOTAL LOST REVENUE FOR THE YEAR	$_____

Source: Adapted from Adams 12 School District in Northglenn, Colorado. Used by permission.

SELECTED REFERENCES

AARP. 1998. *A Profile of Older Americans.* Washington, DC: AARP.

Bender, Betty. 1987. "Dayton Schools Move Toward Entrepreneurship." *School Food Service Journal* 4(4):80.

"Final Rules: Grant for State and Community Programs on Aging." 1988. *Federal Register* 53, No. 169: 3358-79

National Association of Area Agencies on Aging. 1987. *Guidelines for Food Purchasing for Nutrition Programs for the Elderly.* Washington, DC: National Association of Area Agencies on Aging.

National Association of State Units on Aging. 1985. *An Orientation to the Older Americans Act.* 2d ed., edited by Susan Coombs Ficke. Washington, DC: National Association of State Units on Aging.

Subcommittee on Human Services of the House Select Committee on Aging. 1984. *Older Americans Act: A Staff Summary.* Com. Pub. No. 98-482. Washington, DC: House Select Committee on Aging.

U. S. Bureau of the Census. 1998. "United States Population Estimates, by Age, Sex, Race, and Hispanic Origin, 1990-1997.

U. S. Department of Agriculture (USDA). n.d. Series of Six Manuals. Part I, *Nutrition Programs Elderly in Perspective*: Part II, *Purchasing Methods;* Part III, Documents for Formal Bid Purchasing; Part IV, *Reviews and Audits of Contracts*; Part V, *Management of Meal Costs;* and Part VI, *Meal Production Contracts.* Washington, DC: U. S. Department of Agriculture.

U. S. Department of Health and Human Services. 1996. *Serving Elders at Risk the Older Americans Act Nutrition Programs: National Evaluation of the Elderly Nutrition Program 1993-1995.* Prepared by Mathematica Policy Research, Inc. Washington, DC: U. S. Department of Health and Human Services.

16
MARKETING AND PROMOTING
SCHOOL FOODSERVICE

Marketing and Promoting School Foodservice

Managing Marketing

Branding

Food Courts
    "Re-Imaging" or "Make-Overs" of the School Dining Area

Managing Promotions

Managing Advertising and Publicity

Meeting the Press

Merchandising

Communicating With Customers

Selling

Selected References

MARKETING AND PROMOTING SCHOOL FOODSERVICE

Marketing and promoting school foodservices in the 1990s has become important to maintaining program participation. The customer has changed over the years, and today's customer, whether restaurant food or school food, wants the food brought to them and they want it to be "fun." It has become obvious with high school students that serving good food at low prices is not enough. Today's students have grown up with thousands of commercials telling them what they ought to eat in order to be big, strong, popular, or "in." Since fast foods are a central part of their lives, to them the perfect lunch may be a Big Mac, fries, and a Coke—not a cafeteria sliced turkey and gravy, mashed potatoes, fruit cup, and milk. As a result, many school foodservice managers are beginning to look at the students as "customers," and "marketing" what they have to sell. If this is not done, a school foodservice can lose out to neighborhood fast-food restaurants and convenience stores at lunchtime.

The Los Angeles (CA) Unified School District experienced such a decline in school lunch participation in 1988, when only 23 percent of the high school students chose to eat the school lunch, even though 78 percent of them qualified for a free or reduced-priced lunch. These declines seem to be caused by changes in the customers' expectations and because the school foodservice program hadn't changed to keep up with the customer. They have began to take corrective action and seen increasing in participation. Other segments of the foodservice industry were having similar problems in foodservices, e.g., military bases in the early 1980s. Then foodservice management began treating the troops as customers and "marketing" to them, and using "branding" of popular foods.

MANAGING MARKETING

Marketing is the process of promoting, advertising, merchandising, and selling. It includes defining what the customer wants and needs; providing products or services that meet those wants and needs; informing the customer of the availability of the services or products and the benefits that can be gained by using them; and finally, selling products at prices the customer considers fair. The commercial foodservice industry understands the importance of marketing and spends millions of dollars each year on it. McDonald's spent more than a billion in 1998 on marketing their products.

Zimmerman (1985) says that school foodservice management should take a few tips from successful commercial foodservice operations. These same commonalities exist today. When comparing what successful commercial foodservices had in common, Zimmerman found the following:

- Products are promoted.
- Popular foods are served.
- Food is consistently of good quality.
- Atmosphere is pleasant.

- Personnel are friendly.
- Prices fit students' budgets.
- Service is fast.

Every school foodservice has an image. The image of school foodservice may be negative in a community because of adverse publicity or lack of publicity. A foodservice's image is made up of intangible thoughts and impressions that people have about school foodservices. These are influenced by all the senses, and can be changed. In order to make the change the foodservice program needs to be determine what the current image is and what the desired image is.

"Dull cafeteria food is an image to avoid, and one that profoundly affects the financial bottom line" (Boehrer 1993). A dull, institutional-type school foodservice can be turned into a fun place to eat. The image, "fun place to eat," can be created by presenting food in a more contemporary way (e.g., fish and chips in a paper cone), by painting the serving line area and dining room area brighter colors, and by having employees smile while serving customers. Adding a "super sack" (not a brown bag) lunch or a "big lunch in a box" in the spring for eating outside is a possibility. This food can be taken to students in portable serving carts, an option that has been tried successfully by the San Diego (CA) Schools.

The Beaufort County (SC) School District, Brownsville (TX) Independent School District, and Cobb County (GA) Schools have seen participation increase 10-12 percent at the secondary level as a result of their recent changes in atmosphere, menu, and marketing.

There are several factors that influence students regarding food at school, including the following:

- Menu—the single most important variable
- Prices charged students—no longer the single most important variable
- Quality of the food
- Image of the foodservice program held by students—particularly important with high school students
- Value parents place on nutrition, and their perception of how nutritious the meals are at school
- Ages of students—older students participate in school lunch programs less frequently than younger ones
- Sex of students—male students participate more frequently than females
- Location, urban or city—students from rural areas participated more often than students from urban areas
- Attitudes of the foodservice employees

Today's students want food when they want it—convenient and easy to eat. The breakfast may need to be a breakfast in a bag on the school bus.

Before selecting a marketing approach, foodservice personnel should examine the factors associated with nonparticipation. A study of one major school district's foodservice participation in 1988 showed that:

1.   There was the lowest interest in school lunch at the ninth grade level, or at about age 15.
2.   Food variety was more of a concern among senior high students.

3. There were substantial differences in food preferences between different ethnic groups.
4. Some ethnic groups of students were more embarrassed by association with free/discounted programs than other ethnic groups.
5. Breaks in the morning reduced the number who ate lunch.

To increase the participation of female students or others concerned with losing weight, a salad bar might be opened and promoted with a sign saying, "Make it your way" or "You decide how many calories you eat."

To prepare a marketing approach, a school foodservice manager or supervisor also needs to identify and study the competition. It is usually one or more of the following: fast-food establishments nearby, convenience stores, lunches brought from home, going home for lunch, vending machines (if available), or not eating at all.

The marketing approach can be planned and executed in big segments or all at one time—not gradually, the gradual approach does not get attention. Students will not see the marketing approach as anything new. The theme and image to be marketed should be enhanced by the presentation of food, the type of service offered, the appearance of the serving and dining areas, the uniforms the employees wear, and the attitudes the employees display.

Six marketing characteristics are shared by giants in the corporate world that are considered to have the most successful marketing programs, including Mercedes-Benz, Xerox, Federal Express, and Kodak (Lele and Sheth, 1987):

1. *They set themselves "impossibly high" standards.*
2. *They are obsessive about knowing, even better than the customers themselves, what the customers want.*
3. *They create and manage customers' expectations.*
4. *They design their products or services to maximize customer satisfaction.*
5. *They put their money where their mouth is.*
6. *They make customer satisfaction everybody's business.*

BRANDING

A United States General Accounting Office study (1996) showed that "branding" can be found in 13 percent of the public schools and continues to grow. However, the U. S. Department of Agriculture "School Food Purchase Study "(1998) shows that figure much higher with almost 40 percent of all public school districts with national brands offered about twice as frequently as house brands. *School Foodservice & Nutrition* publication (February 1997) defines branding as "relying on name recognition in developing menus, as well as for advertising and promotional strategies." Branding started to be promoted around 1992 in schools, and because it is still around (widespread) today, it is considered a trend, not a fad. However, it hasn't really taken off in the school market as much as one might expect. Some of the reasons may be:

- Fear of paying a higher price

- Resistance to sharing the revenue with a company (franchise fee)
- Perception of poor nutrition quality
- Concern that the "branded food" will take money that otherwise would go to the regular lunch
- Resistance to change

The question is, "why would a school district want to use branding?" It costs more for the "name." Is it worth it? Undoubtedly a lot of colleges and universities think so, which is where branding has really flourished. The answers to the question about why to use branding are name recognition, perceived value, quality assurance of company, marketing support, and, often, increases revenue.

There are three types of branding: (1) "quick-serve" restaurants, (2) manufacturer's brand name products, and (3) in-house, or signature items. Under the first type some of the big quick-serve or fast-food restaurants that are popular with students are Pizza Hut, Domino's, Taco Bell, Subway, and McDonald's. Each of these have tested the school foodservice market, but pulled back because there is not enough business or profits to be realized. They changed their approach to frozen Taco Bell burritos and Pizza Hut now sells the pizza kits.

The San Juan Capistrano School District was one of the first to open a fast-food court in 1992 with Pizza Hut, Taco Bell and Kentucky Fried Chicken (all PepsiCo Food Service) franchise. They serve more than 1200 students in one 35-minute lunch period. The logos of Colonel Sanders, Taco Bell, and Pizza Hut decorate the walls at Capistrano Valley High School. The San Jan Capistrano School District serves on an average day 600 burritos and tacos, 350 pizzas, 300 servings of French fries, and 50 to 90 servings of chicken. Fresh fruit, cookies, snacks, and milk are available. The fruit is free so as to encourage students to eat it. Fifteen employees and 30 student workers operate the program during the lunch periods. The students have been happy over the years with the food offerings.

The Minneapolis (MN) School District has offered a "Taco Bell Express" in one of its high schools since 1994. When Scottsdale (AZ) and Albuquerque (NM) switched to closed campus, they brought in several branded concepts for their high schools. The Henrico County (VA) School District has had on-site franchises for Taco Bell, Domino's, and Subway since 1993. Burger King has one school franchise, in the San Lorenzo (CA) Unified School District, and it is served a la carte.

Manufacturers' brands that are sometimes "advertised" in the school menus or on the signage at the school are: Otis Spunkmeyer, Tony's Pizza, Red Baron, Minute Maid, Kellogg's, and many others. With most school districts Taco Bell and Pizza Hut have resorted to frozen products—Pizza Hut discontinued the school foodservice licensing program for Pizza Hut Express in early 1998. They now have bake-off kits that contain ten 15-inch pies with cheese and toppings and delivery programs. Taco Bell has hard and soft tacos and a variety of flavored burritos that they sell frozen to schools at prices higher than less-known brands charge.

Many of the school districts in a South Carolina buying alliances (with 91 school districts) use brands on their menus, such as: Oscar Mayer, Tony's Pizza, Pillsbury Quaker Oats, Welch's Ocean Spray, Hershey's, Pizza Hut, Domino's, and Subway. Some school districts view this as advertising and won't permit it.

The Fairfax County (VA) Public Schools was one of the first to establish school brands and the logos of "Bite Right," "Lite Bite," "Big Bite," and "Super Sack" back in 1978. They developed logo sandwich wraps, cups, napkins, lunch bags, lunch boxes, and placemats. The school logo was modernized in 1990 to "Energy Zone," and is still used today. The Beaufort County (SC) School District's foodservices is called "Sea Island Foods" and uses palm trees under a bright sun in their logo.

School brands have done fairly well for the Hillsborough County (FL) Public Schools with their freshly baked school brand pizza, and Glendale (CA) Schools switched over to school brands on some items in 1998. Many other school districts have developed logos and school brands. Indianapolis (IN) Public Schools foodservice staff made the decision not to use ready-to-serve brands, such as Pizza Hut, Subway, and Kentucky Fried Chicken, but instead they borrowed concepts from popular brands and developed in-house brands (self-branding).

FOOD COURTS

Though food courts are really a style of service, they are discussed here because they are a break from the norm in a rather traditional program. Atmosphere and food presentation count, and this is seen every time a school district makes the changes from the traditional to a more contemporary approach and starts offering meals in a food court arrangement. Many school districts ventured into this concept in the early 1990s, but in the last three years of the 1990s numerous school districts have opened food courts at their high schools and have experienced success with the changes in the way they serve.

Broward County (FL) high schools have converted their traditional lines to diverse food courts and have lunch, keeping more students on campus. The four different foodservice areas at South Plantation High School are:

Country Kitchen—serves old favorites, traditional lunches
The Grill—offers hamburgers, several other sandwiches, and fries
The Pizzeria—serves 16-inch pizzas prepared from components
The International —features Chinese, Italian, Mexican, and other ethnic dishes

Pizza is the biggest draw at $1.50 a slice with salad and milk (a reimbursable lunch). The Nacho Lunch is another popular item. The students sit at round tables either inside or out on the patio, where an overhang shields from the rain.

The Corona-Norco Unified (CA) School District pioneered "Campus Catering" in 1990 and put the logo on everything, and expanded the service to all students with portable carts for use on school grounds. When the new concepts were first introduced in 1990, the food sales doubled in the Corono-Norco Unified School District's high schools and increased by 25 percent the second year. Annually the school district comes out with creative approaches to serving its customers. The logo/concept has been adopted by a number of other California school districts, as well as school districts across the country. Carts like the one in Figure 16.1 are used by school districts to take the food to students.

"Re-imaging" or "Make-Overs" of the School Dining Area

Many of the school cafeteria look today as they did in 1960, but the students see a much different environment when they go out to eat. Many school districts are changing how the cafeteria looks

Figure 16.1. A Portable Serving Piece Expands Service to Students

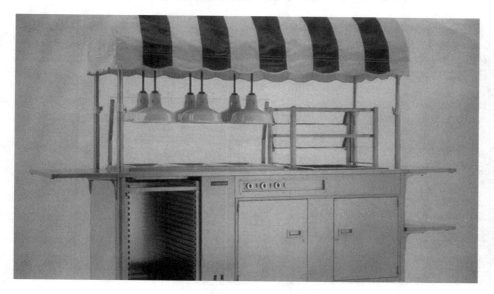

Courtesy of Cres Cor/Crown X, Cleveland, Ohio.

through renovations referred to by some as re-imaging or make-overs.

Greenwich (CT) High School has had a total making-over or "re-imaging," and the results in participation have been significant. They averaged another $100 per day more in a la carte sales and 15% increase in participation immediately. Their revenue averages $6,000 per day. The Bellingham (WA) School District has created the "Mariner Commons Food Court" and has experienced an increase of 24% for reimbursable meals and 9% for a la carte purchases. They have six different stations: Fairhaven Grill, Chuckanut Choices, the Deli, Health Club, Extra! Extra! (for a la carte items), and a self-service pizza station. "The Health Club" offers a selection of premade salads and side dishes.

The Corpus Christi (TX) Independent School District is an example of a school district that has put some money into remodeling the serving and dining areas, and the results speak for themselves. See Figure 16.2 for the before picture and Figure 16.3 for the after. The neon lights, convenience stores, computerized point-of-sale, and many food courts ideas have kept the students happy with eating on campus. School districts are taking advantage of the beauty of nature and eat outside all year around weather permitting.

Albuquerque (NM) Public Schools saw a staggering increase in participation after the "re-imaging" or "make-over" at one of the high schools. See Figure 16.4 for the before picture and Figure 16.5 for the after ones.

School districts can spend a lot or a little to bring about changes and create food court arrangements. The Brownsville (TX) Independent School District probably did the most at the least cost when their high schools went with the inTEAM Food System and established food stations. The

Figure 16.2. The Typical High School Serving Area of the 1950s-1980s—"Before"

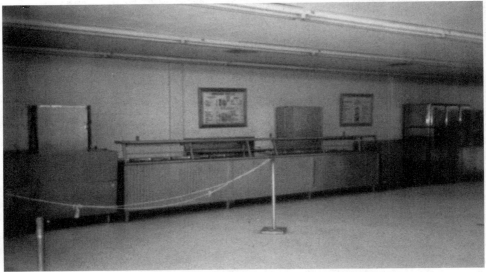

Source: Corpus Christi (TX) Independent School District. Used by permission.

Figure 16.3. The Food Court Arrangement Made From the Typical High School Serving Area— "After"

Source: Corpus Christi (TX) Independent School District. Used by permission.

adult participation soared after the change—a 66 percent increase, and the already high student participation in the school district's lunch program increased by 12 percent.

It takes imagination and determination to bring a change about. Among the best ideas, most creative ideas for change in look of serving and dining areas, can be obtained from professional journals like *FoodService Director*, from a trip to shopping malls food courts, and from university campus foodservices. Also, the inTEAM Food system helps school districts bring about change with step-by-step directions. The System's training program spends nearly half a day on "make overs" and creating food courts. School districts across the United States have put inTEAM Food System ideas to work for them along with the one-week high school menu cycle and food court arrangements.

Food courts can incorporate the outdoors, too. There is no better atmosphere, at as little cost as using the outside of the school building for dining when weather permits. Some school districts have roving barbeque trucks, e.g., the Desert Sands (CA) Unified School District and Los Angeles (CA) Unified School District. The trucks serve different sites each day, but make lunch fun. They are eagerly anticipated, especially by elementary children. Many school districts utilize beautiful weather and warm climates with portable carts and/or trucks, e.g., the Gilroy (CA) School District, the Girl's Preparatory School in Chattanooga (TN), and especially school districts in Florida. Hillsborough County (FL), Corpus Christi (TX), and many California schools have walk-up windows, tables, and umbrellas or other cover for students to be served and for them to eat outside.

Creating interesting dining areas has been discussed above in the form of high school food courts, but the concept should not be limited to high schools. Certainly the high schools are challenging and probably should be the first to re-image. However, the middle and elementary school cafeterias need changes too. Each elementary school in McNairy County (TN) School District has a personality created by the decor. They are successfully using self-service for kindergarten through twelfth grade.

The straight-line, stainless-steel cafeteria serving line of the 1960s era is a dying concept and needs to be replaced at all grade levels with something more customer-friendly and interesting. Small children respond to bright colors, decorations, logos, brands they recognize, and change. Melanie Wood, president of the Color Marketing Group, said, "The best product in the world, if it isn't the right color, it won't sell very well." You could add to that quote "and if it is not packaged well, it won't sell very well."

MANAGING PROMOTIONS

Promotion, or public relations, can be described as the "act of promoting goodwill;" as related to school foodservice. It should result in the public's having a positive image of the operation. Dr. R. W. McIntosh, a sales promoter and merchandising authority, says that the public relations should be "an attitude of management which places first priority on the public interest when making management decisions."

Promoting goodwill can mean something as simple as giving a straw to a child who brings a drink from home. Though "freebies" have to be controlled, the public relations benefits of giving the straw must be considered by management in making the decision to do so. Goodwill may be

Figure 16.4. Albuquerque (NM) Public Schools Typical High School Serving Area
           of the 1980s

Source: Albuquerque (NM) Public Schools. Used by permission.

Figure 16.5. Albuquerque (NM) Public Schools High School After "Re-imaging"

Source: Albuquerque (NM) Public Schools. Used by permission.

something as simple as replacing a student's food because the student did not like what he or she chose.

Since creating goodwill can be costly, it is usually best to establish clearly what services and products can and cannot be provided gratis by foodservice. For example, if a teacher wants free napkins to served food cooked in the classroom and the manager says "no," the results may be negative public relations. The manager is not wrong, but if the rule has not been established that napkins to go with must be paid for, the decision may come across negatively. In such a case, it probably would help if prices for the services and supplies have been previously established and teachers informed about them. For good public relations, it is best to announce what can be provided at what price.

Promotions used in the commercial food industry draw on a wide variety of special marketing techniques, such as special events contests, coupons, "specials" (reduced prices, samples, and bonuses) and giveaways. For example, Hidden Valley Salad Dressings had a very popular salad bar promotion to increase the sale of salad dressings. Their promotions included the popular "rub-off" cards given to each customer who selects the salad lunch. If the rub-off card revealed a salad under all three dots, the customer receives a free salad lunch; if two salads appear, an ice cream. It was fun and created suspense. Students like for eating at school to be fun.

Students like something free—for example, a frequent diner card. A free dessert with six punches or a lunch free for ten punches. Tony's Pizza Company has given CD players to school districts to promote the lunch program and it has worked because it is a reward that student want. Students in Boston suggested giving a free lunch to the 50th student who came through the point-of-sale. Some schools have had drawings for enough pizzas to serve eight. Not all promotions work at all schools, particularly at the high school level. A Nutrition Advisory Council survey showed the favorite premiums to be stickers with the smaller children and free videos/CDS with grades 10 to 12. Figure 16.6 shows the outcome of the Nutrition Advisory Council survey.

The main use of "promotions" in school foodservices can be to keep students interested in eating at the same place each day throughout the school year. The Marriott Corporation Food Services Division calls promotions "monotony breakers." Looking at the commercial industry can provide ideas for school foodservice promotions.

The Parish (KY) Elementary School has invited fathers, brothers, grandfathers, and uncles to attend the "100 Man Lunch." In 1999, 167 men from this small community accepted the invitation. Grandparents day is celebrated in schools across the country, bringing grandparents from across the country to lunch at school.

A school foodservice promotion might involve a contest to name the dining room and pick a theme for different seasons of the year, the sale of a book of lunch tickets for ten meals at a slight savings, or a coupon for a free ice cream with each book of tickets. It might also include capitalizing on holidays and special school events with decorations and menus that create interest, sending home favorite school recipes with the student (adjusted to family size) at Christmas time or during National School Lunch Week, or celebrating birthdays of the month with specially decorated cupcakes. Such efforts will usually result not only in higher participation, but also in more customer satisfaction.

A promotion can have very positive results. It is an excellent way to encourage students to try something new and buy more that just a lunch (if the customers have the money). As an inducement, the foodservice can, for example, offer a non-food item such as a customized school cup with the purchase of a milkshake.

Figure 16.6. Popularity of Favorite Premiums by Grade Level

Premium	Grade K-4	Grade 5-6	Grade 7-9	Grade 10-12
Stickers	55.4%	47.1%	40.2%	27.3%
Free video/CDS	20.4%	45.9%	34.6%	48.9%
T-shirts	36.3%	37.7%	26.8%	44.3%
Stuffed animals/ characters	30.6%	32.7%	32.4%	28.4%
Hats	30.6%	28.4%	22.9%	25.0%
Trading cards	24.2%	32.3%	21.8%	8.0%
Sport sipper bottles	16.6%	31.9%	17.3%	23.9%
Pogs	21.0%	26.1%	11.7%	6.8%
Phone cards	9.6%	18.3%	18.4%	21.6%
Sunglasses	12.1%	21.0%	16.2%	10.2%
Scratch cards	7.6%	16.3%	20.1%	15.9%
Other	12.7%	9.7%	11.2%	15.9%

Source: School Foodservice Journal (February) 1998.

Grandparents' day, secretaries' day, and a special Thanksgiving lunch can be very positive community relations activities. In 1988, the Fairfax County (VA) Public Schools' foodservice program sponsored a very successful "Pizza Read;" students were rewarded with a "pizza party" if they met the reading requirements established by the reading specialist for one month. This proved to be an excellent way to encourage students to read more and to relate classroom efforts to the school foodservice program.

Promoting good nutrition should be a prime goal of any school foodservice. Making information available, such as nutrient analyses of the food served, can be very positive. With the use of the computer, it is possible to provide actual nutrition analyses of the menus served. One of the major commercial management companies, Aramark, has had a successful nutrition promotion involving Nutrisaurus, a registered trademark. It is a grinning, green, dinosaur-like creature with horns, used to extol the virtues of a well-balanced, nutritional lunch.

Some school districts have adopted logos and trademarks that promote good nutrition. The registered trademark of Decatur (GA) schools is "Smart Bites;" Virginia Beach (VA) City Schools', "Might Bite;" and Fairfax County (VA) Public Schools was "Bite Right" and is now "Energy Zone," and the trademark of the Corona-Norco Unified (CA) School District and many other school districts, "Campus Catering."

Armistead (1988) identifies four steps in planning a public relations project: (1) research, (2) planning or analysis, (3) communication, and (4) evaluation. Unfortunately, steps 1, 2, and 4 are frequently omitted in public relations efforts. All four steps are important to planning and managing a successful public relations project.

Some of the characteristics of successful nutrition promotional programs (of some restaurants today) are the following: (1) The promotions clearly communicate to the customer "how" the items meet their needs; (2) they not only are addressing current nutrition needs but also have the built-in flexibility to adapt to future nutrition concerns; and (3) they are promoted "in house" to the staff (production and service) as well as to the customer. Promotions generate enthusiasm for the program.

MANAGING ADVERTISING AND PUBLICITY

Schools have opened their doors to advertising in a big way with Coca Cola, Pepsi, and other companies but it has drawn strong criticism. Some school districts have a policy banning advertising inside the classroom. School foodservices have to work within the restraints of the school board policy and of what is acceptable to the district and the community.

The objectives of publicity and advertising are to create and reinforce an image. Publicity is usually free, while advertising is usually purchased. Both are techniques used to inform and persuade the public or the customers. Both can be used to call attention to, tell about, or praise someone or something. The fact that publicity is free doesn't guarantee that positive publicity will happen. School foodservice management should be assertive and imaginative in obtaining "free publicity." This can be done by preparing feature stories and making them available to small newspapers that have lean budgets—they may be used as fillers, but the story is told.

One sure way to obtain positive publicity, though usually free, is through paid advertising. However, paid advertising is rarely used by school foodservices. Why not purchase an ad in the school newspaper? Why not run a 25-cent-off coupon in the school newspaper? The cents-off coupon is one of the most popular and effective sales promotions used in the retail food market (Schultz and Robinson 1982). School districts in the Phoenix area have been able to purchase time on television and radio by forming a corporation through which companies contribute funds for advertising school foodservice in relationship to products purchased from the companies (Reid, 1988).

Advertising of school foodservice activities and offerings usually qualifies for "free time" or "free space" in the media. Menus are often published in local newspapers. Even the *Washington Post* in Washington, DC, did carry the local school districts' weekly menus. Surveys have shown that students are one of are prime audiences for early-morning television—just prior to leaving for school. With persuasion, the local television channels may be interested in carrying the menus. Cable television and radio is often looking for fillers. The lunch menu presentation will act as an advertisement, if well done.

If book covers are popular, book covers can be printed advertising foodservice offerings and a la carte prices along with the school's football schedule. These book covers can be given away with a lunch served at the beginning of the school year.

MEETING THE PRESS

Since it cannot be expected that all publicity will be positive, it is important to develop a cooperative working relationship with the press. This becomes especially useful in handling unpleasant situations that may arise. For example, reports of food poisoning or high levels of some undesired nutrient or chemical in school lunches can cause very negative publicity. Of note in the late 1980s when CBS in Washington, DC, carried a series of feature news items entitled "Flunking School Lunch," which claimed that school lunches were higher in sodium and fat than fast foods. The reporter was good at "sensationalizing" and turning facts into hot human interest stories during television ratings week.

Most reporters, however, will be fair. Honest responses to a reporter are safer in the long run than attempts to cover up an unfavorable situation. In the case of crises, it is usually wise to take the initiative in disseminating information. Facts can stop rumors and gossip and provide reassurance to the public. The best public relations results come from an "act," not a "reaction." The public can usually be won over by frank, candid responses and a sincere concern for the welfare of the customers.

According to the National Restaurant Association (1988), every operation, no matter how large or small, should have a written "crisis communications" policy. Anyone who is to speak to the press on behalf of the foodservices or school district should be a skilled communicator and have the primary objective of getting the right message to the right audience in a believable way. In the case of a food poisoning outbreak thought to be caused by food eaten in a school cafeteria, the goals should include protecting the well-being of the customer, cooperating fully with any investigation, informing the public, and being truthful at all times.

Some tips for working with reporters in a normal situation (Armistead 1988) include these:

- Be honest.
- Do not be afraid to be interviewed.
- Regularly and systematically offer news and feature story ideas to the media.
- Spend as much time as necessary explaining an idea or program so reporters will understand it.
- Keep your head about errors in the resulting story. (Do they really matter?)
- Understand that when you are talking "off the record," this information may be used by the reporter.

MERCHANDISING

Merchandising is so much a part of food production that it should be on the standardized recipe as a step and discussed under Chapter 10, "Managing Production and Service." Effective merchandising can increase participation in a school foodservice program, and it can particularly increase satisfaction. In narrow terms, merchandising refers to making the customer want to buy a product because of the product itself. In a school foodservice, it involves offering good food that looks attractive at a price the customer considers fair, in a courteous manner and in a pleasant environment.

One of the greatest downfalls of school foodservice has been the lack of merchandising. This may be due to the volume of food being produced, a tight budget, time limits, or the lack of competition, or the lack of knowledge on how to merchandise. (Garnishing and presentation of food is discussed in Chapter 10, "Managing Production and Service.")

The key elements of food presentation are:

1. Color—natural to the food, bright, fresh, crisp
2. Flavor—never too strong or contrasting, clean and crisp
3. Contrast in texture, crisp foods with soft foods, and vice-versa
4. Shapes—varying, e.g., not all mounds or strips
5. Uniformity in size and shape

COMMUNICATING WITH CUSTOMERS

How can a manager know what the students like or dislike? Certainly production records help determine preferences. However, there needs to be ways whereby the manager can get more definite feedback. Techniques that can be used in communicating with customers—students and adults—regarding their likes and dislikes include: (1) formal questionnaires and surveys (see Figure 16.7), (2) informal interviewing of students and adults, (3) small-group discussions, (4) suggestion boxes, and (5) taste parties or sampling.

Small-group discussions with students and adults can be very beneficial if suggestions for improvement are obtained along with help in carrying out the changes. Also, circulating throughout the dining area during lunch time, a manager or designated person can effectively solicit customers' opinions and give them a chance to ask questions in turn. This should be a regular occurrence. In addition, employees on the serving line and in the dishroom window can obtain useful feedback and identify happy and unhappy customers. This information should be communicated to management.

Taste parties can provide an excellent means of determining if a new product will be accepted. They can be formal or informal, small or large, and can involve students, parents and faculty and/or foodservice supervisors or managers. New recipes can be tested this way. The National Dairy Council has materials and ideas on having taste parties in its kit called "Taste Buddies."

For any taste party or sampling of food on the serving line, some type of form for expressing opinions should be provided. For younger children, a simple graphic form with faces to be marked is appropriate. A director can obtain student feedback from elementary with a poster on the wall. Students are to express their opinions as they exit the dining room by marking a happy face or a sad face.

The National Food Service Management Institute has provided and encouraged states to do statewide surveys of students, and the results are still being collected. Local school districts have learned a lot about what is important to their customers and what they need to do to better serve the customer.

The Youth Advisory Council (YAC) and Nutrition Advisory Council (NAC) are organizations made up of students interested in nutrition and school foodservice. It is a national organization sponsored by the American School Food Service Association, but the YAC has almost disappeared

Figure: 16.7. Sample Form for Evaluating the School Cafeteria Atmosphere—Middle and High

Name _____ Date _____

Please place an "X" by your answers.

1. Is the time you spend in line getting your food:
    ☐ too long
    ☐ okay
    ☐ too short

2. How many minutes do you have to eat your meal?
    ☐ less than 15 minutes
    ☐ 15-30 minutes
    ☐ 30-45 minutes
    ☐ more than 45 minutes

3. Is the school cafeteria supervised by friendly people?
    ☐ Yes   ☐ No

4. Are the people who serve the food friendly?
    ☐ Yes   ☐ No

5. Do you think the school cafeteria is:

    a. ☐ well lit   b. ☐ colorful
        ☐ okay   ☐ okay
        ☐ too dark   ☐ drab

    c. ☐ too quiet   d. ☐ messy
        ☐ okay   ☐ okay
        ☐ noisy   ☐ clean

6. Would you like to see improvements in the school cafeteria?
    ☐ Yes   ☐ No

7. Would you like to help make improvements in the school cafeteria?
    ☐ Yes   ☐ No

Figure 16.7. Sample Form for Evaluating School Lunches (continued)

Name _____ Date _____

Please place an "X" by your answers.

1. How often do you eat the school lunch?
    ☐ never
    ☐ sometimes
    ☐ always

2. If never, why?
    ☐ food does not taste good
    ☐ food does not look good
    ☐ too expensive
    ☐ don't like menu choices
    ☐ lines are too long
    ☐ don't like cafeteria
    ☐ my friends don't eat there

3. If always, why?
    ☐ food tastes good
    ☐ food looks good
    ☐ inexpensive
    ☐ like menu choices
    ☐ lines are too long
    ☐ my friends eat there
    ☐ I have no choice

4. What do you prefer for lunch?
    ☐ hot dinner-type lunch
    ☐ soup and sandwiches
    ☐ fast-food-type lunch
    ☐ box or bag lunch
    ☐ salad bar
    ☐ yogurt
    ☐ snack items
    ☐ other

5. List five of your favorite foods that are served for school lunch.
    _____   _____
    _____   _____
    _____

6. List five foods that you would like to see served for school lunch.
    _____   _____
    _____   _____
    _____

in recent years. In the 1980s the Irving (TX) Independent School District was one of the first to form such a group; it developed a manual for its YAC. The American School Food Service Association still has materials available on how to start a YAC. The problem with involving students and parents in the menu planning process today is that it has become so complicated. It is nearly impossible to make this a meaningful, fun experience. After all, the customer does not really care what the federal regulations are when it comes to planning menus.

Federal regulations require that schools participating in the National School Lunch Program have student and parent involvement. The YACs and other student groups have provided excellent ways to involve students. Since parent and student involvement has proven difficult to obtain, the U.S. Department of Agriculture has considered dropping the requirement.

SELLING

"Selling "(like advertising) is a new word to some school foodservice managers. Certainly the schools are no place for high-pressure selling, but using suggestive selling and good business sense in displaying food is appropriate in most school foodservices. For example, chocolate chip cookies next to ice cream cups with the suggestion to make one's own cookie or ice cream sandwich will usually increase the sale of chocolate chip cookies and ice cream cups.

Displaying soft pretzels in a revolving, well-lighted case will increase their sales. Making a la carte food items accessible—easy to see—will make a difference in sales of these items. Self service no longer works because of the theft. Also, how foods are priced will have an effect on sales. For example, if the price of lunch is $1.35, having a 15-cent item such as a cookie will increase the revenue. (Pricing is discussed in Chapter 2, "Financial Management.")

To make the foodservice more effective by increasing participation and serving all students in less time, the manager needs to know what the customer wants. Preferences can be determined through surveys, listening, questioning, and staying in touch with the customer. The student needs to know that the foodservice goals are to deliver a top-quality, nutritious lunch at the best price in town. A good price can be proven to the customer with a poster comparing the prices of key items on the menu with prices charged at popular fast-food restaurants.

In order to keep the customer's interest and maintain the goals of increasing participation and customer satisfaction, the foodservice should design products to provide surprises, give more than is expected, put as much of the revenue as possible into the purchase of good-quality food, and train all employees to be salespersons and act as if the foodservice were their own business.

A friendly, simple survey for evaluating the school cafeteria atmosphere and the lunches served is provided in Figure 16.8. The "bottomline" to successful management of school foodservice in the 21st century is keeping the customers happy with nutritious meals at a price their parents are willing to pay.

SELECTED REFERENCES

"ARA's Marketing Efforts Help Keep Clients Satisfied." 1988. *School Business Affairs* 54(8): 51.

Armistead, L. 1988. "A Practical and Positive Approach to Public Relations." *School Business Affairs* 52(12): 15- 19.

Boehrer, J. 1993. "Managing to Meet the Bottom Line." *School Business Affairs* 57 (11): 3-8.

The Education Foundation of the National Restaurant Association. 1992. *Foodservice Sales Promotions and Marketing.* Washington, DC: Author.

Lele, M., and J. Sheth. 1987. *The Customer Is Key: Gaining an Unbeatable Advantage Through Customer Satisfaction.* New York: John Wiley & Sons.

McKinsey & Company, Inc. 1996. *Foodservice 2005: Satisfying America's Changing Appetite.* Falls Church, VA: Foodservice Distributors International—NAWGA/IFDA, Inc.

McNeal, J. 1987. *Children as Consumers: Insights and Implications.* Lexington, MA.: Lexington Books, D. C. Health and Company.

National Restaurant Association. 1986. *A Nutrition Guide for the Restauranteau.* Washington, D.C.: National Restaurant Association.

——, 1988. *The Foodservice Operator's Crisis Management Manual.* Washington, D.C.: National Restaurant Association.

Rednak, J. 1987. "Building High Participation in School Food Service." *School Business Affairs* 52(11): 22-27.

Reid, J. 1988. "School Lunch in Crisis: An Arizona District Takes an Innovative Approach." *School Business Affairs* 54(11): 32-33.

U. S. Department of Agriculture, Food and Nutrition Services. 1998. *School Food Purchase Study: Final Report.* Washington, DC: Author.

Watkins, E. 1988. "Teaching the School Foodservice Market to Merchandise." *The Foodservice Distributor* (May): 80-82.

Zimmerman, Kathy. 1985. "Changing with the Times." *School Food Service Journal* 39 (6): 28.

APPENDIX A -
EXCERPTS FROM THE
NATIONAL SCHOOL LUNCH ACT
AND THE CHILD NUTRITION ACT OF 1966

AN ACT

DECLARATION OF POLICY

SEC. 2. [1751]

It is hereby declared to be the policy of Congress, as a measure of national security, to safeguard the health and well-being of the nation's children and to encourage the domestic consumption of nutritious agricultural commodities and other food, by assisting the States, through grants-in-aid and other means, in providing an adequate supply of food and other facilities for the establishment, maintenance, operation, and expansion of nonprofit school lunch programs.

◆ ◆ ◆ ◆ ◆ ◆

SEC. 4. [1753]

(a) The sums appropriated for any fiscal year pursuant to the authorizations contained in section 3 of this Act shall be available to the Secretary for supplying agricultural commodities and other food for the program in accordance with the provisions of this Act.

(b) (1) The Secretary shall make food assistance payments to each State educational agency each fiscal year, at such times as the Secretary may determine, from the sums appropriated for such purpose, in a total amount equal to the product obtained by multiplying—

(A) the number of lunches (consisting of a combination of foods which meet the minimum nutritional requirements prescribed by the Secretary under section 9(a) of this Act) served during each fiscal year in schools in such State which participate in the school lunch program under this Act under agreements with such State educational agency; by

(B) the national average lunch payment prescribed in paragraph (2) of this subsection.

(2) The national average lunch payment for each lunch served shall be 10.5 cents (as adjusted pursuant to section 11(a) of this Act) except that for each lunch served in school food authorities in which 60 percent or more of the lunches served in the school lunch program during the second preceding school year were served free or at a reduced price, the national average lunch payment shall be 2 cents more.

◆ ◆ ◆ ◆ ◆ ◆

SEC. 6. [1755]

(a) The funds provided by appropriation or transfer from other accounts for any fiscal year for carrying out the provisions of this Act, and for carrying out the provisions of the Child Nutrition Act of 1966, other than section 3 thereof, less

(1) not to exceed 3 ½ per centum thereof which per centum is hereby made available to the Secretary for the Secretary's administrative expenses under this Act and under the Child Nutrition Act of 1966;

(2) the amount apportioned by the Secretary pursuant to section 4 of this Act and the amount appropriated pursuant to sections 11 and 13 of this Act and sections 4 and 7 of the Child Nutrition Act of 1966; and

(3) not to exceed 1 per centum of the funds provided for carrying out the programs under this Act and the programs under the Child Nutrition Act of 1966, other than section 3, which per centum is hereby made available to the Secretary to supplement the nutritional benefits of these programs through grants to States and other means for nutritional training and education for workers, cooperators, and participants in these programs, for pilot projects and the cash-in-lieu of commodities study required to be carried out under section 18 of this Act, and for necessary surveys and studies of requirements for food service programs in furtherance of the purposes expressed in section 2 of this Act and section 2 of the Child Nutrition Act of 1966,

shall be available to the Secretary during such year for direct expenditure by the Secretary for agricultural commodities and other foods to be distributed among the States and schools and service institutions participating in the food service programs under this Act and under the Child Nutrition Act of 1966 in accordance with the needs as determined by the local school and service institution authorities. Except as provided in the next 2 sentences, any school participating in food service programs under this Act may refuse to accept delivery of not more than 20 percent of the total value of agricultural commodities and other foods tendered to it in any school year; and if a school so refuses, that school may receive, in lieu of the refused commodities, other commodities to the extent that other commodities are available to the State during that year. Any school food authority may refuse some or all of the fresh fruits and vegetables offered to the school food authority in any school year and shall receive, in lieu of the offered fruits and vegetables, other more desirable fresh fruits and vegetables that are at least equal in value to the fresh fruits and vegetables refused by the school food authority. The value of any fresh fruits and vegetables refused by a school under the preceding sentence for a school year shall not be used to determine the 20 percent of the total value of agricultural commodities and other foods tendered to the school food authority in the school year under the second sentence. The provisions of law contained in the proviso of the Act of June 28, 1937, facilitating operations with respect to the purchase and disposition of surplus agricultural commodities under section 32 of the Act approved August 24, 1935, shall, to the extent not inconsistent with the provisions of this Act, also be applicable to expenditures of funds by the Secretary under this Act. In making purchases of such agricultural commodities and other foods, the Secretary shall not issue specifications which restrict participation of local producers unless such specifications will result in significant advantages to the food service programs authorized by this Act and the Child Nutrition Act of 1966.

(b) The Secretary shall deliver, to each State participating in the school lunch program under this Act, commodities valued at the total level of assistance authorized under subsection (c) for each school year for the school lunch program in the State, not later than September 30 of the following school year.

(c) (1) (A) The national average value of donated foods, or cash payments in lieu thereof, shall be 11 cents, adjusted on July 1, 1982, and each July 1 thereafter to reflect changes in the Price Index for Food Used in Schools and Institutions. The Index shall be computed using 5 major food components in the Bureau of Labor Statistics' Producer Price Index (cereal and bakery products, meats, poultry and fish, dairy products, processed fruits and vegetables, and fats and oils). Each component shall be weighed using the same relative weight as determined by the Bureau of Labor Statistics.

(B) The value of food assistance for each meal shall be adjusted each July 1 by the annual percentage change in a 3-month average value of the Price Index for Foods Used in Schools and Institutions for March, April, and May each year. Such adjustment shall be computed to the nearest 1/4 cent.

(C) For each school year, the total commodity assistance of cash in lieu thereof available to a State for the school lunch program shall be calculated by multiplying the number of lunches served in the preceding school year by the rate established by subparagraph (B). After the end of each school year, the Secretary shall reconcile the number of lunches served by schools in each State with the number of lunches served by schools in each State during the preceding school year and increase or reduce subsequent commodity assistance or cash in lieu thereof provided to each State based on such reconciliation.

(D) Among those commodities delivered under this section, the Secretary shall give special emphasis to high protein foods, meat, and meat alternates (which may include domestic seafood commodities and their products).

(E) Notwithstanding any other provision of this section, not less than 75 percent of the assistance provided under this subsection shall be in the form of donated foods for the school lunch program.

(2) To the maximum extent feasible, each State agency shall offer to each school food authority under its jurisdiction that participates in the school lunch program and receives commodities, agricultural commodities and their products, the per meal value of which is not less than the national average value of donated foods established under paragraph (1). Each such offer shall include the full range of such commodities and products that are available from the Secretary to the extent that quantities requested are sufficient to allow efficient delivery to and within the State.

(f) Beginning with the school year ending June 30, 1981, the Secretary shall not offer commodity assistance based upon the number of breakfasts served to children under section 4 of the Child Nutrition Act of 1966 [(42 U.S.C. 1773)].

(g) (1) Subject to paragraph (2), in each school year the Secretary shall ensure that not less than 12 percent of the assistance provided under section 4, this section, and section 11 shall be in the form of commodity assistance provided under this section, including cash in lieu of commodities and administrative costs for procurement of commodities under this section.

(2) If amounts available to carry out the requirements of the sections described in paragraph (1) are insufficient to meet the requirement contained in paragraph (1) for a school year, the Secretary shall, to the extent necessary, use the authority provided under section 14(a) to meet the requirement for the school year.

STATE DISBURSEMENT TO SCHOOLS

SEC. 8. [1757]

(a) funds paid to any State during any fiscal year pursuant to section 4 shall be disbursed by the State educational agency, in accordance with such agreements approved by the Secretary as may be entered into by such State agency and the schools in the State, to those schools in the State which the State educational agency, taking into account need and attendance, determines are eligible to participate in the school lunch program.

(b) The agreements described in subsection (a) shall be permanent agreements that may be amended as necessary.

(c) The State educational agency may suspend or terminate any such agreement in accordance with regulations prescribed by the Secretary.

(d) Use of funds paid to States may include, in addition to the purchase price of agricultural commodities and other foods, the cost of processing, distributing, transporting, storing, or handling thereof.

(e) In no event shall such disbursement for food to any school for any fiscal year exceed an amount determined by multiplying the number of lunches served in the school in the school lunch program under this Act during such year by the maximum per meal reimbursement rate for the State, for the type of lunch served, as prescribed by the Secretary.

(f) In any fiscal year in which the national average payment per lunch determined under section 4 is increased above the amount prescribed in the previous fiscal year, the maximum per meal reimbursement rate for the type of lunch served, shall be increased by a like amount.

(g) Lunch assistance disbursements to schools under this section and under section 11 of this Act may be made in advance or by way of reimbursement in accordance with procedures prescribed by the Secretary.

NUTRITIONAL AND OTHER PROGRAM REQUIREMENTS

SEC. 9. [1758]

(a) (1) (A) Lunches served by schools participating in the school lunch program under this Act shall meet minimum nutritional requirements prescribed by the Secretary on the basis of tested nutritional research, except that the minimum nutritional requirements—

      (i) shall not be construed to prohibit the substitution of foods to accommodate the medical or other special dietary needs of individual students; and

      (ii) shall, at a minimum, be based on the weekly average of the nutrient content of school lunches.

    (B) The Secretary shall provide technical assistance and training, including technical assistance and training in the preparation of lower-fat versions of foods commonly used in the school lunch program under this Act, to schools participating in the school lunch program to assist the schools in complying with the nutritional requirements prescribed by the Secretary pursuant to subparagraph (A) and in providing appropriate meals to children with medically certified special dietary needs. The Secretary shall provide additional technical assistance to schools that are having difficulty maintaining compliance with the requirements.

(2) Lunches served by schools participating in the school lunch program under this Act—

(A) Shall offer students fluid milk; and

(B) Shall offer students a variety of fluid milk consistent with prior year preferences unless the prior year preference for any such variety of fluid milk is less than one percent of the total milk consumed at the school.

(3) Students in senior high schools that participate in the school lunch program under this Act (and, when approved by the local school district or nonprofit private schools, students in any other grade level) shall not be required to accept offered foods they do not intend to consume, and any such failure to accept offered foods shall not affect the full charge to the student for a lunch meeting the requirements of this subsection or the amount of payments made under this Act to any such school for such lunch.

(b) (1) (A) Not later than June 1 of each fiscal year, the Secretary shall prescribe income guidelines for determining eligibility for free and reduced price lunches during the 12-month period beginning July 1 of such fiscal year and ending June 30 of the following fiscal year. The income guidelines for determining eligibility for free lunches shall be 130 percent of the applicable family size income levels contained in the nonfarm income poverty guidelines prescribed by the Office of Management and Budget, as adjusted annually in accordance with subparagraph (B). The income guidelines for determining eligibility for reduced price lunches for any school year shall be 185 percent of the applicable family size income levels contained in the nonfarm income poverty guidelines prescribed by the Office of Management and Budget, as adjusted annually in accordance with subparagraph (B). The Office of Management and Budget guidelines shall be revised at annual intervals, or at any shorter interval deemed feasible and desirable.

(B) The revision required by subparagraph (A) of this paragraph shall be made by multiplying—

(i) the official poverty line (as defined by the Office of Management and budget); by

(ii) the percentage change in the Consumer Price Index during the annual or other interval immediately preceding the time at which the adjustment is made.

Revisions under this subparagraph shall be made not more than 30 days after the date on which the consumer price index data required to compute the adjustment becomes available.

(2) (A) Following the determination by the Secretary under paragraph (1) of this subsection of the income eligibility guidelines for each school year, each State educational agency shall announce the income eligibility guidelines by family size, to be used by schools in the State in making determinations of eligibility for free and reduced price lunches. Local school authorities shall, each year, publicly announce the income eligibility guidelines for free and reduced price lunches on or before the opening of school.

(B) Applications for free and reduced price lunches, in such form as the Secretary may prescribe or approve, and any descriptive material, shall be distributed to the parents or guardians of children in attendance at the school, and shall contain only the family size income levels for reduced price meal eligibility with the explanation that households with incomes less than or equal to these values would be eligible for free or reduced price lunches. Such forms and descriptive material may not contain the income eligibility guidelines for free lunches.

(C) (i) Except as provided in clause (ii), each eligibility determination shall be made on the basis of a complete application executed by an adult member of the household. The Secretary, State, or local food authority may verify any data contained in such application. A local school food authority shall undertake such verification of information contained in any such application as the Secretary may by regulation prescribe and, in accordance with such regulations, shall make appropriate changes in the eligibility determination with respect to such application on the basis of such verification.

(ii) Subject to clause (iii), any school food authority may certify any child as eligible for free or reduced price lunches or breakfasts, without further application, by directly communicating with the appropriate State or local agency to obtain documentation of such child's status as a member of—

(I) a household that is receiving food stamps under the Food Stamp Act of 1977; or

(II) a family that is receiving assistance under the State program funded under part A of title IV of the Social Security Act that the Secretary determines complies with standards established by the Secretary that ensure that the standards under the State program are comparable to or more restrictive than those in effect on June 1, 1995.

(iii) The use or disclosure of any information obtained from an application for free or reduced price meals, or from a State or local agency referred to in clause (ii), shall be limited to—

(I) a person directly connected with the administration or enforcement of this Act or the Child Nutrition Act of 1966, or a regulation issued pursuant to either Act;

(II) a person directly connected with the administration or enforcement of—

(aa) a Federal education program;

(bb) a State health or education program administered by the State or local educational agency (other than a program carried out under title XIX of the Social Security Act; or

(cc) a Federal, State, or local means-tested nutrition program with eligibility standards comparable to the program under this section; and

(III) (aa) the Comptroller General of the United States for audit and examination authorized by any other provision of law; and

(bb) notwithstanding any other provision of law, a Federal, State, or local law enforcement official for the purpose of investigating an alleged violation of any program covered by paragraph (1) or this paragraph.

(IV) Information provided under clause (iii)(II) shall be limited to the income eligibility status of the child for whom application for free or reduced price meal benefits was made or for whom eligibility information was provided under clause (ii), unless the consent of the parent or guardian of the child for whom application for benefits was made is obtained.

(V) A person described in clause (iii) who publishes, divulges, discloses, or makes known in any manner, or to any extent not authorized by Federal law (including a regulation), any information obtained under this subsection shall be fined not more than $1,000 or imprisoned not more than 1 year, or both.

(D) FREE AND REDUCED PRICE POLICY STATEMENT—After the initial submission, a school food authority shall not be required to submit a free and reduced price policy statement to a State educational agency under this Act unless there is a substantive change in the free and reduced price policy of the school food authority. A routine change in the policy of a school food authority, such as an annual adjustment of the income eligibility guidelines for free and reduced price meals, shall not be sufficient cause for requiring the school food authority to submit a policy statement.

(3) Any child who is a member of a household whose income, at the time the application is submitted, is at an annual rate which does not exceed the applicable family size income level of the income eligibility guidelines for free lunches, as determined under paragraph (1), shall be served a free lunch. Any child who is a member of a household whose income, at the time the application is submitted, is at an annual rate greater than the applicable family size income level of the income eligibility guidelines for free lunches, as determined under paragraph (1), but less than or equal to the applicable family size income level of the income eligibility guidelines for reduced price lunches, as determined under paragraph (1), shall be served a reduced price lunch shall not exceed 40 cents.

(4) No physical segregation of or other discrimination against any child eligible for a free lunch or a reduced price lunch under this subsection shall be made by the school nor shall there be any overt identification of any child by special tokens or tickets, announced or published list of names, or by other means.

(5) Any child who has a parent or guardian who (A) is responsible for the principal support of such child and (B) is unemployed shall be served a free or reduced price lunch, respectively, during any period (i) in which such child's parent or guardian continues to be unemployed and (ii) the income of the child's parents or guardians during such period of unemployment falls within the income eligibility criteria for free lunches or reduced price lunches, respectively, based on the current rate of income of such parents or guardians. Local school authorities shall publicly announce that such children are eligible for free or reduced price lunch, and shall make determinations with respect to the status of any parent, or guardian of any child under clauses (A) and (B) of the preceding sentence on the basis of a statement executed in such form as the Secretary may prescribe by such parent or guardian. No physical segregation of, or other discrimination against, any child eligible for a free or reduced price lunch under this paragraph shall be made by the school nor shall there be any overt identification of any such child by special tokens or tickets, announced or published lists of names, or by any other means.

(6) (A) A child shall be considered automatically eligible for a free lunch and breakfast under this Act and the Child Nutrition Act of 1966, respectively, without further application or eligibility determination, if the child is—

(i) a member of a household receiving assistance under the food stamp program authorized under the Food Stamp Act of 1977;

       (ii) a member of a family (under the State program funded under part A of title IV of the Social Security Act that the Secretary determines complies with standards established by the Secretary that ensure that the standards under the State program are comparable to or more restrictive than those in effect on June 1, 1995, or

       (iii) enrolled as a participant in a Head Start program authorized under the Head Start Act on the basis of a determination that the child is a member of a family that meets the low-income criteria prescribed under section 645(a)(1)(A) of the Head Start Act.

    (B) Proof of receipt of food stamps or assistance under the State program funded under part A of title IV of the Social Security Act that the Secretary determines complies with standards established by the Secretary that ensure that the standards under the State program are comparable to or more restrictive than those in effect on June 1, 1995, or of enrollment or participation in a Head Start program on the basis described in subparagraph (A)(iii), shall be sufficient to satisfy any verification requirement imposed under paragraph (2)(C).

(c) School lunch programs under this Act shall be operated on a nonprofit basis. Commodities purchased under the authority of section 32 of the Act of August 24, 1935, may be donated by the Secretary to schools in accordance with the needs as determined by local school authorities, for utilization in the school lunch program under this Act as well as to other schools carrying out nonprofit school lunch programs and institutions authorized to receive such commodities. The requirements of this section relating to the service of meals without cost or at a reduced cost shall apply to the lunch program of any school utilizing commodities donated under any provision of law.

(d) (1) The Secretary shall require as a condition of eligibility for receipt of free or reduced price lunches that the member of the household who executes the application furnish the social security account number of the parent or guardian who is the primary wage earner responsible for the care of the child for whom the application is made, or that of another appropriate adult member of the child's household, as determined by the Secretary. The Secretary shall require that social security account numbers of all adult members of the household be provided if verification of the data contained in the application is sought under subsection (b)(2)(C).

  (2) No member of a household may be provided a free or reduced price lunch under this Act unless—

    (A) appropriate documentation relating to the income of such household (as prescribed by the Secretary) has been provided to the appropriate local school food authority so that such authority may calculate the total income of such household;

    (B) documentation showing that the household is participating in the food stamp program under the Food Stamp Act of 1977 has been provided to the appropriate local school food authority; or

    (C) documentation has been provided to the appropriate local school food authority showing that the family is receiving assistance under the State program funded under part A of title IV of the Social Security Act that the Secretary determines complies with standards established by the Secretary that ensure that the standards under the State program are comparable to or more restrictive than those in effect on June 1, 1995.

(e) A school or school food authority participating in a program under this Act may not contract with a food service company to provide a la carte food service unless the company agrees to offer free, reduced price, and full-price reimbursable meals to all eligible children.

(f) (1) NUTRITIONAL REQUIREMENTS—Except as provided in paragraph (2), not later than the first day of the 1996-1997 school year, schools that are participating in the school lunch or school breakfast program shall serve lunches and breakfasts under the program that—

    (A) are consistent with the goals of the most recent Dietary Guidelines for Americans published under section 301 of the National Nutrition Monitoring and Related Research Act of 1990; and

    (B) provide, on the average over each week, at least—

        (i) with respect to school lunches, 1/3 of the daily recommended dietary allowance established by the Food and Nutrition Board of the National Research Council of the National Academy of Sciences; and

        (ii) with respect to school breakfasts, 1/4 of the daily recommended dietary allowance established by the Food and Nutrition Board of the National Research Council of the National Academy of Sciences.

(2) State educational agencies may grant waivers from the requirements of paragraph (1) subject to criteria established by the appropriate State educational agency. The waivers shall not permit schools to implement the requirements later than July 1, 1998, or a later date determined by the Secretary.

(3) To assist schools in meeting the requirements of this subsection, the Secretary—

    (A) shall—

        (i) develop, and provide to schools, standardized recipes, menu cycles, and food product specification and preparation techniques; and

        (ii) provide to schools information regarding nutrient standard menu planning, assisted nutrient standard menu planning, and food-based menu systems; and

    (B) may provide to schools information regarding other approaches, as determined by the Secretary.

(4) USE OF ANY REASONABLE APPROACH.—

    (A) IN GENERAL.—A school food service authority may use any reasonable approach, within guidelines established by the Secretary in a timely manner, to meet the requirements of this subsection, including—

        (i) using the school nutrition meal pattern in effect for the 1994-1995 school year; and

        (ii) using any of the approaches described in paragraph (3).

    (B) NUTRIENT ANALYSIS.—The Secretary may not require a school to conduct or use a nutrient analysis to meet the requirements of this subsection.

(5) WAIVER OF REQUIREMENT FOR WEIGHTED AVERAGES FOR NUTRIENT ANALYSIS.—During the period ending on September 30, 2003, the Secretary shall not require the use of weighted averages for nutrient analysis of menu items and foods offered or served as part of a meal offered or served under the school lunch program under this Act or the school breakfast program under section 4 of the Child Nutrition Act of 1966.

(g) Not later than 1 year after the date of enactment of this subsection, the Secretary shall provide a notification to Congress that justifies the need for production records required under section 210.10(b) of title 7, Code of Federal Regulations, and describes how the Secretary has reduced paperwork relating to the school lunch and school breakfast programs.

(h) FOOD SAFETY INSPECTIONS.—

    (1) IN GENERAL.—Except as provided in paragraph (2), a school participating in the school lunch program under this Act or the school breakfast program under section 4 of the Child Nutrition Act of 1966 shall, at least once during each school year, obtain a food safety inspection conducted by a State or local governmental agency responsible for food safety inspections.

    (2) EXCEPTION.—Paragraph (1) shall not apply to a school if a food safety inspection of the school is required by a State or local governmental agency responsible for food safety inspections.

(i) SINGLE PERMANENT AGREEMENT BETWEEN STATE AGENCY AND SCHOOL FOOD AUTHORITY; COMMON CLAIMS FORM.—

    (1) IN GENERAL.—If a single State agency administers any combination of the school lunch program under this Act, the school breakfast program under section 4 of the Child Nutrition Act of 1966, the summer food service program for children under section 13 of this Act, or the child and adult care food program under section 17 of this Act, the agency shall—

        (A) require each school food authority to submit to the State agency a single agreement with respect to the operation by the authority of the programs administered by the State agency; and

        (B) use a common claims form with respect to meals and supplements served under the programs administered by the State agency.

    (2) ADDITIONAL REQUIREMENT.—The agreement described in paragraph (1)(A) shall be a permanent agreement that may be amended as necessary.

DISBURSEMENT TO SCHOOLS BY THE SECRETARY

SEC. 10. [1759]

(a) The Secretary shall withhold funds payable to a State under this Act and disburse the funds directly to schools, institutions, or service institutions within the State for the purposes authorized by this Act to the extent that the Secretary has so withheld and disbursed such funds continuously since October 1, 1980, but only to such extent (except as otherwise required by subsection (b)). Any funds so withheld and disbursed by the Secretary shall be used for the same purposes, and shall be subject to the same conditions, as applicable to a State disbursing funds made available under this Act. If the Secretary is administering (in whole or in part) any program authorized under this Act, the State in which the Secretary is administering the program may, upon request to the Secretary, assume administration of that program.

(b) If a State educational agency is not permitted by law to disburse the funds paid to it under this Act to any of the nonpublic schools in the State, the Secretary shall disburse the funds directly to such schools within the State for the same purposes and subject to the same conditions as are authorized or required with respect to the disbursements to public schools within the State by the State educational agency.

SPECIAL ASSISTANCE

SEC. 11. [1759a]

(a) (1) (A) Except as provided in section 10 of this Act, in each fiscal year each State educational agency shall receive special assistance payments in an amount equal to the sum of the product obtained by multiplying the number of lunches (consisting of a combination of foods which meet the minimum nutritional requirements prescribed by the Secretary pursuant to subsection 9(a) of this Act) served free to children eligible for such lunches in schools within that State during each fiscal year by the special assistance factor for free lunches prescribed by the Secretary for such fiscal year and the product obtained by multiplying the number of lunches served at a reduced price to children eligible for such reduced price lunches in schools within that State during such fiscal year by the special assistance factor for reduced price lunches prescribed by the Secretary for such fiscal year.

(B) Except as provided in subparagraph (C), (D), or (E), in the case of any school which determines that at least 80 percent of the children in attendance during a school year (hereinafter in this sentence referred to as the "first school year") are eligible for free lunches or reduced price lunches, special assistance payments shall be paid to the State educational agency with respect to that school, if that school so requests for the school year following the first school year, on the basis of the number of free lunches or reduced price lunches, as the case may be, that are served by that school during the school year for which the request is made, to those children who were determined to be so eligible in the first school year and the number of free lunches and reduced price lunches served during that year to other children determined for that year to be eligible for such lunches.

(C) (i) Except as provided in subparagraph (D), in the case of any school that—

(I) elects to serve all children in the school free lunches under the school lunch program during any period of 4 successive school years, or in the case of a school that serves both lunches and breakfasts, elects to serve all children in the school free lunches and free breakfasts under the school lunch program and the school breakfast program established under section 4 of the Child Nutrition Act of 1966 during any period of 4 successive school years; and

(II) pays, from sources other than Federal funds, for the costs of serving the lunches or breakfasts that are in excess of the value of assistance received under this Act and the Child Nutrition Act of 1966 with respect to the number of lunches or breakfasts served during the period;

special assistance payments shall be paid to the State educational agency with respect tot he school during the period on the basis of the number of lunches or breakfasts determined under clause (ii) or (iii).

(ii) For purposes of making special assistance payments under clause (i), except as provided in clause (iii), the number of lunches or breakfasts served by a school to children who are eligible for free lunches or breakfasts or reduced price lunches or breakfasts during each school year of the 4-school-year period shall be considered to be equal to the number of lunches or breakfasts served by the school, to children eligible for free lunches or breakfasts or reduced price lunches or breakfasts during the first school year of the period.

(iii) For purposes of computing the amount of the payments, a school may elect to determine on a more frequent basis the number of children who are eligible for free or reduced price lunches or breakfasts who are served lunches or breakfasts during the 4-school-year period.

(D) (i) In the case of any school that is receiving special assistance payments under this paragraph for a 4-school-year period described in subparagraph (C), the State may grant, at the end o f the 4-school-year period an extension of the period for an additional 4 school years, if the State determines, through available socioeconomic data approved by the Secretary, that the income level of the population of the school has remained stable.

(ii) A school described in clause (i) may reapply to the State at the end of the 4-school-year period, and at the end of each 4-school-year period thereafter for which the school receives special assistance payments under this paragraph, for the purpose of continuing to receive the payments for a subsequent 4-school-year period.

(iii) If the Secretary determines after considering the best available socioeconomic data that the income level of families of children enrolled in a school has not remained stable, the Secretary may require the submission of applications for free and reduced price lunches, or for free and reduced price lunches and breakfasts, in the first school year of any 4-school-year period for which the school receives special assistance payments under this paragraph, for the purpose of calculating the special assistance payments.

(iv) For the purpose of updating information and reimbursement levels, a school described in clause (i) that carries out a school lunch or school breakfast program may at any time require submission of applications for free and reduced price lunches or for free and reduced price lunches and breakfasts.

(E) (i) In the case of any school that—

(I) elects to serve all children in the school free lunches under the school lunch program during any period of 4 successive school years, or in the case of a school that serves both lunches and breakfasts, elects to serve all children in the school free lunches and free breakfasts under the school lunch program and the school breakfast program during any period of 4 successive school years; and

(II) pays, from sources other than Federal funds, for the costs of serving the lunches or breakfasts that are in excess of the value of assistance received under this Act and the Child Nutrition Act of 1966 with respect to the number of lunches or breakfasts served during the period;

total Federal cash reimbursements and total commodity assistance shall be provided to the State educational agency with respect to the school at a level that is equal to the total Federal cash reimbursements and total commodity assistance received by the school in the last school year for which the school accepted applications under the school lunch or school breakfast program, adjusted annually for inflation in accordance with paragraph (3)(B) and for changes in enrollment, to carry out the school lunch or school breakfast program.

(ii) A school described in clause (i) may reapply to the State at the end of the 4-school-year period described in clause (i), and at the end of each 4-school-year period thereafter for which the school receives reimbursements and assistance under this subparagraph, for the purpose of continuing to receive the reimbursements and assistance for a subsequent 4-school-year period. The State may approve an application under this clause if the State determines, through available socioeconomic data approved by the Secretary, that the income level of the population of the school has remained consistent with the income level of the population of the school in the last school year for which the school accepted the applications described in clause (i).

(2) The special assistance factor prescribed by the Secretary for free lunches shall be 98.75 cents and the special assistance factor for reduced price lunches shall be 40 cents less than the special assistance factor for free lunches.

(3) (A) The Secretary shall prescribe on July 1, 1982, and on each subsequent July 1, an annual adjustment in the following:

    (i) The national average payment rates for lunches (as established under section 4 of this Act).

    (ii) The special assistance factor for lunches (as established under paragraph (2) of this subsection.)

    (iii) The national average payment rates for breakfasts (as established under section 4(b) of the Child Nutrition Act of 1966.

    (iv) The national average payment rates for supplements (as established under section 17(c) of this Act).

(B)COMPUTATION OF ADJUSTMENT.—

    (i) IN GENERAL.—The annual adjustment under this paragraph shall reflect changes in the cost of operating meal programs under this Act and the Child Nutrition Act of 1966, as indicated by the change in the series for food away from home of the Consumer Price Index for all Urban Consumers, published by the Bureau of Labor Statistics of the Department of Labor.

    (ii) BASIS.—Each annual adjustment shall reflect the changes in the series for food away from home for the most recent 12-month period for which such data are available.

    (iii) ROUNDING.—

        (I) THROUGH JUNE 30, 1999.—For the period ending June 30, 1999, the adjustments made under this paragraph shall be computed to the nearest one-fourth cent, except that adjustments to payment rates for meals and supplements served to individuals not determined to be eligible for free or reduced price meals and supplements shall be computed to the nearest lower cent increment and based on the unrounded amount for the preceding 12-month period.

        (II) JULY 1, 1999, AND THEREAFTER.—On July 1, 1999, and on each subsequent July 1, the national average payment rates for meals and supplements shall be adjusted to the nearest lower cent increment and shall be based on the unrounded amounts fore the preceding 12-month period.

(b) Except as provided in section 10 of the Child Nutrition Act of 1966, the special assistance payments made to each State agency during each fiscal year under the provisions of this section shall be used by such State agency to assist schools of that State in providing free and reduced price lunches served to children pursuant to subsection 9(b) of this Act. The amount of such special assistance funds that a school shall from time to time receive, within a maximum per lunch amount established by the Secretary for all States, shall be based on the need of the school for such special assistance. Such maximum per lunch amount established by the Secretary shall not be less than 60 cents.

(c) Special assistance payments to any State under this section shall be made as provided in the last sentence of section 7 of this Act.

(d) (1) The Secretary, when appropriate, may request each school participating in the school lunch program under this Act to report monthly to the State educational agency the average number of children in the school who received free lunches and the average number of children who received reduced price lunches during the immediately preceding month.

(2) On request of the Secretary, the State educational agency of each State shall report to the Secretary the average number of children in the State who received free lunches and the average number of children in the State who received reduced price lunches during the immediately preceding month.

(e) Commodity only schools shall also be eligible for special assistance payments under this section. Such schools shall serve meals free to children who meet the eligibility requirements for free meals under section 9(b) of this Act, and shall serve meals at a reduced price, not exceeding the price specified in section 9(b)(3) of this Act, to children meeting the eligibility requirements for reduced price meals under such section. No physical segregation of, or other discrimination against, any child eligible for a free or reduced price lunch shall be made by the school, nor shall there by any overt identification of any such child by any means.

(f) INFORMATION AND ASSISTANCE CONCERNING REIMBURSEMENT OPTIONS—
  (1) IN GENERAL.—From funds made available under paragraph (3), the Secretary shall provide grants to not more than 10 State agencies in each of fiscal years 2000 and 2001 to enable the agencies, in accordance with criteria established by the Secretary, to—
    (A) identify separately in a list—
      (i) schools that are most likely to benefit from electing to receive special assistance under subparagraph (C) or (E) of subsection (a)(1); and
      (ii) schools that may benefit from electing to receive special assistance under subparagraph (C) or (E) of subsection (a)(1);
    (B) make the list of schools identified under this subsection available to each school district within the State and to the public;
    (C) provide technical assistance to schools, or school districts containing the schools, to enable the schools to evaluate and receive special assistance under subparagraph (C) or (E) of subsection (a)(1);
    (D) take any other actions the Secretary determines are consistent with receiving special assistance under subparagraph (C) or (E) of subsection (a)(1) and receiving a grant under this subsection; and
    (E) as soon as practicable after receipt of the grant, but not later than September 30, 2001, take the actions described in subparagraphs (A) through (D).

  (2) REPORT.—
    (A) IN GENERAL.—Not later than January 1, 2002, the Secretary shall submit to the Committee on Education and the Workforce of the House of Representatives and the

Committee on Agriculture, Nutrition and Forestry of the Senate a report on the activities of the State agencies receiving grants under this subsection.

(B) CONTENTS.—In the report, the Secretary shall specify—

(i) the number of schools identified as likely to benefit from electing to receive special assistance under subparagraph (C) or (E) of subsection (a)(1);

(ii) the number of schools identified under this subsection that have elected to receive special assistance under subparagraph (C) or (E) of subsection (a)(1); and

(iii) a description of how the funds and technical assistance made available under this subsection have been used.

(3) FUNDING.—Out of any moneys in the Treasury not otherwise appropriated, the Secretary of the Treasury shall provide to the Secretary $2,250,000 for each of fiscal years 2000 and 2001 to carry out this subsection. The Secretary shall be entitled to receive the funds and shall accept the funds, without further appropriation.

MISCELLANEOUS PROVISIONS AND DEFINITIONS

SEC. 12. [1760]

(a) States, State educational agencies, and schools participating in the school lunch program under this Act shall keep such accounts and records as may be necessary to enable the Secretary to determine whether the provisions of this Act are being complied with. Such accounts and records shall be available at any reasonable time for inspection and audit by representatives of the Secretary and shall be preserved for such period of time, not in excess of five years, as the Secretary determines is necessary.

(b) The Secretary shall incorporate, in the Secretary's agreements with the State educational agencies, the express requirements under this Act with respect to the operation of the school lunch program under this Act insofar as they may be applicable and such other provisions as in the Secretary's opinion are reasonably necessary or appropriate to effectuate the purpose of this Act.

(c) In carrying out the provisions of this Act, the Secretary shall not impose any requirement with respect to teaching personnel, curriculum, instruction, methods of instruction, and materials of instruction in any school.

(d) For the purposes of this Act—

(1) CHILD.—

(A) IN GENERAL.—The term "child" includes an individual, regardless of age, who—

(i) is determined by a State educational agency, in accordance with regulations prescribed by the Secretary, to have one or more disabilities; and

(ii) is attending any institution, as defined in section 17(a), or any nonresidential public or nonprofit private school of high school grade or under, for the purpose of participating in a school program established for individuals with disabilities.

(B) RELATIONSHIP TO CHILD AND ADULT CARE FOOD PROGRAM.—No institution that is not otherwise eligible to participate in the program under section 17 shall be considered eligible because of this paragraph.

(2) "Commodity only schools" means schools that do not participate in the school lunch program under this Act, but which receive commodities made available by the Secretary for use

by such schools in nonprofit lunch programs.

(3) "School" means

    (A) any public or nonprofit private school of high school grade or under, and

    (B) any public or licensed nonprofit private residential child care institution (including, but not limited to, orphanages and homes for the mentally retarded, but excluding Job Corps Centers funded by the Department of Labor). For purposes of this paragraph, the term "nonprofit," when applied to any such private school or institution, means any such school or institution which is exempt from tax under section 501(c)(3) of the Internal Revenue Code of 1986.

(4) "School year" means the annual period from July 1 through June 30.

(5) "Secretary" means the Secretary of Agriculture.

(6) "State" means any of the fifty States, the District of Columbia, the Commonwealth of Puerto Rico, the Virgin Islands, Guam, American Samoa, or the Commonwealth of the Northern Mariana Islands.

(7) "State educational agency" means, as the State legislature may determine,

    (A) the chief State school officer (such as the State superintendent of public instruction, commissioner of education, or similar officer), or

    (B) a board of education controlling the State department of education.

(8) DISABILITY.—The term "disability" has the meaning given the term in the Rehabilitation Act of 1973 for purposes of title II of that Act.

(e) The value of assistance to children under this Act shall not be considered to be income or resources for any purposes under any Federal or State laws, including laws relating to taxation and welfare and public assistance programs.

(f) In providing assistance for breakfasts, lunches, suppers, and supplements served in Alaska, Hawaii, Guam, American Samoa, Puerto Rico, the Virginia Islands of the United States, and the Commonwealth of the Northern Mariana Islands, the Secretary may establish appropriate adjustments for each such State to the national average payment rates prescribed under sections 4, 11, 13, and 17 of this Act and section 4 of the Child Nutrition Act of 1966, to reflect the differences between the costs of providing meals and supplements in those States and the costs of providing meals and supplements in all other States.

(g) Whoever embezzles, willfully misapplies, steals, or obtains by fraud any funds, assets, or property that are the subject of a grant or other form of assistance under this Act or the Child Nutrition Act of 1966, whether received directly or indirectly from the United States Department of Agriculture, or whosoever receives, conceals, or retains such funds, assets, or property to personal use or gain, knowing such funds, assets, or property have been embezzled, willfully misapplied, stolen, or obtained by fraud shall, if such funds, assets, or property are of the value of $100 or more, be fined not more than $25,000 or imprisoned not more than five years, or both, or, if such funds, assets, or property are of a value of less than $100, shall be fined not more than $1,000 or imprisoned for not more than one year, or both.

(h) No provision of this Act or of the Child Nutrition Act of 1966 shall require any school receiving funds under this Act and the Child Nutrition Act of 1966 to account separately for the cost incurred in the school lunch and school breakfast programs.

(i) Facilities, equipment, and personnel provided to a school food authority for a program authorized under this Act or the Child Nutrition Act of 1966 may be used, as determined by a local educational agency, to support a nonprofit nutrition program for the elderly, including a program funded under the Older Americans Act of 1965.

(j) (1) Except as provided in paragraph (2), the Secretary may provide reimbursements for final claims for service of meals, supplements, and milk submitted to State agencies by eligible schools, summer camps, family day care homes, institutions, and service institutions only if—

(A) the claims have been submitted to the State agencies not later than 60 days after the last day of the month for which the reimbursement is claimed; and

(B) the final program operations report for the month is submitted to the Secretary not later than 90 days after the first day of the month.

(2) The Secretary may waive the requirements of paragraph (1) at the discretion of the Secretary.

(k) (1) Not later than June 1, 1995, the Secretary shall issue final regulations to conform the nutritional requirements of the school lunch and breakfast programs with the guidelines contained in the most recent "Dietary Guidelines for Americans" that is published under section 301 of the National Nutrition Monitoring and Related Research Act of 1990. The final regulations shall include—

(A) rules permitting the use of food-based menu systems; and

(B) adjustments to the rule on nutrition objectives for school meals published in the Federal Register on June 10, 1994.

(2) No school food service authority shall be required to implement final regulations issued pursuant to this subsection until the regulations have been final for at least 1 year.

(l) (1) (A) Except as provided in paragraph (4), the Secretary may waive any requirement under this Act or the Child Nutrition Act of 1966, or any regulation issued under either such Act, for a State or eligible service provider that requests a waiver if—

(i) the Secretary determines that the waiver of the requirement would facilitate the ability of the State or eligible service provider to carry out the purpose of the program;

(ii) the State or eligible service provider has provided notice and information to the public regarding the proposed waiver; and

(iii) the State or eligible service provider demonstrates to the satisfaction of the Secretary that the waiver will not increase the overall cost of the program to the Federal Government, and, if the waiver does increase the overall cost to the Federal Government, the cost will be paid from non-Federal funds.

(B) The notice and information referred to in subparagraph (A)(ii) shall be provided in the same manner in which the State or eligible service provider customarily provides similar notices and information to the public.

(2) (A) To request a waiver under paragraph (1), a State or eligible service provider (through the appropriate administering State agency) shall submit an application to the Secretary that—

(i) identifies the statutory or regulatory requirements that are requested to be waived;

(ii) in the case of a State requesting a waiver, describes actions, if any, that the State has undertaken to remove State statutory or regulatory barriers;

(iii) describes the goal of the waiver to improve services under the program and the expected outcomes if the waiver is granted; and

(iv) includes a description of the impediments to the efficient operation and administration of the program.

(B) An application described in subparagraph (A) shall be developed by the State or eligible service provider and shall be submitted to the Secretary by the State.

(3) The Secretary shall act promptly on a waiver request contained in an application submitted under paragraph (2) and shall either grant or deny the request. The Secretary shall state in writing the reasons for granting or denying the request.

(4) The Secretary may not grant a waiver under this subsection that increases Federal costs or that relates to—

(A) the nutritional content of meals served;

(B) Federal reimbursement rates;

(C) the provision of free and reduced price meals;

(D) limits on the price charged for a reduced price meal;

(E) maintenance of effort;

(F) equitable participation of children in private schools;

(G) distribution of funds to State and local school food service authorities and service institutions participating in a program under this Act and the Child Nutrition Act of 1966.

(H) the disclosure of information relating to students receiving free or reduced price meals and other recipients of benefits;

(I) prohibiting the operation of a profit producing program;

(J) the sale of competitive foods;

(K) the commodity distribution program under section 14;

(L) the special supplemental nutrition program authorized under section 17 of the Child Nutrition Act of 1966; or

(M) enforcement of any constitutional or statutory right of an individual, including any right under—

    (i) title VI of the Civil Rights Act of 1964;

    (ii) section 504 of the Rehabilitation Act of 1973;

    (iii) title IX of the Education Amendments of 1972;

    (iv) the Age Discrimination Act of 1975;

    (v) the Americans with Disabilities Act of 1990; and

    (vi) the Individuals with Disabilities Education Act.

(5) The Secretary shall periodically review the performance of any State or eligible service provider for which the Secretary has granted a waiver under this subsection and shall terminate the waiver if the performance of the State or service provider has been inadequate to justify a continuation of the waiver. The Secretary shall terminate the waiver if, after periodic review, the Secretary determines that the waiver has resulted in an increase in the overall cost of the program to the Federal Government and the increase has not been paid for in accordance with paragraph (1)(A)(iii).

(6) The Secretary shall annually submit to the Committee on Education and Labor of the House of Representatives and the Committee on Agriculture, Nutrition, and Forestry of the Senate, a report—

(A) summarizing the use of waivers by the State and eligible service providers;

(B) describing whether the waivers resulted in improved services to children;

(C) describing the impact of the waivers on providing nutritional meals to participants; and

    (D) describing how the waivers reduced the quantity of paperwork necessary to administer the program.

   (7) As used in this subsection, the term "eligible service provider" means—

    (A) a local school food service authority;

    (B) a service institution or private nonprofit organization described in section 13; or

    (C) a family or group day care home sponsoring organization described in section 17.

(m) (1)   The Secretary, acting through the Administrator of the Food and Nutrition Service or through the Extension Service, shall award on an annual basis grants to a private nonprofit organization or educational institution in each of 3 States to create, operate, and demonstrate food and nutrition projects that are fully integrated with elementary school curricula.

   (2)   Each organization or institution referred to in paragraph (1) shall be selected by the Secretary and shall—

    (A) assist local schools and educators in offering food and nutrition education that integrates math, science, and verbal skills in the elementary grads;

    (B) assist local schools and educators in teaching agricultural practices through practical applications, like gardening;

    (C) create community service learning opportunities or educational programs;

    (D) be experienced in assisting in the creation of curriculum-based models in elementary schools;

    (E) be sponsored by an organization or institution, or be an organization or institution, that provides information, or conducts other educational efforts, concerning the success and productivity of American agriculture and the importance of the free enterprise system to the quality of life in the United States; and

    (F) be able to provide model curricula, examples, advice, and guidance to schools, community groups, States, and local organizations regarding means of carrying out similar projects.

   (3) Subject to the availability of appropriations to carry out this subsection, the Secretary shall make grants to each of the 3 private organizations or institutions selected under this subsection in amounts of not less than $100,000, nor more than $200,000, for each fiscal years 1995 through 2003.

   (4)   The Secretary shall establish fair and reasonable auditing procedures regarding the expenditure of funds under this subsection.

   (5)   There are authorized to be appropriated to carry out this subsection such sums as are necessary for each of fiscal years 1995 through 2003.

(n) BUY AMERICAN.—

   (1) DEFINITION OF DOMESTIC COMMODITY OR PRODUCT.—In this subsection, the term "domestic commodity or product" means—

    (A) an agricultural commodity that is produced in the United States; and

    (B) a food product that is processed in the United States substantially using agricultural commodities that are produced in the United States.

   (2) REQUIREMENT.—

    (A) IN GENERAL.—Subject to subparagraph (B), the Secretary shall require that a school food authority purchase to the maximum extent practicable, domestic commodities or products.

(B) LIMITATIONS.—Subparagraph (A) shall apply only to—
(i) a school food authority located in the contiguous United States; and
(ii) a purchase of a domestic commodity or product for the school lunch program under this Act or the school breakfast program under section 4 of the Child Nutrition Act of 1966.
(3) APPLICABILITY TO HAWAII.—Paragraph (2)(A) shall apply to a school food authority in Hawaii with respect to domestic commodities or products that are produced in Hawaii in sufficient quantities to meet the needs of meals provided under the school lunch program under this Act or the school breakfast program under section 4 of the Child Nutrition Act of 1966.
(o) PROCUREMENT CONTRACTS.—In acquiring a good or service for programs under this Act or the Child Nutrition Act of 1966 (other than section 17 of that Act), a State, State agency, school, or school food authority may enter into a contract with a person that has provided specification information to the State, State agency, school, or school food authority for use in developing contract specifications for acquiring such good or service.

SUMMER FOOD SERVICE PROGRAM FOR CHILDREN

SEC. 13.

(a) (1) The Secretary is authorized to carry out a program to assist States, through grants-in-aid and other means, to initiate and maintain nonprofit food service programs for children in service institutions. For purposes of this section,
(A) "program" means the summer food service program for children authorized by this section;
(B) "service institutions" means public or private nonprofit school food authorities, local, municipal, or county governments, public or private nonprofit higher education institutions participating in the National Youth Sports Program, and residential public or private nonprofit summer camps, that develop special summer or school vacation programs providing food service similar to that made available to children during the school year under the school lunch program under this Act or the school breakfast program under the Child Nutrition Act of 1966;
(C) "areas in which poor economic conditions exist" means areas in which at least 50 percent of the children are eligible for free or reduced price school meals under this Act and the Child Nutrition Act of 1966, as determined by information provided from departments of welfare, zoning commissions, census tracts, by the number of free and reduced price lunches or breakfasts served to children attending public and nonprofit private schools located in the area of program food service sites, or from other appropriate sources, including statements of eligibility based upon income for children enrolled in the program;
(D) "children" means individuals who are eighteen years of age and under, and individuals who are older than eighteen who are
(i) determined by a State educational agency or a local public educational agency of a State, in accordance with regulations prescribed by the Secretary, to have a disability, and

(ii) participating in a public or nonprofit private school program established for individuals who have a disability; and

(E) "State" means any of the fifty States, the District of Columbia, the Commonwealth of Puerto Rico, the Virgin Islands of the United States, Guam, American Samoa, and the Northern Mariana Islands.

(2) To the maximum extent feasible, consistent with the purposes of this section, any food service under the program shall use meals prepared at the facilities of the service institution or at the food service facilities of public and nonprofit private schools. The Secretary shall assist States in the development of information and technical assistance to encourage increased service of meals prepared at the facilities of service institutions and at public and nonprofit private schools.

(3) Eligible service institutions entitled to participate in the program shall be limited to those that—

(A) demonstrate adequate administrative and financial responsibility to manage an effective food service;

(B) have not been seriously deficient in operating under the program;

(C) (i) conduct a regularly scheduled food service for children from areas in which poor economic conditions exist; or

(ii) qualify as camps; and

(D) provide an ongoing year-round service to the community to be served under the program (except that an otherwise eligible service institution shall not be disqualified for failure to meet his requirement for ongoing year-round service if the State determines that its disqualification would result in an area in which poor economic conditions exist not being served or in a significant number of needy children not having reasonable access to a summer food service program).

(4) The following order of priority shall be used by the State in determining participation where more than one eligible service institution proposes to serve the same area;

(A) Local schools.

(B) All other service institutions and private nonprofit organizations eligible under paragraph (7) that have demonstrated successful program performance in a prior year.

(C) New public institutions.

(D) New private nonprofit organizations eligible under paragraph (7).

The Secretary and the States, in carrying out their respective functions under this section, shall actively seek eligible service institutions located in rural areas, for the purpose of assisting such service institutions in applying to participate in the program.

(5) Camps that satisfy all other eligibility requirements of this section shall receive reimbursement only for meals served to children who meet the eligibility requirements for free or reduced price meals, as determined under this Act and the Child Nutrition Act of 1966.

(6) Service institutions that are local, municipal, or county governments shall be eligible for reimbursement for meals served in programs under this section only if such programs are operated directly by such governments.

(7) (A) Private nonprofit organizations, as defined in subparagraph (B) (other than organizations eligible under paragraph (1)), shall be eligible for the program under the same terms and conditions as other service institutions.

(B) As used in this paragraph, the term "private nonprofit organizations" means those organizations that—

    (i) operate—

        (I) not more than 25 sites, with not more than 300 children being served at any one site; or

        (II) with a waiver granted by the State agency under standards developed by the Secretary, with not more than 500 children being served at any one site;

    (ii) exercise full control and authority over the operation of the program at all sites under their sponsorship;

    (iii) provide ongoing year-around activities for children or families;

    (iv) demonstrate that such organizations have adequate management and the fiscal capacity to operate a program under this section; and

    (v) meet applicable State and local health, safety, and sanitation standards.

(b) SERVICE INSTITUTIONS

    (1) PAYMENTS.—

    (A) IN GENERAL.—Except as otherwise provided in this paragraph, payments to service institutions shall equal the full cost of food service operations (which cost shall include the costs of obtaining, preparing, and serving food, but shall not include administrative costs).

    (B) MAXIMUM AMOUNTS.—Subject to subparagraph (c), payments to any institution under subparagraph (A) shall not exceed—

        (i) $1.97 for each lunch and supper served:

        (ii) $1.13 for each breakfast served; and

        (iii) 46 cents for each meal supplement served.

    (C) ADJUSTMENTS.—Amounts specified in subparagraph (B) shall be adjusted on January 1, 1997, and each January 1 thereafter, to the nearest lower cent increment to reflect changes for the 12-month period ending the preceding November 30 in the series for food away from home of the Consumer Price Index for All Urban Consumers published by the Bureau of Labor Statistics of the Department of Labor. Each adjustment shall be based on the unrounded adjustment for the prior 12-month period.

    (2) Any service institution may only serve lunch and either breakfast or a meal supplement during each day of operation, except that any service institution that is a camp or that serves meals primarily to migrant children may serve up to 3 meals, or 2 meals and 1 supplement, during each day of operation, if

    (A) the service institution has the administrative capability and the food preparation and food holding capabilities (where applicable) to serve more than one meal per day, and

    (B) the service period of different meals does not coincide or overlap.

    (3) Every service institution, when applying for participation in the program, shall submit a complete budget for administrative costs related to the program, which shall be subject to approval by the State. Payment to service institutions for administrative costs shall equal the full amount of State approved administrative costs incurred, except that such payment to service institutions may not exceed the maximum allowable levels determined by the Secretary pursuant to the study prescribed in paragraph (4) of this subsection.

    (4) (A) The Secretary shall conduct a study of the food service operations carried out under the program. Such study shall include, but shall not be limited to—

(i) an evaluation of meal quality as related to costs; and

(ii) a determination whether adjustments in the maximum reimbursement levels for food service operation costs prescribed in paragraph (1) of this subsection should be made, including whether different reimbursement levels should be established for self-prepared meals and vendored meals and which site-related costs, if any, should be considered as part of administrative costs.

(B) The Secretary shall also study the administrative costs of service institutions participating in the program and shall thereafter prescribe maximum allowable levels for administrative payments that reflect the costs of such service institutions, taking into account the number of sites and children served, and such other factors as the Secretary determines appropriate to further the goals of efficient and effective administration of the program.

(C) The Secretary shall report the results of such studies to Congress not later than December 1, 1977.

(c) (1) Payments shall be made to service institutions only for meals served during the months of May through September, except in the case of service institutions that operate food service programs for children on school vacation at any time under a continuous school calendar or that provide meal service at non-school sites to children who are not in school for a period during the months of October through April due to a natural disaster, building repair, court order, or similar cause.

(2) Children participating in National Youth Sports Programs operated by higher education institutions shall be eligible to participate in the program under this paragraph on showing residence in areas in which poor economic conditions exist or on the basis of income eligibility statements for children enrolled in the program.

(d) Not later than April 15, May 15, and July 1 of each year, the Secretary shall forward to each State a letter of credit (advance program payment) that shall be available to each State for the payment of meals to be served in the month for which the letter of credit is issued. The amount of the advance program payment shall be an amount which the State demonstrates, to the satisfaction of the Secretary, to be necessary for advance program payments to service institutions in accordance with subsection (e) of this section. The Secretary shall also forward such advance program payments, by the first day of the month prior to the month in which the program will be conducted, to States that operate the program in months other than May through September. The Secretary shall forward any remaining payments due pursuant to subsection (b) of this section not later than sixty days following receipt of valid claims therefor.

(e) (1) Not later than June 1, July 15, and August 15 of each year, or, in the case of service institutions that operate under a continuous school calendar, the first day of each month of operation, the State shall forward advance program payments to each service institution. The State shall not release the second month's advance program payment to any service institution (excluding a school) that has not certified that it has held training sessions for its own personnel and the site personnel with regard to program duties and responsibilities. No advance program payment may be made for any month in which the service institution will operate under the program for less than ten days.

(2) The amount of the advance program payment for any month in the case of any service institution shall be an amount equal to

(A) the total program payment for meals served by such service institution in the same calendar month of the preceding calendar year,

(B) 50 percent of the amount established by the State to be needed by such service institution for meals if such service institution contracts with a food service management company, or

(C) 65 percent of the amount established by the State to be needed by such service institution for meals if such service institution prepares its own meals, whichever amount is greatest: *Provided*, That the advance program payment may not exceed the total amount estimated by the State to be needed by such service institution for meals to be served in the month for which such advance program payment is made or $40,000, whichever is less, except that a State may make a larger advance program payment to such service institution where the State determines that such larger payment is necessary for the operation of the program by such service institution and sufficient administrative and management capability to justify a larger payment is demonstrated. The State shall forward any remaining payment due a service institution not later than seventy-five days following receipt of valid claims. If the State has reason to believe that a service institution will not be able to submit a valid claim for reimbursement covering the period for which an advance program payment has been made, the subsequent month's advance program payment shall be withheld until such time as the State has received a valid claim. Program payments advanced to service institutions that are not subsequently deducted from a valid claim for reimbursement shall be repaid upon demand by the State. Any prior payment that is under dispute may be subtracted from an advance program payment.

(f) (1) Service institutions receiving funds under this section shall serve meals consisting of a combination of foods and meeting minimum nutritional standards prescribed by the Secretary on the basis of tested nutritional research.

(2) The Secretary shall provide technical assistance to service institutions and private nonprofit organizations participating in the program to assist the institutions and organizations in complying with the nutritional requirements prescribed by the Secretary pursuant to this subsection.

(3) Meals described in paragraph (1) shall be served without cost to children attending service institutions approved for operation under this section, except that, in the case of camps, charges may be made for meals served to children other than those who meet the eligibility requirements for free or reduced price meals in accordance with subsection (a)(5) of this section.

(4) To assure meal quality, States shall, with the assistance of the Secretary, prescribe model meal specifications and model food quality standards, and ensure that all service institutions contracting for the preparation of meals with food service management companies include in their contracts menu cycles, local food safety standards, and food quality standards approved by the State.

(5) Such contracts shall require

(A) periodic inspections, by an independent agency or the local health department for the locality in which the meals are served, of meals prepared in accordance with the contract in order to determine bacteria levels present in such meals, and

(B) conformance with standards set by local health authorities.

(6) Such inspections and any testing resulting therefrom shall be in accordance with the

practices employed by such local health authority.

(7) OFFER VERSUS SERVE.—A school food authority participating as a service institution may permit a child to refuse one or more items of a meal that the child does not intend to consume, under rules that the school uses for school meals programs. A refusal of an offered food item shall not affect the amount of payments made under this section to a school for the meal.

(g) The Secretary shall publish proposed regulations relating to the implementation of the program by November 1 of each fiscal year, final regulations by January 1 of each fiscal year, and guidelines, applications and handbooks by February 1 of each fiscal year. In order to improve program planning, the Secretary may provide that service institutions be paid as startup costs not to exceed 20 percent of the administrative funds provided for in the administrative budget approved by the State under subsection (b)(3) of this section. Any payments made for startup costs shall be subtracted from amounts otherwise payable for administrative costs subsequently made to service institutions under subsection (b)(3) of this section.

(h) Each service institution shall, insofar as practicable, use its food service under the program foods designated from time to time by the Secretary as being in abundance. The Secretary is authorized to donate to States, for distribution to service institutions, food available under section 416 of the Agriculture Act of 1949, or purchased under section 32 of the Act of August 24, 1935, or section 709 of the Food and Agriculture Act of 1965. Donated foods may be distributed only to service institutions that can use commodities efficiently and effectively, as determined by the Secretary.

[(i) Repealed]

(j) Expenditures of funds from State and local sources for the maintenance of food programs for children shall not be diminished as a result of funds received under this section.

(k) (1) The Secretary shall pay to each State for its administrative costs incurred under this section in any fiscal year an amount equal to

(A) 20 percent of the first $50,000 in funds distributed to that State for the program in the preceding fiscal year;

(B) 10 percent of the next $100,000 distributed to that State for the program in the preceding fiscal year;

(C) 5 percent of the next $250,000 in funds distributed to that State for the program in the preceding fiscal year, and

(D) 2 ½ percent of any remaining funds distributed to that State for the program in the preceding fiscal year: *Provided,* That such amounts may be adjusted by the Secretary to reflect changes in the size of that State's program since the preceding fiscal year.

(2) The Secretary shall establish standards and effective dates for the proper, efficient, and effective administration of the program by the State. If the Secretary finds that the State has failed without good cause to meet any of the Secretary's standards or has failed without good cause to meet any of the Secretary's standards or has failed without good cause to carry out the approved State management and administration plan under subsection (n) of this section, the Secretary may withhold from the State such funds authorized under this subsection as the Secretary determines to be appropriate.

(3) To provide for adequate nutritional and food quality monitoring, and to further the implementation of the program, an additional amount, not to exceed the lesser of actual costs or 1 percent of program funds, shall be made available by the Secretary to States to pay for State

or local health department inspections, and to reinspect facilities and deliveries to test meal quality.

(l) (1) Service institutions may contract on a competitive basis with food service management companies for the furnishing of meals or management of the entire food service under the program, except that a food service management company entering into a contract with a service institution under this section may not subcontract with a single company for the total meal, with or without milk, or for the assembly of the meal. The Secretary shall prescribe additional conditions and limitations governing assignment of all or any part of a contract entered into by a food service management company under this section. Any food service management company shall, in its bid, provide the service institution information as to its meal capacity.

(2) Each State may provide for the registration of food service management companies.

(3) In accordance with regulations issued by the Secretary, positive efforts shall be made by service institutions to use small businesses and minority-owned businesses as sources of supplies and services. Such efforts shall afford those sources the maximum feasible opportunity to compete for contracts using program funds.

(4) Each State, with the assistance of the Secretary, shall establish a standard form of contract for use by service institutions and food service management companies. The Secretary shall prescribe requirements governing bid and contract procedures for acquisition of the services of food service management companies, including, but not limited to, bonding requirements (which may provide exemptions applicable to contracts of $100,000 or less), procedures for review of contracts by States, and safeguards to prevent collusive bidding activities between service institutions and food service management companies.

(m) States and service institutions participating in programs under this section shall keep such accounts and records as may be necessary to enable the Secretary to determine whether there has been compliance with this section and the regulations issued hereunder. Such accounts and records shall be available at any reasonable time for inspection and audit by representatives of the Secretary and shall be preserved for such period of time, not in excess of five years, as the Secretary determines necessary.

(n) Each State desiring to participate in the program shall notify the Secretary by January 1 of each year of its intent to administer the program and shall submit for approval by February 15 a management and administration plan for the program for the fiscal year, which shall include, but not be limited to,

(1) the State's administrative budget for the fiscal year, and the State's plans to comply with any standards prescribed by the Secretary under subsection (k) of this section;

(2) the State's plans for use of program funds and funds from within the State to the maximum extent practicable to reach needy children;

(3) the State's plans for providing technical assistance and training eligible service institutions;

(4) the State's plans for monitoring and inspecting service institutions, feeding sites, and food service management companies and for ensuring that such companies do not enter into contracts for more meals than they can provide effectively and efficiently;

(5) the State's plan for timely and effective action against program violators; and

(6) the State's plan for ensuring fiscal integrity by auditing service institutions not subject to auditing requirements prescribed by the Secretary.

(o) (1) Whoever, in connection with any application, procurement, recordkeeping entry, claim for reimbursement, or other document or statement made in connection with the program, knowingly and willfully falsifies, conceals, or covers up by any trick, scheme, or device a material fact, or makes any false, fictitious, or fraudulent statements or representations, or makes or uses any false writing or document knowing the same to contain any false, fictitious or fraudulent statement or entry, or whoever, in connection with the program, knowingly makes an opportunity for any person to defraud the United States, or does or omits to do any act with intent to enable any person to defraud the United States, shall be fined not more than $10,000 or imprisoned not more than five years, or both.

(2) Whoever being a partner, officer, director, or managing agent connected in any capacity with any partnership, association, corporation, business, or organization, either public or private, that receives benefits under the program, knowingly or willfully embezzles, misapplies, steals, or obtains by fraud, false statement, or forgery, any benefits provided by this section or any money, funds, assets, or property derived from benefits provided by this section, shall be fined not more than $10,000 or imprisoned for not more than five years, or both (but, if the benefits, money, funds, assets, or property involved is not over $200, then the penalty shall be a fine or not more than $1,000 or imprisonment for not more than one year, or both).

(3) If two or more persons conspire or collude to accomplish any act made unlawful under this subsection, and one or more of such persons to any act to effect the object of the conspiracy or collusion, each shall be fined not more than $10,000 or imprisoned for not more than five years, or both.

(p) (1) In addition to the normal monitoring of organizations receiving assistance under this section, the Secretary shall establish a system under which the Secretary and the States shall monitor the compliance of private nonprofit organizations with the requirements of this section and with regulations issued to implement this section.

(2) In the fiscal year 1990 and each succeeding fiscal year, the Secretary may reserve for purposes of carrying out paragraph (1) not more than ½ of 1 percent of amounts appropriated for purposes of carrying out this section.

(q) For the fiscal year beginning October 1, 1977, and each succeeding fiscal year ending before October 1, 2003, there are hereby authorized to be appropriated such sums as are necessary to carry out the purposes of this section.

◆ ◆ ◆ ◆ ◆ ◆

COMMODITY DISTRIBUTION PROGRAM

SEC. 14. [1762]

(a) Notwithstanding any other provision of law, the Secretary, during the period beginning July 1, 1974, and ending September 30, 2003, shall—

(1) use funds available to carry out the provisions of section 32 of the Act of August 24, 1935 which are not expended or needed to carry out such provisions, to purchase (without regard to the provisions of existing law governing the expenditure of public funds) agricultural commodities and their products of the types customarily purchased under such section (which may include domestic seafood commodities and their products, for donation to maintain the annually programmed level of assistance for programs carried on under this Act, the Child Nutrition Act of 1966 and title III of the Older Americans Act of 1965; and

(2) if stocks of the Commodity Credit Corporation are not available, use the funds of such

Corporation to purchase agricultural commodities and their products of the types customarily available under section 416 of the Agricultural Act of 1949, for such donation.

(b) (1) The Secretary shall maintain and continue to improve the overall nutritional quality of entitlement commodities provided to schools to assist the schools in improving the nutritional content of meals.

(2) The Secretary shall—

(A) require that nutritional content information labels be placed on packages or shipments of entitlement commodities provided to the schools; or

(B) otherwise provide nutritional content information regarding the commodities provided to the schools.

(c) The Secretary may use funds appropriated from the general fund of the Treasury to purchase agricultural commodities and their products of the types customarily purchased for donation under section 311(a)(4) of the Older Americans Act of 1965 or for cash payments in lieu of such donations under section 311(b)(1) of such Act. There are hereby authorized to be appropriated such sums as are necessary to carry out the purposes of this subsection.

(d) In providing assistance under this Act and the Child Nutrition Act of 1966 for school lunch and breakfast programs, the Secretary shall establish procedures which will—

(1) ensure that the views of local school districts and private nonprofit schools with respect to the type of commodity assistance needed in schools are fully and accurately reflected in reports to the Secretary by the State with respect to State commodity preferences and that such views are considered by the Secretary in the purchase and distribution of commodities and by the States in the allocation of such commodities among schools within the States;

(2) solicit the views of States with respect to the acceptability of commodities;

(3) ensure that the timing of commodity deliveries to States is consistent with State school year calendars and that such deliveries occur with sufficient advance notice;

(4) provide for systematic review of the costs and benefits of providing commodities of the kind and quantity that are suitable to the needs of local school districts and private nonprofit schools; and

(5) make available technical assistance on the use of commodities available under this Act and the Child Nutrition Act of 1966.

Within eighteen months after the date of the enactment of this subsection [enacted on November 10, 1977], the Secretary shall report to Congress on the impact of procedures established under this subsection, including the nutritional, economic, and administrative benefits of such procedures. In purchasing commodities for programs carried out under this Act and the Child Nutrition Act of 1966, the Secretary shall establish procedures to ensure that contracts for the purchase of such commodities shall not be entered into unless the previous history and current patterns of the contracting party with respect to compliance with applicable meat inspection laws and with other appropriate standards relating to the wholesomeness of food for human consumption are taken into account.

(e) Each State agency that receives food assistance payments under this section for any school year shall consult with representatives of schools in the State that participate in the school lunch program with respect to the needs of such schools relating to the manner of selection and distribution of commodity assistance for such program.

(f) Commodity only schools shall be eligible to receive donated commodities equal in value to the sum of the national average value of donated foods established under section 6(c) of this Act and the national average payment established under section 4 of this Act. Such schools shall be eligible to receive up to 5 cents per meal of such value in cash for processing and handling expenses related to the use of such commodities. Lunches served in such schools shall consist of a combination of foods which meet the minimum nutritional requirements prescribed by the Secretary under section 9(a) of this Act, and shall represent the four basic food groups, including a serving of fluid milk.

(g) (1) As used in this subsection, the term "eligible school district' has the same meaning given such term in section 1581 (a) of the Food Security Act of 1985.

(2) In accordance with the terms and conditions of section 1581 of such Act, the Secretary shall permit an eligible school district to continue to receive assistance in the form of cash or commodity letters of credit assistance, in lieu of commodities, to carry out the school lunch program operated in the district.

◆ ◆ ◆ ◆ ◆ ◆

ELECTION TO RECEIVE CASH PAYMENTS

SEC. 16. [1765]

(a) Notwithstanding any other provision of law, where a State phased out its commodity distribution facilities prior to June 30, 1974, such State may, for purposes of the programs authorized by this Act and the Child Nutrition Act of 1966, elect to receive cash payments in lieu of donated foods. Where such an election is made, the Secretary shall make cash payments to such State in an amount equivalent in value to the donated foods that the State would otherwise have received if it had retained its commodity distribution facilities. The amount of cash payments in the case of lunches shall be governed by section 6(c) of this Act.

(b) When such payments are made, the State educational agency shall promptly and equitably disburse any cash it receives in lieu of commodities to eligible schools and institutions, and such disbursements shall be used by such schools and institutions to purchase United States agricultural commodities and other foods for their food service programs.

SEC. 17A. [1766a] MEAL SUPPLEMENTS FOR CHILDREN IN AFTERSCHOOL CARE.

(a) GENERAL AUTHORITY.—

(1) GRANTS TO STATES.—The Secretary shall carry out a program to assist States through grants-in-aid and other means to provide meal supplements under a program organized primarily to provide care for children in afterschool care in eligible elementary and secondary schools.

(2) ELIGIBLE SCHOOLS.—For the purposes of this section, the term "eligible elementary and secondary schools" means schools that—

(A) operate school lunch programs under this Act;

(B) sponsor afterschool care programs; and

(C) operate afterschool programs with an educational or enrichment purpose.

(b)   ELIGIBLE CHILDREN.—Reimbursement may be provided under this section only for supplements served to school children who are not more than 18 years of age, except that the age limitation provided by this subsection shall not apply to a child described in section 12(d)(1)(A).

(c)   REIMBURSEMENT.—

(1)   AT-RISK SCHOOL CHILDREN.—In the case of an eligible child who is participating in a program authorized under this section operated at a site located in a geographical area served by a school in which at least 50 percent of the children enrolled are certified as eligible to receive free or reduced price school meals under this Act or the Child Nutrition Act of 1966, a supplement provided under this section to the child shall be—

(A)   reimbursed at the rate at which free supplements are reimbursed under section 17(c)(3); and

(B)   served without charge.

(2)   OTHER SCHOOL CHILDREN.—In the case of an eligible child who is participating in a program authorized under this section at a site that is not described in paragraph (1), for the purposes of this section, the national average payment rate for supplements shall be equal to those established under section 17(c)(3) (as adjusted pursuant to section 11(a)(3)).

(d)   CONTENTS OF SUPPLEMENTS.—The requirements that apply to the content of meal supplements served under child care food programs operated with assistance under this Act shall apply to the content of meal supplements served under programs operated with assistance under this section.

SEC. 21. [1769b-1] TRAINING, TECHNICAL ASSISTANCE, AND FOOD SERVICE MANAGEMENT INSTITUTE.

(a)   GENERAL AUTHORITY.—The Secretary—

(1)   subject to the availability of, and from, amounts appropriated pursuant to subsection (e)(1), shall conduct training activities and provide technical assistance to improve the skills of individuals employed in—

(A)   food service programs carried out with assistance under this Act;

(B)   school breakfast programs carried out with assistance under section 4 of the Child Nutrition Act of 1966; and

(C)   as appropriate, other federally assisted feeding programs; and

(2)   from amounts appropriated pursuant to subsection (e)(2), is authorized to provide financial and other assistance to the University of Mississippi, in cooperation with the University of Southern Mississippi, to establish and maintain a food service management institute.

(b)   MINIMUM REQUIREMENTS.—The activities conducted and assistance provided as required by subsection (a)(1) shall at least include activities and assistance with respect to—

(1)   menu planning;

(2)   implementation of regulations and appropriate guidelines; and

(3)   compliance with program requirements and accountability for program operations.

(c)   DUTIES OF FOOD SERVICE MANAGEMENT INSTITUTE.—

(1)   IN GENERAL.—Any food service management institute established as authorized ⊦ subsection (a)(2) shall carry out activities to improve the general operation and quality of

(A) food service programs assisted under this Act;

(B) school breakfast programs assisted under section 4 of the Child Nutrition Act of 1966; and

(C) as appropriate, other federally assisted feeding programs.

(2) REQUIRED ACTIVITIES.—Activities carried out under paragraph (1) shall include—

(A) conducting research necessary to assist schools and other organizations that participate in such programs in providing high quality, nutritious, cost-effective meal service to the children served;

(B) providing training and technical assistance with respect to—

   (i) efficient sue of physical resources;

   (ii) financial management;

   (iii) efficient use of computers;

   (iv) procurement;

   (v) sanitation;

   (vi) safety;

   (vii) food handling;

   (viii) meal planning and related nutrition activities;

   (ix) culinary skills; and

   (x) other appropriate activities;

(C) establishing a national network of trained professionals to present training programs and workshops for food service personnel;

(D) developing training materials for use in the programs and workshops described in subparagraph (C);

(E) acting as a clearinghouse for research, studies, and findings concerning all aspects of the operation of food service programs, including activities carried out with assistance provided under section 19 of the Child Nutrition Act of 1966;

(F) training food service personnel to comply with the nutrition guidance and objectives established by the Secretary through a national network of instructors or other means;

(G) preparing informational materials, such as video instruction tapes and menu planners, to promote healthier food preparation; and

(H) assisting State educational agencies in providing additional nutrition and health instructions and instructors, including training personnel to comply with the nutrition guidance and objectives established by the Secretary.

(d) COORDINATION.—

(1) IN GENERAL.—The Secretary shall coordinate activities carried out and assistance provided as required by subsection (b) with activities carried out by any food service management institute established as authorized by subsection (a)(2).

(2) USE OF INSTITUTE FOR DIETARY AND NUTRITION ACTIVITIES.—The Secretary shall use any food service management institute established under subsection (a)(2) to assist in carrying out dietary and nutrition activities of the Secretary.

(e) AUTHORIZATION OF APPROPRIATIONS.—

(1) TRAINING ACTIVITIES AND TECHNICAL ASSISTANCE.—There are authorized to be appropriated to carry out subsection (a)(1) $3,000,000 for fiscal year 1990, $2,000,000 for fiscal year 1991, and $1,000,000 for each of fiscal years 1992 through 2003.

(2) FOOD SERVICE MANAGEMENT INSTITUTE.—

(A) FUNDING.—In addition to any amounts otherwise made available for fiscal year 1995, out of any moneys in the Treasury not otherwise appropriated, the Secretary of the Treasury shall provide to the Secretary $147,000 for fiscal year 1995, $2,000,000 for each of fiscal years 1996 through 1998, and $3,000,000 for fiscal year 1999 and each subsequent fiscal year, to carry out subsection (a)(2). The Secretary shall be entitled to receive the funds and shall accept the funds, without further appropriation.

(B) ADDITIONAL FUNDING.—In addition to amounts made available under subparagraph (A), there are authorized to be appropriated to carry out subsection (a)(2) such sums as are necessary for fiscal year 1995 and each subsequent fiscal year. The Secretary shall carry out activities under subsection (a)(2), in addition to the activities funded under subparagraph (A), to the extent provided for, and in such amounts as are provided for, in advance in appropriations Acts.

(C) FUNDING FOR EDUCATION, TRAINING, OR APPLIED RESEARCH OR STUDIES.—In addition to amounts made available under subparagraphs (A) and (B), from amounts otherwise appropriated to the Secretary in discretionary appropriations, the Secretary may provide funds to any food service management institute established under subsection (a)(2) for projects specified by the Secretary that will contribute to implementing dietary or nutrition initiatives. Any additional funding under this subparagraph shall be provided noncompetitively in a separate cooperative agreement.

SEC. 22. [1796c] COMPLIANCE AND ACCOUNTABILITY.

(a) UNIFIED ACCOUNTABILITY SYSTEM.—There shall be a unified system prescribed and administered by the Secretary for ensuring that local food service authorities that participate in the school lunch program under this Act comply with the provisions of this Act. Such system shall be established through the publication of regulations and the provision of an opportunity for public comment, consistent with the provisions of section 553 of title 5, United States Code.

(b) FUNCTIONS OF SYSTEM.—

(1) IN GENERAL.—Under the system described in subsection (1), each State educational agency shall—

(A) require that local food service authorities comply with the provisions of this Act; and

(B) ensure such compliance through reasonable audits and supervisory assistance reviews.

(2) MINIMIZATION OF ADDITIONAL DUTIES.—Each State educational agency shall coordinate the compliance and accountability activities described in paragraph (1) in a manner that minimizes the imposition of additional duties on local food service authorities.

(c) ROLE OF SECRETARY.—In carrying out this section, the Secretary shall—

(1) assist the State educational agency in the monitoring of programs conducted by local food service authorities; and

(2) through management evaluations, review the compliance of the State educational agency and the local school food service authorities with new regulations issued under this Act.

(d) AUTHORIZATION OF APPROPRIATIONS.—There is authorized to be appropriated for purposes of carrying out the compliance and accountability activities referred to in subsection (c) $3,000,000 for each of the fiscal years 1994 through 2003.

EXCERPTS FROM THE
CHILD NUTRITION ACT OF 1966

Excerpts from the Child Nutrition Act of 1966

As Amended Through P. L. 105-394, November 13, 1988

DECLARATION OF PURPOSE

SEC. 2. [(42 U.S.C. 1771)]
In recognition of the demonstrated relationship between food and good nutrition and the capacity of children to develop and learn, based on the years of cumulative successful experience under the national school lunch program with its significant contributions in the field of applied nutrition research, it is hereby declared to be the policy of Congress that these efforts shall be extended, expanded, and strengthened under the authority of the Secretary of Agriculture as a measure to safeguard the health and well-being of the Nation's children, and to encourage the domestic consumption of agricultural and other foods, by assisting States, through grants-in-aid and other means, to meet more effectively the nutritional needs of our children.

SPECIAL MILK PROGRAM AUTHORIZATION

SEC. 3.
(a) (1) There is hereby authorized to be appropriated for the fiscal year ending June 30, 1970, and for each succeeding fiscal year such sums as may be necessary to enable the Secretary of Agriculture, under such rules and regulations as the Secretary may deem in the public interest, to encourage consumption of fluid milk by children in the United States in (A) nonprofit schools of high school grade and under, except as provided in paragraph (2), which do not participate in a meal service program authorized under this Act or the National School Lunch Act, and (B) nonprofit nursery schools, child-care centers, settlement houses, summer camps, and similar nonprofit institutions devoted to the care and training of children, which do not participate in a meal service program authorized under this Act or the National School Lunch Act.

(2) The limitation imposed under paragraph (1)(A) for participation of nonprofit schools in the special milk program shall not apply to split-session kindergarten programs conducted in schools in which children do not have access to the meal service program operating in schools the children attend as authorized under this Act or the National School Lunch Act.

(3) For the purposes of this section "United States" means the fifty States, Guam, the Commonwealth of Puerto Rico, the Virgin Islands, American Samoa, the Commonwealth of the Northern Mariana Islands, and the District of Columbia.

(4) The Secretary shall administer the special milk program provided for by this section to the maximum extent practicable in the same manner as the Secretary administered the special milk program provided for by Public Law 89-642, as amended, during the fiscal year ending June 30, 1969.

(5) Any school or nonprofit child care institution which does not participate in a meal service program authorized under this Act or the National School Lunch Act shall receive the special

milk program upon its request.

(6) Children who qualify for free lunches under guidelines established by the Secretary shall, at the option of the school involved (or of the local educational agency involved in the case of a public school), be eligible for free milk upon their request.

(7) For the fiscal year ending June 30, 1975, and for subsequent school years, the minimum rate of reimbursement for a half-pint of milk served in schools and other eligible institutions shall not be less than 5 cents per half-pint served to eligible children, and such minimum rate of reimbursement shall be adjusted on an annual basis each school year to reflect changes in the Producer Price Index for Fresh Processed Milk published by the Bureau of Labor Statistics of the Department of Labor.

(8) Such adjustment shall be computed to the nearest one-fourth cent.

(9) Notwithstanding any other provision of this section, in no event shall the minimum rate of reimbursement exceed the cost to the school or institution of milk served to children.

(10) The State educational agency shall disburse funds paid to the State during any fiscal year for purposes of carrying out the program under this section in accordance with such agreements approved by the Secretary as may be entered into by such State agency and the schools in the State. The agreements described in the preceding sentence shall be permanent agreements that may be amended as necessary. Nothing in the preceding sentence shall be construed to limit the ability of the State educational agency to suspend or terminate any such agreement in accordance with regulations prescribed by the Secretary.

(b) Commodity only schools shall not be eligible to participate in the special milk program under this section. For the purposes of the preceding sentence, the term "commodity only schools" means schools that do not participate in the school lunch program under the National School Lunch Act, but which receive commodities made available by the Secretary for use by such schools in nonprofit lunch programs.

SCHOOL BREAKFAST PROGRAM AUTHORIZATION

SEC. 4.

(a) There is hereby authorized to be appropriated such sums as are necessary to enable the Secretary to carry out a program to assist the States and the Department of Defense through grants-in-aid and other means to initiate, maintain, or expand nonprofit breakfast programs in all schools which make application for assistance and agree to carry out a nonprofit breakfast program in accordance with this Act. Appropriations and expenditures for this Act shall be considered Health and Human Services functions for budget purposes rather than functions of Agriculture.

APPORTIONMENT TO STATES

(b) (1) (A) (i) The Secretary shall make breakfast assistance payments to each State educational agency each fiscal year, at such times as the Secretary may determine, from the sums appropriated for such purpose, in an amount equal to the product obtained by multiplying—

(I) The number of breakfasts served during such fiscal year to children in schools in such States which participate in the school breakfast program under agreements with such State educational agency; by

(II) The national average breakfast payment for free breakfasts, for reduced price breakfasts, or for breakfasts served to children not eligible for free or reduced price meals, as appropriate, as prescribed in clause (B) of this paragraph.

(ii) The agreements described in clause (i)(I) shall be permanent agreements that may be amended as necessary. Nothing in the preceding sentence shall be construed to limit the ability of the State educational agency to suspend or terminate any such agreement in accordance with regulations prescribed by the Secretary.

(B) The national average payment for each free breakfast shall be 57 cents (as adjusted pursuant to section 11(a) of the National School Lunch Act). The National average payment for each reduced price breakfast shall be one-half of the national average payment for each free breakfast, except that in no case shall the difference between the amount of the national average payment for a free breakfast and the national average payment for a reduced price breakfast exceed 30 cents. The national average payment for each breakfast served to a child not eligible for free or reduced price meals shall be 8.25 cents (as adjusted pursuant to section 11(a) of the National School Lunch Act).

(C) No school which receives breakfast assistant payments under this section may charge a price of more than 30 cents for a reduced price breakfast.

(D) No breakfast assistance payment may be made under this subsection for any breakfast served by a school unless such breakfast consists of a combination of foods which meet the minimum nutritional requirements prescribed by the Secretary under subsection (e) of this section.

(E) FREE AND REDUCED PRICE POLICY STATEMENT.—After the initial submission, a school food authority shall not be required to submit a free and reduced price policy statement to a State educational agency under this Act unless there is a substantive change in the free and reduced price policy of the school food authority. A routine change in the policy of a school food authority, such as an annual adjustment of the income eligibility guidelines for free and reduced price meals, shall not be sufficient cause for requiring the school food authority to submit a policy statement.

(2)   (A) The Secretary shall make additional payments for breakfasts served to children qualifying for a free or reduced price meal at schools that are in severe need.

(B) The maximum payment for each such free breakfast shall be the higher of—

(i) the national average payment established by the Secretary for free breakfasts plus 10 cents, or

(ii) 45 cents (as adjusted pursuant to section 11(a)(3)(B) of the National School Lunch Act).

(C) The maximum payment for each such reduced price breakfast shall be thirty cents less than the maximum payment for each free breakfast as determined under clause (B) of this paragraph.

(3) The Secretary shall increase by 6 cents[1] the annually adjusted payment for each breakfast served under this Act and Section 17 of the National School Lunch Act. These funds shall be used to assist States, to the extent feasible, in improving the nutritional quality of the breakfasts.

---

[1]Became effective on July 1, 1989.

(4) Notwithstanding any other provision of law, whenever stocks of agricultural commodities are acquired by the Secretary of the Commodity Credit Corporation and are not likely to be sold by the Secretary of the Commodity Credit Corporation or otherwise used in programs of commodity sale or distribution, the Secretary shall make such commodities available to school food authorities and eligible institutions serving breakfasts under this Act in a quantity equal in value to not less than 3 cents for each breakfast served under this Act and section 17 of the National School Lunch Act.

(5) Expenditures of funds from State and local sources for the maintenance of the breakfast program shall not be diminished as a result of funds or commodities received under paragraph (3) or (4).

STATE DISBURSEMENT TO SCHOOLS

(c) Funds apportioned and paid to any State for the purpose of this section shall be disbursed by the State educational agency to schools selected by the State educational agency to assist such schools in operating a breakfast program and for the purpose of subsection (d). Disbursement to schools shall be made at such rates per meal or on such other basis as the Secretary shall prescribe. In selecting schools for participation, the State educational agency shall, to the extent practicable, give first consideration to those schools drawing attendance from areas in which poor economic conditions exist, to those schools in which a substantial proportion of the children enrolled must travel long distances daily, and to those schools in which there is a special need for improving the nutrition and dietary practices of children of working mothers and children from low-income families. Breakfast assistance disbursements to schools under this section may be made in advance or by way of reimbursement in accordance with procedures prescribed by the Secretary

[SEVERE NEED ASSISTANCE]

(d) (1) Each State educational agency shall provide additional assistance to schools in severe need, which shall include only—

(A) those schools in which the service of breakfasts is required pursuant to State law; and

(B) those schools (having a breakfast program or desiring to initiate a breakfast program) in which, during the most recent second preceding school year for which lunches were served, 40 percent or more of the lunches served to students at the school were served free or at a reduced price, and in which the rate per meal established by the Secretary is insufficient to cover the costs of the breakfast program.

The provision of eligibility specified in clause (A) of this paragraph shall terminate effective July 1, 1983, for schools in States where the State legislatures meet annually and shall terminate effective July 1, 1984, for schools in States where the State legislatures meet biennially.

(2) A school, upon the submission of appropriate documentation about the need circumstances in that school and the school's eligibility for additional assistance, shall be entitled to receive 100 percent of the operating costs of the breakfast program, including the costs of obtaining, preparing, and serving food, or the meal reimbursement rate specified in paragraph (2) of section 4(b) of this Act, whichever is less.

NUTRITIONAL AND OTHER PROGRAM REQUIREMENTS

(e) (1) (A) Breakfasts served by schools participating in the school breakfast program under this section shall consist of a combination of foods and shall meet minimum nutritional requirements prescribed by the Secretary on the basis of tested nutritional research, except that the minimum nutritional requirements shall be measured by not less than the weekly average of the nutrient content of school breakfast. Such breakfasts shall be served free or at a reduced price to children in school under the same terms and conditions as are set forth with respect to the service of lunches free or at a reduced price in section 9 of the National School Lunch Act.

(B) The Secretary shall provide through State educational agencies technical assistance and training, including technical assistance and training in the preparation of foods high in complex carbohydrates and lower-fat versions of foods commonly used in the school breakfast program established under this section, to schools participating in the school breakfast program to assist the schools in complying with the nutritional requirements prescribed by the Secretary pursuant to subparagraph (A) and in providing appropriate meals to children with medically certified special dietary needs.

(2) At the option of a local school food authority, a student in a school under the authority that participates in the school breakfast program under this Act may be allowed to refuse not more than one item of a breakfast that the student does not intend to consume. A refusal of an offered food item shall not affect the full charge to the student for a breakfast meeting of the requirements of this section or the amount of payments made under this Act to a school for the breakfast.

STATE ADMINISTRATIVE EXPENSES

SEC. 7.

(a) (1) Each fiscal year, the Secretary shall make available to the States for their administrative costs an amount equal to not less than 1 ½ percent of the Federal funds expended under sections 4, 11, and 17 of the National School Lunch Act and sections 3 and 4 of this Act during the second preceding fiscal year. The Secretary shall allocate the funds so provided in accordance with paragraphs (2), (3), and (4) of this subsection. There are hereby authorized to be appropriated such sums as may be necessary to carry out the purposes of this section.

(2) The Secretary shall allocate to each State for administrative costs incurred in any fiscal year in connection with the programs authorized under the National School Lunch Act or under this Act, except for the programs authorized under section 13 or 17 of the National School Lunch Act or under section 17 of this Act, an amount equal to not less than 1 percent and not more than 1 ½ percent of the funds expended by each State under sections 4 and 11 of the National School Lunch Act and sections 3 and 4 of this Act during the second preceding fiscal year. In no case shall the grant available to any State under this subsection be less than the amount such State was allocated in the fiscal year ending September 30, 1981, or $100,000, whichever is larger.

(3) The Secretary shall allocate to each State for its administrative costs incurred under the

program authorized by section 17 of the National School Lunch Act in any fiscal year an amount, based upon funds expended under that program in the second preceding fiscal year, equal to

(A) 20 percent of the first $50,000,

(B) 10 percent of the next $100,000,

(C) 5 percent of the next $250,000, and

(D) 2 ½ percent of any remaining funds.

If an agency in the State other than the State educational agency administers such a program, the State shall ensure that an amount equal to no less than the funds due the State under this paragraph is provided to such agency for costs incurred by such agency in administering the program, except as provided in paragraph (5). The Secretary may adjust any State's allocation to reflect changes in the size of its program.

(4) The remaining funds appropriated under this section shall be allocated among the States by the Secretary in amounts the Secretary determines necessary for the improvement in the States of the administration of the programs authorized under the National School Lunch Act and this Act, except for section 17 of this Act, including, but not limited to, improved program integrity and the quality of meals served to children.

(5) (A) Not more than 25 percent of the amounts made available to each State under this section for the fiscal year 1991 and 20 percent of the amounts made available to each State under this section for the fiscal year 1992 and for each succeeding fiscal year may remain available for obligation or expenditure in the fiscal year succeeding in the fiscal year for which such amounts were appropriated. Funds available to States under this subsection and under section 13(k)(1) of the National School Lunch Act shall be used for the costs of administration of the programs for which the allocations are made, except that States may transfer up to 10 percent of any of the amounts allocated among such programs.

(6) USE OF ADMINISTRATIVE FUNDS.—Funds available to a State under this subsection and under section 13(k)(1) of the National School Lunch Act may be used by the State for the costs of administration of the programs authorized under this Act (except for the programs authorized under sections 17 and 21) and the National School Lunch Act without regard to the basis on which the funds were earned and allocated.

(7) Where the Secretary is responsible for the administration of programs under this Act or the National School Lunch Act, the amount of funds that would be allocated to the State agency under this section and under section 13(k)(1) of the National School Lunch Act shall be retained by the Secretary for the Secretary's use in the administration of such programs.

(8) In the fiscal year 1991 and each succeeding fiscal year, in accordance with regulations issued by the Secretary, each State shall ensure that the State agency administering the distribution of commodities under programs authorized under this Act and under the National School Lunch Act is provided, from funds made available to the State under this subsection, an appropriate amount of funds for administrative costs incurred in distributing such commodities. In developing such regulations, the Secretary may consider the value of commodities provided to the State under this Act and under the National School Lunch Act.

(9) (A) If the Secretary determines that the administration of any program by a State under this Act (other than section 17) or under the National School Lunch Act, or compliance with a regulation issued pursuant to either of such Acts, is seriously deficient, and the State fails to correct the deficiency within a specified period of time, the Secretary may withhold from the State some or all of the funds allocated to the State under this section or under section 13(k)(1) or 17 of the National School Lunch Act.

(B) On a subsequent determination by the Secretary that the administration of any program referred to in subparagraph (A), or compliance with the regulations issued to carry out the program, is no longer seriously deficient and is operated in an acceptable manner, the Secretary may allocate some or all of the funds withheld under such subparagraph.

(b) Funds paid to a State under subsection (a) of this section may be used to pay salaries, including employee benefits and travel expenses, for administrative and supervisory personnel; for support services; for office equipment; and for staff development.

(c) If any State agency agrees to assume responsibility for the administration of food service programs in nonprofit private schools or child care institutions that were previously administered by the Secretary, an appropriate adjustment shall be made in the administrative funds paid under this section to the State not later than the succeeding fiscal year.

(d) Notwithstanding any other provision of law, funds made available to each State under this section shall remain available for obligation and expenditure by that State during the fiscal year immediately following the fiscal year for which such funds were made available. For each fiscal year the Secretary shall establish a date by which each State shall submit to the Secretary a plan for the disbursement of funds provided under this section for each such year, and the Secretary shall reallocate any unused funds, as evidenced by such plans, to other States as the Secretary considers appropriate.

(e) Each State shall submit to the Secretary for approval by October 1 of the initial fiscal year a plan for the use of State administrative expense funds, including a staff formula for State personnel, system level supervisory and operating personnel, and school level personnel. After submitting the initial plan, a State shall be required to submit to the Secretary for approval only a substantive change in the plan.

(f) Payments of funds under this section shall be made only to States that agree to maintain a level of funding out of State revenues, for administrative costs in connection with programs under this Act (except section 17 of this Act) and the National School Lunch Act (except section 13 of that Act), not less than the amount expended or obligated in fiscal year 1977, and that agree to participate fully in any studies authorized by the Secretary.

(g) For the fiscal years beginning October 1, 1977, and each succeeding fiscal year ending before October 1, 2003, there are hereby authorized to be appropriated such sums as may be necessary for the purposes of this section.

UTILIZATION OF FOODS

SEC. 8.

Each school participating under section 4 of this Act shall, insofar as practicable, utilize in its program foods designated from time to time by the Secretary as being in abundance, either nationally or in the school area, or foods donated by the Secretary. Foods available under section 416 of the Agricultural Act of 1949, as amended, or purchased under section 32 of the Act of August 24, 1935, as amended, or section 709 of the Food and Agriculture Act of 1965, may be donated by the Secretary to schools, in accordance with the needs as determined by local school authorities, for utilization in their feeding programs under this Act.

NONPROFIT PROGRAMS

SEC. 9.

The food and milk service programs in schools and nonprofit institutions receiving assistance under this Act shall be conducted on a nonprofit basis.

REGULATIONS

SEC. 10.

(a) The Secretary shall prescribe such regulations as the Secretary may deem necessary to carry out this Act and the National School Lunch Act, including regulations relating to the service of food in participating schools and service institutions in competition with the programs authorized under this Act and the National School Lunch Act.

(b) The regulations shall not prohibit the sale of competitive foods approved by the Secretary in food service facilities or areas during the time of service of food under this Act or the National School Lunch Act if the proceeds from the sales of such foods will inure to the benefit of the schools or of organizations of students approved by the schools.

(c) In such regulations the Secretary may provide for the transfer of funds by any State between the programs authorized under this Act and the National School Lunch Act on the basis of an approved State plan of operation for the use of the funds and may provide for the reserve of up to 1 percentum of the funds available for apportionment to any State to carry out special developmental projects.

◆ ◆ ◆ ◆ ◆ ◆

PRESCHOOL PROGRAMS

SEC. 12.

(a) The Secretary may extend the benefits of all school feeding programs conducted and supervised by the Department of Agriculture to include preschool programs operated as part of the school system.

◆ ◆ ◆ ◆ ◆ ◆

ACCOUNTS AND RECORDS

SEC. 16.

(a) States, State educational agencies, schools, and nonprofit institutions participating in programs under this Act shall keep such accounts and records as may be necessary to enable the Secretary to determine whether there has been compliance with this Act and the regulations hereunder. Such accounts and records shall at all times be available at any reasonable time for inspection and audit by representatives of the Secretary and shall be preserved for such period of time, not in excess of three years, as the Secretary determines is necessary.

(b) With regard to any claim arising under this Act or under the National School Lunch Act, the Secretary shall have the authority to determine the amount of, to settle and to adjust any such claim, and to compromise or deny such claim or any part thereof. The Secretary shall also have the authority to waive such claims if the Secretary determines that to do so would serve the purposes of either such Act. Nothing contained in this subsection shall be construed to diminish the authority of the Attorney General of the United States under section 516 of title 28, United States Code, to conduct litigation on behalf of the United States.

NUTRITION EDUCATION AND TRAINING

SEC. 19.

(a) Congress finds that effective dissemination of scientifically valid information to children participating or eligible to participate in the school lunch and related child nutrition programs should be encouraged.

PURPOSE

(b) It is the purpose of this section to establish a system of grants to State educational agencies for the development of comprehensive nutrition education and training programs. Such nutrition education programs shall fully use as a learning laboratory the school lunch and child nutrition programs.

DEFINITIONS

(c) For purposes of this section, the term "nutrition education and training program" means a multidisciplinary program by which scientifically valid information about foods and nutrients is imparted in a manner that individuals receiving such information will understand the principles of nutrition and seek to maximize their well-being through food consumption practices. Nutrition education programs shall include, but not be limited to, (A) instructing students with regard to the nutritional value of foods and the relationship between food and human health; (B) training school food service personnel in the principles and practices of food service management; (C) instructing teachers in sound principles of nutrition education; (D) developing and using classroom materials and curricula; and (E) providing information to parents and caregivers regarding the nutritional value of food and the relationship between food and health.

NUTRITION INFORMATION AND TRAINING

(d) (1) The Secretary is authorized to formulate and carry out a nutrition education and training program, through a system of grants to State educational agencies, to provide for
> (A) the nutritional training of educational and food service personnel,
> (B) training school food service personnel in the principles and practices of food service management, in cooperation with materials developed at any food service management institute established as authorized by section 21 of the National School Lunch Act, and
> (C) the conduct of nutrition education activities in schools and child care institutions, and institutions offering summer food service programs under section 13 of the National School Lunch Act, and the provision of nutrition education to parents and caregivers.

(2) The program is to be coordinated at the State level with other nutrition activities conducted by education, health, and State Cooperative Extension Service agencies. In formulating the program, the Secretary and the State may solicit the advice and recommendations of the State educational agencies, the Department of Health and Human Services, and other interested groups and individuals concerned with improvement of child nutrition.

(3) If a State educational agency is conducting or applying to conduct a health education program which includes a school-related nutrition education component as defined by the Secretary, and that health education program is eligible for funds under programs administered by the Department of Health and Human Services, the Secretary may make funds authorized in this section available to the Department of Health and Human Services to fund the nutrition education component of the State program without requiring an additional grant application.

(4) The Secretary, in carrying out the provisions of this subsection, shall make grants to State educational agencies who, in turn, may contract with land-grant colleges eligible to receive funds under the Act of July 2, 1862, or the Act of August 30, 1890, including the Tuskegee Institute, other institutions of higher education, and nonprofit organizations and agencies, for the training of educational, school food service, child care, and summer food service personnel with respect to providing nutrition education programs in schools and the training of school food service personnel in school food service management, in coordination with the activities authorized under section 21 of the National School Lunch Act. Such grants may be used to develop and conduct training programs for early childhood, elementary, and secondary educational personnel and food service personnel with respect to the relationship between food, nutrition, and health, educational methods and techniques, and issues relating to nutrition education; and principles and skills of food service management for cafeteria personnel.

(5) The State, in carrying out the provisions of this subsection, may contract with State and local educational agencies, land-grant colleges eligible to receive funds under the Act of July 2, 1862, or the Act of August 30, 1890, including the Tuskegee Institute, other institutions of higher education, and other public or private nonprofit educational or research agencies, institutions, or organizations to pay the cost of pilot demonstration projects in elementary and secondary schools, and in child care institutions and summer food service institutions, with respect to nutrition education. Such projects may include, but are not limited to, projects for the

development, demonstration, testing, and evaluation of curricula for use in early childhood, elementary, and secondary education programs.

AGREEMENTS WITH STATE AGENCIES

(e) The Secretary is authorized to enter into agreements with State educational agencies incorporating the provisions of this section, and issue such regulations as are necessary to implement this section.

USE OF FUNDS

(f) (1) The funds available under this section may, under guidelines established by the Secretary, be used by State educational agencies for—

   (A) employing a nutrition education specialist to coordinate the program, including travel and related personnel costs;

   (B) undertaking an assessment of the nutrition education needs of the State;

   (C) developing a State plan of operation and management for nutrition education;

   (D) applying for and carrying out planning and assessment grants;

   (E) pilot projects and related purposes;

   (F) the planning, development, and conduct of nutrition education programs and workshops for food service and educational personnel;

   (G) coordinating and promoting nutrition information and education activities in local school districts (incorporating, to the maximum extent practicable, as a learning laboratory, the child nutrition programs);

   (H) contracting with public and private nonprofit educational institutions for the conduct of nutrition education instruction and programs relating to the purposes of this section; and

   (I) related nutrition education purposes, including the preparation, testing, distribution, and evaluation of visual aids and other informational and educational materials.

   (J) other appropriate related activities, as determined by the State.

(2) A State agency may use an amount equal to not more than 15 percent of the funds made available through a grant under this section for expenditures for administrative purposes in connection with the program authorized under this section if the State makes available at least an equal amount for administrative or program purposes in connection with the program.

ACCOUNTS, RECORDS, AND REPORTS

(g) (1) State educational agencies participating in programs under this section shall keep such accounts and records as may be necessary to enable the Secretary to determine whether there has been compliance with this section and the regulations issued hereunder. Such accounts and records shall be available at any reasonable time for inspection and audit by representatives of the Secretary and shall be preserved for such period of time, not in excess of five years, as the Secretary determines to be necessary.

(2) State educational agencies shall provide reports on expenditures of Federal funds, program participation, program costs, and related matters, in such form and at such times as the Secretary may prescribe.

STATE COORDINATORS FOR NUTRITION; STATE PLAN

(h) (1) In order to be eligible for assistance under this section, a State shall appoint a nutrition education specialist to serve as a State coordinator for school nutrition education. It shall be the responsibility of the State coordinator to make an assessment of the nutrition education needs in the State, prepare a State plan, and coordinate programs under this Act with all other nutrition education programs provided by the State with Federal or State funds.

(2) Upon receipt of funds authorized by this section, the State coordinator shall prepare an itemized budget and assess the nutrition education and training needs of the State.

(i) AUTHORIZATION OF APPROPRIATIONS.—

(1) IN GENERAL.—

(A) FUNDING.—There are authorized to be appropriated such sums as are necessary to carry out this section for each of fiscal years 1997 through 2003.

(B) GRANTS.—

(i) IN GENERAL.—Grants to each State from the amounts made available under subparagraph (A) shall be based on a rate of 50 cents for each child enrolled in schools or institutions within the State, except that no State shall receive an amount less than $75,000 per fiscal year.

(ii) INSUFFICIENT FUNDS.—If the amount made available fro any fiscal year is insufficient to pay the amount to which each State is entitled under clause (i), the amount of each grant shall be ratably reduced.

(2) Funds made available to any State under this section shall remain available to the State for obligation in the fiscal year succeeding the fiscal year in which the funds were received by the State.

(3) Enrollment data used for purposes of this subsection shall be the latest available as certified by the Department of Education.

DEPARTMENT OF DEFENSE OVERSEAS DEPENDENTS' SCHOOLS

SEC. 20.

(a) For the purpose of obtaining Federal payments and commodities in conjunction with the provision of breakfasts to students attending Department of Defense dependents' schools which are located outside the United States, its territories or possessions, the Secretary of Agriculture shall make available to the Department of Defense, from funds appropriated for such purpose, the same payments and commodities as are provided to States for schools participating in the school breakfast program in the United States.

(b) The Secretary of Defense shall administer breakfast programs authorized by this section and shall determine eligibility for free and reduced price breakfasts under the criteria published by the Secretary of Agriculture, except that the Secretary of Defense shall prescribe regulations governing computation of income eligibility standards for families of students participating in the school breakfast program under this section.

(c) The Secretary of Defense shall be required to offer meals meeting nutritional standards prescribed by the Secretary of Agriculture; however, the Secretary of Defense may authorize deviations from Department of Agriculture prescribed meal patterns and fluid milk requirements when local conditions preclude strict compliance or when such compliance is highly impracticable.

(d) Funds are hereby authorized to be appropriated for any fiscal year in such amounts as may be necessary for the administrative expenses of the Department of Defense under this section.

(e) The Secretary of Agriculture shall provide the Secretary of Defense with technical assistance in the administration of the school breakfast programs authorized in this section.

◆ ◆ ◆ ◆ ◆ ◆

APPENDIX B -
AN EXAMPLE OF AN AUDIT FORM
FOR THE SCHOOL MEALS
INITIATIVE (SMI)

APPENDIX B - School Meals Initiative

SCHOOL MEALS INITIATIVE (SMI) FORM

School Food Authority Profile

1. SFA: _____

    Agreement Number: _____

Type of Meal Planning System	Number of Schools in SFA Using System
Enhanced Food Based	
Traditional Food Based	
NSMP	
Assisted NSMP	
Any Reasonable Method (Describe)	
Total Number of Schools	

1. Contact Name/Title: _____
   Address: _____
   Telephone Number: _____

2. Menu Planner(s) Names(s): _____
   Menu Planning Conducted: Centrally _____   At School Level _____
                   By a Consultant _____

3. Reviewer(s) Name(s): _____

SCHOOL MEALS INITIATIVE (SMI) FORM

School Profile

1. School: _____
2. Contact Name/Title: _____
    Address: _____
    Telephone Number: _____
3. Menu Planner(s) Name(s): _____
    Menu Planning Conducted: Centrally _____   At School Level _____
                        By a Consultant _____
4. Menu Planning Option Used:

    [X]   Enhanced Food Based   Traditional Food Based
          NSMP   ANSMP   Any Reasonable Method
5. Reviewer(s) Name(s): _____
6. Period of Analysis: _____
7. Date of On-site Visit: _____
8. Type(s) of Food Service Program:
    Self-Operated _____   Vended: All _____   Part _____   Management Company _____
9. Type of Site Where Food is Prepared:
    On-Site Preparation _____   Central Kitchen _____
    Satellite Kitchen _____   Other _____
10. Ages/Grades Participating in NSLP/SBP _____
11. Age/Grade Grouping(s) Used to Plan Menus in School _____
12. Program Reviewed   NSLP _____   SBP _____
13. Weighting   Yes _____   No _____
14. Simple Averaging   Yes _____   No _____
15. Combined B/L Analysis   Yes _____   No _____
16. Offer vs. Serve   Yes _____   No _____ (If Yes, see instructions)
17. A La Carte Available   Yes _____   No _____
18. Adult Meals   Yes _____   No _____
19. Special Needs Meals   Yes _____   No _____

SCHOOL MEALS INITIATIVE (SMI) FORM

Food Based Menu Planning - Nutrient Analysis

SFA/School: _____

Before Nutrient Analysis	Yes	No	N/A	Comments
1. Has a nutrient analysis been conducted on the school's menus? If yes, was USDA approved software used?				
2. Are necessary materials available? Menus Production records including Grades/portion sizes Standardized recipes Processed foods information (CN Database/Nutrition Facts Label/Nutrient Analysis Data Form) Food Product Information/Specifications Estimates of a la carte sales and adult meals				
3. Based on available information, can a nutrient analysis be conducted?				

SCHOOL MEALS INITIATIVE (SMI) FORM

Food Based Menu Planning - Nutrient Analysis (Continued)

SFA/School: _____

Conduct the nutrient analysis of a minimum of one school week (3-7 days) as defined in regulations.
Complete the chart below or attach a copy of computer generated analysis.

Nutrient Analysis				Data Analysis Conducted			
Nutrient	Nutrient Standard for Grades K-6	Average for Grades K-6	Nutrient Standard for Grades 7-12	Average for Grades 7-12	Nutrient Standard for K-3	Average for K-3	Nutrient Standard for Grades 4-12	Average for Grades 4-12
Calories (KCal)	664		825		633		785	
Protein (g)	10		16		9		15	
Calcium (mg)	286		400		267		370	
Iron (mg)	3.5		4.5		3.3		4.2	
Vitamin A (RE)	224		300		200		285	
Vitamin C (mg)	15		18		15		17	
Total fat	≤ 30%		≤ 30%		≤ 30%		≤ 30%	
Saturated fat	< 10%		< 10%		< 10%		< 10%	
Cholesterol (mg)*								
Sodium (mg)*								
Fiber (g)*								

*There are no RDA standards established for these nutrients.

Comments:

SCHOOL MEALS INITIATIVE (SMI) FORM

Food Based Menu Planning - Menu Evaluation

SFA/School: _____

Based on the menus and production records for the period of evaluation, determine the following:

Working Toward the Goals of the Dietary Guidelines and Nutrition Standards	Yes	No	N/A	Comments

1. Did the school:
 	
    Offer a variety of meat/meat alternates?
 	
    Offer a variety of fruits/vegetables?
 	
    Offer a variety of grains/breads?
 	
    Offer a variety of milk choices?				

2. Were accepted menu planning principles followed:				
3. Were portion sizes sufficient for established grade groupings?				
4. Were the required servings of grains/breads for each grade group planned for the week?				
5. Was no more than one serving of grains-based dessert credited per day for the grain/bread component? (Enhanced Food Based Only)				
6. Were the required servings of fruits/vegetables planned for the day? For the week? (Enhanced K-6 only)				

SCHOOL MEALS INITIATIVE (SMI) FORM

Food Based Menu Planning - On Site Menu Evaluation

SFA/School: _____

Obtain and record the planned menu(s) for the day of the on-site visit.

Menu of the Day	Grades Served:

Based on the Menu and Meal Service	Yes	No	N/A	Comments
1. Were planned portion sizes sufficient for the established grade groupings?				
2. Were portion sizes served as planned?				
3. Did planned food items/components satisfy meal pattern requirements?				
4. Was no more than one grains-based dessert planned to meet the grain/bread component for the day? (Enhanced food based only)				
5. Is offer versus served correctly implemented?				

SCHOOL MEALS INITIATIVE (SMI) FORM

Review the production record and observe preparation the day of the on-site visit.

	Yes	No	N/A	Comments
1.				
2.				

Review a copy of the recipes used in preparing the menu(s)

Standardized Recipes	Yes	No	N/A	Comments
1. Based on reviewer observation: a. Was the food prepared according to the recipe that was standardized for the school? b. Was the food served according to the recipe that has been standardized for the school?				

Interview school staff about nutrition education activities.

Nutrition Education	Comments
1. Describe what the school/SFA is doing to promote a healthy lifestyle for students. a. Training efforts: For school staff For school district staff b. Nutrition education for students c. Team Nutrition activities d. Outreach efforts (including community, parent organizations, school boards) e. Nutrition information displayed in cafeteria	

SCHOOL MEALS INITIATIVE (SMI) FORM

Summary of Review Findings

SFA/School: _____

Period of Analysis: _____

Commendations: Progress made toward meeting the Nutrition Standards and the Dietary Guidelines
Areas Needing Improvement:

Source: U. S. Department of Agriculture

GLOSSARY OF TERMS

GLOSSARY OF TERMS RELATED TO
SCHOOL FOODSERVICES

AccuClaim is a review process formerly by state agencies that administer Child Nutrition Programs.

ADA is the acronym for average daily attendance.

ADP is the acronym for average daily participation.

A la carte refers to the sale of food items sold individually, separate from a complete meal.

Appropriation is money allocated by the federal government for various child nutrition programs.

ASFSA is the acronym for American School Food Service Association, a national professional association.

Attendance factor is the average number of students present at the school. (If the school's attendance factor is not available, the national attendance factor is used.)

Audit of Child Nutrition Programs, refers to a financial and/or program examination by the USDA's Office of Audit, a state audit office or a certified public accountant of an organization's claim for reimbursement, cost records and/or financial condition for a completed accounting period.

Audit trail is a procedure that traces through all stages of an accounting system or data-processing operation, starting from the source document (at point of sale) and ending with the final report (monthly claim for reimbursement).

Average daily attendance (ADA) is a figure representing a school or school district's attendance per day averaged over a period of time.

Average daily participation (ADP) is the number served and can be arrived at by dividing the total lunches served during a reporting period by the operating days in the same period.

Balance sheet is a financial statement that shows the financial condition of a fund at a given point, a "snapshot."

Baseline budget is a budget based on the assumption that all the previous year's expenditures were necessary and will be duplicated.

Beginning inventory is the food and supplies on hand and available for use at the beginning of the accounting period (usually a month).

Block grant is specified amounts of money provided without being earmarked for specific use.

Bonus commodities are food products that the USDA purchases in addition to the entitlement commodities. (The quantity available each year is not guaranteed and varies from year to year.)

Bottom-up budget is a decentralized budget where each cost center (school) plans a budget and the school district's budget is made up by combining all the budgets together.

Break-even point (BEP) is the point in time when enough revenue has been received to cover all costs.

Breakfast (federal) is a meal served in the morning of a school day that must meet federal meal and regulatory requirements to receive federal funding.

Budget is an organized financial plan for a specified period of time (usually a year), that forecasts sales and services, revenue and expenditures.

CACFP is the acronym for Child and Adult Care Food Program.

Cash in lieu of commodities refers to monies issued for purchase of foods instead of donated commodities.

Cash reimbursement rates are monies received for serving meals that meet the federal meal requirements.

Central kitchen is a type of meal preparation facility that prepares meals for children at that location for delivery to other sites. (Sometimes referred to as a commissary or satellite production kitchen.)

Child nutrition label (CN label) is a label statement identifying the specific contribution that a product makes toward meeting the requirements of Section 210.10 of the National School Lunch Act for one or more components of a meal.

Claim assessment is action taken by auditors to recover overpayment made, a "fiscal action."

Claims for reimbursement is a claim submitted to a state agency or USDA, Food and Nutrition Services regional office (where applicable) on a monthly basis by a school food authority for reimbursement for meals and milk served under the National School Lunch, School Breakfast, or Special Milk Program.

CNA is the acronym for Child Nutrition Act of 1966, the federal law that authorizes and funds several of the Child Nutrition Programs.

CNP is the acronym for Child Nutrition Program.

Commodity letter of credit (CLOC) is monies issued by the federal government in place of USDA commodity foods for purchase of specific foods instead of receiving donated commodities.

Commodity only schools are schools not participating in the National School Lunch Program but that receive commodities for a nonprofit lunch program.

Competitive foods are those foods sold to students at school before or during breakfast or lunch periods in competition with the National School Lunch or School Breakfast programs.

Convenience foods are food items that have been processed before being received at the school and may or may not require additional preparation before serving.

Cooperative purchasing involves a group of school district joining together to accomplish the purchasing task.

Distribution agency is the state, federal, or private agency distributing donated commodities.

Donated commodities are food items made available by the US Department of Agriculture to Child Nutrition Programs.

Error-prone school is a school that claims a high percentage (90-95%) of those who qualify for free and reduced-price meals.

Escalator clause is an automatic increase or decrease of reimbursement rates based on consumer index for food away from home.

Fair labor laws are laws that protect the employee in the workplace.

Federal register is a federal document that provides a uniform system for making available to the public regulations and legal notices issued by federal agencies.

Finishing kitchen is a kitchen that receives prepared foods for reconstituting or heating, assembling, portioning, and serving on site.

FNS is the acronym for Food and Nutrition Service, the department under USDA that administers the Child Nutrition Programs (named Food and Consumer Service for a short while).

Focused sampling is the selection of free and reduced-price meal applications for verification of one percent or 1,000 (the lesser of the two) approved applications, plus .5% or 500 (the lesser of the two) of applications approved based on food stamp/TAN case numbers.

Food component means one of the four food groups that compose the reimbursable school breakfast/lunch, i.e., meat or meat alternate, milk, fruit/vegetable, and bread/grain, under the food-based menu planning system.

Food distribution agency is the agency in the state government responsible for distribution of USDA-donated commodities.

Food item means one of the five foods that compose the reimbursable school breakfast/lunch, i.e., meat or meat alternate, milk, bread/grain, and two servings of vegetables or fruits or a combination of both.

Free meals are meals served to students at no cost to the recipient because they qualify for free meals under federal regulations.

GAO is the acronym for Government Accounting Office, a federal watchdog agency.

HACCP is the acronym for Hazard Analysis Critical Control Point System.

Income eligibility is the range of income within which students qualify for free or reduced price meal.

Income statement (see "profit and loss statement).

Indirect costs are those costs that cannot be directly identified to exact costs but must be prorated across several programs, e.g., utilities.

Law is a bill that has been passed by both Houses of Representatives and the Senate and signed by the president.

Loss leader is pricing low what is for sale for a reason, e.g., French fries at a fast-food restaurant priced low to increase the amount of money spent by the customer.

Management companies are commercial enterprises that contract with school districts to operate foodservice programs.

Mandate is legislation or regulation that demand that something be done.

Meals on Wheels is a program that is responsible for home-delivered meals to people confined to their home and often delivered by volunteers

National School Lunch Program (NSLP) is the federally subsidized child nutrition program that provides lunches at school.

National School Lunch Week is the seven-day period beginning on the second Sunday of October each year as designated by Congress (PL 87-780).

Nonprofit lunch program is a program maintained for the benefits of children with the income used solely for the food service operation.

NET is the acronym for Nutrition Education and Training, which is funded by money made available by Congress for educational and training purposes.

Offer versus serve is a serving method used in schools participating in the Child Nutrition Program that allows students to turn down food items in the lunch or breakfast if they do not intend to eat them.

On-site preparation refers to food prepared in the school where it will be served.

Overclaim is that portion of a school food authority's claim for reimbursement which exceeds the federal financial assistance that is properly payable.

Point-of-service means that point in the foodservice operation where a determination can accurately be made that a reimbursable free, reduced-price or paid lunch has been served to an eligible child and where the type meal for federal reimbursement is determined.

Postcosting is the process of determining the actual cost of a recipe, a portion, a menu item, or meal, after it has been prepared and served.

Precosting is the process of determining the cost of a recipe, a portion, a menu item, or meal prior to preparation or service.

Processing contracts are agreements entered into with companies by school districts, groups of school districts, or state agencies to turn donated commodities into another or similar product, e.g., ground beef into hamburger patties.

Productivity rate is the ratio of measurement of labor's efficiency, arrived at by dividing the output (food and services) by the input (labor hours).

Profit is the revenue that exceeds expenditures.

Profit and loss statement is a financial report that indicates how the school foodservice program is doing financially during a period of time (generally done monthly and year-to-date). This report is also known as an "income statement" and "statement of income."

Reauthorization is the process of re-approving programs to continue to operate a specific period of time.

Rebate program is provided to the state agencies or school district in the form of cash (from a processor) to cover costs of commodities used as ingredients.

Receiving kitchen is the foodservice location that receives food ready to serve.

Reduced-price meals are the meals served to students who do not qualify (because of family income) for free meals but do not have sufficient family income to pay full price.

Reimbursable meal (lunch or breakfast) is a meal meeting the USDA meal pattern served to an enrolled child, priced as an entire meal rather than based on individual items. (Such a meal qualifies for reimbursement with federal funds.)

Revenue is income or sales.

Satellite foodservice is a system whereby food is prepared in one location and transported to other locations to be served.

SBP is an acronym for School Breakfast Program.

School food authority (SFA) means the governing body that is responsible for the administration of one or more schools; and has the legal authority to operate the program therein or be otherwise approved by FNS, to operate the program.

Section 4 funds refer to federal funds appropriated for all lunches.

Section 11 funds refer to federal funds appropriated for free and/or reduced-price meals.

Section 32 commodities refers to commodities purchased with funds received by the Secretary of Agriculture from 30 percent of the custom receipts.

Severe Need Breakfast School is a school that in the second preceding school year served 40 percent or more of the lunches free or at a reduced price and can receive additional federal subsidies for each free or reduced-price breakfast meal served if costs justify.

Severe Need Lunch School District is a school district that in the second preceding year served more than 60 percent of the lunches free or at a reduced price and is reimbursed for meals at a higher rate. (In 1999 school year it was two cents).

Special Milk Program provides milk to children in schools and child care institutions that do not participate in other federal Child Nutrition meal service programs.

State Administrative Expense (SAE) is funding used by states to administer the school food service programs.

State agency is the agency in a state that has been designated by the governor to administer the child nutrition programs.

Statement of income (see profit and loss statement).

Subsidy is the monetary or commodity assistance provided by the USDA to school food service programs.

Summer Food Service Program is a nutrition program that operates during the summer months and at other times when school is not in session.

Top-down budget is a centralized budget planned for more than one cost center.

Turnover rate of employees is the ratio of employees who have left employment when compared with those in the workforce. The turnover rate is arrived at by dividing the number of separations (employees who have left) by the average number of employees for the period of time.

Universal Breakfast Program is a determination made by the school district that allows all students in the school to have a breakfast free.

USDA is the acronym for United States Department of Agriculture.

Variable costs are the costs affected by sales that vary in direct proportion with volume of sales or number of customers served, e.g., food and disposable products.

Verification is the confirmation of eligibility for free and reduced-price meal benefits under the National School Lunch Program or School Breakfast Program.

Weighted average refers to the average portions served of each item when different components make up the menus.

Work simplification is the process of finding the easiest and most efficient way to do a job.

Zero-based budget is a budget planned as if for the first time by determining revenue by forecasted number of customers and established prices and determining expenditures by costing out all items.

INDEX